AF707500

HANDBOOK OF ENVIRONMENTAL AND GREEN FINANCE

Toward a Sustainable Future

Transformations in Banking, Finance and Regulation

Print ISSN: 2752-5821
Online ISSN: 2752-583X

Series Editors: Sabri Boubaker
(*EM Normandie Business School, France*)
Duc Khuong Nguyen
(*EMLV Business School, France*)

Presently, the banking and finance sectors evolve within a globalized and highly uncertain environment. Each business and financial decision requires careful consideration of country-specific and international factors due to high levels of shock transmission and volatility spillovers. Furthermore, it would be remiss to omit the COVID-19 health crisis, which caused harmful effects to all areas of the real economy and made profound changes in the way our firms, economies, and markets used to function.

Many other already well-known aspects, including the repercussions of quantitative easing policies, disruptive technologies in finance (e.g., FinTech, Big Data, Data Analytics, Artificial Intelligence, and Blockchains), as well as innovative financing instruments for startups (e.g., ICOs and crowdfunding) are currently revolutionizing banking and finance and posing numerous challenges to regulatory bodies and policymakers. Climate change emergencies also put pressure on governments and firms worldwide to improve policy on governance, corporate social responsibility, and sustainability practices.

This book series "Transformations in Banking, Finance and Regulation" attempts to address these issues by focusing on transformative perspectives in banking and finance. Accordingly, it provides evidence-based guidance, recommendations, and pathways to assist businesses and policy decision-makers through an interdisciplinary and in-depth understanding of ongoing changes in the behavior of economic agents.

Published

Vol. 11 *Handbook of Environmental and Green Finance: Toward a Sustainable Future*
edited by Sabri Boubaker and Thai-Ha Le

Vol. 10 *Banking Resilience and Global Financial Stability*
edited by Sabri Boubaker and Marwa Elnahass

Vol. 9 *Banking Resilience: New Insights on Corporate Governance, Sustainability and Digital Innovation*
edited by Sabri Boubaker and Marwa Elnahass

Vol. 8 *Political Corruption and Corporate Finance*
by Quoc Trung Tran and Duc Khuong Nguyen

For the complete list of volumes in this series, please visit
www.worldscientific.com/series/tbfr

Transformations in Banking, Finance and Regulation
Volume 11

HANDBOOK OF ENVIRONMENTAL AND GREEN FINANCE

Toward a Sustainable Future

Editors

Sabri Boubaker
EM Normandie Business School, France

Thai-Ha Le
VinFuture Foundation, Vietnam

World Scientific

NEW JERSEY • LONDON • SINGAPORE • BEIJING • SHANGHAI • HONG KONG • TAIPEI • CHENNAI • TOKYO

Published by

World Scientific Publishing Europe Ltd.
57 Shelton Street, Covent Garden, London WC2H 9HE
Head office: 5 Toh Tuck Link, Singapore 596224
USA office: 27 Warren Street, Suite 401-402, Hackensack, NJ 07601

Library of Congress Cataloging-in-Publication Data
Names: Boubaker, Sabri, editor. | Le, Thai-Ha, editor.
Title: Handbook of environmental and green finance : toward a sustainable future / editors, Sabri Boubaker, EM Normandie Business School, France, Thai-Ha Le, VinFuture Foundation, Vietnam.
Description: Hackensack, NJ : World Scientific, [2024] | Series: Transformations in banking, finance and regulation, 2752-5821 ; volume 11 | Includes bibliographical references and index.
Identifiers: LCCN 2023039674 | ISBN 9781800614444 (hardcover) | ISBN 9781800614451 (ebook for institutions) | ISBN 9781800614468 (ebook for individuals)
Subjects: LCSH: Finance--Environmental aspects. | Sustainable Development Goals.
Classification: LCC HG101 .H35 2024 | DDC 332--dc23/eng/20231002
LC record available at https://lccn.loc.gov/2023039674

British Library Cataloguing-in-Publication Data
A catalogue record for this book is available from the British Library.

Copyright © 2024 by World Scientific Publishing Europe Ltd.

All rights reserved. This book, or parts thereof, may not be reproduced in any form or by any means, electronic or mechanical, including photocopying, recording or any information storage and retrieval system now known or to be invented, without written permission from the Publisher.

For photocopying of material in this volume, please pay a copying fee through the Copyright Clearance Center, Inc., 222 Rosewood Drive, Danvers, MA 01923, USA. In this case permission to photocopy is not required from the publisher.

For any available supplementary material, please visit
https://www.worldscientific.com/worldscibooks/10.1142/Q0426#t=suppl

Desk Editors: Nambirajan Karuppiah/Rosie Williamson/Shi Ying Koe

Typeset by Stallion Press
Email: enquiries@stallionpress.com

© 2024 World Scientific Publishing Europe Ltd.
https://doi.org/10.1142/9781800614451_fmatter

About the Editors

Sabri Boubaker is a Professor of Finance at EM Normandie Business School (Paris, France) and the University of Swansea (Swansea, Wales, United Kingdom). Professor Boubaker holds a Ph.D. in Finance from the University of Paris Est (2006) and an HDR degree (Habilitation for Supervising Doctoral Research) in 2010 from the same university. Professor Boubaker is the Editor-in-Chief of the *Journal of International Financial Management & Accounting* (Wiley, IF: 5.1, Scopus Q1, Clarivate Q1). He is the recipient of "The Economic Research Foundation's Research Award 2022" from the "Centrum for Forskning om Ekonomiska Relationer, Sweden" and the best corporate finance paper award at the 2023 Asian Finance Conference. He was/is visiting professor/researcher at Cass Business School (London, UK), University of Birmingham (Birmingham, UK), Dalhousie University (Halifax, Canada), University of Cranfield (Bedford, UK), University of Portsmouth (Portsmouth, UK), University of Brunel (London, UK), University of Bologna (Bologna, Italy), University of Napoli Parthenope (Napoli, Italy), University of Canterbury (Christchurch, New Zealand), Rabat Business School (Morocco, France), University of Tunis (Tunis, Tunisia), and the Vietnam National University (VNU-IS, Hanoi, Vietnam). Sabri Boubaker has recently published many academic papers (more than 100 papers) in international refereed journals, including the *Journal of Corporate Finance, Journal of Banking and Finance,*

Journal of International Money and Finance, *Financial Management*, *Journal of Business Ethics*, *Journal of Economic Dynamics and Control*, *Auditing: A Journal of Theory & Practice*, and *British Journal of Management*. He has also edited 12 books on corporate finance, corporate governance, and corporate social responsibility (Emerald Group Publishing, Springer-Verlag, World Scientific Publishing, Palgrave Macmillan, Elsevier, Edward Elgar, etc.) and is also the co-director of the book series *Transformations in Banking, Finance, and Regulation* (World Scientific Publishing). Professor Boubaker serves on the editorial boards of several accounting and finance academic journals such as the *British Journal of Management*, *Journal of International Financial Markets, Institutions, and Money* (Subject Editor), *International Review of Economics and Finance* (Associate Editor), *International Journal of Finance & Economics* (Associate Editor), *Emerging Markets Review* (Associate Editor), *Global Finance Journal* (Senior Editor), and *Finance Research Letters* (Associate Editor). He is the co-founder and co-chair of the annual Paris Financial Management Conference (2013–), Vietnam Symposium in Banking and Finance (2016), the Annual Meeting of the International Society for the Advancement of Financial Economics (2022–) and the President of the International Society for the Advancement of Financial Economics (ISAFE).

Thai-Ha Le is the Managing Director at the VinFuture Foundation, Vietnam. She holds a Bachelor of Arts (Hons) and Ph.D. in Economics from Nanyang Technological University, Singapore, where she completed her Ph.D. within two years at the age of 24. Prior to joining VinFuture Foundation, Dr. Le was the Director of Research and a Senior Faculty member at the Fulbright School of Public Policy and Management, Fulbright University Vietnam, for nearly three years and was a tenured Senior Lecturer at RMIT University Vietnam for seven years. She was also a guest lecturer for several programs at Dartmouth College (the US) and the Young Southeast Asian Leaders Initiative (YSEALI), sponsored by the U.S. Bureau of Educational and Cultural Affairs. Her primary research fields include energy economics, environmental economics, and applied economics.

Dr. Le is an active researcher who has published about 70 scholarly research articles in international, peer-reviewed journals such as *Energy Economics*, *Energy Journal*, *Energy Policy*, *Renewable Energy*, *Resources Policy*, *Economic Modelling*, *International Review of Financial Analysis*, *Empirical Economics*, *Annals of Operations Research*, *Applied Economics*, and *Australian Tax Forum*.

According to rankings compiled by Stanford University and published in *PLoS Biology* in 2021 and Elsevier in 2022, Dr. Le is in the world's top 1% most influential scientists across all scientific fields, and is the only Vietnamese female researcher based in Vietnam in this ranking. She is also the youngest (and the only female) member of the Scientific Committee in Economics for the term 2022–2024 of the National Foundation for Science and Technology Development (NAFOSTED) (under Vietnam's Ministry of Science and Technology).

Dr. Le has consulted for the World Bank, UNDP, Asian Development Bank (ADB), ADB Institute (ADBI), and the Economic Research Institute for ASEAN and East Asia (ERIA). She is a recipient of multiple competitive research grants and fellowships such as the Pacific Trade and Development (PAFTAD) Fellowship for Young Scholars in 2013; the Public Diplomacy Federal Assistance Award by The U.S. Consulate General in Ho Chi Minh City; Vietnam's Public Affairs Section in 2018; and the National Foundation for Science and Technology Development (NAFOSTED) funds for research in social sciences and humanities in 2019 and 2023 as the principal investigator.

Dr. Le was an external reviewer for the Vici Social Sciences and Humanities programme under the NWO Talent Programme, the Dutch Research Council (NWO). She was the founding Editor-in-Chief of the *Fulbright Review of Economics and Policy* and holds associate editor/editorial roles with several other scholarly journals including the *Journal of Economic Asymmetries* (Elsevier); *Journal of Economic Development* (sponsored by the National Research Foundation of Korea); *Singapore Economic Review* (one of the oldest and most respected economics journals in the Asia-Pacific region); and *Springer New Monograph Series, New Frontiers in Regional Science: Asian Perspectives* (Springer Nature).

© 2024 World Scientific Publishing Europe Ltd.
https://doi.org/10.1142/9781800614451_fmatter

About the Contributors

Silvio Andrae is an economist. Most of his professional experience has been in the financial sector. Since 2000, he has worked as a senior consultant in various green finance projects in Latin America, Africa, and Asia. For example, he worked on interdisciplinary rainforest projects in Amazonia (Brazil) for many years. Silvio Andrae is currently a senior advisor. He studied and received his Ph.D. at the Free University Berlin.

Roberto Barontini, Ph.D. in economics and management, is a Professor of Corporate Finance at Scuola Superiore Sant'Anna in Pisa, Italy. He has held research positions and professorships at Catholic University (Milan and Piacenza) and Pisa University, where he teaches Corporate Finance, International and Sustainable Finance, and Finance for Innovation. His research focuses on corporate governance, sustainability management, and innovation financing. He has published many academic papers in international refereed journals, including *Entrepreneurship Theory and Practice*, *Family Business Review*, *Business Strategy and the Environment*, *European Financial Management Journal*, *R&D Management*, *Journal of Cleaner Production*, *Journal of Management and Governance*, *Journal of Small Business and Enterprise Development*, *Economic Notes*, and *Journal of Economics and Business.*

John V. Duca is a Danforth-Lewis Professor of Economics at Oberlin College and Vice President (part-time) at the Federal Reserve Bank of Dallas, United States. He holds a Ph.D. in Economics from

Princeton University (1986) and a B.A. from Yale University (1982). He has published over 50 academic papers in international refereed journals, including the *Journal of Economic Literature*, *American Economic Review*, *Economic Journal*, *Journal of Money, Credit, and Banking*, *Journal of Economics and Dynamics and Control*, *International Economic Review*, *Economic Inquiry*, *Journal of Financial Stability*, and *Contemporary Economic Policy*. He has also published over 50 articles and working papers in Federal Reserve publications. From 1991 to 2017, he worked full-time at the Federal Reserve Bank of Dallas, last as the associate director of research. From 1986 to 1991, he was at the Federal Reserve Board, where he briefed the chairmen of the Board of Governors of the Federal Reserve System, Paul Volcker and Alan Greenspan, as well as Federal Reserve governors. Duca has taught part-time at Southern Methodist University and the University of Maryland.

Sebastian Goers has worked as a Researcher since April 2008 and as a Senior Researcher since December 2013 at the Department of Energy Economics of the Energieinstitut at the Johannes Kepler University Linz, Austria. After his studies in Bonn (Rheinische Friedrich-Wilhelm University), Germany, and Córdoba (Universidad Católica de Córdoba), Argentina, he graduated in economics with a focus on international macroeconomics and environmental economics. His dissertation at the Johannes Kepler University Linz, Austria, dealt with selected aspects of the effectiveness and efficiency of the European Emissions Trading Scheme. His research focuses mainly on the macro-econometric analysis of energy issues at the regional and national levels and on evaluating European energy and climate policies. In addition, since mid-2013 he has acted as the scientific coordinator of Upper Austria within the RLS-Energy Network of the partner regions of Bavaria, Georgia, Western Cape, Upper Austria, Québec, São Paulo, and Shandong in which he initiates and coordinates multiregional research cooperations about energy transitions.

Ikram Ullah Khan has received a Ph.D. in Business Administration from the School of Management, University of Science and Technology of China (USTC), Hefei, China. He currently serves as Assistant Professor at the Institute of Management Sciences, University of Science and Technology Bannu, KP, Pakistan. His research interests include digital banking/finance, behavioral finance, green banking/finance, e-learning/health, and information/technology management. He has published several articles in top-tier journals, such as *Journal of Behavior and Information Technology, Telematics and Informatics, Information Technology and People, Journal of Global Information Management, International Journal of Hospitality Management, Environment, Development and Sustainability*, and the *International Journal of Finance & Economics.*

Elaine Laing is an Assistant Finance Professor at Trinity Business School, Trinity College, Ireland. Previously, she worked in Australia, Hong Kong, and Singapore, lecturing undergraduate and postgraduate students on finance. Dr. Laing has also been a visiting scholar at the HEC Paris, France, and the Toulouse School of Economics, France. Dr. Laing obtained her Ph.D. degree from University College Dublin, Ireland, examining the foreign exchange exposure, multinationality, and corporate governance of U.S. firms. Her main research interests are risk management, corporate governance, international finance, and sustainable finance. Dr. Laing has been awarded several competitive research grants and her research has been published in the *Journal of Corporate Finance, Journal of Banking and Finance, International Review of Financial Analysis, Small Business Economics, Finance Research Letters, Research in International Business and Finance*, and *Journal of International Financial Markets, Institutions, and Money.* Dr. Laing is a recipient of the Trinity Business School Research Excellence Award, Performance Excellence Award, and Teaching Excellence Awards.

Wenling Li works as an Analyst at Marathon Capital, an investment bank serving clean power, sustainable technologies and infrastructure markets in the areas of mergers and acquisitions, capital raising, project finance, and tax equity advisory. Wenling is responsible for conducting research and due diligence, authoring marketing and offering materials, preparing financial analysis, and creating financial models. Previously, she worked as a research intern at Climate Bonds Initiative, where she contributed to the completion of the report "Transition Finance in China's Guangdong Hong Kong–Macao Greater Bay Area." In January 2022, Wenling received her B.A. in Economics and Environmental Studies, graduating Phi Beta

Kappa with Honors in Economics from Oberlin College, United States.

K. Thomas Liaw is a Professor of Finance in the Economics and Finance Department at St. John's University, New York, United States. Professor Liaw has published articles on green bonds, investment strategies of university endowments, repurchase agreements, smart beta exchange-traded funds (ETFs), and Brexit and risk contagion in global financial markets. He has also published books on financial technology, investment banking, and capital markets. His current research projects include green mortgages, property-assessed clean energy programs, university endowments, and fintech innovations. His principal areas of teaching and research include fintech, green finance, capital markets, investment management, and investment banking. He regularly participates in professional and academic activities. Professor Liaw received his Ph.D. from Northwestern University, United States.

Céline Louche is a Professor of Business & Society at Audencia Business School, France. Building on organizational, institutional, and strategic perspectives, her research examines the interplay between business and society. It includes topics such as corporate responsibility, sustainable development, business models for sustainability, and responsible finance. Her work appeared in top-tier journals, such as *Human Relations*, *Business & Society*, *Journal of Business Ethics*, *Organization & Environment*, *World Development*, *Journal of Management Development*, and *The International Journal of Human Resource Management*. Céline is Deputy Editor of *Business & Society* and Associate Editor of *Sustainability Accounting, Management and Policy Journal*. She also serves on several editorial boards, including *Organization & Environment*, *Journal of Sustainable Finance & Investment*, and *Management* and professional committees, such as the Towards Sustainability Initiative in Belgium.

Anastasiya Luzgina is an Associate Professor with a Ph.D. in Economics. She has work experience at the Belarusian State University, the National Bank of the Republic of Belarus, and as the IMF Resident Representative office in Minsk. Since 2010, she has worked at the Belarusian Economic Research and Outreach Center (BEROC). In 2015, Anastasiya participated in the BOFIT (Research

Center of the Central Bank of Finland) Visiting Researchers Program. She also completed the Fulbright Visiting Scholar Program (United States, 2018). In 2016 and 2018–2019, Anastasiya attended IMF/WB Spring Meetings in Washington, DC. She is the author of practice-oriented research papers in fields like monetary policy, green financing, fintech, currency market, cryptoassets and their regulation, social entrepreneurship, and food banks. She was involved in developing the FinTech Map of the Republic of Belarus and the Startup Heart mentor program. Anastasia Luzgina conducted a series of webinars for banks on green banking and sustainable finance.

Alain Neher is an Associate Head of School and Senior Lecturer at Charles Sturt University, Australia, and a Research Fellow and Adjunct Lecturer at the School of Business of the University of Applied Sciences and Arts Northwestern Switzerland. He earned his Doctoral degree in Business Administration from Charles Sturt University and was awarded the Outstanding Thesis Prize for the academic year 2016. He also holds two Master's degrees from the Lucerne University of Applied Sciences and Arts and a Bachelor's degree from the University of Applied Sciences in Business Administration, Zurich, Switzerland. His research interests include organizational culture and values, business ethics, and environmental, social, and corporate governance (ESG). Dr. Neher has published in various academic management journals, such as the *International Journal of Productivity and Performance* and *European Business Review* and is an editorial board member of the *Journal of Business Research*, with a focus on Corporate Social Responsibility and Business Ethics. He has also served as a referee for various high-quality international peer-reviewed journals.

Xuan-Hoa Nghiem received his Ph.D. in Economics from the School of Economics, Finance, and Marketing, College of Business, RMIT University, Melbourne, Australia. He is currently a lecturer in Economics at the International School, Vietnam National University, Hanoi, Vietnam. His research interests include macroeconomics, technology and growth, monetary policy, international finance, corporate finance, green finance, energy economics, and environmental economics. He has published in the *Bulletin of Monetary Economics and Banking* and has been actively involved in other research projects.

Dr. Nghiem used to work as a lecturer at Foreign Trade University, Hanoi, Vietnam; in the banking sector, as a researcher at Deposit Insurance of Vietnam (DIV) — a bank regulator, and as a risk management officer at PVcomBank — a commercial bank in Vietnam.

Benjamin Le Pendeven is Associate Professor at Audencia Business School (France). He holds a Ph.D. from Conservatoire National des Arts & Métiers (CNAM), France. His main research areas are entrepreneurial finance (venture capital, crowdfunding, corporate venture capital) and sustainable innovation financing (impact investing, social/environmental impact bonds, discrimination in funding entrepreneurs). On these topics, he heads the "Finance for Innovation" Chair in Audencia, and closely works with entrepreneurs, investors, intermediaries, and policymakers. He recently published papers in the *British Journal of Management*, *Venture Capital: An International Journal of Entrepreneurial Finance*, *Economics Bulletin*, and also contributed several book chapters.

Julia Margarete Puaschunder holds a Master's degree in Psychology, Business, Public Administration, and Economics, as well as Doctorates in Social and Economic Sciences, Natural Sciences, and Economics from the Inter-University Consortium (courses at Columbia, Princeton, and The New School, United States). Julia M. Puaschunder has over 20 years of empirical experience in applied behavioral and social sciences research in the international arena. Julia has published 10 books, which are held in thousands of libraries around the world. Since 2018 she has been listed in the "Marquis Who's Who in America and the World" among the top 3% of professionals around the globe and was awarded Lifetime Achievement Awards and Outstanding Leadership Awards from academic and professional communities. As a Friends of the International Institute of Applied Systems Analysis (IIASA) board member, she currently advances science diplomacy in cooperation with the United States National Academy of Sciences. Julia Puaschunder's work on climate justice was honorably mentioned in a Nobel Peace Prize nomination.

Vasja Rant is a Professor of Money and Finance at the School of Economics and Business, University of Ljubljana, Slovenia. He received a Ph.D. in economics from the University of Ljubljana in 2008, with additional training from the IMF Institute, Centro de

Estudios Monetarios y Financieros, and Barcelona Graduate School of Economics. His research focuses on budgetary aspects of European Union (EU) integration, bank regulation, international finance, and, more recently, sustainable finance. He published several articles in peer-reviewed journals and contributed book chapters, including in the *Journal of Financial Stability*, *Finance Research Letters*, *Journal of Common Market Studies*, *CESifo Economic Studies*, *Southeast European and Black Sea Studies*, and *Panoeconomicus*. He also serves as an editorial board member of the *Slovenian Journal of Banking*. Professionally, he participated in multiple rounds of negotiations about the EU multiannual financial framework (2007–2013, 2014–2020, and 2021–2021) at the European Council level and was involved in negotiating the NextGenerationEU recovery package in response to the COVID-19 crisis.

Mario Reisinger studied Industrial Economics at Universidad Carlos III de Madrid, Madrid, Spain. He has specialized in industrial economics, regulation, and competition policy with a focus on energy, transport, and telecommunication economics. Mario Reisinger graduated in September 2013 with honors. He worked at Iberdrola in Madrid and for the National Competition Authority Spain. Back in Austria, Mario Reisinger worked at Robotron, the Industrial Economics Institute, and for the Austrian Regulation and Competition Authority for Electricity and Gas E-Control. He was an active member of the energy intervention group at E-Control and was involved in designing ordinances for Market Monitoring, Statistics, and the Energy Intervention Act. Besides his academic and professional experience in Spain, he gained further international experience working as an expert in EU Twinning Projects in Georgia and the Eastern Partnership Programme. His fields of work at the Energy Institute of the Johannes Kepler University in Linz include regulation topics in the energy sector and macroeconomic simulation analyses.

Bart Reumkens is a Finance Ph.D. Candidate at Queen's University Belfast, UK. He holds an M.Sc. in Investment and Treasury from Dublin City University, Ireland. He is also a financial services professional with over 20 years of industry experience, particularly in risk management, data analytics, and sustainable finance. His career includes a wide range of roles spanning a number of different financial organizations in both the public and private sectors and firms such as HSBC, Morgan Stanley, and the Central Bank of Ireland.

Friedrich Schneider was a Professor of Economics at the Johannes Kepler University of Linz, Austria, from January 1986 to September 2017. He has been retired since October 2017. He obtained his Ph.D. in Economics from the University of Konstanz in 1977 and has held numerous visiting and honorary positions at many universities. He was the European editor of *Public Choice* from 1991 to 2004 and has published extensively in leading Economics journals, including *The Quarterly Journal of Economics*, *The American Economic Review*, *The Economic Journal*, and *Kyklos*. He has published (1974–2021) 82 books, 238 articles in refereed scientific journals, and 196 articles in edited volumes. His main research areas are Public Finance, Public Choice, and Environmental Economics. He has specialized in the shadow/informal economy, tax evasion, organized crime, and finances of terrorist organizations.

Lisa Sheenan is Lecturer at Queen's University Belfast, UK. She has published many academic papers in peer-reviewed top-tier academic journals, such as the *European Journal of Finance*, *Journal of Banking & Finance*, *Economics Letters*, and *The North American Journal of Economics and Finance*. She was the recipient of many prizes, such as the "Best Speaker Award" (2014) and the "Harry Murray Prize for Finance" (2008).

Jonathan Taglialatela, Ph.D., is a Postdoctoral Research Fellow at the Institute of Management of Scuola Superiore Sant'Anna in Pisa, Italy. He obtained a Ph.D. degree in "Management of Innovation, Sustainability, and Healthcare" (2017) from the same university under the supervision of Professor Roberto Barontini. He has been a visiting scholar at the Centre for Business Research, Judge Business School at the University of Cambridge, UK. Since 2020, he has been a lecturer at the University of Pisa, Italy, in Entrepreneurial Finance; since 2022, he also teaches Corporate Finance. His research interests include Sustainable Finance, Corporate Governance, and Innovation Financing.

Francesco Testa is a Full Professor of Sustainability of Management at the Scuola Superiore Sant'Anna in Pisa, Italy, where he coordinates the research group on Life cycle Management. He is also the Vice-Director of the Institute of Management, and a partner of the Spin-off Ergo srl. His main research concerns the relationship between institutional pressures, motivational drivers, environmental and economic performance, circular economy business models, and sustainable entrepreneurship. He has participated in numerous research projects promoted by the European Commission in environmental management. He is an Associate Editor of *Business Strategy & Environment* and a member of the Editorial Board of *Organization & Environment* and *Corporate Social Responsibility and Environmental Management.* He is the author of more than 90 articles, books, and book chapters on these topics.

Robert Tichler is a (macro-)economist and expert in energy and environmental economic analyses. His methodological research focuses on macroeconomic, techno-economic, socioeconomic, and systemic analyses of energy policy and economic issues and on assessing technologies, measures, regulations, and market developments. His main areas of expertise are hydrogen/power-to-X, complex energy systems, energy regulations, and external effects. He has been active at Energieinstitut an der JKU Linz in various functions since 2004, and in between also worked at the Institute for Operational and Regional Environmental Economics at JKU. Since 2019, Robert Tichler has served as managing director of Energieinstitut an der JKU Linz and as sole managing director since 2021.

Maya Tira is a Ph.D. student from Audencia Business School and Angers University (France). Her Ph.D. project is funded by the French Agency for Environmental and Energy Management (ADEME). Building from sustainable finance and public management perspectives, her research project explores the use of outcome-based contracts, such as Environmental Impact Bonds (EIBs) to fund environmental public policies. As part of her Ph.D. project, Maya participated in the launch of the first EIBs in France and continues to follow the project very closely. She also contributed to the selection and design of European Investment Bank-compatible projects for World Wildlife Fund (WWF). Prior to academia, Maya worked as a management consultant in financial services and the public sector.

She also holds a Master's degree in International Public Management from Sciences Po, Paris.

Hai Hong Trinh is a Doctoral Researcher in sustainable and climate finance at the School of Economics and Finance, Massey University, New Zealand, where his Ph.D. studies focus on the interactions between climate risks and financial markets. Hai is the executive board committee member of the Interdisciplinary Perspectives Special Interest Group (SIG) of the British Accounting and Finance Association (BAFA). Also, he has been a regular organizing member of Financial Management Association (FMA) International. His research papers have been published in several A-ABDC/CABS 3* journals and books, such as *Pacific-Basin Finance Journal*, *Applied Economics*, and *Business Strategy and the Environment*. His scientific engagement and memberships involve leading associations across the world, such as the British Accounting & Finance Association, American Finance Association, British Academy of Management, European Association of Environmental and Resource Economists, and Economic Research Forum. Hai is a member of Association of Vietnamese Scientists and Experts (AVSE) Global, where he is also part of the economic advisory board contributing to economic policies for Ho Chi Minh City, Vietnam, for financial centers, financial development, and the economy.

Han Wang is a Ph.D. student in Finance at Trinity Business School, Trinity College, Ireland, and she obtained her Master's degree in Finance from the same university. Her research focuses on the interface between corporate governance and sustainable finance with a particular focus on green bonds, examining the role of multiple governance mechanisms in corporate green bond choices and bond market performances.

Alfred Wong is a Senior Lecturer at the School of Business at Charles Sturt University and a Research Fellow at the School of Business of the University of Applied Sciences and Arts Northwestern Switzerland. He earned a Ph.D. in Finance from RMIT University in Melbourne, Australia, where he was awarded the University Research Prize. He also holds postgraduate and undergraduate degrees from the University of Queensland Business School in Brisbane, Australia.

His main research interests include the volatility of financial markets and sustainability. His expertise is in corporate finance, financial risk management, portfolio management, and applied economics. His recent work focuses on the role of ESG in executive compensation, stock return resiliency, and valuation of renewable projects. He has published in various academic journals, including the *Journal of Futures Markets, Finance Research Letters, and Sustainability.* He holds the Financial Risk Manager (FRM) designation certified by the Global Association of Risk Professionals, United States.

© 2024 World Scientific Publishing Europe Ltd.
https://doi.org/10.1142/9781800614451_fmatter

Contents

Part I
Green and Impact Bonds

© 2024 World Scientific Publishing Europe Ltd.
https://doi.org/10.1142/9781800614451_0001

Chapter 1

Green Bonds: A Tool Against Climate Change

Han Wang[*,†] **and Elaine Laing**[‡]

Trinity Business School, Trinity College Dublin,
University of Dublin, Dublin 2, Ireland
[†]*hwang1@tcd.ie*
[‡]*elaing@tcd.ie*

Abstract

This chapter aims to analyze the development of the green bond market from industry and academic perspectives. We provide an overview of green bonds, focusing on definitions, international green bond market frameworks, and risks and benefits for market participants. We raise awareness about the harmonization of green bond definitions and standards, the enhancement of green issuers' information disclosure quality, and transparency in the market. A comprehensive survey of the green bond empirical literature pertinent to both investors and issuers is provided, highlighting five research streams: (i) the drivers of green bond market/issuances, (ii) the impact of green bond issuances on issuers' performances, (iii) the existence of green bond premium, (iv) the determinants of green bond yields/premium, and (v) the correlations and diversification associated with the green bond market, contributing to comparisons across multi-divisional green studies. This chapter concludes with suggestions for future research directions.

[*]Corresponding author.

1. Introduction

As environmental, social, and governance (ESG) considerations and sustainability concerns are increasingly integrated into capital markets, green bonds have emerged as one of the most innovative and impactful financial instruments to channel capital flows toward climate change adaptation. A green bond is a fixed-income instrument whereby the funds raised are used to support specific climate-related or environmental projects. The pressure of climate change has fueled the demand for sustainable investments, and green bonds have become an integral element of sustainable financing (Nanayakkara & Colombage, 2021).

This chapter begins with a discussion of green bond basics, including definitions and governance regimes, calling for a unified regulatory framework and greater transparency of green bond practices. We then present a comprehensive survey of the green bond empirical literature. Drawing from related streams of corporate social responsibility (CSR) and conventional bond literature, we divide the mainstream green bond studies into five specific streams: (i) the drivers of green bond market/issuances (e.g., Barua & Chiesa, 2019; Nanayakkara & Colombage, 2021), (ii) the impact of green bond issuances on issuers' performances (e.g., Tang & Zhang, 2020; Wang *et al.*, 2020), (iii) the existence of green bond premium (e.g., Flammer, 2021; Zerbib, 2019), (iv) the determinants of green bond yields and premiums (e.g., Hyun *et al.*, 2021; Immel *et al.*, 2021), and (v) the correlations and diversification associated with the green bond market (e.g., Pham, 2021; Reboredo *et al.*, 2020). Our survey of the green bond literature helps compare the results for the different research streams and demonstrates the development of the green bond market. We conclude by identifying the gaps within the green bond literature and suggest an array of future research pathways.

2. Green bond basics

2.1. *Definition of green bonds*

To date, there is no consensus on the definition of green bonds. According to the Green Bond Principles (GBPs), green bonds are defined as "any type of bond instrument where the proceeds or an equivalent amount will be exclusively applied to finance or re-finance, in part or in full, new and/or existing eligible green projects and which are aligned with the four core components of the GBPs" (ICMA, 2021a). Bloomberg defines a green bond as "a bond specifically earmarked to be used for climate and environmental projects" (Bloomberg, 2021) and the Organization for Economic Co-operation and Development (OECD) defines it as follows: "a green bond is differentiated from a regular bond by its commitment to exclusively use the funds raised to finance or refinance "green" projects, assets, or business activities" (OECD, 2017). Although these definitions commonly acknowledge the differences between green bonds and conventional bonds, they also highlight the divergences in the use of green proceeds and what constitutes the funded green project category. Following the general guidelines above, the Climate Bonds Initiative (CBI) has constructed a green bond database based on two strict filtering criteria: (i) 100% net proceeds of bonds financing or refinancing green projects, and (ii) bonds aligned with self-defined Climate Bonds Taxonomy (see CBI, 2021). This helps provide a more practical definition, contributing to greater transparency and consistency in the market.

2.2. *International guidelines on green bonds*

The GBPs were introduced by the International Capital Market Association (ICMA), a not-for-profit organization under Swiss law aimed at offering services and recommendations to international security markets. It is the most recognized international framework for the global green bond market. As its green bond definition implies, the GBPs intend to promote integrity and transparency in the green bond market. The four core components for the GBPs, alignment are as follows: (i) use of proceeds, (ii) process for project evaluation and selection, (iii) management of proceeds, and (iv) reporting.

Furthermore, it outlines 10 eligible green project categories: (i) renewable energy, (ii) energy efficiency, (iii) pollution prevention and control, (iv) environmentally sustainable management of living natural resources and land use, (v) terrestrial and aquatic biodiversity, (vi) clean transportation, (vii) sustainable water and wastewater management, (viii) climate change adaptation, (ix) circular economy adapted products, production technologies and processes, and (x) green buildings.[1]

The GBP also recommends external reviews to strengthen the transparency of green bonds, which take the form of appointing independent verifiers to assure compliance. There are three major types of external reviews in practice.[2] The first is a second-party opinion which declares whether a bond's intended use of proceeds and intended governance framework comply with the GBPs. One disadvantage of this method is the lack of a standard process and comparability. Second is third-party verification and certification against a declared set of industry-specific criteria, including the assessment of issuers' internal tracking method, whether the projects being funded are green, and the use of proceeds during project implementation. The third type of review is green bond ratings (or scores), which take a form similar to bond credit ratings that are evaluated by third parties, such as rating agencies, researchers, or specialists, and which are based on an established methodology. The ratings take unique 'green' features into consideration to assess bond performances.

Among the various types of external reviews, certification is considered to be the most rigorous form of assessment.[3] One popular and recognized certification framework was developed by the CBI, which launched the Climate Bonds Standard and Certification Scheme. To meet the CBI standard, green bond issuers need to appoint an independent reviewer who is certified by the CBI to provide a pre-issuance verification statement along with the bond documentation and statement that are reviewed by the Climate Bonds Standard Board (Hyun *et al.*, 2020).

The European green bond standard (EUGBS) established by the European Commission is another significant sustainability framework followed by the international community (Fatica & Panzica, 2020). It is a voluntary standard aimed at scaling the green bond market and

---

[1]Refer to ICMA (2021a) for further details.
[2]Refer to ICMA (2021b) for further details.
[3]Refer to ICMA (2021a) for further details.

Table 1. Green bond development event timeline.

Events	Agency/organization	Year (version)
The first ever green bond, also labeled as Climate Awareness Bond	European Investment Bank (EIB)	2007
The first U.S. municipal green bond	Commonwealth of Massachusetts	2013
The first corporate green bond	Vasakronan (Swedish company)	2013
Green Bond Principles (GBPs)	ICMA	2014 (v1) 2018 (v2) 2021 (v3)
The Paris Agreement of 2015	UNGCCC	2015
Climate Bonds Standard	CBI	2015 (2.0) 2017 (2.1) 2019 (3.0)
ASEAN Green Bond Standards	ASEAN Capital Market Forum (ACMF)	2018
EU Green Bond Standard	European Commission	2019

Source: Created by authors with reference to Cortellini & Panetta (2021).

meeting the European Union (EU) sustainability goals. Under this framework, four key requirements are proposed: (i) taxonomy and classification alignment; (ii) transparency; (iii) external reviews; and (iv) supervision by the European Securities and Markets Authority (ESMA) of reviewers (EU Technical Expert Group on Sustainable Finance, 2020). The standardization of green bond criteria by the EU enables the European green market to be estimated with greater transparency, credibility, and effectiveness (Table 1).

2.3. *Benefits and risks associated with green bonds*

2.3.1. *Benefits associated with green bonds*

Climate change has been the catalyst for sustainable development in finance. Green bonds originally emerged as an innovative fixed-income instrument to meet the demand for climate investments. They have grown explosively to finance the fight against climate change (Piñeiro-Chousa *et al.*, 2021a).

In recent years, there has been regulatory pressure to develop the green bond market and mitigate environmental impact. The Paris Agreement of 2015 under the United Nations Framework Convention on Climate Change (UNGCCC) pioneered the first legally binding international deal on climate policy. It was adopted by 195 countries, with the agreement of maintaining the rise in the global average temperature to well below 2°C above the pre-industrial level, preferably to 1.5°C (United Nations, 2017). During the 2016 G20 summit held in Hangzhou, world leaders reached an agreement supporting the development of local green bond markets and enhancing international collaboration to facilitate cross-border investments in green bonds. In response to international calls, there is a growing interest in country-level policies toward green bonds. In 2017, Singapore launched the Sustainable Bond Grant Scheme to encourage the issuance of green-related bonds. Hong Kong also announced the Green Bond Grant Scheme (GBGS) in 2018, subsidizing eligible green projects.

Issuers can potentially benefit from green bond issuances. By declaring themselves as green, issuers confirm their compliance with the Paris Agreement goals, which can attract sustainable investors, thereby broadening their investor base (Maltais & Nykvist, 2020). Another incentive for issuers is the potential of enjoying long-term pricing advantages and lowering their funding costs. Though some recent papers argue that the green pricing benefit is essentially zero, indicating that there are no pricing advantages at issuance (Flammer, 2021; Larcker & Watts, 2020), there is no unanimity on this strand of literature. Gianfrate & Peri (2019) and Hyun *et al.* (2020) report that stronger green signals to investors, such as certification by the CBI, can offer economic benefits to issuers. Moreover, MacAskill *et al.* (2021), when conducting a systematic review of green pricing literature, find that green bonds are more financially efficient in the secondary market. This suggests that, even if offering yields are not attractive at issuance, issuers can still choose green bonds because excessive demands in the secondary market may push up prices with higher liquidity so that issuers pay a lower rate at the end, which offsets higher financing costs at inception.

For investors who intend to 'green' their portfolios, green bonds provide them with the opportunity to meet ESG mandates. From an environmental viewpoint, incorporating green bonds into portfolios can diversify investment risks, thus lowering financial and transition risks (Naeem *et al.*, 2021a; Pham & Nguyen, 2021; Tiwari *et al.*, 2022).

2.3.2. *Risks associated with green bonds and green bond market barriers*

The risk of "greenwashing" exists for green bond investors. Broadly speaking, "greenwashing" refers to the deceptive corporate behavior of using an environmentally friendly appearance to cover its environmentally unfriendly substance to mislead stakeholders (Du, 2015). Firms adopting "greenwashing" as their corporate strategy may issue green bonds without undertaking actual environment-friendly actions. Such 'sin' bonds will severely impact investors' confidence in investing in green bonds.

The capital raised via green bonds can also be at risk of being misused during the project implementation phase. This arises from the fact that green bond projects have long operational periods and require new technologies, timely assessment, and supervision that may be unavailable at times (Agliardi & Agliardi, 2021). Appropriate institutional arrangements for green bond management are also lacking, and the key barriers to the development of the green bond market include restrictions on minimum issue size and high transaction costs (Banga, 2019). Nanayakkara and Colombage (2019) report that the green bond market is limited by low creditability caused by the lack of standardized definitions and transparent procedures.

To further develop the green bond market, international agencies and regional governments are recommended to facilitate the harmonization and taxonomy of green standards, construct a unified international green bond framework rather than voluntary regional regimes, and conduct grant schemes or offer subsidies to green issuers. Risk perception in the green bond market can be lowered by enhancing transparency in the monitoring process and assessment of the use of proceeds throughout a green project's lifecycle.

3. Green bond literature review

In recent years, there has been a rapid growth in the green bond market, and literature on this field has developed in parallel. A keyword search utilizing words such as "green bond", "climate bond" and "green finance" was conducted on two databases: Scopus and Google Scholar. The search results were then restricted to English-language empirical academic papers published in the finance area between January 2015 and February 2022.

In Table 2, we first divide the literature into macro- and micro-finance categories, and then, drawing from the conventional bond and CSR literature, we highlight five main literature streams: (i) the drivers of green bond market/issuances, (ii) the impact of green bond issuances on issuers' performances, (iii) the existence of green bond premium, (iv) the determinants of green bond yields/premium, and (v) the correlations and diversification associated with the green bond market. We discuss each of the literature streams in further detail in Sections 3.1–3.5. In Table 3, we provide a summary of the literature review papers that have been published to date. Most of the review papers have covered green bonds from a micro-finance perspective, except Bhutta *et al.* (2022), who develop a systematic review covering all research strands and outline several research venues that can be further explored. Bhutta *et al.* (2022) also summarize the main theoretical literature on the drivers of the green bond market and empirical literature on the impact of green bond issuances on issuers' performances, recommending that future examinations can focus on the impact of governance issues and business life cycle on green–conventional bond performance comparisons.

3.1. *Drivers of green bond market/issuances*

Despite the rapid growth of the global green bond market, Agliardi and Agliardi (2021) suggest that there is still a limited supply of green debt and plenty of scope for the green bond market to develop further. Hence, research on the drivers of green bonds could identify favorable variables that promote the green bond market, and can offer policy implications. Relevant research has shown that the factors that impact green issuances are multi-faceted and can be divided into issuers' attributes, bond, market, sectoral characteristics, and

Table 2. Categories of green bond literature.

Financial perspectives	Sub-category	Specific strands	Perspectives from market participants	Representatives
Micro-finance	CSR/sustainability-related	(1) Drivers of green bond market/issuances	Both issuers and investors (market)	Barua & Chiesa (2019); Chiesa & Barua (2019); Dan & Tiron-Tudor (2021)
		(2) The impact of green bond issuances on issuers' performances	Issuers (supply)	Fatica & Panzica (2020); Tang & Zhang (2020); Wang & Li (2020); Zhang *et al.* (2021)
	Bond literature	(3) The existence of green bond premium	Market	Flammer (2021); Nanayakkara & Colombage (2019); Zerbib (2019)
		(4) Green bond yield/premium determinants	Issuers (supply)	Hyun *et al.* (2020); Immel *et al.* (2021); Russo *et al.* (2021)
Macro-finance	Correlations and diversification associated with green bond market/index	(5) Correlations and diversification associated with the green bond market	Market	Broadstock & Cheng (2019); Naeem *et al.* (2021a); Pham (2021); Piñeiro-Chousa *et al.* (2021a); Reboredo *et al.* (2020)

Table 3. Literature reviews on green bonds.

Author (year)	Title	Methodology	No. of selected articles	Specific strand no.	Key findings/ suggested directions
Bhutta *et al.* (2022)	Green bonds for sustainable development: Review of literature on development and impact of green bonds	Systematic review	53	(1)–(5)	Regulatory environment and disclosure transparency are essential to scale up the green bond market. More studies are expected to provide insights into the determinants and consequences of green bonds.
MacAskill *et al.* (2021)	Is there a green premium in the green bond market? Systematic literature review revealing premium determinants	Systematic review	30	(3)–(4)	"Greenium" is more pronounced in the secondary markets, for government bonds and bonds with high investment grade.
Cortellini & Panetta (2021)	Green bond: A systematic literature review for future research agenda	Systematic review and qualitative synthesis	53	(1)–(4)	Further research can be done to investigate the green bond market performances.
Gilchrist *et al.* (2021)	The limits of green finance: A survey of literature in the context of green bonds and green loans	Selected literature	N.A.	(2)–(3)	Mixed evidence on green yield spreads can be explained by two competing motives for green bond issues: financial motives and non-pecuniary motives.
Liaw (2020)	Survey of green bond pricing and investment performance	Selected literature	N.A.	(3)–(4)	Mixed conclusions on "greenium" can be attributed to differences in samples, time domains, adopted methodologies, and bond types.

the macro-environment. Barua and Chiesa (2019) and Chiesa and Barua (2019) state that issuers' credit quality and profitability are positively related to the supply size of green bonds. Their findings also analyze the impact of bond characteristics: bonds with a higher coupon rate are associated with smaller size, while Euro-denominated bonds and those with a higher bond rating tend to be larger in size. Issuers' reputational risk is also an important factor (Sartzetakis, 2020). Apart from the supply size, macroeconomic variables, such as inflation, interest rates, and exchange rates, significantly affect the green bond market as well (Tu *et al.*, 2020). Maltais and Nykvist (2020) and Monk and Perkins (2020) illustrate that a supportive regulatory environment and sustainable policies favor the growth of green bond issuances. From the perspectives of green projects, Taghizadeh-Hesary and Yoshino (2019) highlight the role of project assessors in reducing risk, thereby accelerating green finance. Dan and Tiron-Tudor (2021) document a positive relationship between firm-level ESG ratings, fiscal balance, and inflation rates and the volume of green bond issuances in the EU. Within the Chinese context, Dou and Qi (2019) find that the likelihood of enterprise green bond issuances increases with the proportion of funds used for green projects through the examination of the logit model.

Nanayakkara and Colombage (2021) use bid–ask spreads and yield spreads to proxy for investor demands for green bonds and document a positive relationship between compliance with the GBPs and investor demands in G20 countries. Their conclusions suggest that greater transparency and trustworthiness of market participants contribute to higher demands in the green bond market.

3.2. *The impact of green bond issuances on issuers' performances*

While the relevance of green bonds is widely recognized, their economic benefit for issuers is still a subject of debate. The impact of CSR on shareholder value has been extensively debated for decades. Similarly, the issuance of green bonds, as an organizational CSR practice (Maltais & Nykvist, 2020), cannot escape the controversy of the tradeoff between economic and environmental benefits. There are two competing views in place. On the one hand, issuing a new green bond may serve as an information signal to investors on their social responsibility (Flammer, 2021) in line with issuers' long-term business model and market expectations, thereby creating economic value. On the other hand, CSR-centered strategies may also cause higher uncertainty in the short run, and shareholders are not sure whether they can remain profitable compared to economic-centered strategies.

One aspect of the economic benefits that green bonds may carry is reflected post-issuance, which can be divided into immediate reactions (i.e., stock price reactions toward the announcement of green bonds) using event study methodology and long-term corporate benefits (e.g., the changes in institutional ownership and CSR rating) employing the difference-in-differences (DID) approach. Baulkaran (2019) studies positive and significant cumulative abnormal returns (CARs) to green bond announcements, and found that CARs are positively impacted by issuers' firm size and Tobin's Q, and negatively affected by operating cash flows. Flammer (2021) and Tang and Zhang (2020) find that positive CARs are pronounced for certified and first-time green issues and corporate issuers, especially for issuers whose operations are closely related to the environment. However, Lebelle *et al.* (2020) argue that stock market reactions can be negative using an international merged dataset.

Tang and Zhang (2020) also find that the issuance of green bonds is associated with increased domestic institutional ownership and stock liquidity in the long run via the DID approach. Furthermore, Flammer (2020, 2021) utilizes the Bloomberg green bond datasets and reports that green issuers benefit from certified green bond issuances and exhibit long-term improvements in financial performance and reducing environmental footprints. Similar conclusions have been drawn by Yeow and Ng (2021) using green bond samples from CBI and Cbonds databases. Based on the agency and stakeholder views, positive announcement returns and CSR rating enhancement following green issues are also identified in the Chinese green bond market (Wang *et al.*, 2020; Zhou & Cui, 2019). Within the same Chinese context, Zhou and Cui (2019) show that the issues of green bonds can help strengthen issuers' innovation capacity, profitability, and operating performance. Apart from *ex-post* financial and environmental performances, Zhang *et al.* (2021) apply the DID approach to examine the impact of green bond issues on issuers' implied cost of capital and document that it relieves information asymmetry and reduces firms' perceived risks.

3.3. *The existence of green bond premiums*

Another aspect of economic benefit debates is the relative pricing of green bonds, in other words, whether green bonds are a cheaper financing tool when compared with conventional bonds. The yield differential between a green bond and a conventional bond is the green premium. The so-called "greenium" means that the yield of a green bond is lower than that of the equivalent conventional bond, which is also the negative premium. A "greenium" at issuance indicates lower funding costs for issuers while investors would like to pay higher prices for issuers' green behavior.

The research on "greeniums" offers mixed conclusions, depending on issuer types, time horizons, and geographical scopes. Pioneering academic work detects "greeniums" in both primary and secondary markets: Baker *et al.* (2018) and Ehlers and Packer (2017) employ mixed municipal and corporate bonds when examining the bond at-issuance yields; Karpf and Mandel (2018) and Hachenberg and Schiereck (2018) focus on the secondary market using the U.S. and global green bond sample, respectively. Karpf and Mandel (2018) also apply the Oaxaca–Blinder decomposition methodology and show that municipal issuers did not enjoy a "greenium" until 2017. Gianfrate and Peri (2019) support "greeniums" on both primary and secondary markets for 121 European senior labeled green bonds with stronger green benefits on the secondary market. As green bond research surges, recent papers question the existence of a green premium. Larcker and Watts (2020) report that, in 85% of the cases, the expected green premium is essentially zero for the U.S. municipal market, and Flammer (2021) and Tang and Zhang (2020) provide further evidence that the yield differential between global green bonds and conventional counterparts within the same issuer is nearly zero. Hyun *et al.* (2020, 2021), relying on the secondary global green market, show that green bonds do not necessarily have a lower yield compared to similar conventional bonds. Yet, for the Chinese green bond market, one of the representative papers, Wang *et al.* (2020) support a negative green premium of 34 basis points (bps) at issuance (Table 4).

Table 4. Literature related to green bond yields/premiums from micro-finance perspectives.

Author (year)	Green databases	Scope	Primary/ secondary market	No. green bonds	Method	Time period	Green premiums	Determinants of green premiums/ yield (spreads)
Preclaw & Bakshi (2015)	CBI	Euro and US	Secondary	N.A.	OLS	Mar 2014–Aug 2015	Approximate –20 bps	
Ehlers & Packer (2017)	CBI	Pari passu fixed rate	Primary	21	Yield Curve	2014–2017	–18 bps	
Karpf & Mandel (2018)	Bloomberg & EMMA[a]	US municipal	Secondary	1880	Oaxaca-Blinder decomposition	2010–2017	+7.8 bps until 2016; –23 bps later	
Baker *et al.* (2018)	Bloomberg & Mergent	US corporate and municipal	Primary	2083 municipals and 19 corporates	OLS	2010–2016 (municipal), 2014–2016 (corporate)	(–6 bps) – (–8 bps)	
Hachenberg & Schiereck (2018)	Bloomberg	Global	Secondary	63	OLS	Oct 2015–March 2016	Full sample (no spread); financials (tighter spread) & government (wider)	Dependent variable (DV): delta of I-spreads; issuer type; existence of ESG rating & government (+)
Partridge & Medda (2018)	EMMA	US municipal	Primary & secondary	548	Yield curve	June 2013–Jan 2018	–5 bps	
Febi *et al.* (2018)	Secondary	London Stock Exchange	Secondary	64 labeled green bonds	Pooled and fixed-effects OLS	2013–2016	No greenium until 2015; –69.2 bps in 2016	DV: difference between bond yield and government bond yield; maturity (–), liquidity (+), leverage (+)
Gianfrate & Peri (2019)	Bloomberg	Europe senior bullet	Primary & secondary	121 labeled	PSM + OLS	2013–2017	(–18 bps) – (–21 bps)	
Bachelet *et al.* (2019)	CBI	Global	Primary & secondary	89 selected bond couples	Matching	Jan 2013–Dec 2017	(+2.06 bps) – (+5.9 bps)	Institutional issues (negative premium); private (positive premium), unless certified

Zerbib (2017, 2019)	TRACE	Global	Secondary	110 matched	Liquidity control + OLS	July 2013–Dec 2017	–2 bps	Financial & low-rated bonds (–)
Kapraun & Scheins (2019)	Bloomberg & Thomson Reuters Eikon	Global Fixed coupon	Primary & secondary	658 matched	OLS	2009–2018	Government green bonds (–5 bps) – (–18 bps)	Certification (–)
Nanayakkara & Colombage (2019)	Bloomberg	Global – 25 countries	Secondary	125	Hybrid model	2016–2017	Tighter spread of 62.7 bps	
Wang *et al.* (2019)	WIND & CSMAR	China	Primary	305	OLS	Jan 2016–Dec 2018	N.A.	DV: yield spread; Green certification (–); issue size (–), market rate (+), ROE (–)
Larcker & Watts (2020)	Bloomberg & Mergent	US municipal	Primary/ secondary	640 matched	Matching	2013–2018	GB premium essentially 0	
Tang & Zhang (2020)	CBI & Bloomberg	Global 28 countries	Primary	132 unique issuers	OLS	2007–2017	Similar firms (–6.94 bps); same issuer (0)	
Hyun *et al.* (2020)	Bloomberg & CBI	Global	Secondary	60 matched	Liquidity control + OLS	2010–2017	No significant greenium	Certification/external review (–): external review (–6 bps), CBI (–15 bps)
Wang & Li (2020)	CSMAR	China	Primary	159	Multivariate	Jan 2016–June 2019	–34 bps	
Partridge & Medda, (2020)	CBI & EMMA	US municipal	Primary & secondary	N.A.	Index bench-marking	2009–2018	Nearly –4 bps in secondary; 0 in primary	
Li *et al.* (2020)	WIND	China	Primary	114		Jan 2016–Sept 2018	N.A.	DV: initial YTM spread with Treasury yield; issuer rating & certification & bond rating (–)

(*Continued*)

Table 4. (*Continued*)

Author (year)	Green databases	Scope	Primary/ secondary market	No. green bonds	Method	Time period	Green premiums	Determinants of green premiums/ yield (spreads)
Flammer (2021)	Bloomberg	Global	Primary	565	Matching within the same issuer	Jan 2013–Dec 2018	Almost 0	
Hyun *et al.* (2021)	Bloomberg & CBI	Global	Secondary	282 unlabeled & 3,296 labeled	PSM + OLS	Jan 2014–Dec 2017	Labeled green bonds (–24 bps) – (–36 bps)	Certification (–)
Immel *et al.* (2021)	3 indexes	Global	Secondary	466	Matching within the same issuer	Jan 2007–Oct 2019	(–8 bps) – (–14 bps)	DV: yield spread; Credit rating (–), time to maturity (+), amount issued (–), callability (–), USD (+), ESG rating (–)
Löffler *et al.* (2021)	Refinitiv	Global	Primary & secondary	2000	PSM & CEM + OLS	2007–Oct 2019	(–15 bps) – (–24 bps)	DV: ask yield; maturity (no sig)
Dorfleitner *et al.* (2021)	Environmental Finance & CBI	Global	Secondary	250 matched triplets	Matching + hybrid regression	2011–2020	Appropriate –1 bps	DV: green premium; verification (–), credit rating (+), maturity (+)
Russo *et al.* (2021)	Bloomberg & CBI	Global	Secondary	85 green issuers	OLS	2013–2016	N.A.	DV: long-term YTM; country rating (–); company's strategic orientation (+)
Sheng *et al.* (2021)	Xinhua Green Finance	China	Primary	418	PSM + OLS	2016–2018	Financials (−22.2 bps); corporates (+0.3 bps)	DV: green premium on offering yield; third-party (–); SOEs (–)

Note: [a]Electronic Municipal Markets Access.

3.4. *The determinants of green bond yields/premiums*

Febi *et al.* (2018) demonstrate that firms' leverage ratio and liquidity measures are positively associated with the green bond yield spread on the secondary market, and green bonds demonstrate stronger liquidity than conventional bonds. By focusing on bonds constituting three green bond indices, Immel *et al.* (2021) highlight that higher bond credit ratings and ESG ratings lower the yield spread and suggest that firms' MSCI governance scores are found to be the main driver.

Issuer types and external reviews play an important role in "greeniums". Bachelet *et al.* (2019) suggest that although institutional and public issuers enjoy negative green premiums, private issuers bear a higher green financing cost than "brown" financing unless their issues are certified when examining 89 matched bonds in both primary and secondary markets. This suggests that bond investors compensate green issuers for certification and external monitoring, which mitigates information asymmetry and their associated investment risks. Hyun *et al.* (2020, 2021) distinguish unlabeled and labeled bonds by the external certification and justify that the external review or stricter certification can offer a "greenium" of around 6–15 bps. Their analysis demonstrates that without certification, there is no significant evidence of yield differentials between green bonds and similar regular bonds. Wang *et al.* (2019) emphasize that third-party green certification can significantly lower issuers' financing costs indicated by the green bond risk premium as the difference between yield-to-maturity and the risk-free rate.

3.5. *Correlations and diversification associated with the green bond market*

In recent years, from the macro-perspective, market determinants and/or diversification benefits associated with green bonds have attracted scholars' attention. As ICMA (2017) outlines, the Solactive green bond index (SOLGREEN) was introduced in March 2014, followed by the S&P Dow Jones Green Bond index (SPGB) in July 2014 and the Bank of America Merrill Lynch Green Bond Index (GREN) in October 2014, and finally, in November 2014, a family of green bond-related indices was created by MSCI and Barclays, with the inclusion of multi-country local currency debt markets.[4] The comparison of green bond indices that track green market performances may help illustrate divergent results in the macro green bond research.

As shown in Table 5, three green bond indices are mainly employed in academic research: S&P Green Bond Index (SPGB), Solactive Green Bond index (SOLGREEN), and GB Global Ltd. index (GBGL). The SPGB covers bonds from corporates, governments, and multilateral issuers around the world, subject to those used to financing environmentally friendly projects (S&P Dow Jones Indices, 2022), while the SOLGREEN selects green bonds defined by the CBI (Solactive Green Bond Index, 2022). As indicated by the inclusion criteria, the SPGB includes self-labeled bonds, whereas the SOLGREEN does not. In contrast to the other two indices, the GBGL is a multi-currency global index and incorporates investment-grade-only bonds, including treasury, corporate, government-related, securitized bonds, and taxable municipals (MSCI, 2019).

Guo and Zhou (2021) suggest that monetary policy and green technological progress are vital determinants for the overall green market development. Piñeiro-Chousa *et al.* (2021a, 2021b) find evidence of investor sentiment influencing the green market. The spillover effects and diversification of green bonds associated with other financial markets vary across asset classes, time horizons, and market conditions. Regarding the diversification benefits of green bonds, there are mixed conclusions on the connectedness between the green bond market and other markets (e.g., stock, Treasury, currency, and commodity markets). Liu *et al.* (2021) find evidence of mutual spillover effects between the green bond and clean energy markets. A weak connectedness of short-term dependency between crude oil and green bonds is documented in Naeem *et al.* (2021a, 2021b), indicating a short-term hedging tool for the oil market. While Arif *et al.* (2021) and Nguyen *et al.* (2020) suggest that the green bond can be a

[4]The index family includes Bloomberg Barclays MSCI Global Index (GBGL), which tracks performances for the aggregate global green bond market, and single-currency green indexes, including Barclays MSCI USD-only index (GBUS) and Barclays MSCI EURO-only index (GBEU).

Table 5. Correlations and diversification associated with the green bond market from macro-finance perspectives.

Author (year)	Time period	Scope/green indexes	Methodology	Key findings
Broadstock & Cheng (2019)	Nov 2008–July 2018	SPGB	DCC and dynamic model averaging (DMA) model	Changes in financial market volatility, economic policy uncertainty, daily economic activity, oil prices, and positive and negative news-based sentiment toward green bonds are important determinants of the connection between green bonds and black bonds.
Reboredo (2018)	Oct 2014–Aug 2017	SPGB, GBGL, SOL-GREEN, GBEN	Copula	Green bonds have sizeable diversification benefits for investors in stock and energy markets but negligible effects in corporate and Treasury markets.
Reboredo *et al.* (2020)	Oct 2014–Dec 2018	GBEU and GBUS	Wavelet-based and VAR models	Green bonds are strongly connected with Treasury and corporate bonds but weakly connected with high-yield corporate bonds, stock, and energy assets, suggesting a useful vehicle for portfolio hedging and risk diversification over different investment horizons.
Reboredo & Ugolini (2020)	Oct 2014–June 2019	GBGL	Structural VAR	Green bonds are weakly connected with stock, energy, and high-yield corporate bond markets; fixed-income and currency markets transmit sizeable effects to the green market, but the effect of green bonds on other markets is negligible.

(*Continued*)

Table 5. (*Continued*)

Author (year)	Time period	Scope/green indexes	Methodology	Key findings
Kanamura (2020)	Nov 2014–Dec 2018	GBGL, SPGB, SOL-GREEN	Correlation and DCC model parameter estimation	Green bonds are superior to conventional bonds but superiority decays over time, and different indices have different correlations with oil prices: the first two indices tend to be positively correlated with WTI and Brent oil prices, while the last one has a negative relationship.
Hammoudeh *et al.* (2020)	July 2014–Feb 2020	SPGB	Three time-varying causality algorithms	There is significant time-varying causality from CO_2 emission allowances price to green bonds, suggesting its predictive power in the green market, but there is no significant causality running from green bonds to other assets.
Nguyen *et al.* (2020)	Dec 2008–Dec 2019	SPGB series	Wavelet-based	Green bonds can provide hedging implications for both stock and commodity markets at all investment horizons.
Jin *et al.* (2020)	Dec 2008–Aug 2018	SPGB	DCC-APGARCH, DCC-TGARCH, DCC-GJR-GARCH	The connectedness between carbon futures returns and green returns is highest and most noticeable during volatile conditions, indicating that the green bond index is an effective and inexpensive hedge for carbon risk.
Pham & Luu Duc Huynh (2020)	Oct 2014–Nov 2019	SPGB, SOL-GREEN, GBUS, GBEU	Static VAR using 200-day rolling window	The impact of investor attention on green bond index volatility and returns is time-varying.

Pham (2021)	Aug 2014–Aug 2020	SPGB	Generalized forecast error variance decomposition (GFEVD) and cross-quantilogram approach	During extreme market conditions, spillovers between green bonds and green equity are significant, but they are insignificant during normal conditions; the spillovers depend on investment horizons and market conditions.
Pham & Nguyen (2021a)	Oct 2014–Nov 2020	SPGB, SOL-GREEN, GBUS, GBEU	Markov-switching dynamic regression and TVP-VAR models	The connectedness between green bonds and uncertainty is found to be time-varying and state-dependent: the green bond can work as a tool to hedge uncertainty during times of low uncertainty, but its diversification benefits are lower during high uncertain times.
Pham & Nguyen (2021b)	Oct 2014–Feb 2021	GBUS, GBEU	Cross-quantilogram	Hedging benefits of green bonds against conventional assets differ across extreme market conditions: conventional bond and stock markets have significant impacts (spillover effects) on the green bond market after COVID-19, while energy market imposes an insignificant impact.
Liu *et al.* (2021)	July 2011–Feb 2020	SPGB	Copula and conditional value-at-risk models	There is a positive time-varying average and tail dependence between green bond and clean energy markets; extreme movements in the clean energy market have a spillover effect on green bonds, which is asymmetric: spillover is greater for downside risks and lesser for upside risks.

(*Continued*)

Table 5. *(Continued)*

Author (year)	Time period	Scope/green indexes	Methodology	Key findings
Naeem *et al.* (2021a)	Dec 2008–Dec 2020	SPGB	Time-varying spillover approach of DY and frequency-domain spillover framework of BK	Gold and silver observe the strongest link with green indices and oil has a strong connectedness with green bonds in the long run; green bond markets can be a hedging vehicle for commodity markets (except precious markets) at various periods.
Naeem *et al.* (2021b)	Dec 2008–June 2020	SPGB	Time-varying optimal copula (TVOC)	Connectedness between green bond and energy markets observes a decreasing trend since 2012; green bonds comove weakly with stock and energy commodities.
Ferrer *et al.* (2021)	Oct 2014–Dec 2019	GBGL	BK framework and DY approach	Green bonds are not a different asset class, i.e., limited connections with other asset classes, but they closely mirror the performance of government and high-quality corporate bonds; the return and volatility connectedness between green bonds and traditional markets (i.e., commodity, currency, bond, and stock markets) mainly occur at shorter time horizons.
Arif *et al.* (2021)	Jan 2008–July 2020	SPGB	BK framework and DY approach	Financial stability can be a significant factor in determining the smooth transition to green investments.

Guo & Zhou (2021)	Aug 2014–Aug 2021	GBUSTRUU & China Green Bond Index (CNGB)	Copula approach based on TGARCH	Green bonds can be a safe haven but were not an effective hedging tool during the COVID-19 pandemic; monetary policy and green technological progress are important determinants for green market development; Green market behaviors in the US and China resemble each other.
Rannou *et al.* (2021)	Jan 2013–Dec 2020	European 86 power firms	Bivariable GJR GARCH and VAR	Green bonds complement carbon futures for short-term hedging yet substitute for long-term hedging.
Piñeiro-Chousa *et al.* (2021b)	July 2016–Nov 2019	GBGLTRUU,[a] SPGB, SOL-GREEN, CFIICGRB[b]	Panel smooth transition regression model (PSTR)	Social media sentiment plays a role in the green bond markets.
Piñeiro-Chousa *et al.* (2021a)	Jan 2018–Nov 2018		GMM	The green bond market is positively related to social sentiment, but negatively correlates with the S&P index.
Adekoya *et al.* (2021)	Nov 2008–Sep 2020	SPGB & select index	Fractional integration approach and 3 GARCH-based models	The impact of the COVID-19 pandemic on the persistence of volatility shocks in the green bond market is stronger than that of the financial crisis.

(Continued)

Table 5. (*Continued*)

Author (year)	Time period	Scope/green indexes	Methodology	Key findings
Leitao *et al.* (2021)	March 2014–Sept 2019; July 2014–Sept 2019	SOLGREEN SPGB	Markov-switching (MS)	The green market has a significant and positive impact on carbon price movements in both low volatility and high volatility regimes; the green assets' characteristics of transparency and less volatility attract higher demand from investors.
Lee *et al.* (2021)	Dec 2013–Jan 2019	GBGL	Granger-causality quantile analysis	The mutual effect between oil and green bond markets depends on market conditions: stronger in bearish states and limited in bullish markets.
Tiwari *et al.* (2022)	Jan 2015–Sept 2020	SPGB	TVP-VAR and LASSO-DY approach	Green bonds are difficult to hedge but can hedge other assets' risks because green bonds transmit lowest shocks to other markets; clean energy is the largest transmitter of shocks to the green bond market.

Notes: [a]Bloomberg Barclays MSCI Global Green Index Total Return Index Value unhedged (GBGLTRUU).
[b]FTSE Chinese (Onshore CNY) Green Bond Index (CFIICGRB) includes the onshore Chinese yuan-denominated, fixed-rate government, agency, and corporate debt issued in mainland China and labeled as green (FTSE Russell, 2021). The inclusion criteria of Chinese green indices are not closely in line with the international Climate Bond Taxonomy because in 2015 the People's Bank of China (PBOC) defined green bonds differently in the use of proceeds and green projects (see CBI (2021) for more details). China has been trying to harmonize its green bond standards with international ones, such as to adopt the "do no significant harm" principle in updating the catalog.

diversifying and safe-haven asset for precious metals due to its weak link with them, Naeem *et al.* (2021a) argue the opposite. Nguyen *et al.* (2020) also highlight the diversification benefits of green bonds with the stock market in line with Reboredo *et al.* (2020), who suggest that green bonds can be a hedging tool for high-yield corporate bonds, stocks, and energy assets, but not for Treasury and corporate bonds. Jin *et al.* (2020) highlight the hedging role of green bonds for the carbon market, and Pham & Nguyen (2021a) state that green bonds can hedge against uncertainty during volatile periods.

4. Concluding remarks and future research avenues

In the beginning of this chapter, we discussed the development of the green bond market and associated risks and benefits for both issuers and investors, shedding light on the consistency in green standards and transparency in the market. Then, this chapter presented a survey of the empirical literature on green bonds and divided green bond research into five specific strands: (i) the drivers of green bonds, (ii) the impact of green bond issuances on issuers' performances, (iii) the existence of green bond premiums, (iv) the determinants of green bond yields/premiums, and (v) the correlations and diversification associated with the green bond market. There are conflicts and crossovers between these streams that could be better interpreted by using one stream to understand another. For instance, exploring the determinants of green premiums could help resolve the conflicting evidence on the existence of green premiums. Despite growth in the green bond literature, theoretical and empirical understanding of the green bond market are still underdeveloped. We conclude by suggesting the following avenues for future research:

(1) Regarding the factors that impact green bond issuances, research has mainly undertaken qualitative studies (e.g., Sartzetakis, 2020; Tu *et al.*, 2020). To date, the limited number of quantitative papers tends to only focus on the green bond market (Barua & Chiesa, 2019; Nanayakkara & Colombage, 2021) with little empirical evidence on the comparison between green bonds and conventional bonds. Future studies could be conducted to analyze the impact of bond issuers and/or market characteristics on the differences between conventional and green issues

(e.g., issue sizes, post-issuance market performances, and yield premiums), which could provide suggestions for attracting private bond issuers, diversifying investor bases, and enhancing the liquidity of the secondary green bond market.

(2) Mixed results on the existence of the green premium can be explained by issuer types, market characteristics, and methodologies. There are multiple procedures to match a similar conventional bond to a particular green issue, subject to different criteria, for instance, within the same issuer and with similar issuers (Flammer, 2021; Tang & Zhang, 2020). Given the specific characteristics of issuers, future research could examine the impact of governance structures of issuers on the green premium for matched similar green-conventional bond pairs. Although numerous papers have investigated the impact of governance mechanisms on conventional bond yields (e.g., Anderson *et al.*, 2004; Elyasiani *et al.*, 2010; Huang & Petkevich, 2016), whether such mechanisms affect green premiums requires further examination.

(3) When examining green bonds, theoretical perspectives can be integrated with empirical research (e.g., signaling, legitimacy, and agency lens). The conflicting nature of the stakeholder–shareholder relationship and principal–agent relationship may be reflected in the green bond choices and market performances. This is because the issuance of green bonds is an environmental strategy signaling organizational efforts toward climate-friendly project investments and funding, which may not be closely aligned with the interests of profit-maximizing shareholders and managers. Applying an integrated theoretical framework could bridge a link between the sustainability/CSR/governance literature and the development of green bonds.

(4) From the macro-perspective, the spillover effects and diversification benefits of green bonds with other asset classes are investigated using various methodologies (e.g., VAR, Copula, wavelet-based, and multivariate GARCH models). More algorithms could be utilized to examine the dynamic effects between the green bond market and other financial markets.

References

Adekoya, O. B., Oliyide, J. A., Asl, M. G., & Jalalifar, S. (2021). Financing the green projects: Market efficiency and volatility persistence of green versus conventional bonds, and the comparative effects of health and financial crises. *International Review of Financial Analysis, 78*, 101954. https://doi.org/10.1016/j.irfa.2021.101954.

Agliardi, E. & Agliardi, R. (2021). Pricing climate-related risks in the bond market. *Journal of Financial Stability, 54*, 100868. https://doi.org/10.1016/j.jfs.2021.100868.

Anderson, R. C., Mansi, S. A., & Reeb, D. M. (2004). Board characteristics, accounting report integrity, and the cost of debt. *Journal of Accounting and Economics, 37*(3), 315–342. https://doi.org/10.1016/j.jacceco.2004.01.004.

Arif, M., Hasan, M., Alawi, S. M., & Naeem, M. A. (2021). COVID-19 and time-frequency connectedness between green and conventional financial markets. *Global Finance Journal, 49*, 100650. https://doi.org/10.1016/j.gfj.2021.100650.

Bachelet, M. J., Becchetti, L., & Manfredonia, S. (2019). The green bonds premium puzzle: The role of issuer characteristics and third-party verification. *Sustainability, 11*(4), 1098. https://doi.org/10.3390/su11041098.

Baker, M., Bergstresser, D., Serafeim, G., & Wurgler, J. (2018). Financing the response to climate change: The pricing and ownership of U.S. green bonds (No. w25194). National Bureau of Economic Research. https://doi.org/10.3386/w25194.

Banga, J. (2019). The green bond market: A potential source of climate finance for developing countries. *Journal of Sustainable Finance & Investment, 9*(1), 17–32. https://doi.org/10.1080/20430795.2018.1498617.

Barua, S. & Chiesa, M. (2019). Sustainable financing practices through green bonds: What affects the funding size? *Business Strategy and the Environment, 28*(6), 1131–1147. Scopus. https://doi.org/10.1002/bse.2307.

Baulkaran, V. (2019). Stock market reaction to green bond issuance. *Journal of Asset Management, 20*(5), 331–340. https://doi.org/10.1057/s41260-018-00105-1.

Bhutta, U. S., Tariq, A., Farrukh, M., Raza, A., & Iqbal, M. K. (2022). Green bonds for sustainable development: Review of literature on development and impact of green bonds. *Technological Forecasting and Social Change, 175*, 121378. https://doi.org/10.1016/j.techfore.2021.121378.

Broadstock, D. C. & Cheng, L. T. W. (2019). Time-varying relation between black and green bond price benchmarks: Macroeconomic determinants for the first decade. *Finance Research Letters*, *29*, 17–22. https://doi.org/10.1016/j.frl.2019.02.006.

CBI (2019). Climate Bonds Taxonomy. https://www.climatebonds.net/standard/taxonomy.

CBI (2021). China Definitions. https://www.climatebonds.net/market/explaining-green-bonds/china-definitions.

Chiesa, M. & Barua, S. (2019). The surge of impact borrowing: The magnitude and determinants of green bond supply and its heterogeneity across markets. *Journal of Sustainable Finance & Investment*, *9*(2), 138–161. https://doi.org/10.1080/20430795.2018.1550993.

Cortellini, G. & Panetta, I. C. (2021). Green bond: A systematic literature review for future research agendas. *Journal of Risk and Financial Management*, *14*(12), 589. https://doi.org/10.3390/jrfm14120589.

Dan, A. & Tiron-Tudor, A. (2021). The determinants of green bond issuance in the European Union. *Journal of Risk and Financial Management*, *14*(9), 446. https://doi.org/10.3390/jrfm14090446.

Dorfleitner, G., Utz, S., & Zhang, R. (2021). The pricing of green bonds: External reviews and the shades of green. *Review of Managerial Science*. https://doi.org/10.1007/s11846-021-00458-9.

Dou, X. & Qi, S. (2019). The choice of green bond financing instruments. *Cogent Business & Management*, *6*(1), 1652227. https://doi.org/10.1080/23311975.2019.1652227.

Du, X. (2015). How the market values greenwashing? Evidence from China. *Journal of Business Ethics*, *128*(3), 547–574. https://doi.org/10.1007/s10551-014-2122-y.

Ehlers, T. & Packer, F. (2017). Green bond finance and certification (SSRN scholarly paper ID 3042378). Social Science Research Network. https://papers.ssrn.com/abstract=3042378.

Elyasiani, E., Jia, J. (Jane), & Mao, C. X. (2010). Institutional ownership stability and the cost of debt. *Journal of Financial Markets*, *13*(4), 475–500. https://doi.org/10.1016/j.finmar.2010.05.001.

EU Technical Expert Group on Sustainable Finance (2020). Usability guide TEG proposal for an EU green bond standard. https://ec.europa.eu/info/sites/default/files/business_economy_euro/banking_and_finance/documents/200309-sustainable-finance-teg-green-bond-standard-usability-guide_en.pdf.

Fatica, S. & Panzica, R. (2020). Green bonds as a tool against climate change? (SSRN scholarly paper ID 3710020). Social Science Research Network. https://doi.org/10.2139/ssrn.3710020.

Febi, W., Schäfer, D., Stephan, A., & Sun, C. (2018). The impact of liquidity risk on the yield spread of green bonds. *Finance Research Letters, 27*, 53–59. https://doi.org/10.1016/j.frl.2018.02.025.

Ferrer, R., Shahzad, S. J. H., & Soriano, P. (2021). Are green bonds a different asset class? Evidence from time-frequency connectedness analysis. *Journal of Cleaner Production, 292*, 125988. https://doi.org/10.1016/j.jclepro.2021.125988.

Flammer, C. (2020). Green bonds: Effectiveness and implications for public policy. *Environmental and Energy Policy and the Economy, 1*, 95–128. https://doi.org/10.1086/706794.

Flammer, C. (2021). Corporate green bonds. *Journal of Financial Economics.* https://doi.org/10.1016/j.jfineco.2021.01.010.

FTSE Russell (2021). FTSE Chinese (Onshore CNY) Green Bond Index. https://research.ftserussell.com/products/downloads/FTSE_Chinese_Green_Bond_Index_RuleBook.pdf.

Gianfrate, G. & Peri, M. (2019). The green advantage: Exploring the convenience of issuing green bonds. *Journal of Cleaner Production, 219*, 127–135. https://doi.org/10.1016/j.jclepro.2019.02.022.

Gilchrist, D., Yu, J., & Zhong, R. (2021). The limits of green finance: A survey of literature in the context of green bonds and green loans. *Sustainability, 13*(2), 478. https://doi.org/10.3390/su13020478.

Guo, D. & Zhou, P. (2021). Green bonds as hedging assets before and after COVID: A comparative study between the US and China. *Energy Economics, 104*, 105696. https://doi.org/10.1016/j.eneco.2021.105696.

Hachenberg, B. & Schiereck, D. (2018). Are green bonds priced differently from conventional bonds? *Journal of Asset Management, 19*(6), 371–383. https://doi.org/10.1057/s41260-018-0088-5.

Hammoudeh, S., Ajmi, A. N., & Mokni, K. (2020). Relationship between green bonds and financial and environmental variables: A novel time-varying causality. *Energy Economics, 92*, 104941. https://doi.org/10.1016/j.eneco.2020.104941.

Huang, K. & Petkevich, A. (2016). Corporate bond pricing and ownership heterogeneity. *Journal of Corporate Finance, 36*, 54–74. https://doi.org/10.1016/j.jcorpfin.2015.11.001.

Hyun, S., Park, D., & Tian, S. (2020). The price of going green: The role of greenness in green bond markets. *Accounting & Finance, 60*(1), 73–95. https://doi.org/10.1111/acfi.12515.

Hyun, S., Park, D., & Tian, S. (2021). Pricing of green labeling: A comparison of labeled and unlabeled green bonds. *Finance Research Letters, 41*, 101816. https://doi.org/10.1016/j.frl.2020.101816.

ICMA (2017). The GBP databases and indices working group — Summary of green fixed income indices providers. https://www.cbd.int/financial/greenbonds/icma-indices2017.pdf.

ICMA (2021a). Green bond principles. https://www.icmagroup.org/assets/documents/Sustainable-finance/2021-updates/Green-Bond-Principles-June-2021-140621.pdf.

ICMA (2021b). Guidelines for green, social, sustainability and sustainability-linked bonds external reviews. https://www.icmagroup.org/assets/documents/Sustainable-finance/Guidelines-for-GreenSocialSustainability-and-Sustainability-Linked-Bonds-External-Reviews-February-2021-170221.pdf.

Immel, M., Hachenberg, B., Kiesel, F., & Schiereck, D. (2021). Green bonds: Shades of green and brown. *Journal of Asset Management*, *22*(2), 96–109. https://doi.org/10.1057/s41260-020-00192-z.

Jin, J., Han, L., Wu, L., & Zeng, H. (2020). The hedging effect of green bonds on carbon market risk. *International Review of Financial Analysis*, *71*, 101509. https://doi.org/10.1016/j.irfa.2020.101509.

Kanamura, T. (2020). Are green bonds environmentally friendly and good performing assets? *Energy Economics*, *88*, 104767. https://doi.org/10.1016/j.eneco.2020.104767.

Kapraun, J. & Scheins, C. (2019). (In)-Credibly green: Which bonds trade at a green bond premium? (SSRN scholarly paper ID 3347337). Social Science Research Network. https://doi.org/10.2139/ssrn.3347337.

Karpf, A. & Mandel, A. (2018). The changing value of the 'green' label on the US municipal bond market. *Nature Climate Change*, *8*(2), 161–165. https://doi.org/10.1038/s41558-017-0062-0.

Larcker, D. F. & Watts, E. M. (2020). Where's the greenium? *Journal of Accounting and Economics*, *69*(2), 101312. https://doi.org/10.1016/j.jacceco.2020.101312.

Lebelle, M., Jarjir, S. L., & Sassi, S. (2020). Corporate green bond issuances: An international evidence. *Journal of Risk and Financial Management*, 13, 25. https://doi.org/10.3390/jrfm13020025.

Lee, C.-C., Lee, C.-C., & Li, Y.-Y. (2021). Oil price shocks, geopolitical risks, and green bond market dynamics. *North American Journal of Economics and Finance*, *55*. Scopus. https://doi.org/10.1016/j.najef.2020.101309.

Leitao, J., Ferreira, J., & Santibanez-Gonzalez, E. (2021). Green bonds, sustainable development and environmental policy in the European Union carbon market. *Business Strategy and the Environment*, *30*(4), 2077–2090. https://doi.org/10.1002/bse.2733.

Li, Z., Tang, Y., Wu, J., Zhang, J., & Lv, Q. (2020). The interest costs of green bonds: Credit ratings, corporate social responsibility, and certification. *Emerging Markets Finance and Trade*, *56*(12), 2679–2692. https://doi.org/10.1080/1540496X.2018.1548350.

Liaw, K. T. (2020). Survey of green bond pricing and investment performance. *Journal of Risk and Financial Management*, *13*(9), 193. https://doi.org/10.3390/jrfm13090193.

Liu, N., Liu, C., Da, B., Zhang, T., & Guan, F. (2021). Dependence and risk spillovers between green bonds and clean energy markets. *Journal of Cleaner Production*, *279*, 123595. https://doi.org/10.1016/j.jclepro.2020.123595.

Löffler, K. U., Petreski, A., & Stephan, A. (2021). Drivers of green bond issuance and new evidence on the "greenium". *Eurasian Economic Review*, *11*(1), 1–24.

MacAskill, S., Roca, E., Liu, B., Stewart, R. A., & Sahin, O. (2021). Is there a green premium in the green bond market? Systematic literature review revealing premium determinants. *Journal of Cleaner Production*, *280*, 124491. https://doi.org/10.1016/j.jclepro.2020.124491.

Maltais, A. & Nykvist, B. (2020). Understanding the role of green bonds in advancing sustainability. *Journal of Sustainable Finance & Investment*, 1–20. https://doi.org/10.1080/20430795.2020.1724864.

Monk, A. & Perkins, R. (2020). What explains the emergence and diffusion of green bonds? *Energy Policy*, *145*, 111641. https://doi.org/10.1016/j.enpol.2020.111641.

MSCI (2019). Bloomberg Barclays MSCI Green Bond Index Consultation. https://www.msci.com/documents/1296102/12275477/Bloomberg+Barclays+MSCI+Green+Bond+Index+Consultation.pdf/e887b067-1513-c94d-4441-e18b39f6170d?t=1561734332189.

Naeem, M. A., Adekoya, O. B., & Oliyide, J. A. (2021a). Asymmetric spillovers between green bonds and commodities. *Journal of Cleaner Production*, *314*, 128100. https://doi.org/10.1016/j.jclepro.2021.128100.

Naeem, M. A., Bouri, E., Costa, M. D., Naifar, N., & Shahzad, S. J. H. (2021b). Energy markets and green bonds: A tail dependence analysis with time-varying optimal copulas and portfolio implications. *Resources Policy*, *74*, 102418. https://doi.org/10.1016/j.resourpol.2021.102418.

Nanayakkara, K. G. M. & Colombage, S. (2021). Does compliance with Green Bond Principles bring any benefit to make G20's 'Green economy plan' a reality? *Accounting & Finance*, *61*(3), 4257–4285. https://doi.org/10.1111/acfi.12732.

Nanayakkara, M. & Colombage, S. (2019). Do investors in green bond market pay a premium? Global evidence. *Applied Economics*, *51*(40), 4425–4437. https://doi.org/10.1080/00036846.2019.1591611.

Nguyen, T. T. H., Naeem, M. A., Balli, F., Balli, H. O., & Vo, X. V. (2020). Time-frequency comovement among green bonds, stocks, commodities, clean energy, and conventional bonds. *Finance Research Letters*, 101739. https://doi.org/10.1016/j.frl.2020.101739.

OECD (2017). Mobilizing bond markets for a low-carbon transition, green finance, and investment. OECD Publishing, Paris. http://dx.doi.org/10.1787/9789264272323-en.

Pham, L. (2021). Frequency connectedness and cross-quantile dependence between green bond and green equity markets. *Energy Economics*, *98*, 105257. https://doi.org/10.1016/j.eneco.2021.105257.

Pham, L. & Luu Duc Huynh, T. (2020). How does investor attention influence the green bond market? *Finance Research Letters*, *35*, 101533. https://doi.org/10.1016/j.frl.2020.101533.

Pham, L. & Nguyen, C. P. (2021a). How do stock, oil, and economic policy uncertainty influence the green bond market? *Finance Research Letters*, 102128. https://doi.org/10.1016/j.frl.2021.102128.

Pham, L. & Nguyen, C. P. (2021b). Asymmetric tail dependence between green bonds and other asset classes. *Global Finance Journal*, *50*, 100669. https://doi.org/10.1016/j.gfj.2021.100669.

Piñeiro-Chousa, J., López-Cabarcos, M. Á., Caby, J., & Šević, A. (2021a). The influence of investor sentiment on the green bond market. *Technological Forecasting and Social Change*, *162*, 120351. https://doi.org/10.1016/j.techfore.2020.120351.

Piñeiro-Chousa, J., López-Cabarcos, M. Á., & Šević, A. (2021b). Green bond market and sentiment: Is there a switching behaviour? *Journal of Business Research*, S0148296321008559. https://doi.org/10.1016/j.jbusres.2021.11.048.

Rannou, Y., Boutabba, M. A., & Barneto, P. (2021). Are green bond and carbon markets in Europe complements or substitutes? Insights from the activity of power firms. *Energy Economics*, *104*, 105651. https://doi.org/10.1016/j.eneco.2021.105651.

Reboredo, J. C. (2018). Green bond and financial markets: Co-movement, diversification and price spillover effects. *Energy Economics*, *74*, 38–50. https://doi.org/10.1016/j.eneco.2018.05.030.

Reboredo, J. C. & Ugolini, A. (2020). Price connectedness between green bond and financial markets. *Economic Modelling*, *88*, 25–38. https://doi.org/10.1016/j.econmod.2019.09.004.

Reboredo, J. C., Ugolini, A., & Aiube, F. A. L. (2020). Network connectedness of green bonds and asset classes. *Energy Economics*, *86*, 104629. https://doi.org/10.1016/j.eneco.2019.104629.

Russo, A., Mariani, M., & Caragnano, A. (2021). Exploring the determinants of green bond issuance: Going beyond the long-lasting debate on performance consequences. *Business Strategy and the Environment*, *30*(1), 38–59. https://doi.org/10.1002/bse.2608.

Sartzetakis, E. S. (2020). Green bonds as an instrument to finance low carbon transition. *Economic Change and Restructuring*. Scopus. https://doi.org/10.1007/s10644-020-09266-9.

Sheng, Q., Zheng, X., & Zhong, N. (2021). Financing for sustainability: Empirical analysis of green bond premium and issuer heterogeneity. *Natural Hazards*, *107*(3), 2641–2651. https://doi.org/10.1007/s11069-021-04540-z.

S&P Dow Jones Indices (n.d.). S&P Green Bond Index | S&P Dow Jones Indices. Retrieved March 19, 2022, from https://www.spglobal.com/spdji/en/indices/esg/sp-green-bond-index/#data.

Taghizadeh-Hesary, F. & Yoshino, N. (2019). The way to induce private participation in green finance and investment. *Finance Research Letters*, *31*, 98–103. https://doi.org/10.1016/j.frl.2019.04.016.

Tang, D. Y. & Zhang, Y. (2020). Do shareholders benefit from green bonds? *Journal of Corporate Finance*, *61*, 101427. https://doi.org/10.1016/j.jcorpfin.2018.12.001.

Tiwari, A. K., Aikins Abakah, E. J., Gabauer, D., & Dwumfour, R. A. (2022). Dynamic spillover effects among green bond, renewable energy stocks and carbon markets during COVID-19 pandemic: Implications for hedging and investments strategies. *Global Finance Journal*, *51*, 100692. https://doi.org/10.1016/j.gfj.2021.100692.

Tu, C. A., Rasoulinezhad, E., & Sarker, T. (2020). Investigating solutions for the development of a green bond market: Evidence from analytic hierarchy process. *Finance Research Letters*, *34*, 101457. https://doi.org/10.1016/j.frl.2020.101457.

Wang, J., Chen, X., Li, X., Yu, J., & Zhong, R. (2020). The market reaction to green bond issuance: Evidence from China. *Pacific-Basin Finance Journal*, *60*, 101294. https://doi.org/10.1016/j.pacfin.2020.101294.

Wang, Q., Zhou, Y., Luo, L., & Ji, J. (2019). Research on the factors affecting the risk premium of China's green bond issuance. *Sustainability*, *11*(22), 6394. https://doi.org/10.3390/su11226394.

Zerbib, O. D. (2017). The green bond premium (SSRN scholarly paper ID 2890316). *Social Science Research Network*. https://doi.org/10.2139/ssrn.2890316.

Zerbib, O. D. (2019). The effect of pro-environmental preferences on bond prices: Evidence from green bonds. *Journal of Banking & Finance*, *98*, 39–60. https://doi.org/10.1016/j.jbankfin.2018.10.012.

Zhou, X. & Cui, Y. (2019). Green bonds, corporate performance, and corporate social responsibility. *Sustainability*, *11*(23), 6881. https://doi.org/10.3390/su11236881.

© 2024 World Scientific Publishing Europe Ltd.
https://doi.org/10.1142/9781800614451_0002

Chapter 2

Corporate Green Bonds and the Cost of Capital*

Wenling Li[†,‡,‖] and John V. Duca[§,¶,]**

[‡]*Marathon Capital, Chicago, IL, USA*

[§]*Oberlin College, Oberlin, OH, USA*

[¶]*Federal Reserve Bank of Dallas, Dallas, TX, USA*

[‖]*wenling.li@oberlin.edu*

[**]*jduca@oberlin.edu*

Abstract

This study examines the effect of issuing the first green bonds on the corporate overall cost of capital. Using a difference-in-differences approach, we compare 191 green with conventional bonds that were issued in 19 countries between 2013q2 and 2020q4. We find that issuing a green rather than a conventional bond lowers the weighted average cost of capital (WACC) by 25 basis points (bps). In a robustness check, we estimate a nearly identical 24 basis point effect using a synthetic control method (SCM) to compare 16 green with 33 control companies in the energy and utility sectors that issued bonds between 2016q4 and 2020q3. The chapter provides empirical evidence that obtaining a "green bond" designation lowers the cost of capital, along with the required rate of return from the investors and the perceived riskiness of a firm's debt. The results are consistent with the view that climate change poses systemic risk to bond investors.

---

*The views expressed are those of the authors and do not necessarily reflect the views of Marathon Capital, the Federal Reserve Bank of Dallas, or the Federal Reserve System. We thank Paul Brehm, Barbara Craig, Martin Saavedra, Evan Kresch, and seminar participants at Oberlin for comments, input, and suggestions. Any remaining errors are those of the authors.

[†]Corresponding author.

The green bond market has expanded rapidly, with total issuance surging from under \$50 billion in 2015 to over \$250 billion in 2019 (Climate Bonds Initiative, 2020). This study examines whether green bond issuance reduces the overall cost of capital for a company. When a firm first issues a green bond, the green label could highlight their efforts to pursue environmental sustainability, which could improve their brand image and expand their investor base by attracting more ESG investors (Climate Bonds Initiative, n.d.*a*). These effects could reduce a company's cost of capital by lowering its risk premium and interest costs. The main hypothesis examined by this chapter is whether issuing green bonds reduces an issuers' overall costs of capital, equity, and debt.

To address the main hypothesis, our study matches 191 public corporate green bond issuers with conventional bond issuers of similar size and profitability in the same industry, country, and currency that issued a conventional bond close to when the corresponding green bond issuers issued their first green bond. The chapter adopts a difference-in-differences (DID) approach to compare the cost of capital of green and conventional bond issuers before and after issuing a bond. DID estimates indicate that being a green issuer lowers the weighted average cost of capital (WACC) by 24.5 basis points (bps), and by 30.3 bps in a pre-COVID sample (before 2019q4). For financial firms, the green bond designation lowers the WACC by 29.2 bps post issuance. Furthermore, these results are robust to using the synthetic control method (SCM). Studying green bond issuers in the energy and utilities sector, we construct a synthetic group of green bond issuers using the cost of capital and other firm traits *ex-ante* of the conventional bond issuers. The SCM estimates a negative treatment effect of 24 bps on the WACC six quarters after the green bond issuance. Consistent with Zhang, Li, and Liu (2021), we find that being designated as a green bond issuer lowers a firm's WACC. Our results from an international sample find a larger effect on WACC than Zhang, Li, and Liu (2021) did for their sample of Chinese firms.

There are many studies that focus on how green bonds can help investors diversify their portfolios (Reboredo, 2018; Wang *et al.*, 2020), analyze the price premium of green bonds (greenium) (Larcker and Watts, 2020; MacAskill *et al.*, 2020; Zerbib, 2019), or assess how the market rewards green bond-issuing companies (Flammer, 2021; Lebelle, Lajili Jarjir, and Sassi, 2020; Tang and Zhang, 2020;

Wang *et al.*, 2020). Yet, few studies have empirically examined the impact of issuing green bonds on a firm's overall cost of capital. Because firms can substitute across different sources of capital (e.g., loans, bonds, and equity), estimating a net effect on their overall capital costs provides a more meaningful estimate of the financial benefits of qualifying as a green bond issuer. Zhang, Li, and Liu (2021) were the first to directly examine the impact of issuing green bonds on a firm's cost of capital using a sample of publicly traded Chinese firms. We complement their research by examining an international sample of firms and utilizing not only a DID approach, but also the SCM as an important robustness check.

As with Zhang, Li, and Liu (2021), we also contribute to the literature by examining the impact of a firm's initial issuance of a green bond on the cost of capital rather than the impact of corporate social responsibility (CSR) (Cooper and Uzun, 2015; El Ghoul *et al.*, 2011; Xu, Liu, and Huang, 2015), environmental externalities (Chava, 2014), and environmental risk management (Sharfman and Fernando, 2008) on a company's costs of debt, equity, or capital. In particular, we use the issuance of green bonds as a more explicit proxy for sustainable initiatives, because (i) being designated a green issuer requires a firm to have adopted sustainability practices and (ii) institutional investors are more apt to face regulatory pressure to hold green assets rather than meet investment targets based on less explicit ESG rankings.

A third contribution is that the study is unusual in using the SCM to analyze the impact of becoming a green bond issuer. When it is feasible to implement, the SCM is generally preferred to — and used as a robustness check on — results from the DID approach, which imposes more restrictive assumptions on the data. In general, there is limited usage of the SCM approach in the empirical literature on business finance.

Understanding how becoming a green bond issuer affects a companies' overall cost of capital has implications for a company's long-term strategic planning. It is also meaningful for the scaling up of the green bond market and climate finance. As green bond issuance lowers the cost of capital, it provides incentives for companies to issue more green bonds from the supply side and subsequently stimulate the pipeline of sustainability projects (Shishlov, Morel, and Cochran, 2016). Furthermore, our results imply that investors require a lower rate of return and the market perceives lower risk on green bond issuers, which is consistent with the view that the complexity of climate change's impact on social, environmental, economic, and political systems implies that climate change poses a "systemic risk" to the market and especially to conventional bonds of higher credit (Centeno *et al.*, 2015).

To present our findings, this chapter is organized as follows. Section 1 provides a background on green bonds and on cost of capital. Section 2 describes the data and Section 3 discusses the empirical identification strategy. Estimation results, robustness checks, and extensions of the main empirical findings are presented in Section 4, and Section 5 concludes.

1. Background

1.1. *Mobilizing capital for a low-carbon economy*

Achieving Nationally Determined Contributions (NDCs) to ameliorate climate change is at the core of the 2015 Paris Agreement on Climate Change, setting country-specific pledges to reduce greenhouse gas emissions and adapt to climate change in a sustainable manner (Tolliver, Keeley, and Managi, 2020a). Prominent NDC target actions include implementing renewable and efficiency-enhancing energy technologies, preserving natural ecosystems, improving land-use practices, upgrading water supply and management systems, and adopting other sustainability-enhancing infrastructures and processes (Tolliver, Keeley, and Managi, 2020a). Around the globe, 193 countries have submitted their NDCs as of March 2022 (UNFCCC, n.d.).

Businesses are also taking action. Companies including Amazon, Apple, and Target have pledged to work toward the metrics established by the Paris Agreement and the United Nations Sustainable Development Goals (Knowledge@Wharton, 2017). By January 2022, 349 firms had joined *RE100*, a global initiative led by The Climate Group in partnership with the Carbon Disclosure Project (CDP), which brings together the world's most influential businesses to drive the transition to 100% renewable electricity (CDP, 2022). Large institutional investors such as CalPERS show a preference for investing in firms that pursue socially responsible activities

(Guenster *et al.*, 2011). There is also a growing emphasis on sustainable investing, socially responsible investing, and, more broadly, impact investing. According to the Global Sustainable Investment Alliance (2019), sustainable investment assets in Europe, the U.S., Japan, Canada, Australia, and New Zealand were worth $30.7 trillion at the start of 2018, a 34% increase since 2016.

The International Energy Agency estimates that $53 trillion in energy-related investments are needed by 2035 to achieve the target of limiting the rise in average global air temperatures to 2°C (International Energy Agency, 2014). Additionally, NDCs could require $97 to $191 billion by 2030 (Hof *et al.*, 2017). A variety of finance mechanisms that leverage both public and private resources could be critical to channel global capital into the Paris Agreement, NDC initiatives, and more generally, to fund the transformation to a low carbon economy (Tolliver, Keeley, and Managi, 2020a).

1.2. *Green bonds*

1.2.1. *Green bond basics*

Against this backdrop, green bonds are gaining prominence. As defined by International Capital Markets Association (2018), a green bond is "any type of bond instrument where the proceeds will be exclusively applied to finance or re-finance, in part or in full, new or/existing eligible green projects", in renewable energy, energy efficiency, green building, transportation, water management, pollution control, etc.

Initially, green bond issuers were mainly supranational and government entities. Indeed, the first green bond was issued in 2007 by the European Investment Bank as a structured bond with proceeds dedicated to fund renewable energy and energy efficiency projects (Rosembuj and Bottio, 2016). The World Bank issued its first green bond in 2008, a Swedish Export Credit (SEK) $2.3 billion bond with a maturity of six years for a group of Scandinavian investors. In March 2013, the International Finance Corporation (IFC) issued a $1 billion benchmarked bond (Rosembuj and Bottio, 2016).

Since 2013, firms have become more active in the green bond market. Apple issued its first green bond of $1.5 billion in February 2016 with a 7-year maturity, a semi-annual coupon of 2.85%, and an

Aa1 rating by Moody's (Kidney, 2016). Apple's first green bond proceeds were used to "Reduce Impact on Climate Change" by financing projects that fell under Apple's eligibility criteria for renewable energy, green buildings, and waste management. Pepsi, Verizon, LG, Barclays are well known among other green bond issuers. According to Flammer (2021), $113.4 billion of corporate green bonds were issued between 2013 and 2017. China, Japan, Netherlands, France, and the United States are among the countries with the largest corporate green bond issuance (Flammer, 2021).

Several characteristics distinguish green from conventional bonds besides their green nature. First, green bonds are typically backed not by the project but by the issuer's entire balance sheet, which reduces investor risk. Second, the great transparency in the green bond issuing process more effectively links the capital raised by a bond to sustainability efforts. Bonds are labeled green by the issuer and are usually qualified as green by an independent party (Climate Bonds Initiative, n.d.*b*). Issuers can commission an external review on the green credentials of the use of proceeds by accounting/audit firms, ESG service providers (e.g., Sustainalytics), and rating agencies. Green bond issuers may also be certified under the Climate Bonds Standard and Certification Scheme. The Green Bond Principles (GBP) promote the transparency and disclosure of green bonds (International Capital Markets Association, 2018). The GBP provide issuers with guidance on the key components involved in launching a credible green bond. They also encourage issuers to provide investors with more information to evaluate the environmental impact of their green bond investments.

On the demand side, a large investor appetite for green bonds is manifested by the oversubscription of green bond auctions. According to PwC (2022), "asset managers globally are expected to increase their ESG-related assets under management to US$33.9tn by 2026, from US$18.4tn in 2021. With a projected compound annual growth rate of 12.9%, ESG assets are on pace to constitute 21.5% of total global assets under management (AuM) in less than 5 years." These demands come from mainstream institutional investors, specialist ESG and responsible investors, corporate treasurers (including those at Barclays and Apple), sovereign and municipal governments, and retail investors. The Climate Bonds Initiative's "Green Bond Pricing in the Primary Market H2 2021" report reveals that green bonds attracted larger book cover with average oversubscription of 3 times for green bonds in USD and 3.4 times for those in EUR (Harrison, 2022).

1.2.2. *Literature review*

Upon their emergence, nonprofit organizations and scholars started to study green bonds systematically in the context of global climate action. The Institute for Climate Economics (I4CE) published the report "Beyond Transparency: Unlocking the Full Potential of Green Bonds," which summarized the opportunities and identified two major challenges for green bonds: protecting the environmental integrity and enhancing the financial benefits of green bonds (Shishlov, Morel, and Cochran, 2016). The 2016 study also concluded that to date, green bonds have not directly stimulated green investments by lowering the cost of capital, while admitting that growing climate commitment and demand for green bonds could ultimately result in better borrowing conditions. Employing a difference-in-differences (DID) analysis using panel dataset of $25 billion in green bond proceeds in 66 countries between 2008 and 2017, Tolliver, Keeley, and Managi (2020b) find that beyond conventional economic policy supports, climate commitments (i.e., NDCs) can drive global emissions reductions by inducing greater green bond finance for the renewable energy projects.

For investors, the substantial expansion of the market for green bonds has fueled research on them as a diversification instrument for investors. Reboredo (2018) finds that the green bond market weakly co-moves with stock and energy commodity markets; green bonds provide diversification benefits for stock and energy market investors; green bonds are affected by substantial price spillovers from corporate and Treasury fixed-income markets; and that large price swings in stock and energy markets negligibly affect green bond prices. Naeem *et al.* (2021) find hedging and diversification benefits of including green bonds in commodity portfolios.

There is a rich literature studying the premium of green bonds (or "greenium"), the lower yield on green bonds compared to that on similar conventional bonds. Its existence implies that investors are willing to accept a lower yield on green assets. A 2020 "Green Bond Pricing in the Primary Market" report of Climate Bonds Initiative reveals "increasing signs of greenium in both public and private sector bond issuance in the second half of the year". Several studies document the existence of green premium as well (Harrison, 2021). Hyun, Park, and Tian (2020) compare the yield premium of green bonds versus synthetic conventional bonds and conclude a −15 bps green premium for green bonds with Climate Bonds Initiatives certificates. Preclaw and Bakshi (2015) and Zerbib (2019) find similar results. There is also a pronounced green premium in emerging market economies. Wang *et al.* (2020) show a 34 bps lower at-issue yield for green bonds in China. In contrast to a number of studies, Larcker and Watts (2020) study municipal green bonds and find no evidence of a greenium. They conclude that investors appear entirely unwilling to forgo wealth to invest in environmentally sustainable projects. MacAskill *et al.* (2020)'s review of the literature confirms a consensus on the existence of a green premium, with support from 56% of studies of primary market issuance and 70% of research studying secondary market bonds. Meanwhile, studies find that the green premium is more evident among investment-grade bonds, and when the definition of a green bond is based on more standard and official designations or criteria.

The evidence on whether the market rewards companies issuing green bonds is more mixed. Flammer (2021) and Tang and Zhang (2020) find a positive stock price reaction (positive cumulative abnormal returns (CARs) to green bond issuance using an event study approach. Wang *et al.* (2020) also find a positive stock price reaction in emerging markets. By contrast, Lebelle, Lajili Jarjir, and Sassi (2020) estimate a −0.5% and −0.2% CAR on the green bond announcement date and the day after. Taking the perspective of a project finance sponsor, Alonso-Conde and Rojo-Suárez (2020) confirm that green bond financing constitutes a strong financial incentive for sponsors as it delivers higher returns for shareholders than conventional financing.

1.3. *The cost of capital*

1.3.1. *Cost of capital basics*

The overall cost of capital is typically derived from the WACC formula that accounts for the cost of all capital sources or the cost of equity and debt. The standard definitions of $WACC$, cost of equity (R_E), and cost of debt (R_D) are as follows (Damodaran, 2015):

$$WACC = R_E \times \frac{E}{V} + R_D \times \frac{D}{V} \tag{1}$$

$$R_E = R_f + \beta_i \times [E(R_m) - R_f] \tag{2}$$

$$R_D = (R_f + \text{Credit Spread}) \times (1 - T_c) \tag{3}$$

In Eq. (1), E is the market cap of the firm, D is the market value of the firm's debt, $V = E + D$, E/V is the weight of equity in a firm's total capital, and D/V is the weight of debt. The cost of equity reflects the rate of return demanded by equity investors. It is derived using the capital asset pricing model (CAPM) shown in Eq. (2), where R_f is the risk-free rate of return (e.g., on a 10-year Treasury note), β_i is the beta of firm i, $E(R_m)$ is the expected market return, and $E(R_m) - R_f$ is the equity risk premium. The cost of debt reflects a firm's default and liquidity risk, market interest rates, and the corporate tax rate, T_c. The cost of debt is measured on an after-tax basis to reflect the tax deductibility of interest expense.

1.3.2. *Literature review*

Several empirical studies examine how sustainable initiatives or lack of sustainable initiatives affect a company's cost of capital. Using the implied cost of capital and the LIBOR-Treasury spread as the cost of equity and debt, Chava (2014) finds that companies with environmental concerns face significantly higher required rates of return on securities and a significantly higher interest rate on bank loans, while voluntary environmental initiatives do not reduce the cost of equity or debt capital. Cooper and Uzun (2015) conclude that firms with strong CSR have a lower cost of debt, and the result is more significant for manufacturing and financial firms. El Ghoul *et al.* (2011) find that U.S. firms with higher CSR scores have cheaper equity financing. Likewise, Xu, Liu, and Huang (2015) conclude that Chinese listed companies with higher CSR scores have a significantly lower cost of equity capital. Xu, Liu, and Huang also find that the CSR reduction in the cost of capital is greater and more significant during recessions than in economic booms.

1.4. *How a green designation could affect the cost of capital*

There are several channels through which a green designation may affect the cost of capital. Each channel works in the cost of equity (Eq. (2)) and/or cost of debt (Eq. (3)), subsequently affecting the WACC.

1.4.1. *Lower risk premium*

A green designation could lower the cost of capital by lowering the risk premium on a firm, which reflects market expectations of future cash flows, tax policy, regulatory policy, and public policy.

First, a green designation lowers investor perceptions of a company's risk. Issuing green bonds provides a high-profile market signal that a firm is taking sustainability seriously and that it adapts better to impending social and public policy trends than otherwise comparable companies. Previous literature suggests that investors perceive socially irresponsible firms as having a higher level of risk (El Ghoul *et al.*, 2011; Hong and Kacperczyk, 2009).

Second, the issuance of green bonds lowers a firm's risk premium by improving its transparency and reducing informational asymmetries, as the green designation requires third-party evaluations and certifications as well as the disclosure of information about how a firm will use and manage funds raised from green bonds. Easley and O'Hara (2004) find that investors demand a higher return on stocks with greater private information ostensibly because investors are less able to shift their portfolios to incorporate new information. With more accessible information from green bonds issuance, private information is less of a problem, thereby lowering risk premiums. Diamond and Verrecchia (1991) show that revealing public information to reduce information asymmetry can lower a firm's cost of capital by increasing the liquidity of its securities, thereby boosting demand from large investors. El Ghoul *et al.* (2011) confirm reducing information asymmetry is one of the channels through which CSR lowers the cost of equity capital.

Third, a green designation lowers the bond risk premium by increasing the liquidity of debt in other ways, as suggested by Diamond and Verrecchia (1991). Governments might provide more liquidity support for green debt. For example, central banks could require less collateral on discount loans to banks that are collateralized by securities of green designated firms. In addition, many public sector pension funds are pressured by governments to invest minimum percentages of their portfolios in green securities. Finding increased institutional ownership and improved stock liquidity after green bond issuance, Tang and Zhang (2020) confirm two ways in which green bond issuance lowers risk premium. Likewise, Ortiz-Molina and Phillips (2014) find that green bond issuers have a lower cost of capital in industries with more liquid assets and during periods of high asset liquidity.

1.4.2. *Interest costs*

Green labeling could also induce lower interest rates on bond and bank debt. As mentioned earlier, MacAskill *et al.* (2020) find a weak consensus across studies about a green premium within the green bond market. However, this potentially cheaper debt financing has a limited direct impact on a firm's overall cost of capital, as green bonds account for a small share of a company's overall capital. Nevertheless, the green designation could have other indirect effects (e.g., branding and connoting less systemic risk) that lower its overall cost of capital.

Banks have increasingly considered social and environmental issues in their lending decisions. Approximately 80% of global banks by lending volume have adopted the Equator principles, are signatories to the United Nations Environment Programme's Statement, and have agreed to consider social and environmental issues in project finance (Chava, 2014). As noted by Chava (2014), "some lenders may price the risk and charge a higher interest rate on loans issued to firms with environmental concerns to compensate for the potential liability and reputation risk they get exposed to by lending to these firms." The aggregate cost of debt could be affected by green considerations if a significant number of lenders adopt environmentally sensitive lending policies.

2. Data

2.1. *Sample*

The chapter extracts bond data from Bloomberg's fixed income database for which the field "use of proceed" is "Green Bond/Loan" and excludes bonds whose issuer's Bloomberg Industry Classification System (BICS) is "Government" (BICS Level 1). Following Flammer (2021), Zhang, Li, and Liu (2021), and Tang and Zhang (2020), our study focuses on the first issuance of green bonds as the initial issuance generates the greatest impact. Using these criteria we identify 674 corporate green bonds denominated in 31 different currencies, issued between 2013 and 2020 by firms located in 42 countries and spanning 10 industry sectors. Limiting the issues to those from public companies and those providing complete data, the sample of the green bond issuers is reduced to 191 firms. These issuers are from 10 industries (BICS Level 1), corresponding to 37 industry groups (BICS Level 2) with the majority from Banks, Real Estate, Power Generation, Utilities, and Renewable Energy. Most green issuers are from China, Italy, Japan, Sweden, and the United States. Detailed industry and country information on the sample is presented in Tables 1 and 2.

The chapter adopts a matching methodology to build the control group following Flammer (2021). Specifically, each green bond issuer is matched to a non-green bond issuer from the same country, industry, currency, and who has announced bond issuance within 3 quarters before or after the first green bond's issuance. Such a non-green bond issuer has not issued a green bond up through the construction of our sample. Within the pool of candidate non-green bond issuers, the nearest neighbor was selected based on the magnitude of current market capitalization,[1] the closeness of the bond announcement date, and other traits. For example, PepsiCo Inc is matched with Coca-Cola Co., Verizon with AT&T, LG with Sony, Apple with Microsoft Corp, and China Datang Corp Renewable Power is matched with Inner Mongolia MengDian HuaNeng Thermal Power.

When there are a limited number of candidates matching a green issuer, adjustments were made based on country, industry group (BICS Level 2), and currency, but not for industry sector (BICS Level 1) and market capitalization. For instance, some Chinese firms are registered in the Cayman Islands or Bermuda, yet operate in mainland China. These firms are matched with companies registered

[1]For instance, a company with a market capitalization of 4.69E+11 is matched with those of the range 3E+11 to 6E+11.

Table 1. Company sample by industry.

BICS Level 1	BICS Level 2	Green issuer	Others	Total
Communications	Cable and satellite	1	1	2
Communications	Wireline telecommunications services	3	2	5
Consumer discretionary	Airlines	1	1	2
Consumer discretionary	Apparel and textile products	1	1	2
Consumer discretionary	Automobiles manufacturing	1	1	2
Consumer discretionary	Department stores	1	1	2
Consumer discretionary	Home improvement	1	1	2
Consumer discretionary	Retail — consumer discretionary	1	0	1
Consumer discretionary	Travel and lodging	4	4	8
Consumer staples	Food and beverage	4	3	7
Consumer staples	Retail — consumer staples	1	1	2
Consumer staples	Supermarkets and pharmacies	0	1	1
Energy	Refining and marketing	1	1	2
Energy	Renewable energy	9	14	23
Financials	Banks	45	45	90
Financials	Commercial finance	10	8	18
Financials	Consumer finance	2	4	6
Financials	Diversified banks	14	4	18
Financials	Financial services	2	9	11
Financials	Life insurance	2	2	4
Financials	Real estate	24	33	57
Health care	Medical equipment and devices manufacturing	1	1	2

(*Continued*)

Table 1. *(Continued)*

BICS Level 1	BICS Level 2	Green issuer	Others	Total
Industrials	Electrical equipment manufacturing	2	2	4
Industrials	Industrial other	6	7	13
Industrials	Manufactured goods	1	1	2
Industrials	Transportation and logistics	5	5	10
Industrials	Waste, environment services, and equipment	1	3	4
Materials	Chemicals	4	4	8
Materials	Construction materials manufacturing	2	2	4
Materials	Containers and packaging	1	1	2
Materials	Forest and paper products manufacturing	3	3	6
Technology	Communications equipment	1	0	1
Technology	Hardware	2	2	4
Technology	Semiconductors	1	1	2
Technology	Software and services	1	2	3
Utilities	Power generation	18	18	36
Utilities	Utilities	14	11	25
Total		191	200	391

Notes: This table summarizes the industries of the sample along with the specific number of green bond-issuing companies and conventional bond-issuing companies in each industry. BICS refers to the Bloomberg Industry Classification System. Both BICS Level 1 and Level 2 are considered when matching the green bond issuer with a non-green bond issuer. Information is sourced from Bloomberg.

Table 2. Company sample by country.

Country	Green issuer	Non-green issuer	Total	Country	Green issuer	Non-green issuer	Total
Argentina	0	2	2	Luxembourg	1	2	3
Austria	3	2	5	Malaysia	0	1	1
Belgium	1	2	3	Mauritius	0	1	1
Bermuda	1	0	1	Mexico	0	2	2
Brazil	4	3	7	Netherlands	5	1	6
Britain	3	3	6	Nigeria	1	0	1
Canada	3	5	8	Norway	5	4	9
Cayman Islands	0	3	3	Philippines	2	1	3
Chile	2	3	5	Poland	1	8	9
China	35	43	78	Portugal	1	0	1
Czech	0	1	1	Russia	0	4	4
Denmark	3	0	3	Singapore	1	0	1
Finland	3	1	4	South Korea	2	15	17
France	7	0	7	Spain	5	3	8
Germany	7	6	13	Sweden	19	10	29
Iceland	0	2	2	Switzerland	0	3	3
India	5	10	15	Taiwan	3	0	3
Indonesia	0	4	4	Thailand	3	2	5
Italy	10	1	11	Turkey	3	2	5
Japan	37	26	63	UAE	1	1	2
Lithuania	2	0	2	United States	12	23	35
				Total	191	200	391

Notes: This table displays the countries in which the sample companies are registered. The countries in which a green bond issuing company is registered and operates in are considered when matching it to a non-green bond issuer. Information is sourced from Bloomberg.

in China due to a lack of candidates in the Cayman Islands and Bermuda. When matching the United Urban Investment Corporation from Japan in the real estate sector, its large market capitalization limits the pool of candidates from the same country. In this case, we examined firms in China and South Korea and selected China Vanke Co. Ltd. from the real estate sector based on its similar market capitalization. For European firms, the pool of matchable candidates spanned firms in Europe in general rather than firms from only one European country.

The matching methodology produces a control group of 200 conventional bond issuers.[2] The major uses of proceeds from bonds in the control group are acquisition financing, capital expenditures, project finance, stock buyback refinance, working capital refinance, and general corporate purposes. Detailed industry and country information on the conventional issuer sample is presented in Tables 1 and 2. A visual comparison of green and conventional bond issuers by their bond announcement year is shown in Figure 1.

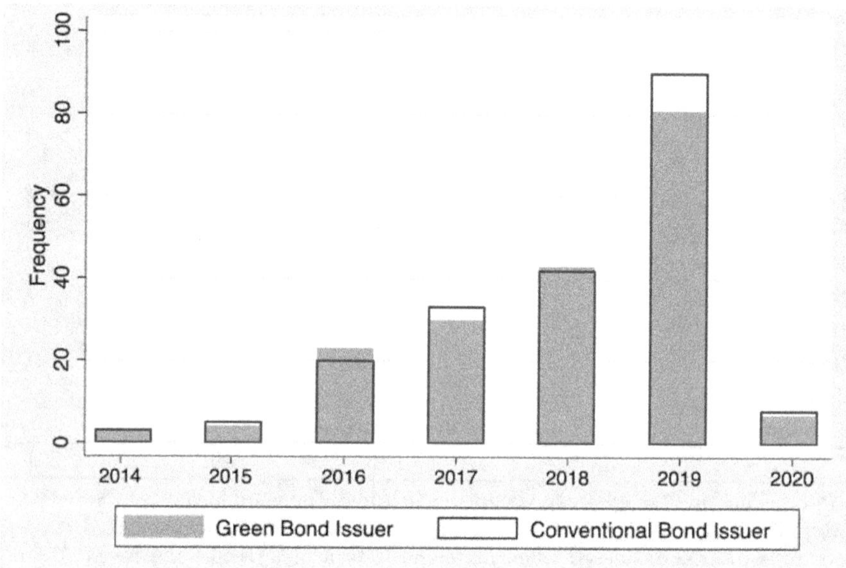

Figure 1. Sample by bond announcement year.
Notes: This figure summarizes the bond announcement year of the green bond issuers and conventional bond issuers in the sample. Each green bond issuer is matched to a non-green bond issuer in the same country, industry, and currency, is similar in size, and has announced bond issuance within 3 quarters before or after the first green bond's issuance.

[2]Over 200 public green issuers were initially used as the treated groups and were matched with conventional bonds. Missing data reduced the final sample to 191 green and 200 conventional bond issuers.

One challenge is the endogeneity of green bond issuance with respect to firm outcomes. Companies with certain traits, for instance, higher profit margin or greater free cash flow, are more likely to issue green bonds, implying that firms do not issue green bonds randomly (Flammer, 2021). As outlined by Flammer (2021), the endogeneity concern should ideally be addressed using "an instrument for the issuance of green bonds". Yet it is difficult to find such an instrument and construct "an empirical setting in which companies (quasi-)randomly issue green bonds" (Flammer, 2021). The matching methodology helps address this issue.

2.2. *Firm-level data*

The data source for firm-level characteristics is Bloomberg. The WACC, cost of equity, and cost of debt are measured based on calculations from Bloomberg.[3]

Following Flammer (2021) and Chava (2014), our company controls include firm size, profitability, leverage, net income, liquidity, market capitalization, and price-to-book ratio. Company size is tracked by the natural logarithm of the book value of total assets. Profitability is measured using the return on assets (ROA) defined as the ratio of operating income before depreciation to total assets. Leverage is the ratio of debt to the book value of total assets. A company's liquidity is measured by its ratio of cash to current assets. The market-to-book ratio compares a business' net assets that are available to the firm's stock market cap.

The firm-level dataset is constructed on a quarterly basis, as the WACC of most companies is calculated at this frequency by Bloomberg. Firm-level data span 2013q2 to 2020q4. To ensure

[3]Bloomberg calculates the WACC by $[\mathrm{KD} \times (\mathrm{TD}/V)] + [\mathrm{KP} \times (P/V)] + [\mathrm{KE} \times (E/V)]$. Where KD = cost of debt, TD = total debt, V = total capital, $V = \mathrm{TD} + P + E$, KP = cost of preferred stock, P = preferred equity, KE = cost of equity, E = equity capital. Figures are drawn from the company's most recent report, annual or interim. The Bloomberg cost of equity is derived based on the Capital Asset Pricing Model (CAPM) as explained in Section 1 — Background. Bloomberg calculates the cost of debt by $[[(\mathrm{SD}/\mathrm{TD}) * (\mathrm{CS} * \mathrm{AF})] + [(\mathrm{LD}/\mathrm{TD}) * (\mathrm{CL} * \mathrm{AF})]] * [1 - \mathrm{TR}]$. Where SD = short-term debt, TD = total debt, CS = before-tax cost of short-term debt, AF = debt adjustment factor, LD = long-term debt, CL = before-tax cost of long-term debt, TR = effective tax rate.

sufficient time trend information comparing the cost of capital in the pre- and post-bond issuance periods, only bonds issued before 2020q1 are included in the sample as shown in Figure 1.

2.3. *Country-level data*

To control for cross-country differences, we include metrics ranging from country-level risk premiums, inflation (GDP deflator), current account balance, and profit tax rate to GDP growth per capita. Country risk premium data are from Bloomberg. The remaining country-level data are from the World Bank dataset, which amalgamates data from other large sources, including the International Monetary Fund and International Financial Statistics. Country-level data are constructed on an annual basis for 2013 to 2019. Data for 2020 and for Taiwan were unavailable.

2.4. *Summary statistics*

Table 3 provides summary statistics for the entire sample, including the basic variables used to identify the observation, along with company-level and country-level data. Some variables are not included in regressions owing to missing observations. The average WACC of the entire sample (391 companies in numerous quarters) is 6.147, with a standard deviation of 4.004. The cost of equity averages 10.88 with a standard deviation of 4.354, while the cost of debt averages 1.853 with a standard deviation of 2.654.

Table 4 provides the Pearson correlation coefficients between WACC, the cost of equity, the cost of debt, the three dummy variables *GreenIssuer*, *Issued*, and *GI* (*GreenIssuer* $*$ *Issued*), and the control variables. The table indicates that WACC is negatively correlated with the three dummy variables, all at 1% significance level. Likewise, cost of debt is also highly and negatively correlated with the three dummy variables. The cost of equity exhibits less significant correlation with the three dummy variables.

Figure 2 presents the distribution of WACC of the company-quarter-year dataset. Juxtaposing the WACC distribution of green bond issuers and conventional bond issuers, the figure shows that green bond issuers have a slightly lower WACC than conventional bond issuers in the sample.

Table 3. Summary statistics.

Variables	(1) N	(2) Mean	(3) SD	(4) Min.	(5) Max.
Panel A: Sample basics					
Company number	10,642	203.7	116.9	1	410
Dates (quarter-year)	10,642	42,795	814.7	41,305	44,196
GreenIssuer	10,642	0.479	0.500	0	1
Issued	10,642	0.321	0.467	0	1
Panel B: Company-level data					
Bond issuance announcement date	10,642	43,309	461.0	41,739	44,159
Weighted average cost of capital (WACC)	10,642	6.147	4.004	−30.21	207.0
Cost of equity	10,642	10.88	4.354	−71.81	222.8
Cost of debt	10,642	1.853	2.654	−0.881	76.62
Return on assets	10,195	2.697	5.405	−56.37	38.95
Leverage	10,273	8.480	51.00	1.038	5,002
Total assets	10,632	3.635e+06	2.218e+07	33.78	3.484e+08
Net income	10,614	8,074	44,642	−1.801e+06	798,037
Market capitalization	10,355	525,580	2.975e+06	4.090	1.344e+08
Implied credit default swap (CDS) spread	10,220	126.6	107.1	3	1,217
Panel C: Country-level data					
Country risk premium	8,702	9.181	2.411	−1.175	23.82
GDP deflator	9,418	2.017	3.363	−15.48	50.62
Current account balance	9,306	1.816	3.633	−19.37	18.69
Profit tax	9,321	18.03	7.567	−0.200	28.20
GDP growth per capita	9,418	2.353	2.286	−4.351	7.235

Notes: This table summarizes the company-quarter data used throughout the study. Panel A describes the basics of the company-quarter sample. Companies that have issued green bonds during the study's time frame (2013q2–2020q4) have a value of 1 for variable *GreenIssuer* throughout the focused time frame. After issuance of a bond, the *Issued* variable of the company has a value of 1. Panel B summarizes the average company-level data. Panel C describes the country-level data which are included as control variables. Country-level data are sourced from World Bank database and Bloomberg. All other data are from Bloomberg.

Table 4. Correlations of variables.

Variables	*WACC*	*CoE*	*CoD*	*Total assets*	*ROA*	*Leverage*	*Net income*	*Market cap*
WACC	1.000							
CoE	0.623***	1.000						
CoD	0.421***	0.174***	1.000					
Total assets	−0.104***	0.024**	−0.047***	1.000				
ROA	0.181***	−0.155***	0.053***	−0.054***	1.000			
Leverage	−0.058***	0.023**	−0.014	0.029***	−0.063***	1.000		
Net income	0.018*	0.012	0.006	0.439***	0.064***	0.004	1.000	
Market cap	0.056***	0.022**	0.027***	0.261***	0.011	−0.004	0.373***	1.000
log(Net income)	−0.062***	0.046***	−0.102***	0.316***	0.033***	0.015	0.467***	0.229***
log(Market cap)	0.036***	0.064***	−0.087***	0.305***	0.104***	−0.009	0.336***	0.365***
log(Total assets)	−0.186***	0.135***	−0.129***	0.366***	−0.099***	0.043***	0.311***	0.195***
Implied CDS	0.138***	0.172***	0.333***	−0.056***	−0.086***	0.001	−0.057***	−0.059***
GreenIssuer	−0.148***	0.013	−0.117***	0.092***	−0.038***	0.023**	0.022**	0.008
Issued	−0.063***	−0.013	−0.072***	0.043***	−0.075***	−0.001	−0.002	0.012
GI	−0.100***	−0.007	−0.090***	0.086***	−0.029***	0.004	−0.018*	−0.001

Table 4. *(Continued)*

Variables	***log(Net income)***	***log(Market cap)***	***log(Total assets)***	***Implied CDS***	***Green issuer***	***Issued***	***GI***
WACC							
CoE							
CoD							
Total assets							
ROA							
Leverage							
Net income							
Market cap							
log(Net income)	1.000						
log(Market cap)	0.868***	1.000					
log(Total assets)	0.872***	0.835***	1.000				
Implied CDS	−0.271***	−0.324***	−0.257***	1.000			
GreenIssuer	0.006	0.039***	0.081***	−0.151***	1.000		
Issued	0.049***	0.013	0.059***	−0.097***	−0.012	1.000	
GI	0.022**	0.018*	0.059***	−0.113***	0.440***	0.613***	1.000

Notes: The table provides the Pearson correlation coefficients between WACC, cost of equity, cost of debt, the control variables, and the three dummy variables *GreenIssuer*, *Issued*, and *GI*. The WACC and cost of debt are both negatively correlated with the three dummy variables, all at 1% significance level. Cost of equity shows less significant correlation with the dummy variables. Levels of significance are presented as follows: $^{***}p < 0.01$, $^{**}p < 0.05$, $^{*}p < 0.1$.

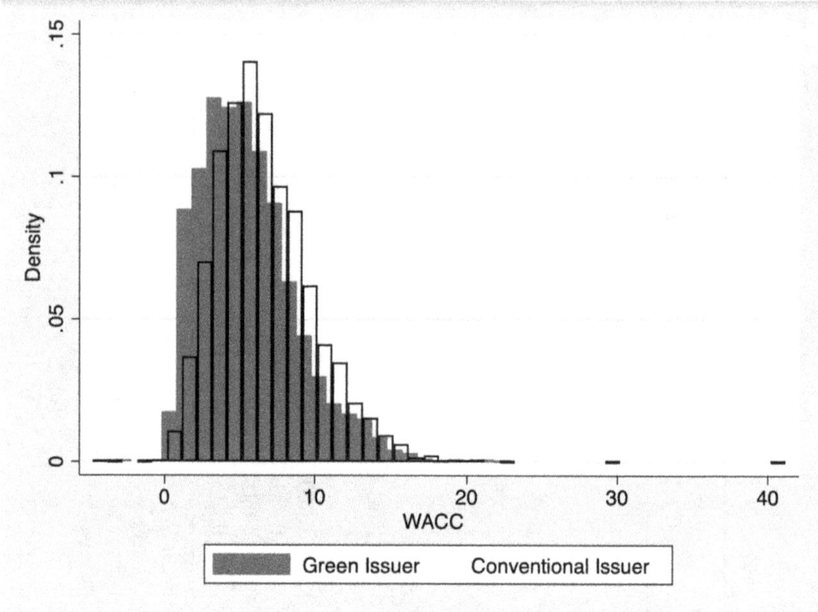

Figure 2. Sample WACC distribution comparison.
Notes: This figure presents the distribution of WACC of the company-quarter-year dataset. Juxtaposing green bond issuers and conventional bond issuers, the figure shows that green bond issuers in the sample have a slightly lower WACC than conventional bond issuers.

3. Empirical strategy

3.1. *Difference in differences*

The chapter primarily employs the DID method to evaluate the effect of issuing green bonds on an issuer's cost of capital. This empirical strategy is often used to analyze green bonds. For example, Tang and Zhang (2020) run a DID analysis to explore whether green bond issuance increases the issuers' liquidity. Flammer (2021) also adopts a DID approach to examine how corporate green bonds affect firm-level outcomes. To estimate the treatment effect of the green bond issuance on the cost of capital, we compare the cost of capital of green and conventional bond issuers before and after the issuance of a bond. In particular, we estimate the following specification:

$$\begin{aligned}\text{WACC}_{ict} = {} & \beta_0 + \beta_1\text{GI}_{it} + \beta_2\text{GreenIssuer}_i + \beta_3\text{Issued}_{it} \\ & + \beta_4\text{FirmControl}_{it} + \text{CountryControl}_{ict} + \text{CountryFE} \\ & + \text{YearFE} + \varepsilon_{it} \qquad (4)\end{aligned}$$

where i indexes firms, c indexes country, t indexes year-quarter. *GI*, *GreenIssuer*, and *Issued* are the three dummy variables following conventional DID settings. $GreenIssuer_i$ always equals one for green issuers and always equals zero for conventional issuers. Issued_{it} equals one if the company has issued the bond by year-quarter t, and zero otherwise, regardless of whether it is a green or a conventional issuer. GI_{it} equals one if firm i has issued a green bond by time t and zero otherwise. GI_{it} equals $\text{Green}_i * \text{Issued}_{it}$, and is the interaction between the treatment and time variables. β_1 is, therefore, the difference-in-differences estimate and the coefficient of interest. It is defined as the treatment effect of green bond issuance on the issuer's cost of capital and measures the change in WACC following the issuance of green bonds. β_1 is expected to be negative for reasons explained in Section 4. FirmControl_{it} and $\text{CountryControl}_{ict}$ include variables defined earlier. Country and year fixed effects are included to control for country and year-specific characteristics that might be endogenous. The cost of equity R_E and the cost of debt R_D are two alternative dependent variables to the WACC. To assess robustness, some regressions omit the country control variables, country FE and/or year FE.

The parallel trend assumption is the most critical assumption for the validity of DID models. It requires that the difference between the treated and control group outcome of interest is constant over time, meaning that the trends of the outcome of interest in the pre-treatment period should be the same (Columbia Public Health, n.d.). Organizing the data according to the number of quarters before and after treatment (bond issuance), Figure 3 plots WACC, cost of equity, and cost of debt of green and conventional bond issuers pre- and post-bond issuance. There are explicitly parallel trends for WACC and cost of debt. While the parallel trend for cost of equity seems less obvious, the difference between the green issuer and conventional issuer's cost of equity does not exceed 0.5% for most pre-treatment periods. This may arise from the greater volatility of stock prices.

3.2. *Synthetic control method*

To further address the limitations posed by the parallel trend assumption of the DID approach, we analyze the causal effect of green bond issuance using SCM, developed by Abadie and Gardeazabal (2003) and Abadie, Diamond, and Hainmueller (2015).[4] The SCM is a data-driven approach to small-sample comparative case studies for estimating treatment effects of treated and untreated units across the event of interest (Galiani and Quistorff, 2017). This method generates a "weighted average of the untreated units that closely matches the treated unit over the pre-treatment period" (Galiani and Quistorff, 2017). It differs from the DID method as it more systematically assigns different weights to the control group, instead of equal weight in DID. Outcomes for this synthetic control are then projected into the post-treatment period using the weights identified from the pre-treatment comparison to best reflect the treated group without the treatment effect. SCM is well suited to study the effects of "interventions that are implemented at an aggregate level affecting a small number of large units (such as cities, regions, or countries) on some aggregate outcome of interest" (Abadie, Diamond, and Hainmueller, 2010).

Assume there are $(p+q)$ firms, where the first (p) firms are green issuers and the remaining (q) firms issue conventional bonds. C'_{it} denotes the cost of capital of green bond issuer i in month t. C^*_{jt} denotes the cost of capital of conventional bond issuer j in month t. The firm issues the bond at a point during periods $t = 1, \dots T$, and the month of the bond issuance is denoted T_0. The firm has been affected by the issuance of the bond for the periods from T_{0+1} to T. Before the issuance of the bond or when $t < T_0$, there should be no difference in cost of capital of the green, C'_{it}, and of the synthetic conventional, C^*_{jt}, bond issuers.

---

[4]Abadie, Diamond, and Hainmueller (2010) released the *synth* Stata command for single equation estimation, and Quistorff and Galiani (2017) developed the *synth runner* Stata package, which automates the process of running multiple synthetic control estimations using *synth*. We use *synth runner*, which allows several units to receive treatment at different time periods and generates the visualization of results.

A group of synthetic conventional bond issuers is constructed for each green bond issuer to let the former's cost of capital, C^*_{jt}, equal the green bond issuer's cost of capital, C'_{it}, before bond issuance with the optimal weights $w_{p+1}, \ldots, w_{p+q}$. Using the same weights to estimate the counterfactual expresses the weighted average of the outcomes of the control group. The cost of capital C^*_{jt} of the synthetic group after the issuance of bonds, or when $t > T_0$, could be estimated using $\sum_{j=p+1}^{p+q} w_j \cdot C^*_{jt}$. Let A denote the treatment effect as follows:

$$A = C'_{it} - \sum_{j=p+1}^{p+q} w_j \cdot C^*_{jt} \tag{5}$$

for $t > T_0$. A should be zero for $t < T_0$.

Using the bond and firm traits *ex-ante*, SCM constructs each synthetic green bond issuer's counterpart as a weighted average of control groups that are similar to the treated green bond issuer. Comparing the cost of capital data of the green issuer and synthetic counterparts, the causal effect of green bond issuance can be assessed.

The synthetic control method requires the data to be strongly balanced, meaning that each company needs to have the same number of observations defined in the same set of time periods. Our study restricts the DID dataset to include only companies in the Energy and Utilities sector. The resulting strongly balanced data are composed of 16 treated firms with 33 control firms from 2016q4 to 2020q3 (16 quarters).

4. Results

4.1. *DID results*

4.1.1. *Main results*

The main DID results on WACC are presented in Table 5. The preferred specification in Column (6) includes company controls, country controls, country fixed effects, and year fixed effects. Consistent with the main empirical hypothesis, estimates of this specification imply that the post-issuance cost of capital of green issuers decreases by a statistically significant 24.5 bps compared to matched conventional bond issuers. Meanwhile, the coefficients on *GI* and *Issued* are also

Table 5. Difference-in-differences regression results on WACC.

Variables	(1) *WACC*	(2) *WACC*	(3) *WACC*	(4) *WACC*	(5) *WACC*	(6) *WACC*
GI	−0.215*	−0.179	−0.247**	−0.198	−0.210**	−0.245**
	(0.127)	(0.137)	(0.115)	(0.135)	(0.0993)	(0.113)
GreenIssuer	−0.496***	−0.315***	−0.203***	−0.312***	−0.159***	−0.196***
	(0.0723)	(0.0683)	(0.0602)	(0.0675)	(0.0604)	(0.0594)
Issued	−0.219**	−0.631***	−0.451***	−0.253**	−0.130	−0.176*
	(0.0889)	(0.0979)	(0.0847)	(0.110)	(0.0891)	(0.0930)
ROA	0.0221**	0.0239***	0.0407***	0.0214**	0.0370***	0.0387***
	(0.00876)	(0.00926)	(0.00797)	(0.00917)	(0.00705)	(0.00787)
Leverage	−0.000400	−0.000142	−4.90e–05	−7.05e–05	−0.000197	−2.11e–06
	(0.000531)	(0.000448)	(0.000373)	(0.000443)	(0.000413)	(0.000368)
log(*Total assets*)	−1.177***	−1.091***	−1.160***	−1.109***	−1.268***	−1.169***
	(0.0319)	(0.0333)	(0.0305)	(0.0330)	(0.0279)	(0.0302)
log(*Net income*)	0.288***	0.287***	0.318***	0.292***	0.251***	0.318***
	(0.0344)	(0.0351)	(0.0307)	(0.0347)	(0.0284)	(0.0303)
log(*Market cap*)	0.982***	0.955***	0.966***	0.971***	1.104***	0.972***
	(0.0297)	(0.0316)	(0.0320)	(0.0313)	(0.0302)	(0.0316)
Implied CDS spread	0.00605***	0.00202***	−0.000899**	0.00122***	−0.00154***	−0.00144***
	(0.000309)	(0.000366)	(0.000430)	(0.000372)	(0.000365)	(0.000436)

Country risk premium		0.0672***	0.269***	0.0570***		0.283***
		(0.0149)	(0.0173)	(0.0148)		(0.0173)
GDP deflator		0.620***	0.149***	0.645***		0.142***
		(0.0165)	(0.0213)	(0.0167)		(0.0220)
Current account balance		−0.120***	−0.0167	−0.105***		0.0915***
		(0.00911)	(0.0221)	(0.00911)		(0.0237)
Profit tax		−0.0201***	0.0778***	−0.0252***		0.0142
		(0.00450)	(0.0148)	(0.00449)		(0.0166)
GDP growth per capita		0.0589***	−0.200***	0.0714***		−0.239***
		(0.0169)	(0.0260)	(0.0172)		(0.0281)
Country FE			Yes		Yes	Yes
Year FE				Yes	Yes	Yes
Constant	7.237***	5.595***	1.831***	6.608***	7.498***	3.309***
	(0.251)	(0.312)	(0.433)	(0.321)	(0.298)	(0.456)
Observations	8,549	6,326	6,326	6,326	8,549	6,326
R-squared	0.305	0.475	0.642	0.488	0.585	0.651

Notes: This table reports DID regressions on WACC with variation in the incorporation of country control variables, country fixed effect (FE), and year FE. When regressing on WACC, the three dummy variables all have negative coefficients and most of them are statistically significant. In the preferred specification in Column (6) where company controls, country controls, country FE, and year FE are all included, the post-issuance cost of capital of green issuers decreases by a statistically significant 24.5 bps compared to matched conventional bond issuers. Standard errors are included in parentheses. Levels of significance are presented as follows: $^{***}p < 0.01$, $^{**}p < 0.05$, $^{*}p < 0.1$.

negative and statistically significant, suggesting green bond issuers have a lower WACC after issuing green bonds. The result is robust as coefficients on these variables are still negative and significant if the two fixed effects and country control variables are omitted in Column (1), if the year fixed effect term is omitted in Column (3), or if only the country control variable is omitted in Column (5).

Replacing the dependent variable in the main specification (Eq. (4)), Table 5 presents regression results on the cost of equity. The coefficients of the three dummy variables are each statistically insignificant in explaining the cost of equity. *GI* is only significant in Column (5), when the country control variables are excluded. Column (5) suggests that after issuing green bonds, issuers have a 36.8 bps lower cost of equity, issuing a bond decreases the cost of equity by 23 bps, and being a green bond issuer raises the cost of equity by 23 bps. Similar signs on the dummy variables also occur in Columns (1), (3), and (6). The lack of significance for being a green issuer on the cost of equity might be due to less obvious parallel trends for the cost of equity, as shown in Figure 3.

Table 6 presents regression results on the cost of debt. Table 7 suggests that being a green issuer does not have a statistically significant effect on the cost of debt. Three out of six regressions in Table 7 suggest a positive, negative, and positive coefficient on *GI*, *GreenIssuer*, and *Issued*, respectively. The R-squares for regressions in Table 7 are generally higher than those in Tables 4 and 5, reflecting a greater ability to explain movements in the cost of debt. For example, Column (6) of Table 7 has a fairly high R-square of 0.912.

The weaker and mixed findings for the separate debt and equity components of capital could plausibly reflect hard on observed aspects of individual firms that affect the composition of their capital. Because it is less affected by the composition of a firm's capital structure and substitution of debt and equity at the firm level, the WACC is less distorted by omitted information and arguably provides a more important gauge of the effect of being designated as a green company.

4.1.2. *Restricting on time and industry*

COVID-19 could plausibly be an external shock and complicate analyzing what affects the cost of capital. For this reason, restricting

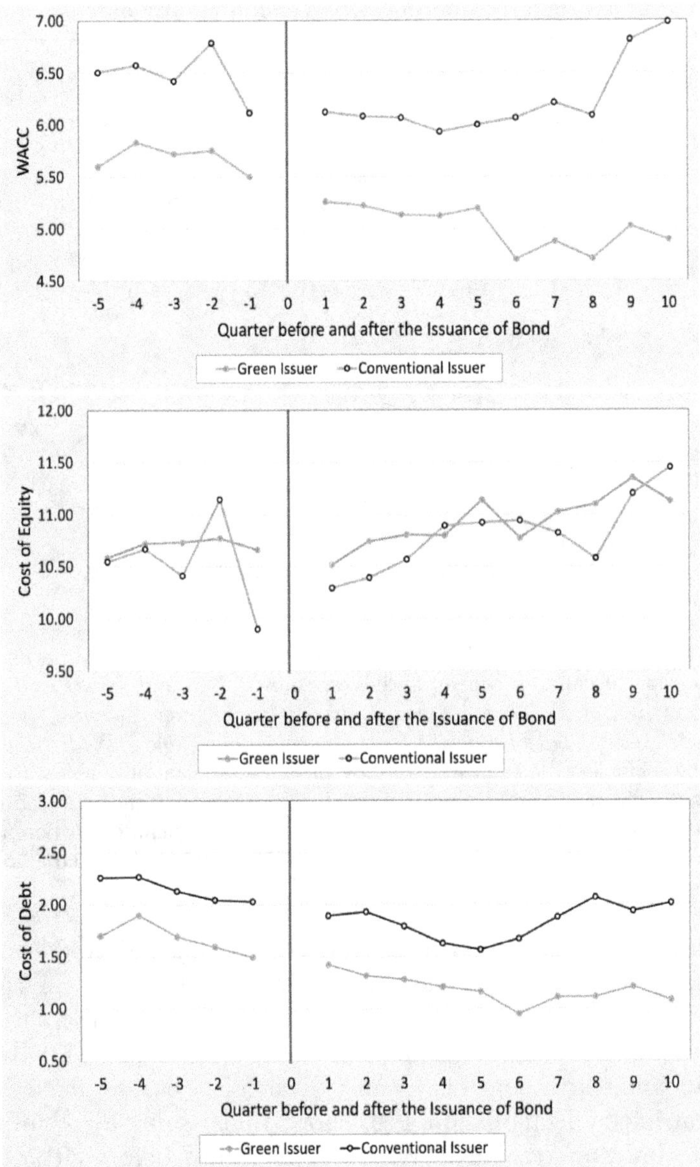

Figure 3. Cost of capital before and after bond issuance.
Notes: This figure displays the cost of capital trends of green issuers and conventional issuers before and after bond issuance. Prior to bond issuance, both WACC and cost of debt of the two groups show explicit parallel trends, while the parallel trend for cost of equity is less obvious.

Table 6. Difference-in-differences regression results on cost of equity.

Variables	(1) Equity	(2) Equity	(3) Equity	(4) Equity	(5) Equity	(6) Equity
GI	−0.0929	0.0547	−0.102	0.0325	0.368***	−0.103
	(0.147)	(0.153)	(0.129)	(0.151)	(0.121)	(0.127)
GreenIssuer	0.244***	0.139*	0.0190	0.142*	0.202***	0.0274
	(0.0837)	(0.0761)	(0.0678)	(0.0750)	(0.0738)	(0.0665)
Issued	−0.110	−0.962***	−0.712***	−0.511***	−0.231**	−0.465***
	(0.103)	(0.109)	(0.0954)	(0.122)	(0.109)	(0.104)
Firm controls	Yes	Yes	Yes	Yes	Yes	Yes
Country controls		Yes	Yes	Yes		Yes
Country FE			Yes		Yes	Yes
Year FE				Yes	Yes	Yes
Constant	5.635***	−1.511***	−3.786***	−0.218	8.997***	−2.237***
	(0.290)	(0.348)	(0.487)	(0.357)	(0.364)	(0.511)
Observations	8,549	6,326	6,326	6,326	8,549	6,326
R-squared	0.119	0.367	0.559	0.386	0.415	0.575

Notes: This table reports DID regressions on cost of equity with variation in the incorporation of country control variables, country FE, and year FE. The firm controls include *ROA*, *Leverage*, log(*Total assets*), log(*Net income*), log(*Market cap*), and *Implied CDS spread*, which are the same as in Table 5. With inconsistent signs, the coefficients of the three dummy variables are generally less statistically significant, which might be due to less obvious parallel trends for the cost of equity data as shown in Figure 3. Standard errors are included in parentheses. Levels of significance are presented as follows: $^{***}p < 0.01$, $^{**}p < 0.05$, $^{*}p < 0.1$.

observations to a pre-COVID sample (before 2019q4) could be more informative or at least provide another robustness check. In Table 8, comparing models (1) to (2), (3) to (4), and (5) to (6) shows that the negative coefficient on *GI* is more pronounced in a pre-COVID sample. Including firm controls, country controls, country fixed effects, and year fixed effects, Column (6) shows that issuing a green bond is likely to lower a company's WACC by 30.3 bps before 2019q4. The result is consistent with the 2020 "Global Sustainable Debt" market report of Climate Bonds Initiative, which noted that the issuance of all types of bonds in March 2020 waned due to the pandemic (Harrison and Muething, 2021). Nevertheless, with government support packages and the ebbing of the first COVID variant, confidence

Table 7. Difference-in-differences regression results on cost of debt.

Variables	(1) Debt	(2) Debt	(3) Debt	(4) Debt	(5) Debt	(6) Debt
GI	−0.0745	0.00576	−0.0180	−0.00382	0.165**	−0.0150
	(0.114)	(0.0841)	(0.0479)	(0.0833)	(0.0665)	(0.0463)
GreenIssuer	−0.336***	0.0731*	0.0524**	0.0764*	−0.0600	0.0556**
	(0.0648)	(0.0419)	(0.0252)	(0.0415)	(0.0405)	(0.0243)
Issued	−0.135*	−0.204***	−0.268***	−0.0904	−0.110*	−0.115***
	(0.0796)	(0.0602)	(0.0354)	(0.0677)	(0.0597)	(0.0381)
Firm controls	Yes	Yes	Yes	Yes	Yes	Yes
Country controls		Yes	Yes	Yes		Yes
Country FE			Yes		Yes	Yes
Year FE				Yes	Yes	Yes
Constant	1.482***	3.761***	1.679***	4.332***	1.530***	2.543***
	(0.225)	(0.192)	(0.181)	(0.197)	(0.200)	(0.187)
Observations	8,549	6,326	6,326	6,326	8,549	6,326
R-squared	0.140	0.702	0.905	0.708	0.713	0.912

Notes: This table reports DID regressions on cost of debt with variation in the incorporation of country controls variables, country FE, and year FE. The firm controls include *ROA*, *Leverage*, log(*Total assets*), log(*Net income*), log(*Market cap*), and *Implied CDS spread*, which are the same as in Table 5. With inconsistent signs, the coefficients of the three dummy variables are generally less statistically significant. Standard errors are included in parentheses. Levels of significance are presented as follows: $^{***}p < 0.01$, $^{**}p < 0.05$, $^{*}p < 0.1$.

returned by September, "resulting in the most prolific third quarter recorded for green issuance" (Harrison and Muething, 2021). It is possible that after the collective experience of the pandemic, more investors prefer more socially responsible assets that would promote greater social resilience to pandemics, climate change, and other societal challenges. How green bonds affect the cost of capital post-COVID is a subject for future research.

Table 9 stratifies regressions into four industry categories including financial, energy, customer-oriented, and business-oriented (see Table A.1 in the Appendix for details). Column (3) shows that the negative treatment effect on WACC is more prominent for financial firms with significantly negative coefficients on all three dummy variables. The WACC of financial firms decreases by 29.2 bps

Table 8. Difference-in-differences regression: Restricting time.

Variables Time restriction	(1) *WACC* Non	(2) *WACC* Before 2019q4	(3) *WACC* Non	(4) *WACC* Before 2019q4	(5) *WACC* Non	(6) *WACC* Before 2019q4
GI	-0.247^{**}	-0.304^{**}	-0.210^{**}	-0.390^{***}	-0.245^{**}	-0.303^{**}
	(0.115)	(0.122)	(0.0993)	(0.122)	(0.113)	(0.121)
GreenIssuer	-0.203^{***}	-0.201^{***}	-0.159^{***}	-0.130^{**}	-0.196^{***}	-0.194^{***}
	(0.0602)	(0.0605)	(0.0604)	(0.0609)	(0.0594)	(0.0597)
Issued	-0.451^{***}	-0.396^{***}	-0.130	-0.0791	-0.176^{*}	-0.158
	(0.0847)	(0.0896)	(0.0891)	(0.0957)	(0.0930)	(0.0964)
Firm controls	Yes	Yes	Yes	Yes	Yes	Yes
Country controls	Yes	Yes			Yes	Yes
Country FE	Yes	Yes	Yes	Yes	Yes	Yes
Year FE			Yes	Yes	Yes	Yes
Constant	1.831^{***}	1.750^{***}	7.498^{***}	7.413^{***}	3.309^{***}	3.144^{***}
	(0.433)	(0.447)	(0.298)	(0.319)	(0.456)	(0.470)
Observations	6,326	6,098	8,549	7,400	6,326	6,098
R-squared	0.642	0.642	0.585	0.589	0.651	0.652

Notes: This table restricts the time included in the regression of WACC. Comparing column (1) to (2), (3) to (4), and (5) to (6) shows that the negative coefficient on *GI* is more negative in a pre-COVID sample without losing statistical significance. Including firm controls, country controls, country fixed effects, and year fixed effects, Column (6) shows that issuing a green bond would likely lower a company's WACC by 30.3 bps before 2019q4. Standard errors are included in parentheses. Levels of significance are presented as follows: $^{***}p < 0.01$, $^{**}p < 0.05$, $^{*}p < 0.1$.

Table 9. Difference-in-differences regression: Restricting industry.

Variables industry	(1) *WACC* all	(2) *WACC* energy	(3) *WACC* financial	(4) *WACC* customer-oriented	(5) *WACC* business-oriented
GI	−0.245**	1.494***	−0.292**	0.560**	−0.145
	(0.113)	(0.293)	(0.115)	(0.238)	(0.245)
GreenIssuer	−0.196***	−0.526*	−0.308***	−0.406***	0.280**
	(0.0594)	(0.300)	(0.0632)	(0.117)	(0.112)
Issued	−0.176*	−1.091***	−0.458***	0.253	−0.243
	(0.0930)	(0.221)	(0.102)	(0.196)	(0.187)
Firm controls	Yes	Yes	Yes	Yes	Yes
Country controls	Yes	Yes	Yes	Yes	Yes
Country FE	Yes	Yes	Yes	Yes	Yes
Year FE	Yes	Yes	Yes	Yes	Yes
Constant	3.309***	12.55***	0.212	1.176	9.533***
	(0.456)	(1.703)	(0.479)	(0.848)	(0.953)
Observations	6,326	592	3,427	1,048	1,259
R-squared	0.651	0.681	0.792	0.726	0.733

Notes: This table stratifies regressions into four industry categories including financial, energy, customer-oriented, and business-oriented (see Table A.1 in the Appendix for details). The negative treatment effect on WACC is more prominent for financial firms with significantly negative coefficients on all three dummy variables. Standard errors are included in parentheses. Levels of significance are presented as follows: $^{***}p < 0.01$, $^{**}p < 0.05$, $^{*}p < 0.1$.

post issuance. Holding all else equal, energy companies face a 1.494% increase in WACC (significant at 1% level) after issuing green bonds, being a green bond issuer, and after issuing a bond. The coefficients on *GreenIssuer* and *Issued* remain negative. Such unexpected results might be due to a relatively low number of energy sector observations or it might reflect that green initiatives conflict with energy firms' prior commitments to or sunk costs in earlier fossil fuel investments. As shown in Column (4), firms in customer-oriented industries experienced a 0.56% increase in WACC (significant at 1% level) after issuing a green bond. The WACC is generally lower for green bond issuers, and higher after issuing a bond. For business-oriented companies, the coefficient on *GI* is not statistically significant.

4.2. *SCM results*

The synthetic control method results on the WACC, cost of equity, and cost of debt are displayed in Figures 4, 5, and 6, respectively. Figures 4 and 5 show that the synthetic group effectively matched the WACC and cost of equity trends of the 16 treated firms in the pre-treatment period. After bond issuance, there is a steady divergence of WACC and the cost of equity between the treated and synthetic control groups, and the negative treatment effects on WACC and cost of equity build up for at least six quarters after the bond issuance. Figure 6 shows that pre-treatment trends are not well aligned between green and non-green matched firms, and the treatment effect shows no specific trends.

Table 10 summarizes the treatment effects, p-values, and standardized p-values for six quarters after the treatment for the WACC, cost of equity, and cost of debt. Column (1) shows a sustained negative treatment effect on WACC after green bond issuance. WACC is likely to decrease by 4.1 bps one quarter after the bond issuance, with a standardized p-value of 0.017. Six quarters after bond issuance, issuance, issuing another green bond lowers the WACC by 24 bps, with a standardized p-value of 0.074. Maintaining standardized p-values smaller than 10% for all six quarters after

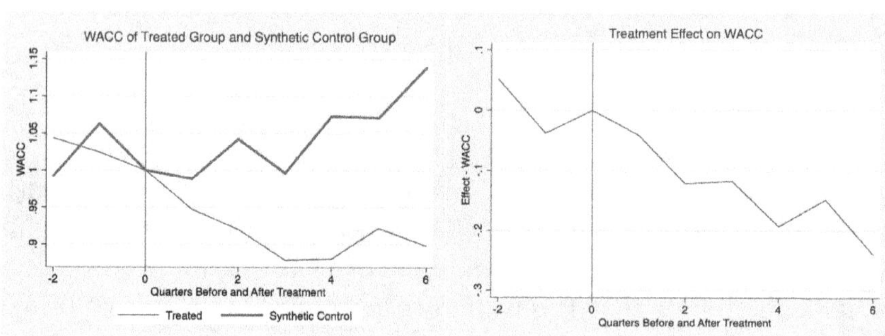

Figure 4. Synthetic control method results for 16 treated firms on WACC.

Notes: This figure shows the WACC of 16 firms in the treated group and synthetic control group two quarters before and six quarters after bond issuance. The synthetic group effectively matches the WACC of the treated firms in the pre-treatment period. The steady divergence of WACC post bond issuance demonstrates a negative treatment effect on WACC. The specific numerical information is presented in column (1) of Table 10.

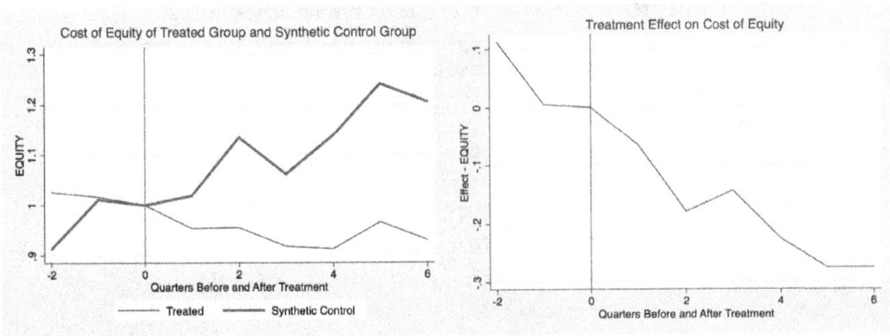

Figure 5. Synthetic control method results for 16 treated firms on cost of equity.

Notes: This figure shows the cost of equity of 16 firms in the treated group and synthetic control group two quarters before and six quarters after bond issuance. The synthetic group effectively matches the cost of equity of the treated firms in the pre-treatment period. The steady divergence of cost of equity post bond issuance demonstrates a negative treatment effect on cost of equity. The specific numerical information is presented in column (2) of Table 10.

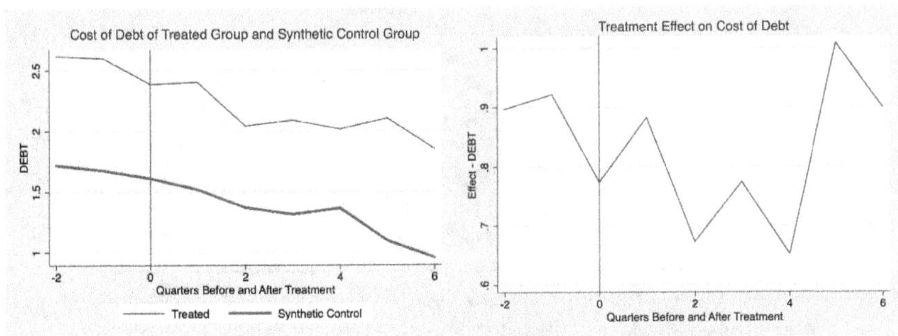

Figure 6. Synthetic control method results for 16 treated firms on cost of debt.

Notes: This figure shows the cost of debt of 16 firms in the treated group and synthetic control group two quarters before and six quarters after bond issuance. It lacks a good pre-treatment alignment, and the treatment effect shows no specific trends. The specific numerical information is presented in column (3) of Table 10.

treatment illustrates that the negative treatment effect on green bond issuance persists for a notable period.

Column (2) of Table 10 shows the SCM results on the cost of equity. One quarter after the bond issuance, the cost of equity is likely to decrease by 6.5 bps with a standardized p-value of 0.017.

Table 10. Synthetic control method results.

Synthetic control methods post-treatment results			
Quarters after treatment	Effects	p-values	Standardized p-values
(1) *WACC*			
c1	−0.0410578	0.427024	0.016816
c2	−0.1219683	0.249003	0.049778
c3	−0.11746	0.209486	0.000168
c4	−0.1927988	0.147483	0.037188
c5	−0.1490977	0.488889	0.035968
c6	−0.2403523	0.246453	0.073764
(2) *Cost of equity*			
c1	−0.0648603	0.234809	0.307103
c2	−0.1790486	0.057089	0.441811
c3	−0.143379	0.042711	0.27973
c4	−0.225073	0.023703	0.142536
c5	−0.275023	0.033353	0.252957
c6	−0.2750257	0.059311	0.365363
(3) *Cost of debt*			
c1	0.8823278	0.474869	0.005655
c2	0.6727045	0.647819	0.058087
c3	0.7744574	0.604773	0.179208
c4	0.6516962	0.620947	0.209174
c5	1.008211	0.314919	0.02056
c6	0.8989118	0.343494	0.03916

Notes: This table summarizes the treatment effects, p-values, and standardized p-values for six quarters after the treatment for the WACC, cost of equity, and cost of debt. Columns (1) and (2) show a sustained negative treatment effect on WACC and cost of equity after green bond issuance, respectively. The negative treatment effect increases in magnitude for at least six quarters after treatment. Column (3) shows a positive and significant treatment effect on the cost of debt. The information of Columns (1), (2), and (3) are presented visually in Figures 4, 5, and 6, respectively. As Figure 6 demonstrates a poor pre-treatment alignment, the results in Column (3) of Table 10 are less reliable.

Six quarters after bond issuance, issuing another green bond lowers the cost of equity by 27.5 bps, with a p-value of 0.06. The negative treatment effect increases in magnitude for at least six quarters after treatment.

As shown in Column (3) of Table 10, SCM results show a positive and significant treatment effect on the cost of debt. Six quarters after issuance, issuing a green bond raises the cost of debt by 89 bps with a standardized p-value of 0.0392. However, because Figure 6 shows a poor alignment of pre-treatment trends across green and non-green matched issuers, the results in Column (3) are less reliable.

To supplement the SCM results, we show the impact on one firm. Figure 7 illustrates the WACC trends for Shenzhen Energy Group Co. Ltd. (000027 CH Equity), which issued its first green bond in 2017q4, and its synthetic counterpart. While the company's WACC kept decreasing after its bond issuance, the WACC of the synthetic control did not. As the synthetic control group uses the weighted combination of data from the conventional issuers' group to best mimic the WACC trends before green bond issuance, the only difference between Shenzhen Energy Group Co. Ltd. and its synthetic counterpart is that the firm issued a green rather than a conventional bond. There is a pronounced negative treatment effect on green bonds post issuance, which reaches about −0.7% in 2020q2.

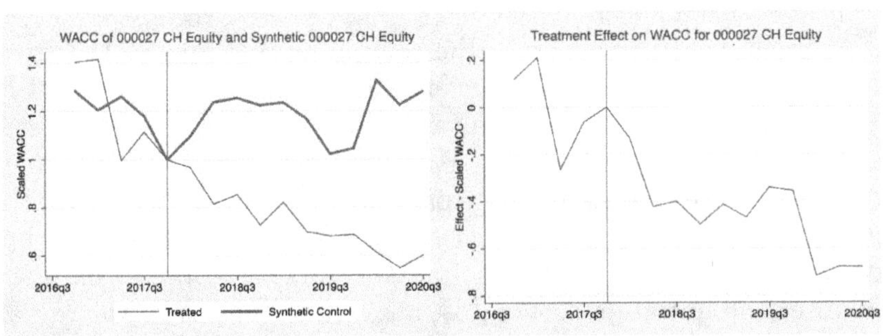

Figure 7. Synthetic control method result for 000027 CH Equity on WACC.

Notes: The figure shows the WACC trends for Shenzhen Energy Group Co. Ltd. (000027 CH Equity), which issued its first green bond in 2017q4, and its synthetic counterpart. While the company's WACC kept decreasing after its bond issuance, the WACC of the synthetic control did not. There is a pronounced negative treatment effect on green bonds post issuance, which reaches about −0.7% in 2020q2.

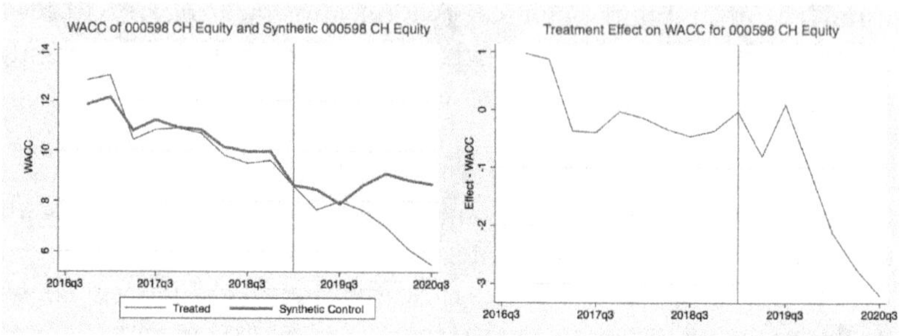

Figure 8. Synthetic control method result for 000598 CH Equity on WACC.

Notes: This figure presents the results for WACC trends of Chengdu Xingrong Environment Co. Ltd. (000598 CH Equity), which issued its first green bond in 2019q1, and its synthetic counterpart. With more data available *ex-ante*, the synthetic counterpart mimics the pre-treatment WACC trend nearly perfectly. The treatment effect reaches −3% in 2020q3, providing compelling evidence for the negative treatment effect of green bond issuance on WACC.

Figure 8 illustrates the WACC trends of Chengdu Xingrong Environment Co. Ltd. (000598 CH Equity), which issued its first green bond in 2019q1, and its synthetic counterpart. With more data available *ex-ante*, the synthetic counterpart mimics the pre-treatment WACC trend nearly perfectly. The treatment effect reaches −3% in 2020q3, providing compelling evidence for the negative treatment effect of green bond issuance on WACC.

As mentioned in Section 3, the sample used in the SCM regressions is limited to firms in the energy and utilities sector. Contrary to the SCM result, the DID result for companies in the energy sector derives a statistically significant positive effect after issuing a green bond. The statistical significance of SCM favors its findings over the stratified DID results. Nevertheless, the SCM finding of a 24 bps decrease in WACC for energy and utility firms combined six quarters after the initial green bond issuance is very close to the overall DID result of 24.5 bps decrease, which demonstrates the robustness of these estimates.

5. Conclusion

This chapter examines the effect of green bond issuance on issuers' cost of capital using data spanning companies around the globe.

Matching green with conventional bond issuers, our analysis shows that green bond issuance has a negative and significant treatment effect estimated using the difference-in-differences (DID) approach and synthetic control method (SCM). The DID finds that green issuance lowers the weighted average cost of capital (WACC) by 24.5 basis points (bps) for 191 green bond issuers in different countries and industries. Restricting observations to a pre-COVID sample (before 2019q4), the WACC decreases by 30.3 bps. The SCM finds a nearly identical negative 24 bps effect six quarters after issuance for 19 green bond issuers in the energy and utilities sector and confirms that the treatment effect of issuing a green bond is increasingly negative for at least six quarters. This chapter contributes to the literature on green bond issuance and the cost of capital by helping fill the gap in examining the impact of green bond issuance on the corporate cost of capital, with the notable exception of Zhang, Li, and Liu's (2021) findings for Chinese firms. Consistent with their seminal contribution, we find that green bond issuance lowers a firm's WACC. While we estimate larger effects, this may reflect that companies in our sample are domiciled in many countries that likely operate in thicker capital markets than in China. We also contribute to the literature on green bonds, which rarely uses the synthetic control method.

Our results have three broad implications. First, the prospect of lowering the cost of capital provides some incentive for private firms to take initiatives to address climate change. Second, as the cost of capital represents the investor's required rate of return on corporate investment, the decrease in the cost of capital after green bond issuance reflects that investors require a lower rate of return from green bond issuers, whom they perceive as less risky. Our findings are consistent with the view that the complexity of climate change's impact on social, environmental, economic, and political systems implies that climate change poses a "systemic risk" to the market and especially to conventional bonds of higher credit (Centeno *et al.*, 2015). Such a systemic risk could heighten credit risk, market risk, and liquidity risk, and undermine the stability of the financial system (Financial Stability Board, 2020). Third, at the granular level, companies could improve their unlevered and levered cash flows by substituting green for conventional bonds. This effect is especially relevant for capital-intensive sustainable projects, including solar and wind farm projects (ARUP, 2018), and for subsequently stimulating the pipeline of projects (Shishlov, Morel, and Cochran, 2016). For energy projects, a lower cost of capital could benefit consumers by lowering energy costs (e.g., lowering the levelized cost of energy (LCOE)).

Nevertheless, there are some issues for future research on green bonds related to sampling and specification. Our study uses a binary classification of companies based on one of their sustainability efforts, namely green versus conventional bond issuance. This approach overlooks any other sustainability efforts of conventional bond issuers, including other forms of engagement with green bonds. For instance, being used to match green issuer Apple Inc., conventional issuer Microsoft Corporation has not issued a green bond *per se* prior to the building of our sample. Yet, Microsoft invested in a large green bond offering of International Finance Corporation as early as 2013 (Nichols, 2013) and is itself a green bond investor. To address such drawbacks, future research could incorporate more graduated measures of sustainability or of issuing green bonds to assess the robustness of results. Such efforts could also see whether there are marginal effects of increasing sustainability other than those associated with crossing the threshold between being designated a conventional versus a green bond issuer.

Our findings also suggest that future research could examine more country-level controls for political, financial, and other factors. For example, the effect of green bond issuance on the cost of capital for US companies may differ following the election of Trump, who campaigned on a US withdrawal from the 2015 Paris Climate Agreement. Such considerations suggest exploring the impact of time-varying country indexes of government climate policies on the private incentives to invest in or issue green bonds. It may also be helpful to control for cross-country variation in the relative importance of bond versus bank debt finance. For example, *ceteris paribus*, ESG scores could have a larger effect on bond issuance in countries with more bond-centric finance (e.g., the US), while ESG requirements on bank lending may be more important in promoting sustainability initiatives of firms in more bank-centric areas such as Europe and Japan.

Appendix

Table A.1. Industry classification in Table 9.

Industry	BICS Level 1	BICS Level 2
Energy	Energy	Renewable Energy
	Utilities	Utilities
Financials	Financials	Banks
	Financials	Commercial Finance
	Financials	Consumer Finance
	Financials	Diversified Banks
	Financials	Financial Services
	Financials	Life Insurance
	Financials	Real Estate
Consumer-Oriented	Communications	Cable and Satellite
	Communications	Wireline Telecommunications Services
	Consumer Discretionary	Airlines
	Consumer Discretionary	Apparel and Textile Products
	Consumer Discretionary	Automobiles Manufacturing
	Consumer Discretionary	Department Stores
	Consumer Discretionary	Home Improvement
	Consumer Discretionary	Retail — Consumer Discretionary
	Consumer Discretionary	Travel and Lodging
	Consumer Staples	Food and Beverage
	Consumer Staples	Retail — Consumer Staples
	Consumer Staples	Supermarkets and Pharmacies
	Industrials	Manufactured Goods
	Industrials	Transportation and Logistics
	Materials	Containers and Packaging
	Technology	Communications Equipment
	Technology	Software and Services
Business-Oriented	Energy	Refining and Marketing
	Health Care	Medical Equipment and Devices Manufacturing
	Industrials	Electrical equipment Manufacturing
	Industrials	Industrial Other
	Industrials	Waste, Environment Services, and Equipment
	Materials	Chemicals
	Materials	Construction materials Manufacturing
	Materials	Forest and Paper Products Manufacturing
	Technology	Hardware
	Technology	Semiconductors
	Utilities	Power Generation

References

Abadie, A., Diamond, A., & Hainmueller, J. (2010). Synthetic control methods for comparative case studies: Estimating the effect of California's tobacco control program. *Journal of the American Statistical Association, 105*(490), 493–505.

Abadie, A., Diamond, A., & Hainmueller, J. (2015). Comparative politics and the synthetic control method. *American Journal of Political Science, 59*(2), 495–510.

Abadie, A. & Gardeazabal, J. (2003). The economic costs of conflict: A case study of the Basque Country. *American Economic Review, 93*(1), 113–132.

Alonso-Conde, A. B. & Rojo-Suárez, J. (2020). On the effect of green bonds on the profitability and credit quality of project financing. *Sustainability, 12*(16), 6695.

ARUP (2018). Cost of capital benefits of revenue stabilisation via a contract for difference.

Baulkaran, V. (2019). Stock market reaction to green bond issuance. *Journal of Asset Management, 20*(5), 331–340.

CDP (2022). RE100 companies need better renewable electricity options from national governments, shows latest report. https://www.cdp.net/en/articles/media/re100-companies-need-better-nenewable-electricity-options-from-national-governments-shows-latest-report.

Centeno, M. A., Nag, M., Patterson, T. S., Shaver, A., & Windawi, A. J. (2015). The emergence of global systemic risk. *Annual Review of Sociology, 41*, 65–85.

Chava, S. (2014). Environmental externalities and cost of capital. *Management Science, 60*(9), 2223–2247.

Climate Bonds Initiative (2020). 2019 Green Bond Market Summary. https://www.climatebonds.net/files/reports/2019_annual_highlights-final.pdf.

Climate Bonds Initiative (n.d.*a*). Explaining green bonds. https://www.climatebonds.net/market/explaining-green-bonds. Accessed 18 March 2022.

Climate Bonds Initiative (n.d.*b*). External review: Bonds are labelled green by the issuer and should be qualified as green by an independent party. https://www.climatebonds. net/market/second-opinion. Accessed 18 March 2022.

Columbia Public Health (n.d.). Difference-in-difference estimation. *Population Health Methods.* https://www.publichealth.columbia.edu/research/population-health-methods/difference-difference-estimation. Accessed 18 March 2022.

Cooper, E. W. & Uzun, H. (2015). Corporate social responsibility and the cost of debt. *Journal of Accounting and Finance*, *15*(8), 11–29.

Damodaran, A. (2015). The cost of capital: Misunderstood, misestimated and misused.

Diamond, D. W. & Verrecchia, R. E. (1991). Disclosure, liquidity, and the cost of capital. *The Journal of Finance*, *46*(4), 1325–1359.

Easley, D. & O'Hara, M. (2004). Information and the cost of capital. *The Journal of Finance*, *59*(4), 1553–1583.

El Ghoul, S., Guedhami, O., Kwok, C. C. Y. & Mishra, D. R. (2011). Does corporate social responsibility affect the cost of capital? *Journal of Banking and Finance*, *35*(9), 2388–2406.

Financial Stability Board (2020). The implications of climate change for financial stability. https://www.fsb.org/wp-content/uploads/P231120.pdf.

Flammer, C. (2021). Corporate green bonds. *Journal of Financial Economics*, *142*(2), 499–516.

Galiani, S. & Quistorff, B. (2017). The synth runner package: Utilities to automate synthetic control estimation using synth. *Stata Journal*, *17*(4), 834–849.

Global Sustainable Investment Alliance (2019). 2018 Global Sustainable Investment Review. http://www.gsi-alliance.org/wp-content/uploads/2019/06/GSIR_Review2018F.pdf.

Guenster, N., Bauer, R., Derwall, J., & Koedijk, K. (2011). The economic value of corporate eco-efficiency. *European Financial Management*, *17*(4), 679–704.

Harrison, C. (2021). Green Bond Pricing in the Primary Market H2 2020. Climate Bonds Initiative. https://www.climatebonds.net/resources/reports/green-bond-pricing-primary-market-h2-2020.

Harrison, C. (2022). Green Bond Pricing in the Primary Market H2 2021. Climate Bonds Initiative. https://www.climatebonds.net/files/reports/cbi_pricing_h2_2021_02g.pdf.

Harrison, C. & Muething, L. (2021). Sustainable Debt Global State of the Market 2020. Climate Bonds Initiative. https://www.climatebonds.net/resources/reports/sustainable-debt-global-state-market-2020.

Hof, A. F., den Elzen, M. G. J., Admiraal, A., Roelfsema, M., Gernaat, D. E. H. J., & van Vuuren, D. P. (2017). Global and regional abatement costs of Nationally Determined Contributions (NDCs) and of enhanced action to levels well below 2°C and 1.5°C. *Environmental Science and Policy*, *71*, 30–40.

Hong, H. & Kacperczyk, M. (2009). The price of sin: The effects of social norms on markets. *Journal of Financial Economics*, *93*(1), 15–36.

Hyun, S., Park, D., & Tian, S. (2020). The price of going green: The role of greenness in green bond markets. *Accounting & Finance*, *60*(1), 73–95.

International Capital Markets Association (2018). Green bond principles: Voluntary process guidelines for issuing green bonds. International Finance Corporation (IFC). https://www.icmagroup.org/assets/documents/Regulatory/Green-Bonds/Green-Bonds-Principles-June-2018-270520.pdf.

International Energy Agency (2014). World energy investment outlook. IEA, Paris.

Kidney, S. (2016). Green bond market report. https://www.climatebonds.net/2016/03/green-bond-market-report-apple-sources-15bn-green-bond-funding-renovate-ameri.

Knowledge@Wharton (2017). How business can take the lead on combating climate change. https://knowledge.wharton.upenn.edu/article/business-can-take-lead-combatting-climate-change/.

Larcker, D. F. & Watts, E. M. (2020). Where's the Greenium? *Journal of Accounting and Economics*, *69*(2–3), 101312.

Lebelle, M., Jarjir, S. L., & Sassi, S. (2020). Corporate green bond issuances: An international evidence. *Journal of Risk and Financial Management*, *13*(2), 25.

MacAskill, S., Roca, E., Liu, B., Stewart, R. A., & Sahin, O. (2020). Is there a green premium in the Green Bond market? Systematic literature review revealing premium determinants. *Journal of Cleaner Production*, 124491.

Naeem, M. A., Nguyen, T. T. H., Nepal, R., Ngo, Q. T., & Taghizadeh-Hesary, F. (2021). Asymmetric relationship between green bonds and commodities: Evidence from extreme quantile approach. *Finance Research Letters*, 101983.

Nichols, W. (2013). Ford and Microsoft invest in $1 billion bond for climate projects. https://www.greenbiz.com/article/ford-and-microsoft-invest-1-billion-bond-climate-projects.

Ortiz-Molina, H. & Phillips, G. M. (2014). Real asset illiquidity and the cost of capital. *Journal of Financial and Quantitative Analysis*, *49*(1), 1–32.

Preclaw, R. & Bakshi, A. (2015). The Cost of Being Green. Barclays U.S. Credit Focus: September 18.

PwC (2022). ESG-focused institutional investment seen soaring 84% to US$33.9 trillion in 2026, making up 21.5% of assets under management: PwC report. https://www.pwc.com/gx/en/news-room/press-releases/2022/awm-revolution-2022-report.html.

Quistorff, B. & Galiani, S. (2017). The synth runner package: Utilities to automate synthetic control estimation using synth. Version 1.6.0.

Reboredo, J. C. (2018). Green bond and financial markets: Co-movement, diversification and price spillover effects. *Energy Economics*, *74*, 38–50.

Rosembuj, F. & Bottio, S. (2016). Mobilizing private climate finance-green bonds and beyond. Encompass No. 25. International Finance Corporation, Washington, DC. https://openknowledge.worldbank.org/handle/10986/30351.

Sharfman, M. P. & Fernando, C. S. (2008). Environmental risk management and the cost of capital. *Strategic Management Journal*, *29*(6), 569–592.

Shishlov, I., Morel, R., & Cochran, I. (2016). Beyond transparency: Unlocking the full potential of green bonds. Institute for Climate Economics. http://www.i4ce.org/download/unlocking-the-potential-of-green-bonds/.

Tang, D. Y. & Zhang, Y. (2020). Do shareholders benefit from green bonds? *Journal of Corporate Finance*, *61*, 101427.

Tolliver, C., Keeley, A. R., & Managi, S. (2020a). Drivers of green bond market growth: The importance of Nationally determined contributions to the Paris agreement and implications for sustainability. *Journal of Cleaner Production*, *244*, 118643.

Tolliver, C., Keeley, A. R., & Managi, S. (2020b). Policy targets behind green bonds for renewable energy: Do climate commitments matter? *Technological Forecasting and Social Change*, *157*, 120051.

UNFCCC (n.d.). NRD Registry. https://www4.unfccc.int/sites/NDCStaging/Pages/All.aspx. Accessed 18 March 2022.

Wang, J., Chen, X., Li, X., Yu, J., & Zhong, R. (2020). The market reaction to green bond issuance: Evidence from China. *Pacific-Basin Finance Journal*, *60*, 101294.

Xu, S., Liu, D., & Huang, J. (2015). Corporate social responsibility, the cost of equity capital and ownership structure: An analysis of Chinese listed firms. *Australian Journal of Management*, *40*(2), 245–276.

Zerbib, O. D. (2019). The effect of pro-environmental preferences on bond prices: Evidence from green bonds. *Journal of Banking & Finance*, *98*, 39–60.

Zhang, R., Li, Y., & Liu, Y. (2021). Green bond issuance and corporate cost of capital. *Pacific-Basin Finance Journal*, *69*, 101626.

© 2024 World Scientific Publishing Europe Ltd.
https://doi.org/10.1142/9781800614451_0003

Chapter 3

Green Bond Market Linkages: An Empirical Study

Bart Reumkens[†] **and Lisa Sheenan**[*,‡]
Queen's University Belfast, Belfast, UK
[†] *breumkens01@qub.ac.uk*
[‡] *l.sheenan@qub.ac.uk*

Abstract

Green bonds are viewed as a powerful tool in the fight against climate change and are rapidly growing in popularity with investors. This chapter provides an overview of green bonds and the green bond market, potential concerns associated with it, and regulatory responses to some of these. We then test for contagion from green bond markets to volatility, fixed income, equity, and gold and sovereign markets using a vector autoregression (VAR) framework as outlined by Longstaff (2010). Our results suggest that green bonds do not serve as a contagion channel to the other markets during higher volatility periods and themselves are significantly affected only by corporate bond markets during such times. This could indicate that these bonds serve as safe haven assets for these markets and have important implications for investors, other market participants, and policymakers seeking to identify and monitor linkages to and from this hugely popular fledgling market.

1. Introduction

Green finance is increasingly being cited as a powerful weapon in the fight against climate change (Sachs *et al.*, 2019). Green bonds, that is bonds which fund environmentally friendly projects and

[*] Corresponding author.

initiatives, are one such green finance tool that have been gaining popularity in recent years (Tolliver *et al.*, 2020). Indeed, 2021 was a record-breaking year for green bonds as the market grew by US$500 billion, following 10 years of consecutive growth (Climate Bonds Initiative, 2022).

However, with this growth has come concerns about "greenwashing", that is the practice of "...misleading consumers about firm environmental performance or the environmental benefits of a product or service" (Delmas and Burbano, 2011). Flammer (2021) hypothesizes that green bonds themselves may act as a type of greenwashing as they enable a company to appear to behave in an environmentally friendly way when that may not be the case in reality.

There are also concerns that there may be a bubble emerging in green markets. Indeed, in September 2021 the Bank for International Settlements warned that the rapid green market growth increases the likelihood of a green bubble developing, which would inevitably burst in the future (BIS, 2021).

Another concern is ensuring that market participants and regulators gain an accurate understanding of this fledgling market in terms of asset construction and interlinkages, particularly considering that the 2007/2008 financial crisis highlighted the need to assess risk transmission between assets and markets at a systemic level (Castrén and Kavonius, 2009). To date, the literature analyzing linkages to and from the green bond market remains sparse.

This chapter aims to begin to fill this gap and add to the literature by empirically investigating the relationship between the green bond market and other major financial markets across two time periods, namely, tranquil market conditions and a relatively higher volatility period. We will begin with a comprehensive overview of green bonds from their creation to the present day, discussing their structure and the global market for these securities.

We will then examine potential issues with green bonds, in particular greenwashing and the potential for a green bubble, along with regulatory responses before moving on to an empirical investigation of how the market for green bonds interacts with other financial markets. We adapt the approach presented in Longstaff (2010), which tests for contagion from the US subprime mortgage-backed securities market during the 2007/2008 financial crisis using a vector-autoregression (VAR) framework. Our results suggest that the green bond market does not act as a channel of contagion to equities, corporate bonds, gold, government bonds, and the Chicago Board Options Exchange Market Volatility Index (VIX) during periods of higher volatility and itself receives contagious effects from only corporate bonds. This indicates that this market may behave in a manner similar to that of a safe haven asset and provides important insights for market participants and regulators.

Section 2 will provide an overview of green bonds and how the market for them has developed since their inception and Section 3 outlines potential issues associated with these assets, such as greenwashing, and regulations applicable to this market. In Section 4, we present the empirical analysis, which includes data, preliminary analysis, methodology, and results. A final section then concludes.

2. Green bonds and the green bond market

Green bonds may be described as "...fixed income securities which finance investments with environmental or climate-related benefits" (Ehlers and Packer, 2017). In 2007, the European Investment Bank (EIB) issued a "Climate Awareness Bond", the proceeds of which were designated to future projects in the areas of renewable energy and energy efficiency and its return was linked to that of the FTSE4Good Environmental Leaders Europe 40 Index. This bond went on to be listed on 27 European domestic markets (Reichelt and Keenan, 2017).

Also, in 2007 the Intergovernmental Panel on Climate Change (IPCC), a group created jointly by the World Meteorological Organization and the United Nations Environment Programme, released a comprehensive report that linked climate change to human behavior (IPCC, 2007). This led a number of Swedish pension funds to express a desire to finance environmentally friendly projects and in 2008 the World Bank issued its first green bond, created with Skandinaviska Enskilda Banken (SEB), which is an AAA-rated investment grade asset and contributes to projects that meet the criteria set out by the World Bank (Reichelt and Keenan, 2017).

While issuances of these bonds were met with much fanfare in terms of media coverage, the market for these assets remained within the realm of a small number of institutional and retail investors until 2013, when interest in green assets began to increase (Kreivi, 2017). In 2014, green bond volume tripled to almost US$37 billion and the original Green Bond Principles were published. The Green Bond Principles are designed and released by the International Capital Market Association (ICMA) and are voluntary, providing recommendations for best practices in green bond markets focusing on transparency and disclosure by breaking the principles into four elements, namely, use of proceeds, project evaluation and selection, management of proceeds, and reporting (ICMA, 2021).[1]

The green bond market has continued to grow rapidly, at an average of 50% annually between 2015 and 2020, as illustrated in Figure 1.

Although the market has grown rapidly, it still only represents about 3% to 3.5% of overall bond issuance. It is forecasted that this market will continue to experience high levels of growth to reach US$1 trillion annual global issuance in 2023 (Climate Bonds Initiative, 2021). However, according to the European Parliament, the green bond market needs to grow more quickly to achieve the targets in the Paris Agreement (European Parliament Briefing, 2022).[2]

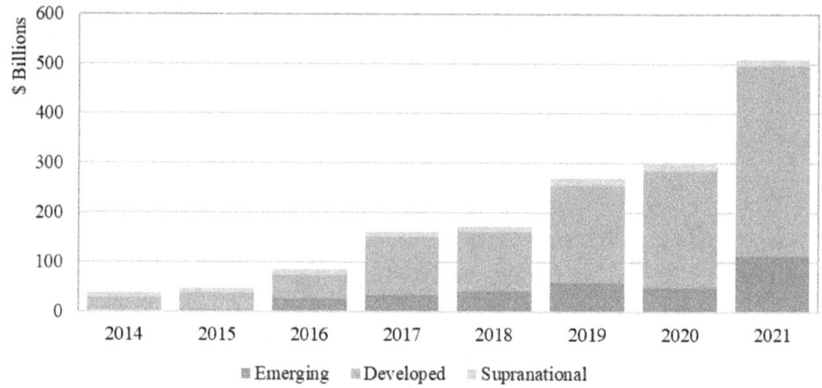

Figure 1. Green bond issuance volume.

Notes: This figure illustrates global green bond issuance volume from 2014 to 2021 in US$ billions. Data are sourced from the Climate Bonds Initiative.

[1]Section 3 will discuss regulation of green bonds in more detail.

[2]The Paris Agreement is an international treaty, adopted by 196 entities, relating to climate change. It is legally binding and was introduced at the COP21 in December 2015 before coming into force in November 2016.

A growing body of literature analyzing green bonds has accompanied this accelerated market growth. This literature is not confined to finance-related topics but spans across disciplines such as economic geography and development economics.

A strand of the literature analyzes whether green bonds actually contribute to the fight against climate change. For example, Ehlers *et al.* (2020) investigate whether green bond issuance is related to a reduction in carbon emissions at the company level, finding that the evidence is mixed. Fatica and Panzica (2021) find that green bond issuers display a decline in the carbon intensity of their assets, which tends to be more pronounced for those issued after the Paris Agreement, as well as those that are subject to external review. Tuhkanen and Vulturius (2020) analyze 20 of the largest green bond issuers in Europe in 2018, identifying a disconnect between their climate targets and green bond frameworks, as well as deficiencies in reporting following issuances.

Literature analyzing green bonds and financial markets encapsulates several topics. For example, from the perspective of corporate finance, Tang and Zhang (2020) conclude that shareholders benefit from firms issuing green bonds. With the focus on pricing, Hachenberg and Schiereck (2018) find that green bonds trade tighter than non-green bonds and Baker *et al.* (2018) state that green municipal bonds are issued at a premium compared to similar non-green bonds. With regards to liquidity, for example, Boutabba and Rannou (2022) find that green bond investors prefer buy and hold strategies as they are compensated for increased liquidity risks.

In terms of risk spillovers and financial contagion to and from the green bond market, the literature to date tends to focus on how this market affects energy markets, such as Liu *et al.* (2021) who find bilateral risk spillovers between clean energy markets and green bonds. Ren *et al.* (2022) conclude that the price of carbon Granger-causes green bonds and Lee *et al.* (2021) analyze the relationships between oil prices, green bonds, and geopolitical risk, finding bilateral causality between green bonds and oil prices. Literature analyzing spillovers from the green bond market to other financial markets is discussed in Section 3.

3. Green bond market issues and regulatory response

As with any fledgling financial market there are a number of potential issues that should be taken into consideration by investors, market participants, and regulators. Here we focus on three areas, specifically greenwashing, the potential for a green bubble, and identifying and assessing interlinkages between markets. We also outline regulatory responses to some of these issues, thus providing an overview of green bond regulation.

The UK Financial Conduct Authority (FCA) defines greenwashing as "... marketing that portrays an organisation's products, activities or policies as producing positive environmental outcomes when this is not the case" (FCA, 2018). Baldi and Pandimiglio (2022) find that the risk of greenwashing is higher among manufacturing firms at the corporate level but is more pronounced in the financial sector. In terms of green bond markets, commentators have raised concerns about greenwashing as investors and regulators fear that the rapid growth in these markets could encourage greenwashing activities (Flood, 2022). The need for transparent and comprehensive regulation surrounding these assets is clear.

We discuss two regulatory perspectives on the standardization and classification of green bonds, namely, from the US and EU, as these two jurisdictions are the largest issuers of green bonds (Climate Bonds Initiative, 2022). Currently, there is a notable lack of a common disclosure framework for green bonds from a regulatory point of view, but private sector-led initiatives are helping industry bodies to address this challenge.

The EU Parliament's resolution on sustainable finance in 2018 noted that green bonds are insufficiently regulated and that the EU lacks a unified standard for these assets, which should be based on a sustainable taxonomy. It also noted that green bonds should be verified and supervised by public authorities, and should include periodic reporting on the environmental impact of the underlying assets. Europe has therefore produced the most substantial legal developments to date toward the standardization of green bonds through the adoption of the EU Taxonomy Regulation, which came into force on July 12, 2020. The EU Taxonomy requires EU member states to apply the criteria from the Regulation to determine whether an economic activity qualifies as environmentally sustainable. In December 2021, the rapporteur of the EU Green Bond Standard (EU GBS) at the European Parliament published a draft report with some suggested amendments, representing a fundamental shift from the Commission's original proposals. This included, among other things, a mandatory versus a voluntary EU GBS and an expansion of the documentation, reporting, and certain other aspects of the EU GBS to cover all types of sustainable bonds.

The US currently lacks a green bond classification system. An introduction of such a system would clearly help to further the US, national climate and environmental goals. The national head of the US Securities and Exchange Commission (SEC) indicated in June 2021 that it plans to introduce new climate-related rules.

A concern closely linked to that of greenwashing is the possibility of a green bubble developing, which could indeed be inflated by greenwashing activities. A number of monetary authorities, experts, and commentators have warned of the potential for a green bubble emerging, the most notable to date being the Bank for International Settlements in their September 2021 Quarterly Report (BIS, 2021). Demidov (2022) links the idea of greenwashing to that of a green bubble, advising that green bond issuance "...should be strictly regulated under obligatory rules of issuance to limit uncontrollable issuance and prevent bursting of a new-bubble of green associated securities."

As stated above, it is crucial that market participants and policymakers acquire an accurate understanding of market linkages because such linkages can increase the possibility of risk spillovers and contagion across financial markets and countries (Chan-Lau *et al.*, 2009). Should a green bubble come to fruition, its inevitable bursting could lead to financial contagion and spillovers, thus it is vital that market practitioners and authorities have a firm grasp on the connections to and from green asset markets.

The financial crisis of 2007/2008 highlighted the importance of assessing and monitoring interlinkages between financial markets as these linkages can strengthen during crisis times leading to financial contagion (Luchtenberg and Vu, 2015). Indeed, studies such as Dungey and Martin (2007) find that cross-market links are important in terms of financial crises and focusing on one market in isolation when assessing spillovers and contagion during crisis times may lead to misspecification.

Following the 2007/2008 crisis central banks and monetary authorities around the world turned toward macroprudential policies, that is policies aimed at mitigating risks to the system as a whole, and issuance of such policies increased (Kahou and Lehar, 2017).

The focus of this chapter, and the strand of literature that we aim to contribute to with our empirical analysis, is on green bond market linkages to other financial markets and testing for contagion among these in order to inform investment strategy and policy discussions regarding this market.

A growing body of work is studying this topic, such as Ferrer *et al.* (2021a) who find that green bonds closely follow the performance of government and high-quality corporate bonds while there is a weaker relationship between green bonds and the stock market, renewable energy equities, and crude oil. Gao *et al.* (2021) analyze spillovers in green bond markets and other financial markets in China, finding significant spillovers between them. Ferrer *et al.* (2021b) find that green bonds are closely connected to Treasury and investment-grade corporate bonds, while green equities are closely linked to general equities. Park *et al.* (2020) investigate spillovers between green bond and equity markets, finding some volatility spillover effects between them but that neither market responds in a significant way to negative shocks in the other.

Next, we present an empirical analysis which will investigate linkages between the green bond market and equities, corporate bonds, government bonds and gold.

4. Empirical analysis

In this chapter, we will empirically assess the interlinkages between green bond markets and other financial markets during tranquil and more volatile market conditions, essentially testing for contagion channels, using the framework presented in Longstaff (2010) and adapted by Sheenan (2014, 2017). By doing so we intend to provide a comprehensive picture of market linkages and inform market participants and policymakers.

Following Longstaff (2010), we utilize the ABX indexes to represent the US subprime mortgage-backed securities market and test for contagion from this market to several fixed-income, equity, and volatility markets using a vector autoregressive (VAR) framework. The sample is divided into three separate one-year periods, the 2006 "pre-crisis" period, the 2007 "subprime-crisis" period, and the 2008 "global-crisis" period, to test for contagion when moving from tranquil "normal" market conditions to a volatile crisis period.

Longstaff (2010) highlights that the literature examining contagion broadly classifies three potential devices though which contagion may be transmitted to financial markets. The first mechanism is termed the "correlated-information channel". In this channel, contagion occurs through the transmission of information by means of price discovery and should cause instantaneous price effects following a crisis. The second channel presented is known as the "liquidity channel". This channel implies that a crisis is related to credit shortages and increased trading in other financial markets. The third outlet is labeled the "risk-premium channel" through which shocks to an affected security may have predictive ability for subsequent returns of other securities. Using a VAR framework, Longstaff (2010) finds strong evidence of contagion in the financial markets examined over the crisis period. It is also found that this contagion is mainly transmitted through liquidity and risk-premium channels, rejecting the correlated information channel. Significant price discovery supports this hypothesis.

We adapt the definition of contagion presented by Forbes and Rigobon (2002), as "an episode in which there is a significant increase in intra-market linkages after a shock occurs in that market".

Because we are testing for significant changes in existing linkages, we are therefore testing for a form of shift contagion[3] and define contagion as linkages over and above those experienced during "normal" market conditions concluding that if there is no significant increase in co-movement over and above what is experienced in tranquil times, it is interdependence, not contagion, that is observed in markets.

[3]Shift contagion is defined as a "... significant change in cross-market linkages after a shock in an individual country or group of countries" (Forbes and Rigobon, 2002).

We test if green bonds Granger-cause returns in other assets, namely, stocks, bonds, gold, sovereign bonds, and the VIX, during periods of higher volatility. We also assess if these assets Granger-cause returns in green bonds, thus analyzing how susceptible they may be to higher volatility periods.

4.1. *Data*

This chapter tests for contagion among six financial markets, as outlined in the following. Data have been obtained from Refinitiv Eikon and daily log returns are used in the analysis. The sample ranges from February 5, 2014 to July 1, 2021, split between a lower volatility period between February 5, 2014 and January 1, 2018 and a higher volatility period between January 1, 2018 and July 1, 2021.[4]

The S&P Green Bond Index is a multi-currency rules-based benchmark that serves as a proxy for the performance of the green bond market. Launched in 2014, the green bonds included present no minimum amount outstanding, and the time to maturity must be at least one year. Nevertheless, the index excludes the following categories of bonds: bills, inflation-linked, and Separate Trading of Registered Interest (STRIPS) bonds. The bonds included are globally issued bonds labeled "green" by the Climate Bonds Initiative. Kanamura (2020) investigates the "greenness", i.e., correlations between green bond prices as environmental value and crude oil prices as fossil fuel value, of green bonds. They find that S&P green bonds, as well as Bloomberg Barclays MSCI, do indeed carry greenness. Due to some MSCI data gaps, the S&P Green Bond Index is used in our analysis. The VIX provides a measure of volatility, known to investors as the "fear gauge" (Whaley, 2000). The S&P 500 is widely regarded as the best single gauge of the large-cap US equity market and is the world's most tracked index by assets under management (AUM). The index includes 500 leading companies and covers approximately 80% of the US equity market's available market cap (Standard & Poor's Global, July 2020). Asem and Alam (2012) investigate the role of the S&P 500 index in tracking the US equity market, finding that it mimics the US equity market performance

[4]The sample period begins in 2014 due to availability of green bond data.

very well and, therefore, serves as an appropriate benchmark for the performance of this market. Gold spot price is a proxy for the performance of gold, which is widely considered a safe haven. Bauer and McDermott (2010) consider the role of gold in the global financial system, finding evidence of the safe haven effect for most developed country stock markets. The Bloomberg Global Aggregate Index is a flagship measure of global investment-grade debt from 24 local currency markets. This multi-currency benchmark includes Treasury, government-related, corporate, and securitized fixed-rate bonds from both developed and emerging market issuers (Bloomberg, 2022). The 10-year US government bond is also included, as it is viewed as a signal of investor sentiment regarding the economy (OECD Data, 2022).

4.2. *Preliminary analysis*

We begin with visual analysis of the raw data, presented in Figure 2. The effect of the COVID-19 pandemic on financial markets is clear as all six variables under analysis display considerable change in early 2020. Our measure of volatility, the VIX, increases as does the spot price of gold, which corresponds to the safe haven theory (Baur and McDermott, 2010). The 10-year sovereign bond prices fell over this period, indicating stress in financial markets (Afonso *et al.*, 2014). The S&P 500 index experiences a fall, but appears to recover quite quickly, which corresponds to the finding by Yilmazkuday (2021) that most negative effects from COVID-19 in the US on the S&P 500 occurred in March 2020. Likewise, global corporate bonds also experience a decline but soon recover.

Similar to equity and corporate bond markets, the green bond market displays a dip in early 2020 but quickly rebounds and continues its upward trajectory as demand for green assets reached new highs, as described earlier.

We calculate daily returns by log-differencing each variable. Table 1 reports summary statistics for these. It reports summary statistics for daily percentage returns for all the series under analysis over the sample period. Mean returns are all close to zero, with low standard deviations, indicating low volatility over the whole sample period. All variables display positive excess kurtosis, which may also be termed leptokurtic. This is very high for the S&P 500 and the

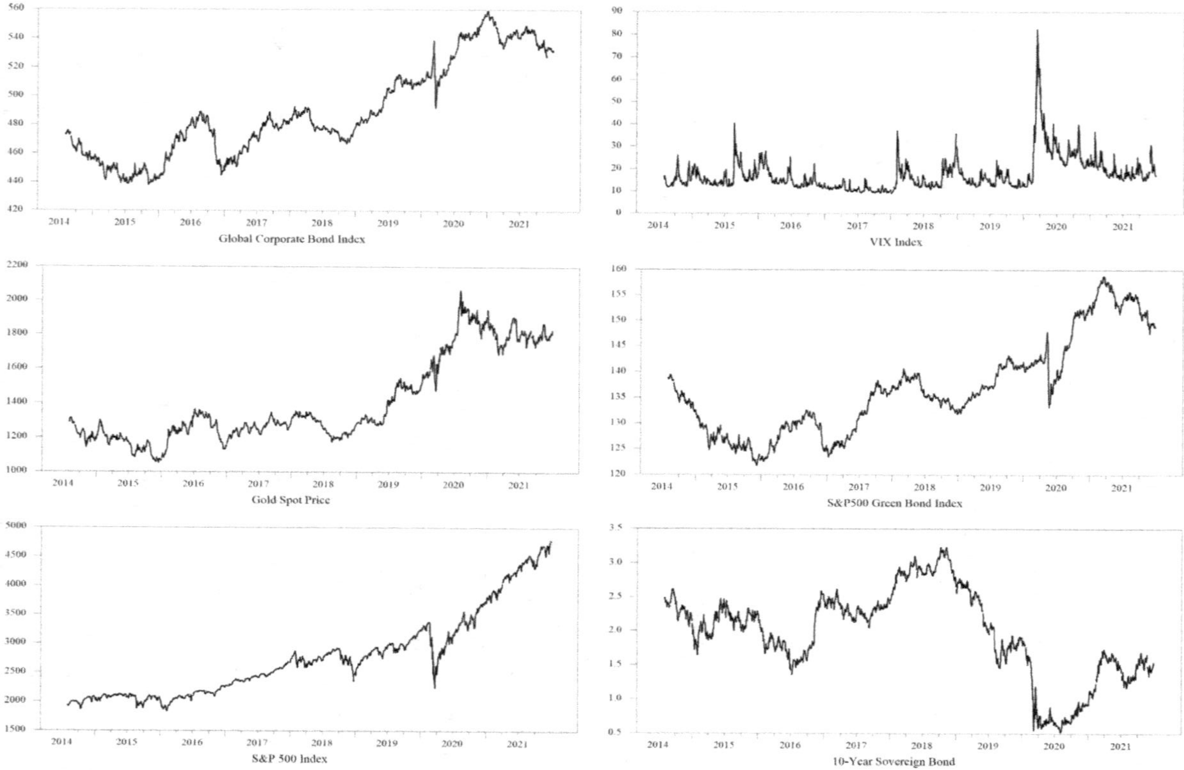

Figure 2. Raw financial market variables.

Notes: This figure illustrates daily raw prices for each of the indicated financial market variables over the sample period. The sample period ranges from February 5, 2014 to July 1, 2021. Data are sourced from Refinitiv Eikon.

Table 1. Summary statistics.

Variable	Obs.	Mean	Std. dev.	Skewness	Kurtosis	Min.	Max.
S&P 500	1923	0.0002	0.0049	−0.9790	19.9412	−0.0554	0.0389
Green bonds	1923	−0.0000	0.0014	−0.5699	5.4545	−0.0104	0.0087
VIX	1923	0.0001	0.0365	1.2672	6.7986	−0.1302	0.3336
Gold	1923	0.0001	0.0038	−0.1941	3.6102	−0.0254	0.0215
10Y government bonds	1923	−0.0000	0.0149	0.2291	32.1407	−0.1482	0.1762
Global bonds	1923	0.0000	0.0013	−0.4839	4.6141	−0.0095	0.0066

Notes: This table reports summary statistics for the daily log returns for the indicated variables. Std. dev. denotes standard deviation; Min. denotes minimum; Max. denotes maximum. The sample period ranges from February 5, 2014 to July 1, 2021.

Table 2. Raw correlations.

Variable	S&P 500	Green bonds	VIX	Gold	10Y government bonds	Global bonds
S&P 500	1	−0.01	−0.74	−0.03	0.46	−0.11
Green bonds	−0.01	1	0.02	0.02	−0.02	0.05
VIX	−0.74	0.02	1	0.06	−0.28	0.15
Gold	−0.03	0.02	0.06	1	−0.29	0.47
10Y government bonds	0.46	−0.02	−0.28	−0.29	1	−0.50
Global bonds	−0.11	0.05	0.15	0.47	−0.50	1

Notes: This table reports raw correlation coefficients for the daily percentage returns for the variables mentioned. The sample period ranges from February 5, 2014 to July 1, 2021.

10-year government bond indicating high probabilities of extreme positive and negative returns. The S&P 500 return distribution is also considered to be moderately negatively skewed, indicating frequent small positive returns and infrequent large negative returns, which is unsurprising for equity returns.

Table 2 reports raw correlations between the variables.

The correlation between green bonds and the other variables can be considered weak, which indicates little or no relationship between these variables. As expected, the S&P 500 has a negative correlation with the VIX, which is unsurprising given that the VIX is a proxy for volatility. The S&P 500 is positively correlated with the 10-year government bond, which is expected as this can be considered as a signal of investor sentiment.

4.3. *Methodology*

As explained earlier, we follow Longstaff (2010), employing a VAR system taking the following form:

$$Y_t = \alpha + \sum_{k=1}^{4}(\beta_k Y_{t-k} + \gamma_k \text{GreenBonds}_{t-k}) + \epsilon_t \tag{1}$$

in which Y_t denotes the financial market included as a dependent variable, so there are six dependent variables and the system is estimated separately for each of these. GreenBonds_{t-k} denotes the Green Bond Index included as an exogenous variable.

As described earlier, the data are broken into two distinct periods, a "low-volatility" period between February 2014 and December 2017 and a "high-volatility" period between January 2018 and July 2021. These regimes are chosen exogenously based on preliminary analysis of the data and market events that occurred at these times. Four lags are suggested by the Akaike Information Criterion (AIC). Despite some limitations to this methodology, which will be discussed later in the chapter, its greatest advantage lies in its ability to incorporate a large number of financial variables simultaneously and thus easily observe relationships between these variables.

4.4. *Results*

Tables 3 and 4 present results from the VAR model depicted as Eq. (1) performed in the low-volatility and high-volatility periods as outlined earlier. As the residuals are likely to have a non-constant variance, we follow Longstaff (2010) by computing Newey–West-adjusted standard errors. We therefore report the Newey–West t-statistics for the γ_k coefficients in Eq. (1) along with the R^2s from

Table 3. Lower volatility period.

Dependent	Independent	Y_1	Y_2	Y_3	Y_4	R^2	P
Green bonds	Global bonds	1.24	−0.30	−0.10	2.34	0.04	0.14
	VIX	−0.37	0.27	0.35	0.19	0.04	0.98
	S&P 500	−1.02	0.80	1.51	−0.09	0.04	0.29
	Gold	0.88	1.25	1.73*	0.45	0.04	0.30
	10Y govt bonds	1.59	1.36	−1.35	1.12	0.04	0.10
Global bonds	Green bonds	0.83	−0.57	0.67	0.15	0.09	0.83
	VIX	0.23	−0.15	0.30	0.30	0.09	0.99
	S&P 500	1.23	0.37	1.29	−0.36	0.09	0.48
	Gold	4.26***	1.98**	0.46	−0.43	0.09	0.00***
	10Y govt bonds	−4.17***	−2.22***	−3.16***	−0.12	0.09	0.00***
VIX	Green bonds	1.21	0.59	0.44	−0.75	0.03	0.63
	Global bonds	1.37	0.60	1.01	−0.03	0.03	0.42
	S&P 500	1.78*	1.14	0.53	−0.56	0.03	0.30
	Gold	1.15	0.92	0.85	−1.74*	0.03	0.21
	10Y govt bonds	0.60	−0.30	0.76	1.88**	0.03	0.31
S&P 500	Green bonds	−2.08***	−0.09	−1.22	0.79	0.02	0.15
	Global bonds	1.88*	0.41	−0.52	0.40	0.02	0.34
	VIX	−1.79*	−1.66*	−1.40	−0.15	0.02	0.06*
	Gold	−0.57	−1.12	−0.27	0.38	0.02	0.83
	10Y govt bonds	0.82	0.73	−0.48	−2.15***	0.02	0.15
Gold	Green bonds	0.56	0.01	1.15	0.57	0.03	0.76
	Global bonds	−0.84	−0.94	−0.68	−0.08	0.03	0.80
	VIX	0.48	0.51	−0.24	−0.33	0.03	0.93
	S&P 500	1.22	1.06	0.87	−1.19	0.03	0.28
	10Y govt bonds	−1.24	−2.83***	−2.98***	0.27	0.03	0.00***

(*Continued*)

Table 3. (*Continued*)

Dependent	Independent	Y_1	Y_2	Y_3	Y_4	R^2	P
10-year government bonds	Green bonds	−1.95**	0.60	−1.60	0.20	0.03	0.12
	Global bonds	2.03***	1.17	1.38	−0.54	0.03	0.12
	VIX	−0.28	1.12	−0.17	0.95	0.03	0.71
	S&P 500	−0.68	0.55	−0.11	1.27	0.03	0.63
	Gold	−1.05	−1.69**	0.05	−0.18	0.03	0.44

Notes: This table reports results for the following VAR equation:

$$Y_t = \alpha + \sum_{k=1}^{4}(\beta_k Y_{t-k} + \gamma_k \text{GreenBonds}_{t-k}) + \epsilon_t$$

in which Y_t denotes the financial market included as a dependent variable, so there are six dependent variables and the system is estimated separately for each of these. GreenBonds_{t-k} denotes the Green Bond Index included as an exogenous variable. Four lags are suggested by the Akaike Information Criterion. The sample runs from February 5, 2014 to January 1, 2018. The superscript * denotes significance at the 10% level; the superscript ** denotes significance at the 5% level; the superscript *** denotes significance at the 1% level.

the VARs and the p-values for the F-test that the γ_k coefficients are jointly zero.[5]

As our definition of contagion states that we must observe "...a significant increase in intra-market linkages after a shock occurs in that market", if we observe a significant relationship in the low-volatility period that continues in the higher volatility period, we conclude that this is not contagion but interdependency that exists in all states of the world. Contagion is detected if we observe a significant relationship in the high-volatility period that did not exist in the low-volatility period. Should we observe a significant relationship

[5]Note that the results for the β coefficients are not reported in order to conserve space and because they do not provide information regarding contagion from the green bond market to the financial market variables. Full results are available on request.

Table 4. Higher volatility period.

Dependent	Independent	Y_1	Y_2	Y_3	Y_4	R^2	P
Green bonds	Global bonds	−1.02	2.09***	−0.94	1.75*	0.09	0.06**
	VIX	−1.41	1.84**	0.37	−0.94	0.09	0.19
	S&P 500	1.19	1.64	0.07	−1.74**	0.09	0.20
	Gold	−0.91	−2.31***	−0.21	−1.51	0.09	0.11
	10Y govt bonds	−1.63	0.45	−1.14	1.01	0.09	0.20
Global bonds	Green bonds	−0.13	0.21	0.53	0.36	0.20	0.95
	VIX	2.51***	2.88***	1.36	2.88***	0.20	0.00***
	S&P 500	6.31***	2.81***	−0.06	−0.68	0.20	0.00***
	Gold	1.65*	1.82*	0.72	−0.89	0.20	0.08**
	10Y govt bonds	−3.64***	0.05	2.40**	0.97	0.20	0.00***
VIX	Green bonds	0.89	−0.01	0.41	−0.79	0.04	0.83
	Global bonds	0.48	−0.81	0.77	−0.63	0.04	0.79
	S&P 500	1.68*	0.19	0.45	−0.31	0.04	0.40
	Gold	−0.82	−0.07	−0.45	1.19	0.04	0.69
	10Y govt bonds	0.47	−0.52	−1.31	0.58	0.04	0.39
S&P 500	Green bonds	−0.57	−0.87	−0.23	0.57	0.15	0.80
	Global bonds	−0.90	1.86**	−0.27	−0.28	0.15	0.35
	VIX	−2.00***	0.14	−1.22	−2.16**	0.15	0.07**
	Gold	1.36	1.37	−0.15	−0.35	0.15	0.20
	10Y govt bonds	−1.12	−0.03	0.80	−1.11	0.15	0.54
Gold	Green bonds	0.05	0.20	0.45	0.07	0.05	0.99
	Global bonds	−0.52	0.23	−1.15	−1.39	0.05	0.53
	VIX	−0.55	0.85	1.74**	−0.97	0.05	0.21
	S&P 500	0.69	2.02***	0.02	0.08	0.05	0.36
	10Y govt bonds	−2.41***	−1.16	0.77	−0.9	0.05	0.15

(*Continued*)

Table 4. (*Continued*)

Dependent	Independent	Y_1	Y_2	Y_3	Y_4	R^2	P
10-year government bonds	Green bonds	−0.3	0.07	−0.28	0.84	0.14	0.94
	Global bonds	−0.95	1.73**	−0.52	−1.63	0.14	0.07**
	VIX	−2.86***	−1.12	−2.19***	−0.43	0.14	0.00***
	S&P 500	−3.79***	0.28	−0.37	−0.26	0.14	0.00***
	Gold	1.29	−0.95	−0.94	−0.31	0.14	0.45

Notes: This table reports results for the following VAR equation:

$$Y_t = \alpha + \sum_{k=1}^{4}(\beta_k Y_{t-k} + \gamma_k \text{GreenBonds}_{t-k}) + \epsilon_t$$

in which Y_t denotes the financial market included as a dependent variable, so there are six dependent variables and the system is estimated separately for each of these. GreenBonds_{t-k} denotes the Green Bond Index included as an exogenous variable. Four lags are suggested by the Akaike Information Criterion. The sample runs from January 1, 2018 to July 1, 2021. The superscript * denotes significance at the 10% level; the superscript ** denotes significance at the 5% level; the superscript *** denotes significance at the 1% level.

in the low-volatility period that is not observed in the high-volatility period, we term this as decoupling.

Turning first to the low-volatility period there is little evidence that green bond returns Granger-cause in the other assets and vice versa, suggesting that during tranquil market conditions, these markets largely behave independently of each other. There is some evidence of interdependencies between corporate bonds and gold, as well as between corporate bonds and the 10-year government bond in this period, while the VIX is not significantly affected by any other asset class under consideration. The S&P 500 is Granger-caused by the VIX, which is unsurprising given that the VIX is derived from the prices of the S&P 500. Gold returns are Granger-caused by returns in the 10-year government bond during this period. These relationships are consistent with what is expected during low-volatility, tranquil markets.

Moving to the high-volatility period, we observe evidence of contagion from the corporate bond market to the green bond market. This could possibly be due to the fact that entities issuing corporate bonds may also issue green bonds. Interestingly, the green bond market does not display any evidence of contagion to the other markets. This is an important finding for investors and regulators as it suggests that green bonds may have safe haven properties, and this is consistent with Kuang (2021), who finds that green bonds act as a safe haven for international equities. Our results suggest that corporate bonds experience contagion from equities and the VIX, while maintaining interdependencies with gold and the 10-year government bond in the high-volatility period. The S&P 500 maintains interdependency with the VIX in this period, which is not surprising given the construction of the VIX as mentioned earlier and the VIX itself remains independent of the other markets analyzed. Gold decouples from the 10-year government bond in the high-volatility period, which is another sign of the commodity's safe haven properties, while the 10-year government bond experiences contagion from every market other than gold and the green bond.

While considering these results it should be kept in mind that in the higher volatility period the volatility is likely to be caused by the effect of COVID-19 on financial markets in early 2020, which was most pronounced on equity markets and was followed by a rebound.

These results are useful for market participants and regulators as they indicate that the green bond market does not serve as a contagion channel during times of market turbulence, and the green bond market itself is significantly impacted by corporate bonds in a high-volatility period. It may be useful to investigate further why this may be in terms of the corporate entities issuing both types of bonds and the intricacies of the linkages between the two markets.

Our results correspond to those reported by Ferrer *et al.* (2021a) (green bonds display linkages to government and high-quality corporate bonds but are only weakly related to the stock market), Ferrer *et al.* (2021b) (green bonds are closely connected to Treasury and investment-grade corporate bonds), and Park *et al.* (2020) (while equity and green bond markets display some volatility spillovers, neither significantly responds to negative shocks in the other), but limitations to our approach must be addressed.

One such limitation is the fact that, following the approach of Longstaff (2010), we exogenously impose regimes on the data. While the data have been chosen based on preliminary analysis of the data and market events at the time, it is possible that a nonlinear model, such as a Markov-switching VAR to endogenously date phases (as per Flavin and Sheenan, 2015; Cronin *et al.*, 2016; Dungey *et al.*, 2021) followed by a multivariate test for contagion introduced by Dungey *et al.* (2005) may provide more accuracy. Leitao *et al.* (2021) utilize a Markov-switching framework for green bonds, conventional bonds, energy commodities, and the European Union carbon market, finding a positive effect from green bonds to the carbon market in both low- and high-volatility regimes.

5. Conclusion

This chapter has provided a comprehensive overview of green bonds from their creation to the present day, discussing the market for these securities and examining potential issues with these assets, in particular greenwashing, and how these are being tackled from a regulatory point of view. To further the discussion, we empirically test for contagion from the green bond market to other major financial markets, namely, markets for equities, volatility, gold, fixed-income securities, and 10-year sovereign bonds. Our results suggest that green bonds may have safe haven properties, as there is no evidence of contagion from this market to these assets in the high-volatility period. Only corporate bonds display contagious effects for green bonds, suggesting that the relationship between these markets should be investigated further.

Other extensions of this work include adapting the methodology to a nonlinear setting with a Markov-switching model as discussed earlier. Other markets could also be included, such as "clean" and "dirty" energy markets to investigate interactions between these and green bonds and other green financial markets could also be investigated using the same framework.

Our results correspond to a number of existing studies in this area and add to the discussion of these assets, clearly having implications for investors and regulators.

References

Afonso, A., Arghyrou, M. G., & Kontonikas, A. (2014). Pricing sovereign bond risk in the European Monetary Union area: An empirical investigation. *International Journal of Finance & Economics, 19*(1), 49–56.

Asem, E. & Alam, S. (2012). The role of the S&P 500 Index constituents in tracking the US equity market. *International Journal of Economics and Finance, 4*(12), 15–22.

Baker, M., Bergstresser, D., Serafeim, G., & Wurgler, J. (2018). Financing the response to climate change: The pricing and ownership of US green bonds (No. w25194). National Bureau of Economic Research.

Baldi, F. & Pandimiglio, A. (2022). The role of ESG scoring and greenwashing risk in explaining the yields of green bonds: A conceptual framework and an econometric analysis. *Global Finance Journal, 52*(C), 100711.

Baur, D. G. & McDermott, T. K. (2010). Is gold a safe haven? International evidence. *Journal of Banking & Finance, 34*(8), 1886–1898.

BIS (2021). *BIS Quarterly Review*, September 2021.

Bloomberg (2022). Bloomberg global-aggregate total return index value unhedged USD. https://www.bloomberg.com/quote/LEGATRUU:IND.

Boutabba, M. A. & Rannou, Y. (2022). Investor strategies in the green bond market: The influence of liquidity risks, economic factors and clientele effects. *International Review of Financial Analysis, 81*, 102071.

Castrén, O. & Kavonius, I. K. (2009). Balance sheet interlinkages and macro-financial risk analysis in the euro area.

Chan-Lau, J. A., Espinosa, M., Giesecke, K., & Solé, J. A. (2009). Assessing the systemic implications of financial linkages. IMF global financial stability report, 2.

Climate Bonds Initiative (2021). Sustainable debt summary Q3 2021, 2 November 2021.

Climate Bonds Initiative (2022). $500bn Green Issuance 2021: Social and sustainable acceleration: Annual green $1tn in sight: Market expansion forecasts for 2022 and 2025. *Climate Bonds Initiative.* Accessed March 2022.

Cronin, D., Flavin, T. J., & Sheenan, L. (2016). Contagion in Eurozone sovereign bond markets? The good, the bad and the ugly. *Economics Letters, 143*, 5–8.

Delmas, M. A. & Burbano, V. C. (2011). The drivers of greenwashing. *California Management Review, 54*(1), 64–87.

Demidov, V. V. (2022). Not for "green": Risks of inflating a "new-bubble" by applying traditional financial mechanisms. In *Industry 4.0* (pp. 269–280). Cham: Palgrave Macmillan.

Dungey, M., Flavin, T., & Sheenan, L. (2021). Banks and sovereigns: Did adversity bring them closer? *The European Journal of Finance*, 1–26.

Dungey, M., Fry, R., González-Hermosillo, B., & Martin, V. L. (2005). Empirical modelling of contagion: A review of methodologies. *Quantitative Finance*, *5*(1), 9–24.

Dungey, M. & Martin, V. L. (2007). Unravelling financial market linkages during crises. *Journal of Applied Econometrics*, *22*(1), 89–119.

Ehlers, T., Mojon, B., & Packer, F. (2020). Green bonds and carbon emissions: Exploring the case for a rating system at the firm level. *BIS Quarterly Review*, September.

Ehlers, T. & Packer, F. (2017). Green bond finance and certification. *BIS Quarterly Review*, September.

European Parliament Briefing (2022). European green bonds: A standard for Europe, open to the world, January 2022.

Fatica, S. & Panzica, R. (2021). Green bonds as a tool against climate change? *Business Strategy and the Environment*, *30*(5), 2688–2701.

FCA (2018). Climate change and green finance. Discussion Paper DP18/8 October 2018.

Ferrer, R., Benítez, R., & Bolós, V. J. (2021a). Interdependence between green financial instruments and major conventional assets: A wavelet-based network analysis. *Mathematics*, *9*(8), 900.

Ferrer, R., Shahzad, S. J. H., & Soriano, P. (2021b). Are green bonds a different asset class? Evidence from time-frequency connectedness analysis. *Journal of Cleaner Production*, *292*, 125988.

Flammer, C. (2021). Corporate green bonds. *Journal of Financial Economics*, *142*(2), 499–516.

Flavin, T. J. & Sheenan, L. (2015). The role of US subprime mortgage-backed assets in propagating the crisis: Contagion or interdependence? *The North American Journal of Economics and Finance*, *34*, 167–186.

Flood, C. (2022). Fears rise over 'greenwash' bonds. *Financial Times.*

Forbes, K. & Rigobon, R. (2002). No contagion, only interdependence: Measuring stock market co-movements. *The Journal of Finance*, *57*(5), 2223–2261.

Gao, Y., Li, Y., & Wang, Y. (2021). Risk spillover and network connectedness analysis of China's green bond and financial markets: Evidence from financial events of 2015–2020. *The North American Journal of Economics and Finance*, *57*, 101386.

Hachenberg, B. & Schiereck, D. (2018). Are green bonds priced differently from conventional bonds? *Journal of Asset Management, 19*(6), 371–383.

ICMA (2021). Green Bond Principles. Voluntary Process Guidelines for Issuing Green Bonds. June 2021.

IPCC (2007). *Climate Change 2007: Impacts, Adaptation and Vulnerability.* Contribution of Working Group II to the Fourth Assessment Report of the Intergovernmental Panel on Climate Change, M. L. Parry, O. F. Canziani, J. P. Palutikof, P. J. van der Linden, & C. E. Hanson (Eds.) (976 pp.). Cambridge: Cambridge University Press.

Kahou, M. E. & Lehar, A. (2017). Macroprudential policy: A review. *Journal of Financial Stability, 29*, 92–105.

Kanamura, T. (2020). Are green bonds environmentally friendly and good performing assets? *Energy Economics, 88*, 104767.

Kuang, W. (2021). Are clean energy assets a safe haven for international equity markets? *Journal of Cleaner Production, 302*, 127006.

Kreivi, E. (2017). Green bond market development and EIB.

Lee, C. C., Lee, C. C., & Li, Y. Y. (2021). Oil price shocks, geopolitical risks, and green bond market dynamics. *The North American Journal of Economics and Finance, 55*, 101309.

Leitao, J., Ferreira, J., & Santibanez-Gonzalez, E. (2021). Green bonds, sustainable development and environmental policy in the European Union carbon market. *Business Strategy and the Environment, 30*(4), 2077–2090.

Liu, N., Liu, C., Da, B., Zhang, T., & Guan, F. (2021). Dependence and risk spillovers between green bonds and clean energy markets. *Journal of Cleaner Production, 279*, 123595.

Longstaff, F. (2010). The subprime credit crisis and contagion in financial markets. *Journal of Financial Economics, 97*(3), 436–450.

Luchtenberg, K. F. & Vu, Q. V. (2015). The 2008 financial crisis: Stock market contagion and its determinants. *Research in International Business and Finance, 33*, 178–203.

OECD Data (2022). Long-term interest rates. https://data.oecd.org/interest/long-term-interest-rates.htm. Accessed March 2022.

Park, D., Park, J., & Ryu, D. (2020). Volatility spillovers between equity and green bond markets. *Sustainability, 12*(9), 3722.

Reichelt, H. & Keenan, C. (2017). The Green Bond Market: 10 years later and looking ahead. World Bank.

Ren, X., Li, Y., Wen, F., & Lu, Z. (2022). The interrelationship between the carbon market and the green bonds market: Evidence from wavelet quantile-on-quantile method. *Technological Forecasting and Social Change, 179*, 121611.

Sachs, J. D., Woo, W. T., Yoshino, N., & Taghizadeh-Hesary, F. (2019). Importance of green finance for achieving sustainable development goals and energy security. *Handbook of Green Finance: Energy security and Sustainable Development, 10*, 1–10.

Sheenan, L. (2014). Four essays investigating the U.S. subprime mortgage-backed securities market. PhD thesis, National University of Ireland, Maynooth.

Sheenan, L. (2017). Analyzing contagion from the US subprime mortgage-backed securities market. *Eurasian Journal of Economics and Finance, 5*(4), 85–123.

SP Global (2020). S&P 500 Overview. https://www.spglobal.com/spdji/en/indices/equity/sp-500/#overview. Accessed March 2022.

Tang, D. Y. & Zhang, Y. (2020). Do shareholders benefit from green bonds? *Journal of Corporate Finance, 61*, 101427.

Tolliver, C., Keeley, A. R., & Managi, S. (2020). Drivers of green bond market growth: The importance of Nationally determined contributions to the Paris agreement and implications for sustainability. *Journal of Cleaner Production, 244*, 118643.

Tuhkanen, H. & Vulturius, G. (2020). Are green bonds funding the transition? Investigating the link between companies' climate targets and green debt financing. *Journal of Sustainable Finance & Investment, 12*(4), 1–23.

Whaley, R. E. (2000). The investor fear gauge. *The Journal of Portfolio Management, 26*(3), 12–17.

Yilmazkuday, H. (2021). COVID-19 effects on the S&P 500 index. *Applied Economics Letters, 30*(1), 1–7.

© 2024 World Scientific Publishing Europe Ltd.
https://doi.org/10.1142/9781800614451_0004

Chapter 4

Funding Climate Justice: Taxation Transfers and Green Bonds

Julia Margarete Puaschunder
Columbia University, The New School Columbia University,
Graduate School of Arts and Sciences,
The New School, Department of Economics,
School of Public Engagement, New York, NY, USA
julia.puaschunder@columbia.edu,
julia.puaschunder@newschool.edu

Abstract

This chapter proposes climate change impact burden-sharing with a taxation-and-bonds strategy. Five indices are empirically created to determine which countries should be using taxation to raise funds for the climate bonds issuance and which countries should be granted transfer payments via climate bonds premiums. Taxation could be imposed on countries with these features: Territories that gain economically from climate change and countries that are climate flexible in terms of a broad range of climate zones available. In addition, countries that have high CO_2 emissions and unchanging CO_2 emissions levels as well as consume goods and services to a higher degree than other countries are also candidates for climate taxation. Those countries that have favorable bank lending rates could also contribute to climate bonds in the issuance to transfer funds via climate bonds to climate-inflexible regions of the world that are losing the most and the fastest from global warming. In addition, those countries should receive transfer payments via bonds that have low CO_2 emissions and/or are lowering CO_2 emissions. Those countries that only produce goods that are then consumed in other places of the world should also be favored by the transfer scheme. For countries that have unfavorable bank lending rates and hence higher industry financing costs the transfer funds could aid climate change mitigation and adaptation.

Keywords: Climate change, CO_2 emissions, green bonds, redistribution, taxation

1. Introduction

The climate change crisis has gained unprecedented urgency in the most recent decade. Overall, climate change has already led to, and will continuously lead to, irreversible tipping points and lock-ins that will degrade the common welfare (Kellett *et al.*, 2019). The extraction and use of non-renewable fossil fuels are attributed as one of the leading causes of human-made global warming and a highly volatile market endeavor (Gevorkyan and Semmler, 2016; Greiner *et al.*, 2012; Maurer *et al.*, 2014; Nyambuu and Semmler, 2014, 2017, 2020). Global warming can be slowed by limiting the total cumulative global CO_2 emissions, which historically viewed, reflect economic development levels (Semmler, 2021).

Historically, the advanced countries have gained welfare and improved living standards through the use of fossil fuel energy and intensive CO_2 emissions, while the developing countries have not and appear nowadays as the most burdened with the climate disasters. In the aftermath of the United Nations Climate Change Conference COP26 meeting, it has been argued that the advanced countries have an obligation and responsibility to finance the low-income countries' adaptation to global warming through direct transfers and credit guarantees (Sachs, 2021). Now the most pressing question arises, what measures should the world community take to determine the relative economic windfall gain reapers and most blatant victims of climate change?

This chapter addresses geographically determined economic prospects in light of climate change and outlines vast inequalities in the distribution of climate-induced economic gain or loss of future economic prospects. Ethical imperatives will be introduced to support the claim for redistributing some of the relative economic windfall gains of global warming into territories that are losing out from climate change the most and the fastest. In the quest for climate justice, five different indices will be provided to allow various global transfer schemes to distribute the gains and losses of global warming throughout the world.

Future economic growth depends on climate change (Hansen, 2014). Macroeconomically, costs arise due to damages exacerbated by extreme temperature and severe weather events (Banerjee, 2014). The measurement of the widespread effects of temperature changes includes catastrophes and response lags as well as slow feedback in the wake of environmentally changing conditions (Bonen *et al.*, 2014; Hansen and Sato, 2016). Climate change risks feature many forms of environmental damage, which cause financial insecurity and overall volatility in financial systems (Semmler, 2021). Currently, the green transition raises expenses and short-term uncertainties. The costs for a transition to renewable energy, however, appear to pay off when considering the tipping points and irreversible lock-ins associated with global warming.

Novel policy efforts are now focused on taxation and bonds strategies (Semmler, 2021). The contribution to the burden-sharing is usually defined in Nordhaus's Regional Integrated model of Climate and the Economy (RICE model). This regional, dynamic, general-equilibrium model of the economy integrates economic activity with emissions levels as the primary driver of human-made climate change (Orlov *et al.*, 2018).

Green Economy Transition Programs that comprise declining CO_2 emissions, expanding green jobs, and a transition of workers and communities previously dependent on fossil fuel industries have been proposed for the United States (Pollin *et al.*, 2017a,b, 2019, 2020a,b, 2021, 2021a,b). A most recent World Bank Report calls for a fair climate taxation and bonds mix worldwide (Semmler *et al.*, 2021). While the World Bank Report presents a global overview of the current state of climate taxation and climate bonds usage around the globe, it calls for more macroeconomic models that enact climate bonds and tax strategies concurrently used coupled with redistribution and burden-sharing (Semmler *et al.*, 2021). In addition, *The New York Times* recently discussed the disparate impacts of climate policies and climate protection attention disparities (Flavelle, 2021a,b). Literature emerges on how the world's richest people are driving global warming (Roston *et al.*, 2022).

In the aftermath of the COP26 annual climate meeting of the United Nations, Jeffrey Sachs put forward an idea of funds for climate change mitigation and adaptation that should be raised by climate tax-funded grants provided by some countries as transfer payments, while other countries should be recipients of green bonds granted to low-income countries (Sachs, 2021). While Sachs (2021) argues that half of the funds raised should be grants (transfers) and half green bonds that help transition to renewable energy in low-income countries, this chapter will refine prioritizing which countries should be grantors and which should be recipients based on data-driven criteria. These factors will determine whether a country will be on the taxation regime for funding mutual climate stabilization or on the receiving end of climate bonds solutions: the country's (1) starting ground on the relative economic climate gains and losses spectrum, (2) climate flexibility, (3) CO_2 emissions that contribute to production and consumption levels, (4) CO_2 emissions level changes and (5) bank lending rate. Incentivizing countries to transition to renewables with a prospect of redistribution gains could turn competitive race-to-the-bottom markets into participants of a race-to-the-top for mutual climate fund allocations (Puaschunder, 2022). Integrating the CO_2 emissions levels changes over time thereby could serve as an innovative market game changer (Puaschunder, 2022).

Overall, this chapter proposes a taxation-and-bonds strategy that outlines a scheme where countries are either climate taxation bonds funders or climate bonds recipients based on economic prospects in light of climate change, CO_2 emissions and consumption-based, trade-adjusted CO_2 emissions, carbon pollution changes, and bank lending rates.

A macroeconomic cost–benefit analysis led to the quest for an optimum solution on how to distribute climate change benefits and burdens within society and over time. As economic gains and losses from a warming Earth are distributed unequally around the globe, ethical imperatives led to the pledge to redistribute economic gains due to climate change to territories that lose from global warming, pursuant to the goal of climate justice. Responsibility for the environment is thereby derived from ethical imperatives and hopes for harmony with the environment for future generations (Jonas, 1979; Nikulin, 2021).

Based on the overall Climate Change Winners and Losers Index (WLTT), global warming benefits for climate change and adaptation efforts are proposed to be redistributed in a fair way to offset countries losing out due to climate change (Puaschunder, 2020). Climate justice comprises fairness within society, between countries, and also over generations in a unique and unprecedented tax-and-bonds climate change gains and losses distribution strategy. Climate change winning countries, or countries benefiting from climate change, are advised to use taxation to raise revenues to offset the losses incurred by climate change in climate change loser countries. Within the winning countries, the gaining GDP sectors and carbon-emitting industries should first be taxed proportional to their CO_2 emissions. Climate justice within a country should also ensure that low- and high-income households share the same burden proportional to their dispensable income, for instance, enabled through a progressive carbon taxation that curbs consumption. Industries that caused climate change could be regulated to bear a higher cost through a carbon tax. In addition, retroactive billing through a corporate inheritance tax during mergers and acquisitions could reap benefits from past industry wealth accumulation that potentially contributed to global warming. Climate change loser countries could raise revenues by issuing bonds that have to be paid back by taxing future generations in order to shift the economic burden of climate stabilization financing in time (Puaschunder, 2020).

The remainder of the chapter is organized as follows: Section 2 covers the theory in green bonds (Section 2.1), climate change gains and losses (Section 2.2), and climate justice ethical and economic foundations (Section 2.3) and brings forward a climate taxation and green bonds solution for burden sharing (Section 2.4) by presenting an index solution to determine an economic gains and losses redistribution scheme among world countries (Section 2.5).

The remainder of the chapter outlines the Results (Section 3) of five indices. Section 3.1 presents the findings of the relative economic climate change windfall gain reaper and victim countries and CO_2 emission index. Section 3.2 offers the findings of the relative economic climate change windfall gain reaper and victim countries' climate flexibility and CO_2 emission index. Section 3.3 holds information on the relative economic climate change windfall gain reaper and victim countries and CO_2 emission change index. Section 3.4 is dedicated to the relative economic climate change windfall gain reaper and victim countries and CO_2 emission and bond lending rate index. Section 3.5 provides the results for the relative economic climate change windfall gain reaper and victim countries and CO_2 emission and consumption-based, trade-adjusted CO_2 emission index. Section 4 features the Discussion of the findings with particular attention to the implications. The conclusion (Section 5) offers insights about the practical policy implications of the proposed strategy (Section 5.1) and their limitations (Section 5.2) as well as the monitoring, evaluation, and accountability of the envisioned redistribution plan (Section 5.3). The Conclusion (Section 5) also pays tribute to future extensions of the current results and provides a future outlook (Section 5.4).

2. Theory

2.1. *Green bonds*

Green bonds have recently been promoted as an innovative climate stabilization strategy (Puaschunder, 2020; Sachs, 2014; Semmler *et al.*, 2021). They are, in most cases, governmental bonds. Issuance of a bond is taking a loan or getting credit to be repaid in the future. The issuer of bonds establishes the bond for bond buyers. Investors who purchase these bonds can expect to make a profit as the bond matures.

Borrowers of green bonds issue securities to finance projects with favorable environmental impact (Puaschunder, 2022). Examples include green bonds which have funded clean energy and sustainability solutions (Puaschunder, 2022). This chapter introduces green bonds as a means of climate stabilization via renewable energy transition. Green bonds are often issued by central banks and brokers, who qualify assets based on sustainability criteria (Puaschunder, 2022). Governments can back a transition to clean energy by granting tax benefits for investing in green bonds (Puaschunder, 2022). Climate bonds and green solutions tend to offer high yields in the market due not only to their innovative character but also to the uncertain outcomes of climate change action (Puaschunder, 2022).

The green bonds implementation offers to raise funds internationally and spread financial flows around the globe. Green bonds also allow for allocating funds over time in between generations (Puaschunder, 2022). In the U.S., the Green New Deal (GND) fosters global governance to fund climate change mitigation and adaptation efforts in light of climate disasters and financing recovery from them

(Braga *et al.*, 2020; Puaschunder, 2022). The GND also funds R&D for absorbing CO_2 and raising ecowellness standards in factoring in natural resources into national accounting. Europe offers the most sophisticated sustainable finance taxonomy to evaluate the ecological footprint of industries.

2.2. *Climate change gains and losses*

Another approach to raising funds for a transition to a green economy takes a closer look at the macroeconomic impacts and economic growth prospects under global warming. Effects of climate change vary around the world and are likely to impose considerable economic prospect changes, which will increase over time as global temperatures rise (Lomborg, 2021). Global warming will likely cause relative economic gains and losses, distributed unequally throughout the world and over time (Lomborg, 2021; Puaschunder, 2020).

Economic research has elucidated the economic impact of climate change on the world and found stark national differences (Burke *et al.*, 2015; Puaschunder, 2020). Burke *et al.* (2015) estimate how climate change will affect GDP per capita. In addition, the International Monetary Fund (IMF) conducted a cross-country analysis of the long-term macroeconomic effects of climate change and found country inequalities in global warming effects (Kahn *et al.*, 2019).

Puaschunder (2020) measured the Gross Domestic Product (GDP) prospect differences under climate change worldwide and found exacerbating climate inequalities. Puaschunder (2020) introduced a Climate Change Winners and Losers index (WLTT), representing relative economic climate change windfall gain reaper and victim countries, based on the economic prospects under climate change around the world and over time. The model assumes that there are relative economic climate change reapers that have a windfall gain from a warming globe while other relative economic climate change victims face immediate disadvantages due to global warming. The model primarily focuses on shedding light on the inequality in countries and regions of the world exacerbated by climate change determining economic prospects. The index attributed relative economic gain and loss prospects based on the medium temperature per country and the optimum temperature for economic productivity per

GDP agriculture, industry, and service sector, and the GDP sector composition per country to determine how far countries are deviating from their optimum productivity levels on a time scale (Puaschunder, 2020). It is to note that the 'relative economic climate change windfall gain reapers and victims' are categories on a spectrum, that the gain and loss perspective addressed only concerns GDP growth and that the gains/losses distribution are windfall/victim categories that countries did not accomplish or chose willingly. Gains and losses are somewhat random distributions throughout the world. It is sheer luck in the birth lottery where one falls into.

2.3. *Climate justice: Ethical and economic foundations*

Climate justice addresses inequalities inherent in global warming with a mandate to alleviate imbalances and enact fairness regarding climate benefits and burden-sharing. To alleviate inequalities in climate change impacts between countries, ethical imperatives such as Immanuel Kant's categorical imperative (1783/1993), John Rawls' veil of ignorance (1971) as well as economic calculus as put forward in the Kaldor–Hicks compensation criteria guide redistribution schemes.

Based on Kant's imperative proposing to "Act only according to that maxim whereby you can at the same time will that it should become a universal law", no climate harm should be done to any country independent of a country's position on the relative economic climate change gains windfall reapers and victims' spectrum (Kant, 1783/1993, p. 30). Passive neglect of action on climate mitigation is an active injustice to others based on the climatorial imperative (Puaschunder, 2020).

Moral and ethical guidelines may be enhanced with the Kaldor–Hicks Compensation Criteria. The Kaldor–Hicks test for improvement potential within a society aims to move an economy closer toward Pareto efficiency (Law and Smullen, 2008). The Kaldor–Hicks criteria assumes that any change usually makes some people better off and others worse off at the same time and tests if this imbalance can be alleviated by relative economic climate change windfall gains reapers compensating climate change victims for the change in conditions. Applying the Kaldor criterion in the context of taxation and bonds would serve as an example by which the economy moves closer to Pareto optimality if the maximum number of gainers are prepared to pay the losers and agree that the change is greater than the minimum amount losers are prepared to accept. In the Kaldor–Hicks criteria, both sides must also agree that the benefits exceed the costs of such action. The fungibility of compensation (money will always be there), while there are irreversible lock-ins and tipping points in environmental degradation (climate may be irreversibly locked in and degrade living conditions in a nonlinear trajectory), point at action against climate change at the expense of repayable monetary costs.

The Kaldor–Hicks compensation can be applied to environmental constraints regarding climate change. As economic gains and losses from a warming Earth are distributed unequally around the globe, ethical imperatives lead to the pledge to redistribute gains to losing territories in the quest for climate justice. Climate justice comprises fairness not only between countries but also over generations in a unique and unprecedented tax-and-bonds climate change gains and losses distribution strategy. Climate change winning countries are advised to use taxation to raise revenues to offset the losses incurred by climate change. Climate change victims could be incentivized to receive bonds that have to be paid back by future generations.

Regarding taxation within the winning countries, foremost, the gaining GDP sectors should be taxed. Those who cause climate change could be regulated to bear a higher cost through carbon tax combined with retroactive billing through a corporate inheritance tax to map benefits from past wealth accumulation that potentially contributed to global warming. A corporate inheritance tax could raise funds if there is a merger and/or acquisition or a takeover of a corporation, which would allow quasi-retroactive taxation of past corporate activities that may have caused greenhouse gas emissions. Climate justice within a country should also pay tribute to the fact that low- and high-income households share the same burden proportional to their dispensable income, for instance, enabled through progressive carbon taxation and a carbon consumption tax.

For the Kaldor compensation to work effectively, the relative economic climate change windfall gain reapers and climate change victims must also agree that the benefits of a commonly agreed-upon compensation scheme exceed the costs of such action. International cooperation and/or significant participation are crucial ways to internalize global externalities, avert climate change, and agree upon a commonly pursued rescue and resilience plan (Nordhaus, 1994; Puaschunder, 2021; Semmler, 2021). Aside from free-rider problems and penalties for non-compliance, this chapter will introduce a novel climate taxation-and-bonds strategy to redistribute climate change gains and raise widespread momentum for a transition to a zero-carbon global economy based on the notion that the redistribution is fair.

2.4. *Climate taxation and green bonds solution for burden-sharing*

This chapter integrates climate gain and loss theories and empirical validations of the unequal climate change impact on countries into contemporary climate taxation and bonds strategies for climate burden-sharing. As a foundation for the redistribution of climate gains and losses, the disparate impact of global warming on countries is considered. A model will be laid out that assumes that if a country has a rising GDP prospect in a warming climate, then this country should be redistributing some of the expected wealth increase to places that have a declining GDP prospect (Puaschunder, 2022). Further, if a country has natural climate flexibility in terms of a range of different temperatures that vary within its territory, then the country is assumed to have more economic degrees of freedom and future trade assets in a changing climate and thus should redistribute some of the expected wealth increase to places that have a declining GDP prospect (Puaschunder, 2022). In order to set positive market incentives not to cause climate change, the model will also integrate human-made contributions to climate change and the ability and willingness of a country to change its CO_2 emissions among others (Puaschunder, 2022). Those countries that contribute to CO_2 emissions and are not changing their CO_2 emissions levels to reduce pollution are therefore required to redistribute some of the expected economic GDP gains to places that have a declining

GDP prospect, are not causing CO_2 emissions, and have been curbing harmful CO_2 emissions in relation to other countries and over time (Puaschunder, 2022). The prevailing bank lending rate regimes will play a role in the model insofar as those countries with low bank lending rates will be advised to redistribute funds to countries with high bank lending rates to even out historically grown hierarchies and economic power dynamics (Puaschunder, 2022). The consumption-based, trade-adjusted CO_2 emissions will be taken into consideration insofar as countries whose citizens consume goods and services that cause high CO_2 emissions in production should redistribute the expected gains from a warming globe into territories losing out from climate change the fastest and the most (Puaschunder, 2022).

A novel policy recommendation for enacting climate justice entails a taxation funding strategy coupled with a climate bonds repayment based on the following influence factors: (F_1) the country's initial position on the relative economic climate change windfall gains and losses index spectrum; (F_2) a country's climate flexibility along a broad economic degree of freedom spectrum and future trade benefit; (F_3) the country's human-made contribution to climate change as measured by CO_2 emissions; (F_4) the ability and willingness of a country to change its CO_2 emissions in relation to others; (F_5) the estimated lending rate of bonds in that country; and (F_6) the consumption-based, trade-adjusted CO_2 emissions of a country. These six drivers in five proposed indices determine a higher or lower burden on carbon taxes (abatement costs) to finance climate bonds to be repaid later.

2.5. *Indices*

Five indices that integrate six components equally will be presented in the following. First, normalized index scales will be created for measured parameters (F_1)–(F_6) as described in Table 1. Then bundles of these parameters (F_1)–(F_6) will be factored into five different indices highlighting various facets. The factoring of normalized indicators is meant to create equity over several measurement factors, e.g., being a relative economic climate change windfall reaper or a victim country having a specific estimated lending rate of bonds.

Table 1 summarizes five different indices that will be introduced in this chapter. All indices rank the world countries on a spectrum

Table 1. Influence variables on climate taxation and bonds strategy.

	Climate taxation bonds strategy	
Index description	**Low values**	**High values**
(1) Relative economic climate change windfall gain reaper and victim countries and CO_2 emission index (integrating normalized values of F_1 and F_3) by multiplication	Climate change economic victim countries with low CO_2 emissions → climate bonds strategy with high discount rates regime and longer-term maturity to spread the burden of climate stabilization financing between generations and a relatively high bond yield-at-issue with relatively high interest rates from subsidies funded by high index value countries.	Climate change economic windfall reaper countries with high CO_2 emissions → taxation strategy coupled with low discount rates regime and short-term maturity to act now to protect future generations from climate change impacts. The higher the index, the more a country should be obliged to fund the climate bond via taxation. The lower the relatively high values of the index, the more likely a country should have access to bonds with growing yield-at-issue instead of taxation.
(2) Relative economic climate change windfall gain reaper and victim countries' climate flexibility and CO_2 emission index (integrating normalized values of F_1, F_2, and F_3) by multiplication	Climate change economic victim countries with low climate flexibility and low CO_2 emissions → climate bonds strategy with high discount rates regime and longer-term maturity to spread the burden of climate stabilization financing between generations and a relatively high bond yield-at-issue with relatively high interest rates from subsidies funded by high index value countries.	Climate change economic windfall reaper countries with high climate flexibility and high CO_2 emissions → taxation strategy coupled with low discount rates regime and short-term maturity to act now to protect future generations from climate change impacts. The higher the index, the more a country should be obliged to fund the climate bond via taxation. The lower the relatively high values of the index, the more likely a country should have access to bonds with growing yield-at-issue instead of taxation.

(3) Relative economic climate change windfall gain reaper and victim countries and CO_2 emission change index (integrating of F_1, F_3, and F_4 by multiplication)	Climate change economic victim countries with low CO_2 emissions and lowering CO_2 emissions → climate bonds strategy with high discount rates regime and longer-term maturity to spread the burden of climate stabilization financing between generations and a relatively high bond yield-at-issue with relatively high interest rates from subsidies funded by high index value countries.	Climate change economic windfall reaper countries with high CO_2 emissions and increasing CO_2 emissions → taxation strategy coupled with low discount rates regime and short-term maturity to act now to protect future generations from climate change impacts. The lower the relatively high values of the index, the more likely a country should have access to bonds with growing yield-at-issue instead of taxation. The yield-to-maturity should depend on a country's CO_2 emission changing behavior insofar as a reduction over time improves the maturity over time.
(4) Relative economic climate change windfall gain reaper and victim countries and CO_2 emission and bond lending rate index (integrating normalized values of F_1, F_3, and F_5 by multiplication)	Climate change economic victim countries with low CO_2 emissions and high bond lending rate → climate bonds strategy with high discount rates regime and longer-term maturity to spread the burden of climate stabilization financing between generations and a relatively high bond yield-at-issue with relatively high interest rates from subsidies funded by high index value countries.	Climate change economic windfall reaper countries with high CO_2 emissions and low bond lending rate → taxation strategy coupled with low discount rates regime and short-term maturity to act now to protect future generations from climate change impacts. The lower the relatively high values of the index, the more likely a country should have access to bonds with growing yield-at-issue instead of taxation.
(5) Relative economic climate change windfall gain reaper and victim countries and CO_2 emission and consumption-based, trade-adjusted CO_2 emission index (integrating normalized values of F_1, F_3, and F_6 by multiplication)	Climate change economic victim countries with low consumption-based, trade-adjusted CO_2 emissions → climate bonds strategy with high discount rates regime and longer-term maturity to spread the burden of climate stabilization financing between generations and a relatively high bond yield-at-issue with relatively high interest rates from subsidies funded by high index value countries.	Climate change economic windfall reaper countries with high consumption-based, trade-adjusted CO_2 emissions → taxation strategy coupled with low discount rates regime and short-term maturity to act now to protect future generations from climate change impacts. The lower the relatively high values of the index, the more likely a country should have access to bonds with growing yield-at-issue instead of taxation.

from climate financing grantors with taxation to subsidized climate bonds recipient countries. The bonds can be seen as loans paid by the high-index countries to the low-index countries. The bonds could be issued and/or overseen by a global governance entity — such as the World Bank, International Monetary Fund (IMF), or United Nations. These bonds may not be tradable without the oversight of the issuing institution to avoid problems of "trading away" risks and responsibilities. The global taxation-and-bonds strategy may entail global governance institutions offering international bonds with inbetween-countries varying yields-at-issue, maturity, and yields-to-maturity based on the outlined parameters in Table 1.

In the following five indices based on the six described drivers, F_1–F_6 are first translated into a scale with every country of the world included in the data. The six drivers are then integrated into the five different indices by multiplying the respective country values indicating the country's position in relation to other countries on the different indexed dimensions of F_1–F_6. The drivers determine the relative weight on a scale from most taxation for climate stabilization to most climate bonds financing.

The presentation of different indices serves as a first introduction to the topics under scrutiny. Other indices that highlight various aspects may aid policymakers in finding the most favorable combination of evaluation criteria and strengthen their awareness of the disparate impact of climate change. In their entirety, the indices highlight what countries should pay for the installment of a global bond based on taxation revenues and what countries should be beneficiaries of transfer payments derived from climate bonds funded by the relative economic climate change gain windfall reaper countries and with repayment schemes in future generations.

The more a country is considered as a relative economic climate change windfall reaper country (high factor F_1) with climate flexibility (high factor F_2), causing climate change by high CO_2 emissions (high factor F_3) while not reducing CO_2 emission levels (high factor F_4) as well as having favorable bank lending conditions (high factor F_5) and consuming CO_2 emissions in respective goods and services (high factor F_6), the more the country is proposed to be obliged to fund a climate bonds solution via taxation and adopt a low discount rates regime to act now to protect future generations from climate change impacts. In the countries that are considered as relative climate change economic victims (low factor F_1) with low climate flexibility (low factor F_2) that have low CO_2 emission levels (low factor F_3) and are reducing CO_2 emissions (low factor F_4) but also feature unfavorable bank lending conditions (low factor F_5) and are not consuming CO_2 emissions in respective goods and services (high factor F_6), the climate bonds should finance the economy with high bond yield rates and debt to be repaid by future generations. The rationale is that countries with a current economic advantage from climate change should grant climate bonds and redistribute some short-term economic gains to losing territories. Only the countries that have lowered economic prospects due to climate change should be able to shift some of the burden of climate change financing to future generations in bonds.

As Puaschunder (2020) found in a worldwide data set over all countries, being a relative economic climate change gain windfall reaper country and contributing high emissions are related. The relation between GDP growth prospects in light of climate change and the percentage of greenhouse gas emissions (GHG) for ratification was investigated based on the percent of GHG emissions communicated by the Paris COP21 Parties to the Convention retrieved in their national communications and displayed in GHG inventory reports as of December 2015. Over a sample of 181 countries globally, a highly significant correlation between a relative economic climate change gain windfall reaper country and the self-reported percentage of GHG emissions for ratification was found. As a cross-validation check, the percentage of GHG emissions for ratification was significantly positively correlated with self-reported GHG emissions per country. This result leads to the conclusion that those countries that emit more GHG are the ones with a positive GDP prospect on the warming Earth until 2100. The more time countries seem to have a favorable production climate, the more likely they are to emit GHG and contribute to global warming (Puaschunder, 2020). All indices build on the insights that relative economic climate change windfall reaper countries are more likely responsible for human-made climate change. Index 3 builds in the incentive to change this unfavorable behavior of GHG emissions and gratify those countries with willingness and action to reduce CO_2 emissions.

The following five indices are meant to provide a basic numerical scheme of how to redistribute the relative economic gains of climate change to those countries that lose out on climate change the first and the most. The higher each index, the more countries are advised to aid in the financing of climate stability by raising funds through taxation that will then be used as transfer payments to offset the costs of climate bonds subsidies in the countries that lose out from global warming. The actual index numbers translate into a numerical key that determines the relative position of each country to other countries on a scale from taxation to raising funds for climate stabilization and subsidized transfer payments enacted by climate bonds. The more a country is considered to relatively economically win from global warming and the more a country is causing climate change by CO_2 emissions production and consumption as well as the more a country is not willing to change CO_2 emissions in relation to other countries, and the lower the bank lending rate of the country, the more this country will likely have high index rates, which can serve as a key to determine taxation of relative economic climate change gain windfall reaper countries. The more a country faces declining economic prospects in light of global warming and the less a country is emitting CO_2 in relation to others and not consuming CO_2, as well as the more a country is curbing its harmful CO_2 emissions over time and faces higher bank lending rates, the more a country should be given helicopter funding for participating in climate bonds that remunerate a transition to a renewable energy solution and can be co-financed via debt to be repaid by future generations. Among the countries funding climate stabilization via bonds, those countries that are the worst off from climate change and have the lowest CO_2 emissions and CO_2 emission consumption levels among others and are changing their CO_2 emissions for the better, as well as have the highest bank lending rates, should have the best-subsidized conditions for climate bonds. Thus, investors should benefit from the highest premium payments.

The separation of six components for determining the degree of taxation or climate bonds financing between countries shows differences in a relative climate change victim compensation model. The different indices accentuate different aspects to be considered when thinking about redistribution — such as being a relative economic climate change gains reaper or victim country, future climate wealth of nations in comparative trade advantages, causing increase in emissions in the process of production and consumption, willingness to change harmful behavior, or even historically determined bank lending regimes that are based on risk estimates. The multiple indices raise predicaments about what aspects to accentuate in compensation schemes. For instance, should a climate losing territory be compensated although having caused climate change before? All these challenging questions arising from the display of multiple facets of the climate dilemma will hopefully instigate essential conversations on the issue in the future.

While standard climate bond strategies assume one discount rate fits all participating agents, this chapter will propose a novel idea to integrate all countries worldwide into an international climate taxation-and-bonds strategy. Diversified financing of common green bonds with a unique incentive scheme for carbon reduction is a new method to share the burden and the benefits of climate change within society in an economically efficient, legally equitable, and practically feasible way.

3. Results

3.1. *Relative economic climate change windfall gain reaper and victim countries and CO_2 emission index*

Climate justice redistribution could enact that countries that contribute to human-made global warming in CO_2 emissions should pay for the establishment and maintenance of climate bonds via carbon taxation (Puaschunder, 2022). Countries that lose out due to climate change could become recipients of transfer payments via a common climate bond (Puaschunder, 2022).

Figure 1 displays countries first that are advised to fund climate bonds with a taxation strategy. These territories benefit from the highest economic climate change windfall gains and emit the most CO_2. Countries that are at the bottom of the bar chart are climate change victims and have less CO_2 emissions per country. The further down below the country is on the list, the higher the bond premiums are advised to be paid out to this country for being a higher climate victim and having less CO_2 emissions, hence contributing less to the climate problem.

Figure 1. Country ranking of $WL_{TT}CCC$ index for 45 countries.

As visible in the bar chart based on the Relative Economic Climate Change Windfall Gain Reaper and Victim Countries and CO_2 Emission index ($WL_{TT}CCC$), a tax-and-bonds strategy is proposed. Countries that have a short-term rising GDP prospect under climate change and cause CO_2 emissions — as ranked high up in Figure 1 — should be obliged to settle for taxation solutions to issue climate bonds that fund redistribution of climate change gains. Those are the countries with highest $WL_{TT}CCC$ index levels. Beneficiaries of high bond interest rate premiums should be those countries with a low index value that have a declining GDP prospect under climate change and do not emit CO_2 at such high levels as the countries at the top in Figure 1. Bond beneficiaries have the lowest $WL_{TT}CCC$ index levels and are found listed toward the bottom of the bar chart. These countries are advised to pay out high bonds interest rate premiums funded by the taxation efforts of the top countries in Figure 1 as well as via debt to be paid back by future generations.

The countries with medium values in the $WL_{TT}CCC$ index are displayed in the middle in Figure 2. These countries tend to be in the middle of the climate winners and losers index and have medium CO_2 emissions levels. The middle value countries are advised to have a mixture strategy between taxation and bonds payments and should offer a medium level bonds premium payment.

In the bonds strategy, countries that have a rising GDP prospect due to global warming and cause CO_2 emissions — these are the countries on top in Figure 1 — should fund climate bonds by taxation to redistribute funds to the climate victim countries that tend to not cause CO_2 emissions.

3.2. *Relative economic climate change windfall gain reaper and victim countries' climate flexibility and CO_2 emission index*

Climate change winning countries with climate flexibility that contribute to human-made global warming with CO_2 emissions should pay into climate bonds via carbon taxation (Puaschunder, 2022). Countries that lose out from climate change with low CO_2 emissions that are also inflexible when it comes to temperature zones could be granted transfer funds via climate bonds (Puaschunder, 2022).

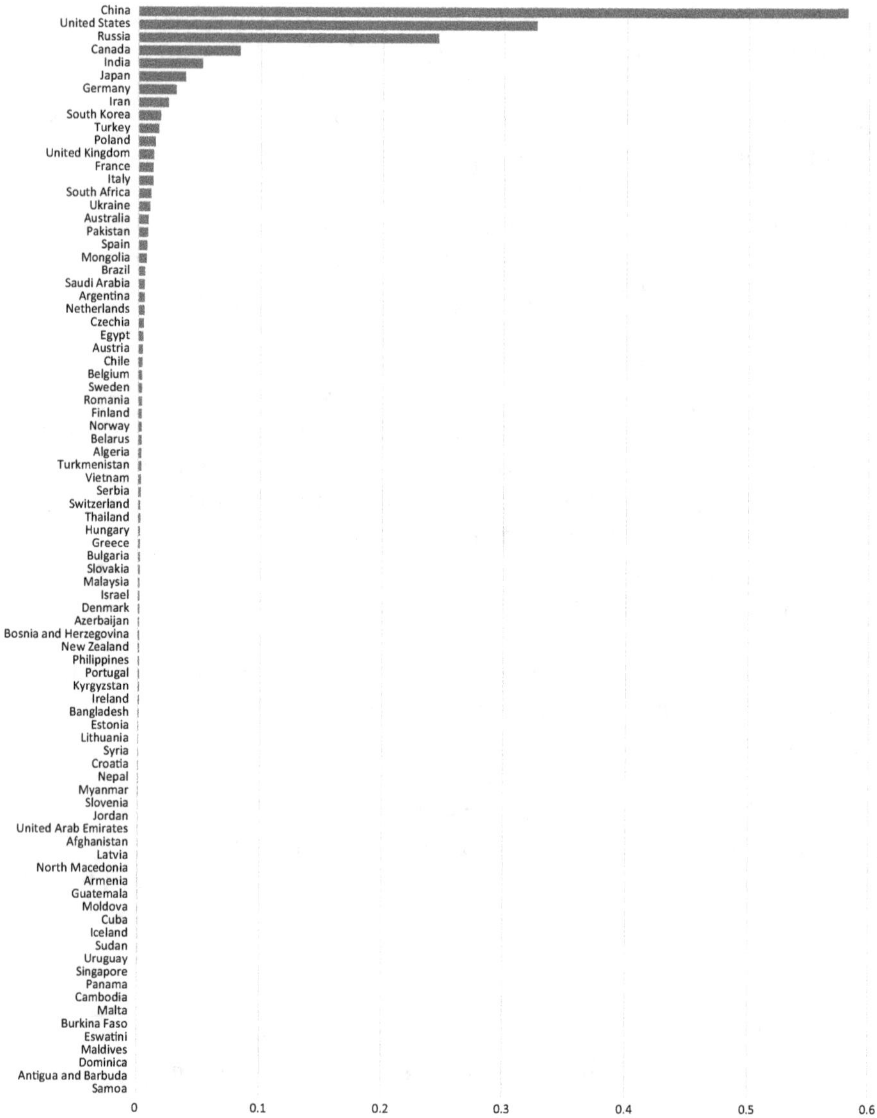

Figure 2. Country ranking of *CFCCC* index for 84 countries.

Figure 2 displays climate change economic windfall gain reapers with high climate flexibility and high CO_2 emissions on top of the bar chart. Climate change victim countries with low climate flexibility and low CO_2 emissions are on the bottom of the bar chart.

Countries in the middle that tend to have medium climate change implications and mean flexibility, and middle levels of CO_2 emissions are in the middle of the bar chart. Countries that are advised to have a high climate taxation strategy are ranked on top, high bonds premium recipients, at the bottom, and countries that are in the middle of the index range are shown in the middle.

Figure 2 displays a bar chart that ranks those countries with advised high taxation strategy on top, high bonds premium recipients on the bottom and countries that are in the middle of the index range in the middle. In Figure 2, countries are ranked toward the top if they are climate change victims and have less climate flexibility, as well as cause less CO_2 emissions per country. The higher a country is, the more likely the country is a relative climate change economic windfall gain reaper that benefits from more climate flexibility as well as is more likely to emit more CO_2. Medium levels of climate change driven economic changes with medium climate flexibility and moderate levels of CO_2 emissions are ranked in the middle. Top countries are advised to have a climate taxation strategy, middle countries a mixed climate taxation and bonds strategy, and the countries toward the bottom, a climate bonds recipient standing among all countries of the world. Countries that have a rising GDP prospect due to global warming and that are climate flexible and emit CO_2 — as ranked on top in Figure 2 — should fund climate bonds via taxation for transfer payments to countries ranked at the bottom. Bottom-ranked countries with a low index value that have a declining GDP prospect and face climate constraints due to low climate flexibility and do not emit CO_2 at such high levels as the countries ranked on top in Figure 2 should be beneficiaries of high bonds interest rate premiums and receive transfer funds via bonds. Green bond beneficiaries have the lowest Relative Economic Climate Change Windfall Gain Reaper and Victim Countries index levels in Figure 2. The countries with medium values in the $CFCCC$ index are displayed in the middle in Figure 2. These countries tend to be in the middle of the climate winners and losers index and have medium levels of climate flexibility and medium CO_2 emissions levels. The middle value countries are advised to have a mixture strategy between taxation and bonds payments and should face a medium level bonds premium payment. The medium $CFCCC$ index countries are ranked in the middle of the country list in Figure 2.

In the bonds strategy, countries that have a rising GDP prospect and appear to be future climate wealth of nations winners based on climate flexibility, but that cause CO_2 emissions — these are the countries ranked on top in Figure 2 — should fund climate bonds by taxation to redistribute relative economic windfall gains due to climate change to the climate victim countries with low climate flexibility that tend to not cause CO_2 emissions. Beneficiaries of the bonds should be countries with a low index value that have a declining GDP prospect in light of climate change, low climate flexibility as well as who do not emit CO_2 at high levels, and are ranked at the bottom in Figure 2. These countries should become beneficiaries of high bonds interest rate premiums funded by the taxation efforts of the top countries in Figure 2 as well as via debt to be paid back by future generations.

3.3. *Relative economic climate change windfall gain reaper and victim countries and CO_2 emission change index*

Countries that reap benefits from climate change and contribute to human-made global warming via CO_2 emissions and have a rising trend of CO_2 emissions should pay for the establishment and maintenance of climate bonds via carbon taxation (Puaschunder, 2022). Countries that lose the most and fastest from global warming with low CO_2 emissions and that have declining CO_2 emissions should become climate bond premium beneficiaries (Puaschunder, 2022). Gratifying CO_2 emission changes over time also incentivize positive changes as countries compete over relative CO_2 emission reductions that are subsidized.

Figure 3 is a graphical display of countries ranked from the highest climate taxation country to the lowest based on the Relative Economic Climate Change Windfall Gain Reaper and Victim Countries and CO_2 Emission Change index ($WL_{TT}CCCG$) index accounting for climate change victim countries as well as those having less CO_2 emissions per country and decreasing CO_2 emissions. Figure 4 ranks 120 countries based on their relative $WL_{TT}CCCG$ index status from the lowest bond payment to the highest bond funding country.

Although the country ranking is meant as a continuum from taxation to bonds solution, Figure 3 displays countries that are

Figure 3. Country ranking of $WL_{TT}CCCG$ index for CO_2 reducing countries.

advised to be climate bonds recipients in the $WL_{TT}CCCG$ index solution, Figure 4 shows the countries that are recommended to finance the climate bonds via taxation in the $WL_{TT}CCCG$ index scheme.

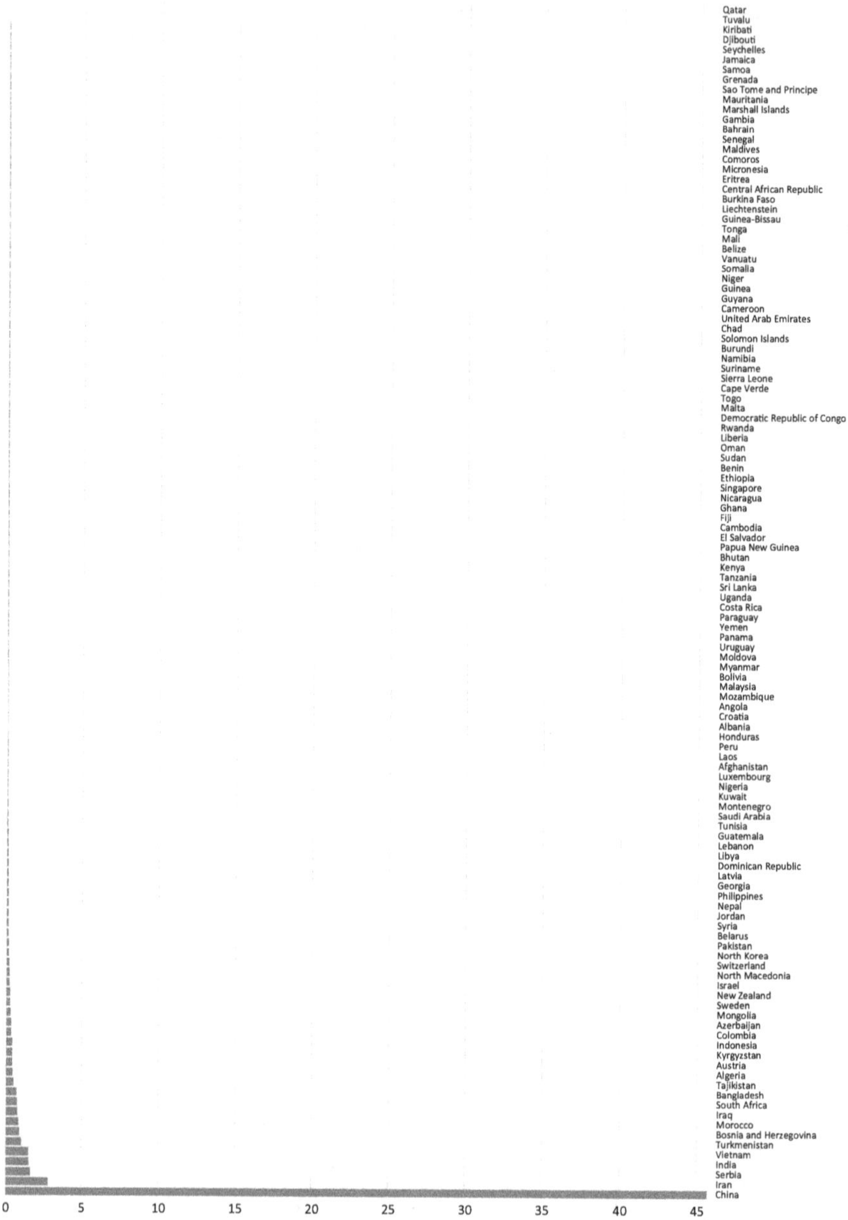

Figure 4. Country ranking of $WL_{TT}CCCG$ index for CO_2 increasing countries.

In Figure 3, the higher a country is ranked, the more likely the country loses from climate change, while having less CO_2 and decreasing CO_2 emissions. High-ranked countries should be made recipients of climate bonds transfer payments. Red territories in Figure 4 are relative climate change winners with rising CO_2 emissions. Red countries should have a climate taxation strategy that funds the common climate bonds solution. Medium levels of climate change economic changes and moderate levels of CO_2 emissions are characteristic for countries that rank at the bottom of Figure 3 and the top of Figure 4. These countries should have a mixed climate taxation and bonds strategy.

In the bonds strategy with incentivization of CO_2 reduction, countries that curb their CO_2 emissions compared to all other countries should become net beneficiaries of the climate bonds premium payments and receive funds for their positive market change, such as the countries at the top in Figure 3. Countries with rising levels of CO_2 emissions in comparison to other countries should be obliged to fund the climate bonds via taxation in order to incentivize a long-term reduction in CO_2 emissions. Under this regime, in the year 2019, countries with rising CO_2 emissions in comparison to the previous year — such as the countries colored in red in Figure 4 — should face low climate bonds interest premium payments and be obliged to fund the bond via taxation. Countries at the bottom of Figure 3 and top of Figure 4 should have a mixture of taxation and climate bonds solutions as these countries tend not to have any relative increase or decrease in CO_2 emissions in relation to the other world countries.

3.4. *Relative economic climate change windfall gain reaper and victim countries, their CO_2 emission levels, and bond lending rate index*

Climate justice between countries could be based on the idea that those countries that have finance expertise have a higher responsibility to protect the Earth with the establishment and maintenance of climate bonds via carbon taxation; while climate change losing territories with low CO_2 emissions that also have less access to capital due to past financial performance should be climate bond recipient beneficiaries (Puaschunder, 2022).

Figure 5 ranks 101 countries based on their Relative Economic Climate Change Windfall Gain Reaper and Victim Countries CO_2 Emission and Bond Lending Rate index ($WL_{TT}CCCL$). It displays countries ranked from the recommended highest climate taxation country to the highest bonds premium recipient country. The higher a country is ranked to contribute to the taxation-and-bonds strategy with taxation, the more the country tends to be economically reaping gains from climate change, have more CO_2 emissions, and a low bank lending rate. The lower a country is ranked on the $WL_{TT}CCCL$ index, the more the country should be a premium bonds rate recipient as the country is likely losing from climate change, has low CO_2 emissions, and a high bank lending rate.

As visible in Figure 5 exhibiting the world countries based on the $WL_{TT}CCCL$ index, a tax-and-bonds strategy is proposed. In the bonds strategy, countries with a rising GDP prospect that are emitting CO_2 and enjoy low bank lending rates — ranked at the top in Figure 5 — should be obliged to raise funds for redistribution via taxation. Beneficiaries of high bonds interest rate premiums, which are ranked at the bottom in Figure 4, should be those countries that have a low $WL_{TT}CCCL$ index value, a declining GDP prospect in light of global warming, that do not emit CO_2 in high levels, and face high lending interest rates. The countries with medium values in the $WL_{TT}CCCL$ index are advised to have a mixture strategy between taxation and bonds payments facing a medium level bonds premium payment due to being in the middle of the climate winners and losers' spectrum and having medium ranges of CO_2 emissions as well as medium bank lending rates in relation to other countries.

3.5. *Relative economic climate change windfall gain reaper and victim countries and their CO_2 emissions and location in the consumption-based, trade-adjusted CO_2 emission index*

If considering trade-adjusted CO_2 emissions per country in relation to other countries, the relative climate change economic windfall gain reaper countries with high CO_2 emissions consumption should fund the bonds solution via climate taxation (Puaschunder, 2022). The lower the index gets, the more the country should be a beneficiary of transfer payments from countries with high CO_2 emissions

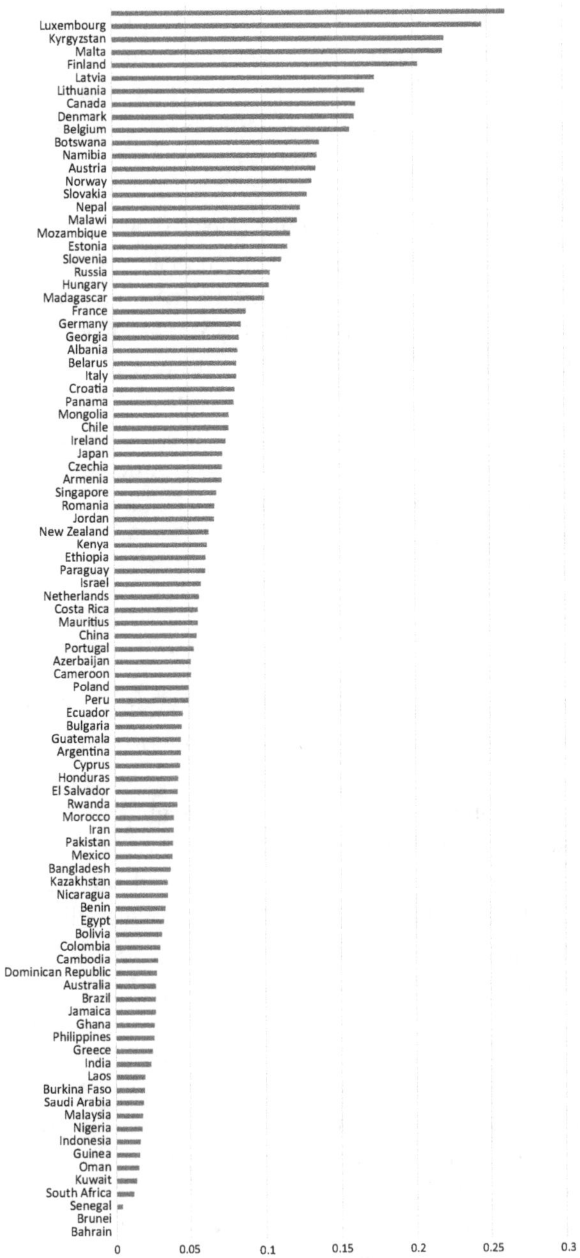

Figure 5. Country ranking of $WL_{TT}CCCL$ index for 101 countries.

consumption (Puaschunder, 2022). This taxation-and-bonds strategy redistributes funds also based on CO_2 emission consumption levels.

Figure 6 ranks 116 countries based on their Relative Economic Climate Change Windfall Gain Reaper and Victim Countries and CO_2 Emissions and Consumption-Based, Trade-Adjusted CO_2 Emission index ($WL_{TT}CBTAE$).

Figure 5 displays all world countries toward the top that are advised to fund climate bonds with a taxation strategy as a result of having a prospect of gaining relatively from climate change, having emissions, and emitting greater CO_2 in the process of consuming goods. Countries at the bottom are climate change victims that have less CO_2 emissions and lesser consumption among other countries. These are advised to be become transfer payment recipients. Countries that lie in the middle in terms of economic prospects and CO_2 emissions as well as goods consumption are displayed in the middle of the bar chart.

4. Discussion

This chapter advanced the idea of a fair distribution of the benefits of global warming that grants climate justice worldwide and over time in proposing a taxation-and-bonds transfer strategy. The novel policy recommendation of this chapter features climate bonds funded by taxation in some countries with differing bonds premium and maturity yield regimes for different countries based on variables such as relative economic climate change gains and losses, climate flexibility, CO_2 emissions production and consumption, as well as greenhouse gas emission changes and bank lending rates. The interest rate of an international green bond could feature either a high or low bond yield to incentivize countries or market actors to lower greenhouse gas emissions and transition to a zero-carbon economy.

Essentially, this chapter proposed a taxation-and-bonds strategy to fund climate change alleviation worldwide. The transfer in the form of tax-debt mechanisms would feature some countries' financing green bonds via carbon taxation revenues, while other countries are climate bonds premium payment recipients. The climate taxation countries would fund the bonds recipients. The proposed climate bond could be tradable, issued, and controlled by global governance institutions, such as the International Monetary Fund, the

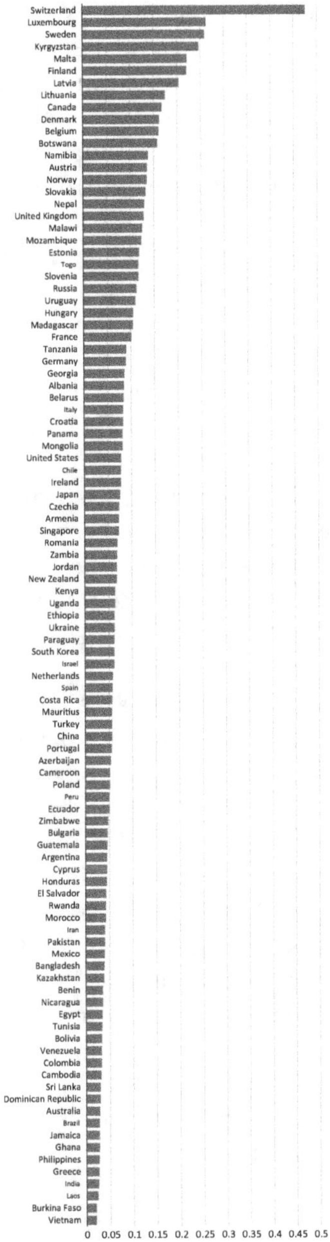

Figure 6. Country ranking of $WL_{TT}CBTAE$ index for 116 countries.

World Bank, the United Nations, or the World Trade Organization. A global governance institution could issue the bond for the entire group of contributors. Based on the six input variables of (1) climate change-related economic prospects, (2) climate flexibility as the range of temperatures a country has, (3) the CO_2 emission production, (4) CO_2 emission consumption levels, (5) the CO_2 emission changes as well as (6) bank lending rates as an indicator for access to capital, the determination of a country falling into two categories will be made: Category 1 includes countries that give the guarantee for climate bonds paid by their taxes when the bond defaults. Category 2 includes countries that get the revenue from the bonds and can invest in a large-scale transition of markets and de-risk their economics. The bonds can be traded in the overall market.

Index 1 addresses climate change-related economic growth prospects coupled with CO_2 emissions as determinants of which countries should be paying for climate bonds and which countries should be beneficiaries of transfer payments. Index 2 integrates climate flexibility as the temperature range a country has as a future trade asset to determine climate bonds payers and transfer beneficiaries worldwide. Index 3 stresses CO_2 emission changes as an incentive for positive market change in determining if a country should pay for climate bonds or be the recipient of transfer payments. Index 4 includes bank lending rates as a key for transfer payments. Index 5 addresses CO_2 emission consumption as the basis for climate change-related market solutions. All six different index input factors highlight different inequality levels contributing to climate injustices. While economic prospect levels and trade advantages cover climate-related inequalities due to favorable climate zones, CO_2 emission production and consumption are more dynamic factors that can be changed by behavior and governmental policies as well as market dynamics over time. Bank lending rates focus on historically grown differences in accessing capital for innovation.

The five indices were empirically created to determine which country should be using a taxation strategy and which country should be granted climate bonds premium yields. Similar to the Euro-bond issued by the Euro country group, the taxation and bonds strategy should feature a transfer payments scheme.

Given the global need for cooperation and intergenerational contract in the eye of the complexity and the long-term impetus of global warming, this chapter put forward a proposal for incentivizing global actors by gaining a share of the relative economic windfall benefits of climate change. Over multiple periods, market actors are thereby brought to cooperate on financing climate change mitigation in competing over CO_2 reduction efforts in the hope of gaining a favorable position on a climate taxation obligation to climate benefits recipient spectrum. Competing over a relatively determined position on the redistribution scale via CO_2 emission reduction will naturally lead to a transition to a zero-carbon economy.

This chapter integrated the original climate winners and losers' model with the climate flexibility model to transition to a green economy model via climate taxation and green bonds (Puaschunder, 2020). In particular, five indices were presented that paid attention to (1) where a country is on the relative climate change economic windfall gains and losses spectrum; (2) the climate flexibility as the range of temperatures available in a country; (3) CO_2 emissions in the process of production and (4) consumption; (5) CO_2 emissions changes over time; and (6) financial lending rates in order to propose a differentiated interest rate as well as the regime for bonds payoffs that pay tribute to (1) future GDP prospects under climate change, (2) who is causing the problem of global warming in production and (3) consumption, the overall (4) willingness to change a country's carbon footprint, and (5) country-specific access to market capital starting levels (Puaschunder, 2020).

The visual results displayed the relative differences among countries on the climate bonds grantor to climate funds recipient spectrum. For Index 1, which focused on relative economic climate change windfall gain reaper and victim countries, and their CO_2 emissions, China, the United States, Russia, Canada, and India were identified as the main climate bond grantors. Qatar, Tuvalu, Kiribati, Djibouti, and Saint Vincent & Grenadines were proposed to become the major climate redistribution fund recipient countries. Further visualization outlined the blatant inequality of only a few countries — respectively, China, the United States, and Russia — accounting for the major relative economic climate change windfall gain reapers with high levels of CO_2 emissions that are disproportionately large in comparison to all other nations of the world.

Index 2 added to estimates of relative economic climate change windfall gain reaper and victim countries' climate flexibility due to the range of temperatures that countries can offer as trade assets and their CO_2 emissions. China, the United States, Russia, Canada, and India were again identified as the main climate bond grantors. Samoa, Antigua, Barbuda, Dominica, Maldives, and Eswatini were proposed as major climate redistribution fund recipient countries. Further visualization outlined the blatant inequality of only a few countries — respectively, China, the United States, Russia, and Canada — accounting for the major windfall gain reapers with high climate flexibility and high levels of CO_2 emissions that are disproportionately large compared to all other nations of the world.

Index 3 integrated relative climate change economic windfall gain reaper or victim countries' CO_2 emissions and CO_2 emission changes to provide incentives to change environmentally damaging behavior. In these calculations, the United States drastically shifted from being a climate bonds grantor to a climate transfer payment recipient due to the high CO_2 emissions reduction in 2019. The top climate fund grantors in this index are China, Iran, Serbia, India, and Vietnam. Climate bonds transfer payment recipients are the United States, Germany, Japan, Russia, and South Korea in this index, which factors in CO_2 emissions changes into the relative climate change economic windfall gain reaper or victim countries' general CO_2 emissions. China is an outlier in this index, requiring to make the highest amount of climate bonds contributions that should be transferred to the United States and Germany foremost.

Index 4 integrated the bank lending rates status of the relative economic climate change windfall gain reaper or victim countries and their CO_2 emissions. China, the United States, Russia, India, and Italy are advised to become the primary climate bond grantors. Major redistributions should be granted to Argentina, Qatar, Gambia, Saint Vincent, the Grenadines, and Samoa in this index solution. As the visual display highlights, first China and the United States should become the main climate bond grantors for their disproportionate advantage with regards to relative windfall climate-related economic growth prospects, but also based on their CO_2 emissions and bank lending rates, which indicate access to financial capital.

The final Index 5 considered relative climate change economic gain windfall reaper or victim countries' consumption-based, trade-adjusted CO_2 emissions. In this index, climate bond grantors should be Switzerland, Luxembourg, Sweden, Kyrgyzstan, and Malta. Climate bond transfer payment recipient countries should be Qatar, Bahrain, Brunei, Trinidad and Tobago, and the United Arab Emirates. Switzerland is thereby the country that should pay the most, while Qatar and Bahrain should receive the most of all world territories.

5. Conclusion

5.1. *Practical policy implications*

In this chapter, an overall redistribution key was introduced to determine transfers per country based on the relative climate change economic windfall gain reaper or victim status and climate flexibility as well as the contribution to the climate change problem measured per country and over time by CO_2 emissions in the process of production and consumption as well as CO_2 emission changes and the bank lending rate per country. For the redistribution scheme to work, those countries with climate change losing prospects and low ranges of climate flexibility as well as low CO_2 emissions in production and consumption, decreasing CO_2 emissions, and high bank lending rates could be granted climate bonds prospects with high bond yield rate that are financed by countries that have relative economic climate change winning prospects and high ranges of climate flexibility as well as high CO_2 emissions in the process of production and consumption, increasing CO_2 emissions trends, and low bank lending rates via taxation. Countries in the middle of the original climate change winners and loser index spectrum with medium climate flexibility levels as well as medium rates of CO_2 emissions in the process of production and consumption, non-changing CO_2 emissions rates, and medium bank lending rates should have a mixture strategy of taxation and bonds with moderate bond yield rates. Those countries that are relatively high climate change economic windfall gain reapers on the winners and loser index spectrum that have high climate flexibility as well as have high rates of CO_2 emissions in the process of production and consumption, increasing CO_2 emissions levels, and low bank lending rates should issue bonds funded by taxation that offer high bond yield rates in countries with climate change losing prospect and low ranges of climate flexibility as well as low CO_2 emissions in the process of production and consumption, decreasing CO_2 emissions, and high bank lending rates.

The idea of differing climate bonds regimes is also extendable to sector-specific bond yield interest rate regimes. On a country level, high CO_2 emitting industries could face a climate taxation in order to set market incentives for a transition to renewable energy. The revenues generated from the taxation of carbon-intensive industries should be used to offset climate change losses and subsidize climate bonds. Within a country, the bonds could be offered by commissioning agents, such as local investment banks, who could install industry-specific premium bonds payments and maturity bond yields based on the environmental sustainability of an industry, e.g., as measured by the European Sustainable Finance Taxonomy. The more sustainably an industry performs, the higher the bond yield that is granted in sector-specific interest rate regimes within a country. This strategy should set positive market incentives via subsidies. Funding industries for not polluting could change the traditional race-to-the-bottom price-cutting behavior driving CO_2 emitting energy supply to have industries compete over subsidies for using clean energy. In this way, bond yield differences between industries could set positive market incentives for transitioning to renewable energy and sustainable productivity solutions.

An in-between country regime could enact fairness on the different starting grounds of countries as relative economic climate change windfall gain reapers or victims coupled with incentivizing countries and/or corporations to compete over better bonds conditions. Incentives could thereby target at lowering CO_2 emissions or subsidizing corporations to move production to places that are climate victims in order to help revitalize economies that have a shrinking prospect under climate change.

The preliminary insights brought forward in this chapter were meant to advance novel understandings of the important role that global governance institutions can play in supporting and implementing a Global Green New Deal that targets at redistribution to overcome global inequalities in regards to climate change. Global governance institutions can shape the conduct and array of international actors to contribute to a commonly agreed upon global scheme. Economically driven indices could aid in taking the political nature out of redistribution politics and historically laden international relations. The chapter was targeted at drawing attention to the need for future research on this nexus and meant as a first step in finding economically driven redistribution schemes.

An international climate change fund could be based on the five indices that integrate the relative country's initial position on the relative economic climate change gains and losses index spectrum, and a country's climate flexibility understood as the future climate wealth of nations trading assets in combination with CO_2 emissions production and consumption levels, changes in CO_2 emissions over time, and the bank lending interest rate per country (Puaschunder, 2020).

Future scientific investigations could learn from previous examples of green bonds for sustainable development focusing on climate.[1] A multilateral organization such as the International Monetary Fund, the World Bank, the United Nations, or the European Union rescue and recovery funds have already worked out specifications on similar bond solutions (Semmler *et al.*, 2021).

5.2. *Limitations*

As for limitations of the proposed ideas, it is to note that bond yields have many drivers, most important being risk (Semmler *et al.*, 2021). In addition, yields are not only incomes by asset holders but also drive capital costs for the issuer — high yields mean high capital costs (Semmler *et al.*, 2021). Bonds are issued conditional on empirical trends and facts that drive the yields in the interest rates they pay (Semmler, 2021).

The combined tax-and-bonds strategy and the incentives to shift from tax net payers into becoming recipients of funds for the transitioning to a renewable economy could de-risk bonds (Braga *et al.*, 2020). The World Bank or the International Monetary Fund could administer such tax-and-bonds redistribution schemes. Global governance institutions would have the power to shift countries from being net taxation-funded creditors to net beneficiaries with high bond yield premium payments from one period to another. Several related proposals have been introduced in the literature — for instance, see

[1] https://treasury.worldbank.org/en/about/unit/treasury/ibrd.

the World Bank Report by Semmler *et al.* (2021) and Braga *et al.* (2020). All these attempts have similarities with a disaster insurance scheme or adaptive model-predictive policies in a multi-country policy setting (Braga *et al.*, 2020; Bréchet *et al.*, 2014).

Additional critiques of bonds are the potential to breed greenwashing. Voluntary characteristics of green bond regulations and a lack of direct coercive pressure on green bond issues, as well as vague goals of green bonds, are additional potential downfalls one may think of and address in precise monitoring, evaluation, and compliance studies. Similar sanction mechanisms as the International Monetary Fund's conditionalities, which stop funding streams if policies are not implemented correctly, as well as clear contract designs, could help as hard law remedies. Soft law diplomacy could feature incentives of certifications of creditors that can face sanction mechanisms of exclusion, as practiced in the United Nations Principles of Responsible Investment and United Nations Global Compact.

5.3. *Monitoring, evaluation, and accountability*

The effectiveness of policies will depend on the national circumstances, the design, interaction, and stringency in the implementation (Kato *et al.*, 2014; Semmler, 2021). Integrating climate policies into broader development agendas will also require to be attentive to the local regulations and standards, the prevailing tax regime and carbon consumption charges, tradable permits, and financial incentives as well as voluntary agreements, information instruments, and future research and development (Semmler, 2021). Especially the improvement of new technologies will be essential for transforming the energy sector and establishing a broad-based renewable energy sector (Mazzucato, 2013; Semmler, 2021). Government initiatives to fund and subsidize the transition to renewable energy via research and development enhanced innovations are needed (Mazzucato, 2013). The respective technologies are expected to become more efficient and less cost-intensive over time (Braga *et al.*, 2020; Mazzucato, 2013; Heine *et al.*, 2019; Semmler *et al.*, 2021).

The recent World Bank Report on green bonds and climate taxation (Semmler *et al.*, 2021) outlines that carbon pricing and green bond initiatives are growing but are still concentrated in high-income countries (especially Europe) and China (classified as upper-middle income). A tax-and-bonds strategy, in which relative climate change gains are redistributed, could open the market and motivate even internationally developing parts of the world to participate in order to be funded for their low CO_2 emissions production and consumption levels in comparison to advanced countries. To this day, most green bonds tend to be project-specific and new infant market operations (Semmler, 2021). Governance on green bonds and the current experience with sustainability and resilience financing in the Green New Deal, European Green Deal, and the Next Generation EU will determine the future of green energy in learning-by-doing of sector-specific but also long-run outcomes (Semmler, 2021).

5.4. *Future studies*

Future studies on climate change impacts may address the different tipping points and disaster drivers of temperature rise, weather extremes, and sea-level rise, as this current model only considered temperature as the primary determinant of economic growth (Dietz *et al.*, 2021). The simplistic model of only prospecting the impact of temperature on GDP growth was chosen as a first starting point to sketch out the potential of a relative climate change economic windfall reaper or victim countries' model for redistribution as an inequality alleviation strategy. Future theoretical work may define and clarify climate argumentations, which served as the basis of the indices. Future index sophistications could feature additional influence factors, such as disaster effects and historical inequalities, to refine the redistribution schemes proposed.

The first model introduced is by no means inclusive of all environmental eventualities and economic drivers. It is yet a first step in balancing out the worldwide climate inequality and provides a first step for relative economic climate change windfall gains redistribution capacities. Future index extensions could also address the CO_2 emission levels per capita and CO_2 emission changes per citizen. The current state of this chapter will hopefully set the stage for future research that refines the variegated impact of climate, weather, and coastal risk as future economic determinants in order to lead toward a more just balance of economic gains and losses around the world, on the most granular, per capita level.

Future comparative studies could compare the costs and effectiveness of various tax and bond designs not only in a cost-effectiveness analysis but also in terms of political feasibility and legal impetus. Forecasting studies should tackle potential obstacles and contingency planning if there are unintended outcomes that raise problems for compensation compliance or if there is a pushback in future generations, or if the plan of redistribution over time does not work. Philosophical problems of bonds should be addressed, specifically that future generations, not having caused the climate problem, will find themselves indebted for stabilizing the climate changes of the past. Counter argumentations of money being fungible and always there but the sustainable stable climate and natural resources' finite character could be underlined. As for future research on implementing the proposed redistribution plan, political and economic insights may inform about bargaining and the role of cartels in reaching favorable common goods allocation outcomes. Historical examples of previous world leaders' negotiations (e.g., after the World Wars or revolutions) may lead to analyzing contemporary negotiation strategies and outcome risk estimate forecasting.

Future Law and Economics extensions should particularly pay attention to the disparate impact of climate policies on marginalized and vulnerable societal groups. In a heterodox opening of the macroeconomic aggregate production and consumption functions, the disproportionately hard effect of policies on gender, race, and other vulnerable populations must be addressed.

For the legal community, the proposed tax-and-bonds strategy is a concrete commitment bond strategy application (Armour *et al.*, 2021; Ayres and Abramowicz, 2011; Bishop, 2019; Omarova, 2020). Corporate legal scholars may add information about the practicality of green bonds and how to avert negative downsides, such as greenwashing, through clear and concrete contracts, economic incentives, and sanction mechanisms.

The aftermath of the Coronavirus crisis offers the unique historical potential to peg all-time-high governmental rescue and recovery packages to environmental long-term causes (Puaschunder, 2021). The United States Green New Deal, as well as the European Green Deal and Sustainable Finance Taxonomy offer unprecedented opportunities to scale up green investments through green bonds as part of a fiscal program to move out of the current pandemic recession (Semmler, 2021). While there has been a macroeconomic debate about the monetary size of the current governmental rescue efforts and if the largess of governmental aid may trigger inflation and unbearable debt levels, the heterodox need for a diversified view and disparate impact of inflation and longest-ever, lowest-ever interest rate regimes become apparent at the same time (Brunnermeier Academy at the Princeton Bendheim Center for Finance; Puaschunder, 2021). Future work could address the normative implications of the developed insights. For instance, in future research, the European Taxonomy for sustainable activities could serve as the basis of CO_2 emissions per industry measurements and thereby lead to a respective redistribution key between industry contributions to the climate change problem (European Union Technical Expert Group on Sustainable Finance, 2020).

As for methodological avenues for future research, redistribution criteria could be sophisticated. For instance, the nature and rate of GDP growth over the following decades, the distributional impacts of funded green projects by income class in countries paying off loans, assessment of climate change windfall gain reapers, and who should pay taxes to pay off bonds but also climate victims and their risks estimates could follow. Different scenarios of net benefits by income class in relative economic climate change windfall gain reaper and victim countries over time with probability estimates would be a grand future endeavor.

Additional layers of inequality should be explored in future Law and Economics analyses of the problem, for instance, in disparate impact studies but also international law and development angles, for example, in the different levels of resilience in watching moving coastlines between the developed and undeveloped nations. Migration as a coping mechanism in regards to climate change may offer additional future prospective research avenues and index parameters to be added in future extensions of the presented model.

Future open research questions are the economic validation and measurement of positive and negative externalities of all these endeavors over time and a disparate impact assessment, which can be granted by a truly heterodox viewpoint (Woo, 2021). Methodological heterodoxy could open the spectrum of macroeconomic models with a more comprehensive treatment of preferences, the climate sensitivity of infrastructure, as well as different technologies' impact on the success of climate mitigation and adaptation policies (Mazzucato, 2013; Semmler, 2021). The overall social context should be explored further in post-Keynesian analyses of the presented problem solutions to estimate the political salience.

Future behavioral research could be dedicated to shifting from a climate change windfall gain reaper ability-to-pay to a voluntary-driven willingness-to-pay, which would also crowd out the negative externalities of greenwashing. Climate change imposing a highly complex collective action problem that faces political realities, and the burden of debt for future generations, are future complicated yet fertile research grounds to be studied that deserve attention.

Overall, introducing the idea of climate taxation and green bonds in an incentives-driven tax-and-bonds strategy is a new heterodox method that establishes green bonds as a possible macroeconomic policy aimed at ensuring the sharing of the burden as well as the benefits of climate change over time, between countries and markets as well as within society, in an economically efficient, legally equitable, and practically feasible way.

Acknowledgment

Part of this chapter is based on the contribution titled "Climate stabilization taxation-and-bonds strategy adjusted for consumption" to the *Proceedings of the 25th Research Association for Interdisciplinary Studies (RAIS) Conference on Social Sciences and Humanities* as well as the 2021 *Scientia Moralitas Conference Proceedings.*

References

Armour, J., Enriques, L., & Wetzer, Th. (2021). Corporate carbon reduction pledges: Beyond greenwashing. Business Law and the Net Zero Economy, *Oxford Business Law Blog*, July 2, 2021. Retrieved at https://www.law.ox.ac.uk/business-law-blog/blog/2021/07/corporate-carbon-reduction-pledges-beyond-greenwashing.

Ayres, I. & Abramowicz, M. (2011). Commitment bonds. *Georgetown Law Journal, 100*, 605–656.

Banerjee, L. (2014). Climate thresholds, weather extremes, and catastrophic losses. In L. Bernard & W. Semmler (Eds.), *The Oxford Handbook of the Macroeconomics of Global Warming* (pp. 567–587). Oxford: Oxford University Press.

Bishop, N. (2019). Green bond governance and the Paris agreement. *New York University Environmental Law Journal*, pp. 377–411. Retrieved at https://www.nyuelj.org/wp-content/uploads/2019/10/Bishop_Green-Bond-Governance-and-the-Paris-Agreement.pdf.

Bonen, A., Klasen, St., & Semmler, W. (2014). *Economic damages from climate change: A review of modeling approaches.* Schwartz Center for Economic Policy Analysis Working Paper 2014-3. Retrieved at https://ideas.repec.org/p/epa/cepawp/2014-3.html.

Braga, J. A., Semmler, W., & Grass, D. (2020). *De-risking of Green Investment Through A Green Bond Market: Empirics and a Dynamic Model.* Laxenburg, Austria: International Institute of Applied Systems Analysis Working Paper WP-20-014. Retrieved at http://pure.iiasa.ac.at/id/eprint/16666/.

Bréchet, T., Camacho, C., & Veliov, V. M. (2014). Adaptive model-predictive policies in a multicountry setting. In L. Bernard & W. Semmler (Eds.), *The Oxford Handbook of the Macroeconomics of Global Warming* (pp. 114–140). Oxford: Oxford University Press.

Brunnermeier Academy at the Princeton Bendheim Center for Finance. Retrieved at https://bcf.princeton.edu/markus-academy/.

Burke, M., Hsiang, S. H., & Miguel, E. (2015). Global non-linear effect of temperature on economic production. *Nature*, *527*, 235–239.

Dietz, S., Rising, J., Stoerk, Th., & Wagner, G. (2021). Economic impacts of tipping points in the climate system. *Proceedings of the National Academy of Sciences*, *118*, 34, 1–9.

European Union Technical Expert Group on Sustainable Finance (2020). *Financing a Sustainable European Economy: Technical Report: Taxonomy: Final Report of the Technical Expert Group on Sustainable Finance March 2020.* Retrieved at https://ec.europa.eu/info/sites/default/files/business_economy_euro/banking_and_finance/documents/200309-sustainable-finance-teg-final-report-taxonomy_en.pdf.

Flavelle, Ch. (2021a). Billions for climate protection fuel new debate: Who deserves it most. *The New York Times*, December 3, 2021. Retrieved at https://www.nytimes.com/2021/12/03/climate/climate-change-infrastructure-bill.html.

Flavelle, Ch. (2021b). The climate bill includes billions in funding: Will it be spent fairly? *The New York Times*, December 8, 2021. Retrieved at https://www.nytimes.com/2021/12/03/climate/climate-change-infrastructure-bill.html.

Gevorkyan, A. & Semmler, A. (2016). Oil price, overleveraging and shakeout in the shale energy sector: Game changers in the oil industry. *Economic Modeling*, *54*, 244–259.

Greiner, A., Mett, T., & Semmler, W. (2012). An economic model of oil exploration and extraction. *Computational Economics*, *40*, 4, 387–399.

Hansen, J. E. (2014). Environment and development challenges: The imperative of a carbon fee and dividend. In L. Bernard & W. Semmler (Eds.), *The Oxford Handbook of the Macroeconomics of Global Warming* (pp. 639–646). Oxford: Oxford University Press.

Hansen, J. E. & Sato, M. (2016). Regional climate change and national responsibilities. *Environmental Research Letters*, *11*, 9–17.

Heine, D., Semmler, W., Mazzucato, M., Braga, J. P., Flaherty, M., Gevorkyan, A., Hayde, E. & Radpour, S. (2019). *Financing Low-carbon Transitions Through Carbon Pricing and Green Bonds.* Washington, DC: World Bank Policy Research Working Paper 8991, August 2019.

Jonas, H. (1979). *Das Prinzip Verantwortung: Versuch einer Ethik für die technologische Zivilisation.* Frankfurt am Main: Insel.

Kahn, M. E., Mohaddes, K., Ng, R. N. C., Pesaran, M. H., Raissi, M., & Yang, J.-Ch. (2019). *Long-term Macroeconomic Effects of Climate Change: A Cross-country Analysis.* International Monetary Fund Working Paper WP/19/215. Retrieved at https://www.imf.org/-/media/Files/Publications/WP/2019/wpiea2019215-print-pdf.ashx.

Kant, I. (1783/1993). *Grounding for the Metaphysics of Morals.* Cambridge: Hackett.

Kato, M., Mittnik, St., Samaan, D., & Semmler, W. (2014). Employment and output effects of climate policies. In L. Bernard & W. Semmler (Eds.), *The Oxford Handbook of the Macroeconomics of Global Warming* (pp. 445–476). Oxford: Oxford University Press.

Kellett, C. M., Weller, E. M., Faulwasser, T., Grüne, L., & Semmler, W. (2019). Feedback, dynamics, and optimal control in climate economics. *Annual Reviews in Control*, *47*, 7–20.

Law, J. & Smullen, J. (2008). *A Dictionary of Finance and Banking.* Oxford: Oxford University Press.

Lomborg, B. (2021). Climate change saves more lives than you'd think: Eight times as many people die from cold as heat, and the fix for both is access to cheap fuel. *The Wall Street Journal*, September 16, 2021. Retrieved at https://www.wsj.com/articles/climate-change-heat-cold-deaths-medical-journal-health-risk-energy-cost-fossil-fuels-11631741045?st=w4h947wjnxd6iio&reflink=article_email_share.

Maurer, H., Preuss, H. J., & Semmler, W. (2014). Scenarios in a model of economic growth and climate change. In L. Bernard & W. Semmler (Eds.), *The Oxford Handbook of the Macroeconomics of Global Warming* (pp. 82–113). Oxford: Oxford University Press.

Mazzucato, M. (2013). *The Entrepreneurial State: Debunking Public vs. Private sector myths.* New York: Anthem.

Nikulin, D. (2021). Responsibility and hope. *Bollettino della Società Filosofica Italiana*, Carocci editore Roma, Nuova Serie n. 232, Gennaio/Aprile 2021.

Nordhaus, W. D. (1994). *Mapping the Global Commons: The Economics of Climate Change.* Cambridge, MA: MIT Press.

Nyambuu, U. & Semmler, W. (2014). Trends in the extraction of non-renewable resources: The case of fossil energy. *Economic Modelling, 37*, 271–279.

Nyambuu, U. & Semmler, W. (2017). Emerging markets' resource booms and busts, borrowing risk and regime change. *Structural Change and Economic Dynamics, 41*, 29–45.

Nyambuu, U. & Semmler, W. (2020). Climate change and the transition to a low carbon economy: Carbon targets and the carbon budget. *Economic Modelling, 84*, 367–376.

Omarova, S. T. (2020). *The Climate Case for a National Investment Authority.* Data for Progress, August 2020. Retrieved at https://www.filesforprogress.org/memos/white-paper-nia.pdf.

Orlov, S., Rovenskaya, E., Puaschunder, J. M., & Semmler, W. (2018). *Green Bonds, Transition to a Low-Carbon Economy, and Intergenerational Fairness: Evidence from an Extended DICE Model.* Laxenburg, Austria: International Institute for Applied Systems Analysis Working Paper WP-18-001, 2018. IIASA, Laxenburg, Austria, European Union.

Pollin, R., Garrett-Peltier, H., & Wicks-Lim, J. (2017a). A green new deal from Washington State. Amherst: Political Economy Research Institute Research Report, University of Massachusetts Amherst.

Pollin, R., Garrett-Peltier, H., & Wicks-Lim, J. (2017b). Clean energy investment for New York State. Amherst: Political Economy Research Institute Research Report, University of Massachusetts Amherst.

Pollin, R., Wicks-Lim, J., Chakraborty, S., & Hansen, T. (2019). A green growth program for Colorado. Amherst: Political Economy Research Institute Research Report, University of Massachusetts Amherst.

Pollin, R., Wicks-Lim, J., Chakraborty, S., Kline, C., & Semieniuk, G. (2021). A program for economic recovery and clean energy transition in California. Amherst: Political Economy Research Institute Research Report, University of Massachusetts Amherst.

Pollin, R., Wicks-Lim, J., Chakraborty, S., & Semieniuk, G. (2020a). A program for economic recovery and clean energy transition in Maine. Amherst: Political Economy Research Institute Research Report, University of Massachusetts Amherst.

Pollin, R., Wicks-Lim, J., Chakraborty, S., & Semieniuk, G. (2020b). Impact of the reimagine Appalachia & clean energy transition programs for Ohio. Amherst: Political Economy Research Institute Research Report, University of Massachusetts Amherst.

Pollin, R., Wicks-Lim, J., Chakraborty, S., & Semieniuk, G. (2021a). Impact of the reimagine Appalachia & clean energy transition programs for Pennsylvania. Amherst: Political Economy Research Institute Research Report, University of Massachusetts Amherst.

Pollin, R., Wicks-Lim, J., Chakraborty, S., & Semieniuk, G. (2021b). Impact of the reimagine Appalachia & clean energy transition programs for West Virginia. Amherst: Political Economy Research Institute Research Report, University of Massachusetts Amherst.

Puaschunder, J. M. (2020). *Governance and Climate Justice: Global South and Developing Nations.* New York, NY: Palgrave Macmillan. Cham, Switzerland: Springer Nature.

Puaschunder, J. M. (2021). Focusing COVID-19 Bailout and Recovery. *Ohio State Business Law Journal, 19*, 91–148.

Puaschunder, J. M. (2022). Governance of climate justice: Taxation transfers and green bonds. In: W. Leal Filho, N. Aguilar-Rivera, B. Borsari, P.R.B. de Brito, B. Andrade Guerra (Eds.) *SDGs in the Americas and Caribbean Region. Implementing the UN Sustainable Development Goals: Regional Perspectives.* Springer, Cham.

Rawls, J. (1971). *A Theory of Justice.* Cambridge, MA: Harvard University Press.

Roston, E., Kaufman, L., & Warren, H. (2022). How the world's richest people are driving global warming. *Bloomberg*, March 24, 2022. Retrieved at https://www.bloomberg.com/graphics/2022-wealth-carbon-emissions-inequality-powers-world-climate/.

Sachs, J. D. (2014). Climate change and intergenerational well-being. In L. Bernard & W. Semmler (Eds.), *The Oxford Handbook of the Macroeconomics of Global Warming* (pp. 248–259). Oxford: Oxford University Press.

Sachs, J. D. (2021). Fixing climate finance. *Social Europe: Politics, Economy and Employment & Labor*, November 17, 2021.

Semmler, W. (2021). *Economics of Climate Change.* Lecture notes, New York: The New School for Social Research.

Semmler, W., Braga, J. A., Lichtenberger, A., Toure, M., & Hayde, E. (2021). *Fiscal Policies for a Low-Carbon Economy.* Washington, DC: World Bank Report. Retrieved at https://documents1.worldbank.org/curated/en/998821623308445356/pdf/Fiscal-Policies-for-a-Low-Carbon-Economy.pdf.

Woo, A. (2021). Environmental fascism and the zero waste movement. Panel on monitoring and evaluation in environmental economics, April 16, 2021, The New School New York.

© 2024 World Scientific Publishing Europe Ltd.
https://doi.org/10.1142/9781800614451_0005

Chapter 5

Environmental Impact Bonds: An Innovative Public–Private Approach to Tackle Climate Challenges

Maya Tira[*,†], **Benjamin Le Pendeven**[‡], **and Céline Louche**[§]

Audencia Business School, Nantes, France
[†]*mtira@audencia.com*
[‡]*blependeven@audencia.com*
[§]*celine.louche@waikato.ac.nz*

Abstract

This chapter explores the emergence of Environmental Impact Bonds (EIBs), an innovative public–private financing mechanism dedicated to environmental projects, as a response to the lack of funding of innovative policies tackling climate change. Building from the Social Impact Bond (SIB) prototypical model and features, and looking at the pioneer experience of DC Water in the USA as well as the EIB experiment by the French Agency for Environmental and Energy Management (ADEME), we identify two distinct models of EIBs that are emerging and compare them in the light of the French and USA experiments. Finally, we discuss the challenges to overcome for a successful and relevant deployment of EIBs.

1. Introduction

On February 28, 2022, the Intergovernmental Panel on Climate Change (IPCC) released its Working Group II contribution to

*Corresponding author.

the Sixth Assessment Report titled "Impacts, Adaptation and Vulnerability". The IPCC report identifies finance constraints as one of the important determinants to the limits of adaptation to climate change (IPCC, 2022). Moreover, the capital allocated to environmental conservation is mainly deployed by the public and philanthropic sectors (Hamrick, 2016). In order to maintain global warming below 1.5°C per year, an estimated amount of $4.13 trillion is needed annually (Climate Policy Initiative, 2021). However, the reality remains far from the current expectations to tackle climate change effects: the annual global climate investment is estimated at $632 billion per year over 2019 and 2020 (Climate Policy Initiative, 2021), which represents less than 15% of the $4.13 trillion target.

Among the financial instruments that could provide an answer to this lack of funding, Environmental Impact Bonds (EIBs) might be an interesting mechanism to explore. Originally designed to tackle social issues such as unemployment, criminal justice, or homelessness, Social Impact Bonds (SIBs) have attracted the interest of several governments and private stakeholders. Since the first SIB experiment aiming at reducing rates of recidivism among short-term prisoners in Peterborough (UK) in 2010, more than 200 SIBs have been issued worldwide for a total of $462.68 million (Brookings Institute, 2022) in more than 20 countries, including UK, USA, France, Australia, Canada, the Netherlands, and Portugal. Almost a hundred academic papers have been published in the past decade on this topic and the characteristics of this financing tool (Buffa and Le Pendeven, 2022). Following this growing interest for SIBs, and despite the technical complexity of the tool, we are currently witnessing the early EIBs, an adaptation of this pay-for-success approach to respond to environmental issues such as climate change and global warming. EIBs have been notably experimented with in the USA by DC Water in Washington DC, the Department of Watershed Management in Atlanta, Georgia, and the city of Hampton, Virginia. They have also been experimented with in France by the French Agency for Environmental and Energy Management (ADEME) in order to fund environmental projects.

Because EIBs are such a recent innovation on the spectrum of payment-by-result mechanisms, they are not yet the subject of an extended dedicated literature. However, there is an undeniable connection between SIBs and EIBs as they both operate along similar lines (Dey and Gibbon, 2018).

This chapter discusses the adaptations of the SIB model as a response to finance projects tackling environmental challenges. First, it draws an overview of its main characteristics: its stakeholders, financial structure, and contract design. The second part explores the emergence of two specific EIB models through the EIB experiments in France and in the USA. Finally, the last section of this chapter discusses the current challenges faced by these experiments in the light of the latest literature findings as well as the French and American experience of EIBs.

2. Understanding environmental impact bonds: Stakeholders, structure, and contract design

2.1. *Definition and stakeholders*

An Environmental Impact Bond is an innovative public–private financing mechanism that uses a pay-for-performance approach to provide capital from private investors for environmental projects (Yonavjak, 2016). EIBs are directly inspired by the SIB model, which originated within the social services sector (Brand *et al.*, 2021).

In EIBs, private investors provide capital to fund a program implemented by an environmental services provider (NGO, social enterprise, etc.). This intervention is limited in time (usually three to five years) and is evaluated using environmental performance indicators. If the program reaches the environmental objectives fixed *ex-ante* by contract, the public payer repays private investors with interests. If the results do not meet the environmental objectives set by the contract, the public authority is not required to fully or partially repay the investors.

EIBs completely differ from Green Bonds (Brand *et al.*, 2021). Indeed, Green Bonds payments are based on realized and measured benefits, mostly for listed companies or public institutions, whereas EIBs are a pay-for-performance mechanism, which means that their payments are indexed to an expected environmental performance of the program.

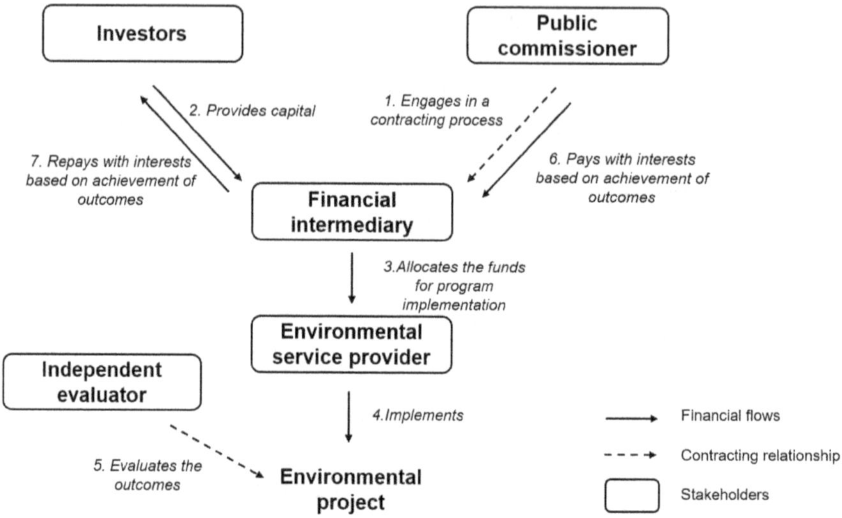

Figure 1. The environmental impact bond model (inspired by Le Pendeven, Nico, and Gachet, 2015).

Typically, an EIB involves exactly the same types of stakeholders as an SIB (Figure 1):

- A service provider that designs a program intended to tackle one or multiple environmental challenges. Usually one or a group of NGOs and/or social companies are implicated;
- Private investors (usually banks, private equity funds, or charities) provide up-front capital in order to finance the program;
- One or multiple public commissioners or final payor(s) that repay the investors if the program ends up being successful and reaches its environmental objectives;
- A financial intermediary that structures the deal, proposes a financial model, and looks for private investors;
- An independent evaluator that assesses whether or not the project outcomes reached the environmental objectives.

2.2. *Financial instruments*

Despite their designation and their fixed-time period, EIBs are not traditional bonds but contracts based on expected environmental outcomes and financed through debt, equity, quasi-equity, or donations (Del Giudice and Migliavacca, 2019). Thus, they can be compared to derivative products where financial return is linked to external evaluation. In the USA, the first EIB — DC Water — was issued privately. However, the following experimentations in Atlanta, Hampton, or Buffalo were issued publicly.

2.3. *Contracting process*

Before the project implementation, the public administration engages in a contracting process by *carefully negotiating* (Balboa, 2016) with the service provider (advised by its financial intermediaries and evaluators) in order to collectively challenge the project and determine the following:

- The environmental performance indicators that will determine the repayment of the bond: Nature (output or outcome), weight, and quantitative objectives related to those key performance indicators (KPIs).
- The financial structure of the bond: Allocation of the budget, payment thresholds, interest rate, amount of the investor's bonus and risk mitigation mechanisms, amount of cost savings for the public entity.
- The evaluation methodology: Identification of the beneficiaries, evaluation's rigor and method, choice of qualitative and/or quantitative tools.

Following the contracting — and only if the negotiation is successful — the financial intermediaries engage in negotiations with potential investors in order to finance the EIB.

2.4. *Cost savings*

As for SIBs in general, particular attention is given during the contracting process to the cost savings that will be realized by the public agencies in issuing an EIB instead of internalizing the experiment. The cost savings represent the amount of money saved by the public authority when choosing to contract an EIB. Indeed, to be considered profitable for the public sector, the cost savings induced by the implementation of an EIB should exceed the outcome payment — including the cost of the intervention and investor return on investment (see Figure 2).

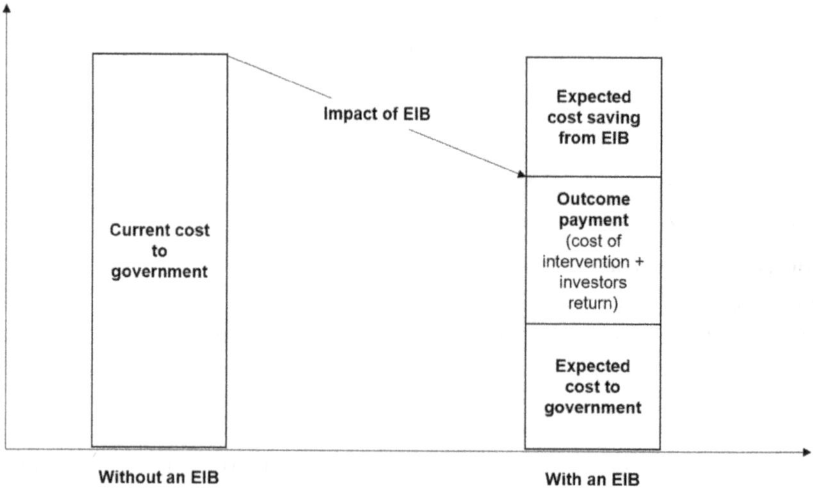

Figure 2. Cost saving of an environmental impact bond (inspired by Balboa, 2016).

2.5. *EIBs as an adaptation of the reference model of SIBs*

SIBs have been established by the literature as the prototypical model of the impact bond logic, and EIBs are portrayed as an adaptation of this SIB model with different settings (Dey and Gibbon, 2018) as it is applied in response to environmental challenges. When it comes to the reference model of SIB, the literature has identified three different levels of compliance to the initial prototypical model of SIBs (Arena *et al.*, 2016). Fully compliant SIBs fund new, innovative, and preventive programs designed on a national scope by multiple service providers, leaving a very marginal role to the commissioner. From a financial point of view, there is an effective transfer of the risk to the private investors without mitigation arrangements. Partially compliant SIBs fund already existing initiatives, usually on a local or regional level, with a successful track record, and thus do not encourage innovation, flexibility in the design of the program, and new forms of public–private collaboration. They act as a substitute to a public policy that responds poorly to a social issue, and often includes risk mitigation mechanisms in order to protect private investors. Finally, marginally compliant SIBs support the scaling of an existing program designed at a local level by a single service provider rather than funding an intervention with specific outcomes. This type of SIB is also characterized by a high level of risk mitigation arrangements for private investors.

Building from the prototypical SIB model, it is interesting to witness the emergence of two EIB models with different characteristics based on the French and US experiments of this tool.

3. EIB experiments in France and in the USA: Toward the emergence of two EIB models

3.1. *The DC Water environmental impact bond*

In 2005, in response to the legal action by local residents of Washington DC, the District of Columbia's Water and Sewer utility (DC Water) signed an agreement with the US Environmental Protection Agency (EPA) in order to address the issue of sewer overflows that were contaminating water in the district. After 10 years, DC Water decided to go further in its commitment by exploring the benefits of green infrastructure (green roofs, rain gardens, permeable pavements...) in storm water management to replace the gray infrastructure that was used at the time. However, the scientific and technical risks associated with green infrastructure management were too high to consider a public financing by DC Water.

DC Water thought of a solution in order to mitigate the performance risk, by transferring it to private investors. This would allow a responsible management of tax-payer funds and the implementation of a large-scale green infrastructure experimentation. Thus, in 2015, DC Water issued the first EIB worldwide. Goldman Sachs and Calvert Impact Capital privately provided the capital for a total amount of $25 million. Prior to the contract implementation, a very rigorous evaluation methodology was designed in order to assess the overflow reduction with green infrastructure compared to the previous gray infrastructure of DC Water. Based on this evaluation, the financial intermediary, Quantified Ventures, worked with DC Water and the investors, and came up with the following three-scenario performance structure:

- *Low-performance scenario*: If the overflow reduction is inferior to 18.6%, the investors owe a claw-back (risk share payment) of $3.3 million to DC Water.

- *Base-performance scenario*: If the overflow reduction is between 18.6% and 41.3%, there is no payment to investors due by DC Water.
- *High-performance scenario*: If the overflow reduction exceeds 41.3%, DC Water repays the private investors with a bonus of $3.3 million.

In 2021, the program funded by the EIB ended. An evaluation conducted by DC Water and an independent evaluator assessed an overflow reduction of nearly 20%, which falls in the base-performance scenario and does not require a repayment to the investors by DC Water. The program allowed the funding of 77 green infrastructure practices and the training of more than a hundred people for green infrastructure jobs. It also generated significant knowledge on green infrastructure management. Thus, it was considered a successful public innovation experimentation by DC Water as well as the private investors that took part in the experiment (DC Water, 2021) and has been replicated in several US municipalities such as Atlanta, Georgia or Hampton, Virginia.

3.2. *The French ADEME experiment*

In France, the development of SIBs has known a significant political momentum since 2019, with the publication of a policy-report requested by the High Commission for the Social Economy and Social Innovation and aiming at developing impact bonds in the country (Lavenir, 2019). One of the specificities of SIBs that emerged through this policy-report in France is the use of thematic calls for interest in order to select the potential SIB-funded programs. Before 2019, service providers had to take the initiative to convince the relevant public agencies in order to build an SIB, which was extremely challenging and time-consuming. Therefore, very few SIBs in France were launched before 2019 (Cazenave, 2022). The French landscape of SIBs has also witnessed a terminological shift: instead of talking about SIBs, the French administration now refers to this mechanism as Impact Bonds (IBs), in order to include both *social* and *environmental* outcomes within those projects, and to encourage the launching of environment-related impact bonds.

Table 1. Description of four EIB experiments in France and the USA.

	DC Water	Label Vie	Envie Autonomie	Toopi Organics
Location	Washington DC, USA	France	France	France
Description of the intervention	Build green infrastructure in order to reduce water overflow, train employees for green infrastructure jobs	Reduce the environmental impact of daycare centers	Collect and distribute medical equipment to facilitate the autonomy of people with disabilities	Collect, transform, and valorize human urine as a resource for agriculture
Amount of the intervention	$25 million	€2.6 million	€5 million	€3.8 million
Bond structure	Three-scenario structure based on one performance indicator	Three-scenario structure based on three performance indicators	Three-scenario structure based on four performance indicators	Three-scenario structure based on five performance indicators
Performance indicators	Percentage of overflow reduction	Number of daycare centers involved in the process Reduction of electricity consumption Reduction of water consumption	Number of jobs created Tons of materials recycled Tons of CO_2 avoided Tons of raw materials avoided	Amount of urine collected Amount of urine sold Amount of water saved Number of facilities equipped with Toopi toilets Diversity of the types of facilities
Estimated cost savings for the public entity	Non-disclosed	€6.24 million	€7.25 million	€5.1 million
Nature of impact	Environmental Social	Environmental	Environmental (80%) Social (20%)	Environmental

Following the Lavenir report, three calls for interest have been published by French agencies at the state level. Among them, the ADEME call for interest was the first one to focus on environmental issues. Launched from September until December 2020, the ADEME call for interest focused on a circular economy and encompassed various topics such as waste sorting of bio-waste, reduction of food waste, or reuse of construction material. Following the end of the call for interest, eight projects have been selected by the French Agency for Environmental and Energy Management to be potentially funded through EIBs. The ADEME call for interest presents two specificities. First, ADEME is a semi-independent public financing agency (called *EPIC* in the French law), and thus, does not have the same accounting and budgetary constraints as the issuing of IBs by a classical public ministry. Second, ADEME is committed to launching a portfolio of eight EIBs selected from the same call of interest. The total envelope of this EIB portfolio reaches €27.3 million. Label Vie, Envie Autonomie, and Toopi Organics were part of the selected projects to be funded through an EIB (Table 1).

Label Vie

Label Vie is a non-profit organization that has designed a program and a label in order to reduce the environmental impact of day care centers. The EIB will fund the program to increase the number of daycare centers involved and, thus, reduce their overall environmental footprint. Label Vie's EIB proposition focuses on the scaling, the digital transformation, and the territorial implementation of its program designed for daycare centers. The purpose of the intervention is to significantly increase the number of daycare centers involved in the labeling program and expand to new French local territories that have not been targeted by Label Vie yet. It aims to develop a digital platform for daycare managers and professionals and give them the adequate tools and documentation in order to contribute to the reduction of their structure's environmental footprint in a more autonomous way.

Envie Autonomie
Envie Autonomie is a social company (*entreprise d'insertion*) that created a program to collect unused medical devices (wheelchairs, sit-to-stand devices, medical beds...), have some of them reconditioned by employees on integration programs, and then distribute them at a fair price, primarily to those who cannot afford medical equipment for economic or administrative reasons. The objective of this EIB intervention is to create a national network to scale the circular economy of such medical devices. The program is expected to create both environmental and social impacts, by helping long-term unemployed persons to re-join the workforce and give them opportunities to re-access a sustainable work activity. Thus, the performance indicators selected are both environmental and social.

Toopi Organics
Among the projects selected by the ADEME call of interest, Toopi Organics is the only one that proposes an unprecedented scientific innovation in France. The start-up launched in 2019 develops a biotechnological process to recycle human urine into agricultural products. The EIB is expected to fund the installation of a specific typology of toilets in facilities such as schools, universities, or shopping centers in order to collect, transform, and valorize important volumes of urine for agricultural purposes.

3.3. *Comparing the French and the USA EIB models*

3.3.1. *Type of risk*

One French specificity compared to the US model is the fact that ADEME has chosen to simultaneously finance several smaller projects (up to 5 million euros) on a more general issue — circular economy — instead of one single big scale project such as DC Water. In that sense, the main risk in France lies in the type and scale of the structures funded through an EIB rather than on the scientific risk induced by the intervention, as the projects financed by ADEME are mainly small social businesses or NGOs offering services. As a result, the environmental impact assessment methodologies are not very technical and do not require robust scientific engineering unlike the EIB experiments in the United States that finance green infrastructure projects.

3.3.2. *Bond structure*

In terms of bond structure, while DC Water bases its financial scenarios on a single environmental performance indicator, the French EIBs are built on a two-level performance structure. First, a three-scenario structure (under-performance, equilibrium, and over-performance) assessing the overall performance of the program. Second, a target performance linked to three to five performance indicators. In that sense, the French model allows the partial reimbursement of the investors depending on the level of performance achieved based on the different indicators.

In terms of nature of the performance indicators, the US and the French models offer the possibility to include both social and environmental objectives for the project. The difference lies in the fact that the French model allows the inclusion of social indicators in the payment scheme, which is not the case in the USA. However, the social indicators should not exceed 20% of the overall payment structure of the bond, as the priority of EIBs for ADEME remains the achievement of an environmental impact taking into consideration the laws related to public funding.

3.3.3. *Nature of evaluation*

In the case of the DC Water EIB, a rigorous three-step evaluation was conducted in order to assess the overall environmental performance of the program. First, DC Water assessed the storm water runoff of the pre-existing gray infrastructures. These pre-monitoring results allowed to build the performance structure of the bond by predicting the reduction runoff with green infrastructure. Finally, a post-intervention evaluation determined the actual runoff reduction that occurred with the construction of green infrastructure compared to the previous gray infrastructure.

In the case of France, the contracting process has highlighted difficulties and already allowed us to learn lessons when it comes to evaluating EIBs. A careful evaluation is based on the availability of data and on the ability to make different sources of data converge during the negotiation. Then, the scale of projects such as the ones financed through the EIB in France can face an additional difficulty in implementing an evaluation methodology because of the lack of resources (such as an efficient IT system to track the impact, for example) as well as the lack of experience in impact measurement and management, which may weaken the rigor and limit the efficiency of the evaluation. This confirms the role of the public entity in the evaluation design and monitoring. As an example, Label Vie has worked closely with the ADEME climate experts in order to find an adequate data correction method in case of climatic hazards.

In both the French and US examples, the impact of an EIB is also to generate significant expertise related to the financed intervention. This points to the utility of EIB and the crucial role of evaluation in order to produce knowledge on innovative and unexplored themes such as the usefulness of human urine in agriculture and the environmental impact of medical devices or construction materials.

3.3.4. *Post-implementation trajectories*

The French and US models also differ in their post-implementation trajectories. While the French model is based on the scaling of small programs from a local to a national level, the US model has been designed to replicate a large-scale infrastructure model in several municipalities around the United States.

Benefiting from its position as a pioneer as well as its high level of innovation, risk transfer to the investors, and robust evaluation methodology, the case of DC Water is established as the prototypical model of EIBs in the USA as it precisely defines what a successful EIB should be for the public commissioner. After DC Water, the trend has been to replicate the same kind of big infrastructure contract addressing the specific environmental issue of water runoff in several municipalities and states such as Atlanta, Georgia or Hampton, Virginia. However, it is important to note that the EIBs launched after DC Water tend to move away from the prototypical model in terms of financial model and risk mitigation arrangement for private investors: in order to make EIBs more accessible for municipalities that were risk-averse, the claw-back (which is the additional payment that the public commissioner would make to investors in case of over-performance) has been suppressed from the subsequent EIBs that were designed. From that perspective, the EIB model in the

Table 2. Comparison of the French and the US EIB models.

	US model	French model
Type of structure financed	Big infrastructure projects	Small businesses or NGOs designing service-based projects
Type of risk	Scientific risk	Type of service provider Regulatory risk
Bond structure	Three-scenario structure based on one environmental performance indicator	Three-scenario structure based on three to five environmental and/or social (up to 20%) performance indicators
Type of impact	Environmental and social	Environmental and/or social
Post-implementation trajectory	Replication on a municipality level	Scaling on a national level

USA has evolved into a comparable framework to issuing municipal bonds. It features a financially less risky structure than the initial EIB model. Moreover, it introduces an added post-evaluation implementation grounded in robust metrics and a disclosed outcome evaluation report. These aspects, which are absent in the traditional municipal bond model, are made accessible to both investors and the public (Quantified Ventures, 2021).

Despite their differences, both the US and the French EIB experiments face converging but also specific challenges that could limit the effectiveness of the tool (Table 2).

4. Challenges and limitations of EIBs: Lessons learned from the French and US experiments

4.1. *The difficult adoption of EIBs by the public entities*

Whether in France or in the United States, environmental impact bonds still struggle to be adopted by the public authorities. This is mainly because EIBs are still perceived as a complex and time-consuming instrument that has not yet proven to be an effective tool to counter issues such as climate change. Another barrier to the adoption of impact bonds could be the complexity of the contracting process that involves a multiplicity of stakeholders and can generate high transaction costs (Liang *et al.*, 2014; Lavenir, 2019; Cazenave, 2022) and even cancel the cost savings that were initially expected with the implementation of an environmental impact bond. Thus, it is possible that the EIBs' initial advantage of fiscal savings will disappear gradually during the contracting process (Hall, 2017).

4.2. *The complex link between impact measurement and saving costs*

Another barrier to the adoption of EIBs lies in the indirect link between impact measurement and saving costs. First, both SIBs and EIBs face the same traceability issue of avoided costs. Indeed, it is a very complex task to identify which public entity will benefit from the financial, social, or environmental impact created through an impact bond, and thus, which public entity will be responsible in case of repayment. This happens especially when several public entities are involved in the same impact bond, resulting in great complexity to allocate the correct level of impact and cost savings to the right beneficiary public entity. A telling example is in *Article 1* SIB tackling school dropouts in the French rural areas: for this intervention, public funds were spread between the Ministry of Agriculture and Food, the Ministry of Ecological Transition as well as the Ministry of Economy and Finance. The presence of three public payors as well as the difficulty of tracking the cost savings of the program (spread between dozens of public entities) amplified the complexity of the contracting process that ended up taking more than 18 months (Article 1, 2019). For EIBs, the case of Envie Autonomie also highlights this difficulty to assess which public entity will benefit from the cost savings: as the project operates within the socio-medical sector, one could wonder if the cost savings generated by the intervention do not also benefit the Ministry of Health, the Ministry of Social Affairs, or even the French social security fund, which are not involved in the repayment of the EIB.

For the specific case of EIBs, complexity can be increased tenfold by the fact that environmental public policies do not depend on one identified public entity and are fragmented at different levels of public governance. The case of France is quite emblematic as the EIB is launched by a national body, while wastewater treatment, waste collection and treatment, or air pollution control are actually part of cities' competencies, resulting in a multiplication of public entities operating at a local level that could potentially benefit from the EIB.

Compared to SIBs, EIBs face an additional complexity to identify. Specifically, the direct beneficiaries of the financed intervention, as environmental impact is diffuse and intangible. As SIBs specifically target specific populations, the impact of a reduction of carbon dioxide or waste emission has a universal character, especially when the intervention is taken care of at a national level such as in the French experiment. For example, it is easier to see concretely the social benefits of SIBs such as the Peterborough One Service SIB aimed at reducing recidivism among short-sentenced prisoners. The intervention allowed a 9% reduction of reoffending (Social Finance, 2017), which can translate easily into avoided costs related to incarceration for the UK Ministry of Justice.

In the case of EIBs, the relationship between an environmental intervention and the generation of cost savings is less evident. This difficulty in identifying beneficiaries has a direct consequence on the monetization of impacts: rather than inducing *avoided costs* for the public authority, EIBs tend to monetize *avoided negative externalities.* In that sense, the avoided costs are indirect and sometimes very difficult to justify. Evaluators use proxies based on international standards on environmental metrics (such as the cost of a ton of carbon dioxide, a ton of food waste management...) to translate the outcomes of the intervention into monetized avoided costs for the public entity, but this translation is sometimes quite vicarious. For example, the Envie Autonomie calculation method consists of assigning a carbon footprint (from the ADEME carbon base) to each material used for each medical device. Then, the cumulative carbon footprint of each medical device is translated into a cost saving linked to the number of tons of avoided carbon dioxide when choosing to reemploy a medical device instead of producing a new one.

Another issue that emerges is the question of saving costs related to environmental degradations that are not, in principle, borne by public entities. Indeed, in some EIB cases, the avoided negative externalities that are created through the intervention are not supposed to be taken care of by the public sector. For example, the intervention of Label Vie to reduce the environmental impact of daycare centers will create avoided negative externalities that are not directly linked to the prerogative of the state, as most of the daycare centers in France are private entities. Even if the avoided negative externalities are translated into cost savings, one could wonder whether those negative externalities were to be taken care of by the public sector in the first place. This difficulty to identify which stakeholder is responsible for the negative externality is quite common in the landscape of EIBs. It applies to many projects tackling, for example, the recycling of construction materials (is the state responsible for the waste generated by construction companies?) or even food waste management (should the externalities of private enterprises such as restaurants or bakeries be taken care of by the public sector?).

In that sense, EIBs become less financially interesting, especially for local authorities that do not benefit from direct cost savings by funding an intervention such as an EIB, and will prefer classic financing mechanisms such as subsidies.

4.3. *Too safe to fail? The tricky innovation–risk couple*

In France and in the USA, the current tendency is to design EIBs that are less and less financially risky compared to the prototypical model of worldwide impact bonds. This is due to the fact that, as identified by the literature, information asymmetry can appear between private and public stakeholders engaged in the contracting process (Maier *et al.*, 2018; Tse and Warner, 2020) and may favor the private investors and disadvantage the public agencies. This is especially true in France where EIBs operate within a small ecosystem of stakeholders that are systematically part of the negotiations.

Moreover, the French case highlights a tendency to mostly (but not only) fund less innovative programs and focus instead on the scaling of existing programs. This can be explained by the regulatory challenges that emerge with funding highly innovative problems, increasing the risk to extend or even jeopardize the contracting process leading to the operationalization of the project.

The complexity and time-consuming character of the contracting process can also harm the service provider, especially in France where the structures funded are usually NGOs, co-ops, or very recent social businesses that are neither financially mature nor capable of absorbing the costs related to the delay in the operationalization of the project (Lavenir, 2019; Cazenave, 2022).

4.4. *The contradictory definition of a "successful" EIB*

At the center of the difficulties encountered by EIBs lies the difficult question of defining a "successful" EIB, as this definition tends to change according to each one of the actors involved in the process. For the private investor, a successful EIB is the one that over-performs and brings a financial benefit. For the public entity, one could wonder whether the definition of a successful EIB is actually an EIB that fails (or at least does not over-perform), resulting in the creation of a limited (but existent) environmental impact and a limited (or even no) reimbursement to the private investors.

The question of "what happens next?" after the end of an EIB is also central to defining a successful EIB: the literature has identified innovation barriers that could potentially hinder the successful scaling of innovations funded by SIBs (Buffa *et al.*, 2022). The specifics of environmental innovations could make the scaling process even more complex (Le Pendeven and Leandri, 2021). The transformative power of EIBs into scalable public policies has yet to be proven. Otherwise, EIBs may result in very short-term solutions to environmental issues as payment is indexed on short-term outcomes. Therefore, EIBs create very little incentive to tackle the underlying source of the issue and create a long-term solution to an installed environmental challenge (Balboa, 2016). Private investors may be encouraged to perpetuate an environmental harm in order to benefit from both the financial and environmental outcomes of multiple EIBs.

5. Conclusion

Despite being a very recent addition to the set of financing mechanisms dedicated to environmental issues, we can already see the emergence of two EIB models, inspired by the two EIB experiments in France and the USA. Those models differ in their settings — such as their type of risk, financial structure, their post-implementation trajectories and scope — but face converging challenges explained by the newness of the instrument as well as its lack of adoption by the public sector, its ecosystemical functioning, and the complexity of its contracting. Those challenges tend to modify EIBs in practice, especially in terms of risk mitigation arrangements in order to attract more investors and contribute to the development of the tool.

However, affirming that EIBs will substitute traditional finance mechanisms funding environmental innovations to tackle climate change would be not only an overstatement, but also an inadequate way to look at the instrument: in essence, an EIB is an innovative instrument meant to fund a specific type of intervention that could potentially transform into an installed environmental public policy. In that sense, the massification of EIBs would lead to a loss of relevance of the tool.

The case of DC Water in the USA is very emblematic of the power of such an instrument to create a long-term environmental impact while aligning the interests of the private and the public sectors. However, the practice tends to further itself from this initial pilot project. In France, it is still too early to draw conclusions on the future of EIB use and impact. However, the French ADEME experiment has already highlighted some tendencies on what the French EIB model would look like, but also the challenges that it could encounter in terms of risk mitigation, robustness of the evaluation, and scaling capacity.

References

ADEME (2021). Lauréats du contrat à impact "économie circulaire". Press Release. https://presse.ademe.fr/wp-content/uploads/2021/03/731-DP-Laureats-Contrats-a-impact-.pdf. Accessed on 15 April 2022.

Arena, M., Bengo, I., Calderini, M., & Chiodo, V. (2016). Social impact bonds: Blockbuster or flash in a pan? *International Journal of Public Administration*, *39*(12), 927–939.

Article 1. (2019). Article 1 lance le premier contrat impact social: Les zones rurales au cœur de l'expérimentation. Press Release. https://article-1.eu/actualites/lassociation-article-1-lance-le-premier-contrat-impact social-les-zones-ruralesau-coeur-de-lexperimentation/#more-1775. Accessed on 15 April 2022.

Balboa, C. (2016). Accountability of environmental impact bonds: The future of global environmental governance? *Global Environmental Politics*, *16*(2), 33–41.

Brand, M. W., Quesnel, K., Saksa, P., Ulibarri, N., Bomblies, A., Mandle, L., & Gibbons, J. P. (2021). Environmental Impact Bonds: A common framework and looking ahead. *Environmental Research: Infrastructure and Sustainability*, *1*(2), 023001.

Brookings Institute (2022). Brookings Institution Global Impact Bond Database. https://www.brookings.edu/wp-content/uploads/2019/01/Impact-Bonds-Snapshot_Apr-2022.pdf (Accessed on 15 April 2022).

Buchner, B., Herve-Mignucci, M., Trabacchi, C., Wilkinson, J., Stadelmann, M., Boyd, R., ...& Micale, V. (2014). Global landscape of climate finance 2015. *Climate Policy Initiative*, 32, 1–38.

Buffa, V. & Le Pendeven, B. (2022). Social Impact Bonds: A Systematic Literature Review of an Emerging Approach to Social Innovation Financing. Working Paper.

Buffa, V., Tira, M., & Pendeven, B. L. (2023). New development: From social impact bonds to impact bonds — an outcomes-based framework. *Public Money & Management*, 1–5.

Cazenave, T. (2022). Propositions pour le développement des contrats à impact en France. Policy Report. https://www.vie-publique.fr/sites/default/files/rapport/pdf/284266.pdf. Accessed on 15 April 2022.

Climate Policy Initiative (2021). Global Landscape of Climate Finance 2021.

DC Water (2021). Water's pioneering Environmental Impact Bond a success. Press Release. https://dcwater.com/sites/default/files/finance/eib-national-pressrelease.pdf. Accessed on 15 April 2022.

Del Giudice, A. & Migliavacca, M. (2019). Social impact bonds and institutional investors: An empirical analysis of a complicated relationship. *Nonprofit and Voluntary Sector Quarterly*, *48*(1), 50–70.

Dey, C. & Gibbon, J. (2018). New development: Private finance over public good? Questioning the value of impact bonds. *Public Money & Management*, *38*(5), 375–378.

Hall, D. (2017). Greening the future: A case for Environmental Impact Bonds. *Policy Quarterly*, *13*(2), 41–48.

Hamrick, K. (2016). State of private investment in conservation 2016: A landscape assessment of an emerging market. Forest Trends.

IPCC (2022). Climate Change 2022: Impacts, Adaptation and Vulnerability. Contribution of Working Group II to the Sixth Assessment Report of the Intergovernmental Panel on Climate Change [H.-O. Pörtner, D.C. Roberts, M. Tignor, E.S. Poloczanska, K. Mintenbeck, A. Alegría, M. Craig, S. Langsdorf, S. Löschke, V. Möller,

A. Okem, B. Rama (eds.)]. Cambridge University Press. Cambridge University Press, Cambridge, UK and New York, NY, USA, 3056 p., doi:10.1017/9781009325844.

Lavenir, F. (2019). Pour un développement du contrat à impact social au service des politiques publiques. Policy Report. https://www.tresor.economie.gouv.fr/Institutionnel/Niveau3/Pages/aea2b118-0d4e-4fd0-8f4e-8c73a1028e01/files/3bc5dab2-6d4d-48f4-bc70-332b20eb0d4e. Accessed on 15 April 2022.

Le Pendeven, B. & Leandri, N. (2021). Et la France inventa les contrats à impact écologique. Le Courrier Financier. https://www.lecourrierfinancier.fr/responsabilite-sociale/opinion/exclusif-et-la-france-inventa-les-contrats-a-impact-ecologique-66763. Accessed on 15 April 2022.

Le Pendeven, B., Nico, Y., & Gachet, B. (2015). Social impact bonds: un nouvel outil pour le financement de l'innovation sociale. Note de l'Institut de l'entreprise.

Liang, M., Mansberger, B., & Spieler, A. C. (2014). An overview of social impact bonds. *Journal of International Business & Law*, *13*, 267.

Maier, F., Barbetta, G. P., & Godina, F. (2018). Paradoxes of social impact bonds. *Social Policy & Administration*, *52*(7), 1332–1353.

Quantified Ventures (2021). Environmental Impact Bonds: Overview + Case Studies. LGAC Quarterly Meeting, Chesapeake Executive Council.

Social Finance (2017). World's 1st social impact bond shown to cut reoffending and to make impact investors a return. Press Release. https://www.socialfinance.org.uk/sites/default/files/news/final-press-release-pb-july-2017.pdf. Accessed on 15 April 2022.

Tse, A. E. & Warner, M. E. (2020). The razor's edge: Social impact bonds and the financialization of early childhood services. *Journal of Urban Affairs*, *42*(6), 816–832.

Yonavjak, L. (2016). Environmental impact bonds pay for performance. Yale Center for Business and the Environment. https://cbey.yale.edu/our-stories/environmental-impact-bonds-pay-for-performance. Accessed on 15 April 2022.

Part II
Green Banking and Financing

© 2024 World Scientific Publishing Europe Ltd.
https://doi.org/10.1142/9781800614451_0006

Chapter 6

Green Mortgages and Green Mortgage-Backed Securities

K. Thomas Liaw
Tobin College of Business, St. John's University, New York, NY, USA
liawk@stjohns.edu

Abstract

Energy-efficient mortgages (EEMs) provide incentives for homeowners to reduce carbon footprints to fight climate change. The chapter surveys recent developments in EEMs (also called green mortgages) and green mortgage-backed securities. The chapter examines the association between green mortgages and default risks and property prices. In addition, the chapter discusses the supply of private capital through securitization of green mortgages to modernize houses to reduce energy consumption. For borrowers, the benefits include savings in energy costs, a lower mortgage rate, a larger loan amount, and a higher house value. For banks, the key factor is about risk reduction. We discuss the benefits of such a green movement in the housing sector and document the evidence that green mortgages reduce credit risk for lenders. We also discuss measures by governments, bank regulators, mortgage lenders, homeowners, and investors to move toward the green transitioning of the housing sector.

1. Introduction and literature review

The housing sector accounts for a significant portion of total energy consumption. The Federal National Mortgage Association (Fannie Mae, 2021) states that in the United States, residential buildings account for roughly 20% of greenhouse gas emissions. In the United Kingdom, homes are responsible for one-quarter of carbon emissions (Intermediary Mortgage Lenders Association, 2020). Billio *et al.* (2021) cite a source from the European Parliament and Council that buildings consume 40% of energy in the European Union. To avoid the adverse consequences of climate change, reducing energy use and transitioning to clean energy are essential to achieving net zero by 2050. Improving the energy efficiency of dwelling properties is an important step in this direction.

1.1. *Introduction and purposes*

Energy-efficient mortgages (EEMs) contribute toward a low-carbon economy. An EEM, also called a green mortgage, is a sustainable credit product that offers the mortgage borrower favorable terms to finance a new energy-efficient home or energy-efficient improvements. Under a green mortgage, the mortgage lender offers the homeowner either a lower mortgage rate or a larger loan amount if the property meets certain environmental standards or the borrower commits to renovating the existing building to improve its energy efficiency. An energy-efficient home lowers utility bills and makes more income available for mortgage payments. As such, the bank or mortgage lender benefits from a potential lower default. Therefore, an EEM presents benefits to both borrower and lender to help finance greener homes. The private market force will unlock capital to support the environment and to meet the goals of the Paris Agreement.

In the United States, the Department of Housing and Urban Development (HUD) initiated a pilot program for EEMs in five states in 1992. HUD expanded the program nationwide in 1995. Federal agencies and local governments have introduced programs to fund or provide incentives for EEMs. In Europe, many countries have also promoted such green mortgages in recent years. The EEMs Action Plan (EeMAP) aims at establishing a market solution to boost private investments in EEMs.

EEMs can be securitized to issue green mortgage-backed securities (green MBS). The green MBS market is a recent development. Federal National Mortgage Association (Fannie Mae) started multifamily green MBS in 2012 and expanded to single-family green MBS in 2020. By 2021, Fannie Mae had issued a total of $100 billion green MBS. The Federal Home Mortgage Corporation (Freddie Mac) is also promoting the EEMs, in financing green mortgages and issuance of green bonds. In Europe, Sinopel 2019 B.V. is among the first green MBS (DBRS, 2019). As the market for EEMs expands, the issuance of green MBS will grow. As the market continues to develop toward more sustainable green finance, green MBS will become a significant segment of the overall green bond market.

The chapter surveys the literature and discusses the impacts of EEMs on mortgage risks and home prices. The findings are conclusive in that EEMs are associated with lower mortgage default risks and higher home prices. In addition, the chapter extends studies of green mortgages to green MBS. The securitization of green mortgages has started and has the potential to grow to a significant segment of the green bond market. As many investors include environmental factors in the investment policy, the supply of funds to the green bond market and thus also to green MBS will continue to increase. To support investor asset allocation to green finance, we stress a new investment analysis to include time and preferences for sustainability (Gambera, Primmer, and Finney, 2021) and show that the support for the environment is consistent with the objectives of a corporation (Business Roundtable, 2019). Furthermore, we discuss actions that homeowners, banks, governments, bank regulators, and investors can take to grow EEMs.

1.2. *Literature review*

The market for EEMs is still young. The literature has focused on the default risks and property prices. Kaza, Quercia, and Tian (2013) examine whether home energy efficiency lowers mortgage default risks. The findings indicate that energy efficiency reduces default and prepayment risks. Kaza, Quercia, and Tian (2015) focus on the Northeast of the United States and the results are similar, that energy-efficient houses have lower defaults and prepayments. Argento, Bak, and Brown (2019) compare default rates and sale prices between energy-efficiency-rated and -unrated homes. The empirical results evidence a lower default rate for loans in high debt-to-income buckets of the rated homes. In addition, the results show property value on average is 2.7% higher with energy efficiency rating.

In other parts of the globe, Richardson and Drinkwater (2017) review energy use in the European Union (EU) and discuss the impact of energy efficiency on mortgage default rate. They conclude that a lower probability of default is associated with energy-efficient homes and energy efficiency has positive impacts on a building's cash flows and valuations. Eves and Kippes (2010) examine buyer awareness and acceptance of energy efficiency of residential property in New Zealand. The awareness of energy efficiency is growing in the residential property market, but it is only a major consideration for young and older buyers in the high-income brackets. Guin and Korhonen (2020) investigate residential mortgages in the United Kingdom. Their analyses reach a similar conclusion that green mortgages are less frequently in payment arrears. Billio *et al.* (2021) find that energy efficiency decreases mortgage default risk in the Dutch market.

In addition to mortgage risks, other studies examine energy efficiency and property sale prices. For example, Argento, Bak, and Brown (2019) use a US national sample and show property value on average is 2.7% higher with energy efficiency rating. Bruegge, Carrión-Flores, and Pope (2016) research single-family property sales in Gainesville, Florida. They find that homeowners are willing to pay a premium for new energy-efficient houses, though such a premium declines in the resale market. Walls *et al.* (2017) study energy efficiency and home prices in three US metropolitan areas. The findings are that green buildings are associated with higher sales prices. Kahn and Kok (2014) examine the impact of energy efficiency or green features on the value of single-family dwellings. The results show that green labels increase transaction prices. Additionally, the results suggest that a green label adds more value in hotter climates. Ankamah-Yeboah and Rehdanz (2014) perform meta-analysis on 30 primary studies. The results indicate the global average of estimated premia for energy efficiency certification is 7.6%. Furthermore, the estimates indicate higher valuation premium in Europe, followed by the US, with the lowest in Australia. Shimizu (2013) examines the new condominium market in Tokyo. The green labels command a positive premium both in asking prices and in transaction prices. Onishi, Deng, and Shimizu (2021) estimate the green premium in Tokyo office market. Green labels show a significant positive effect of 6.5% on new contract rents. The results also indicate the premium varies by market segment. Zhang, Liu, and Wu (2016) investigate official green labels on the price premium in the residential sector in China. The green-labeled new houses have a price premium of 6.9%, compared to the non-labeled counterparts.

In policy area to support EEMs, Esposito *et al.* (2022) emphasize the key role of the financial system to provide funding for the green transition. They propose a method of environmental risk-weighted assets for banks to calculate capital requirements. Their analysis of the Italian banking system shows the proposed method would provide an effective incentive for banks to fund the green transition in the construction sector. To promote the development of the green mortgage market, the Intermediary Mortgage Lenders Association (2020) surveys the market of EEMs in the United Kingdom, identifies barriers to success, and outlines several measures for future growth of green mortgages. The Green Finance Institute (2021) launched Green Home Finance Principles, which provide a transparent methodology for allocating finance for retrofitting UK homes.

In green MBS, Devine and McCollum (2021) provide evidence that EEM-backed green bonds have lower mortgage rates, lower debt service ratios, and higher leverage ratios than their "brown" counterparts. An and Pivo (2018) also show green buildings in their data on commercial mortgage-backed securities carry a lower default rate. Akinlusi (2021) examines the sustainable MBS market in Canada and discusses ways that the sustainable MBS market can become a relevant source for retrofitting financing.

Green MBS are part of the fast-growing green bond market. Liaw (2020) provides a survey of green bond pricing in the primary markets and documents evidence of many issues with green premium while some without. In addition, the investment performance in the secondary markets is also discussed. Cortellini and Panetta (2021) provide a systematic review of the green bond literature and discuss the role of investments in sustainability in reshaping the financial markets.

1.3. *Organization of the chapter*

The chapter is organized as follows. Section 1 covers the introduction and literature review. Section 2 discusses green mortgages, default rates, and price premium. Section 3 examines securitization of green mortgages. Section 4 focuses on the issuance of green MBS.

Section 5 concludes the chapter and discusses measures to grow the EEM market.

2. Green mortgages, default risks, and property prices

EEMs offer favorable terms for home buyers and owners to go green and save energy costs. The loans are for two purposes. One is to purchase or build an energy-efficient home in which the lender takes into consideration energy savings when determining the amount of the loan. Second, there is also an energy-improvement mortgage to pay for improvements on the existing home. The lender can increase the loan amount to an existing mortgage to pay for the upgrade.

EEMs save energy costs. Thus, homeowners have more money available for mortgage payments. The literature has provided evidence that those savings lead to lower mortgage risks. EEMs also have a positive effect on the property sale prices. The following documents result from many studies of lower mortgage risks and premia in home prices.

2.1. *Energy-efficient mortgages and default*

Kaza, Quercia, and Tian (2013) compare the risks of mortgage default on Energy Star homes for which a Home Energy Rating System (HERS) Index Score is available. The data sample includes 71,000 loans and covers single-family owner-occupied houses with loan origination from January 2002 and for purchases in the United States. The multinormal logit model is used to estimate the risks of prepayment and default. The results show that Energy Star certification is associated with lower default and prepayment risks. More energy efficiency, measured by a point decrease in the HERS score, reduces default by 4% and prepayment by 2%. Similar research, by Kaza, Quercia, and Tian (2015), focuses on the Northeast of the United States. The default probability for Energy Star homes is lower, but the prepayment probability is higher. The results are based on a smaller sample of about 1,700 mortgages.

Argento, Bak, and Brown (2019) compare default rates and sale prices between energy-efficiency-rated and -unrated homes.

The analysis is based on a national random sample of 70,000 homes rated by Residential Energy Services Network and 6,500 homes by Department of Energy between 2013 and 2017. The authors apply propensity score matching techniques to select unrated homes for comparisons. To examine the impact of energy efficiency on loan performance, a logistic regression is performed. For the impact on sale prices, the hedonic model is utilized. They find a lower default rate is associated with loans in the high debt-to-income bucket of the rated homes, but not for all rated homes. In addition, the results show property value on average is 2.7% higher with energy efficiency rating and better efficiency leads to higher sale prices.

Several studies provide evidence with data from other countries. Richardson and Drinkwater (2017) review energy use in the European Union (EU) and document the impact of energy efficiency on mortgage default risk from previous works. In addition, the report summarizes the impacts of energy efficiency on rents, sale prices, and investor risk premia. They conclude that a lower probability of default is associated with energy-efficient homes and energy efficiency has positive impacts on a building's cash flows and valuations. The report also promotes reduced capital charges for banks as EEMs increase loss mitigation capacity, enhance loan-to-value, and lower probability of default.

Guin and Korhonen (2020) use logistic regressions based on data of more than 1.8 million outstanding residential mortgages in the United Kingdom at yearend 2017 to investigate the association of energy efficiency and mortgage default risks. The data show that the default rate is 0.93% for energy-efficient properties, which is 0.21% lower than for energy-inefficient houses. The results from logistic regressions, controlling for other relevant explanatory variables, show that green mortgages are less frequently in payment arrears.

Billio *et al.* (2021) investigate the correlation between energy efficiency and the probability of default in the Dutch residential mortgage market. The sample, covering the period January 2014 to May 2018, includes mortgages on more than 120,000 dwellings and data on energy efficiency ratings. The empirical findings through logit regressions and the extended Cox model show energy efficiency decreases mortgage default. The results hold after accounting for other control variables. In addition, the empirical results indicate such a negative relationship is stronger for lower-income borrowers.

2.2. *Energy-efficient home and sale prices*

In addition to the lower mortgage default risks, energy-efficient homes also contribute to higher property sale prices. Bruegge, Carrión-Flores, and Pope (2016) employ the hedonic method to study single-family property sales in Gainesville, Florida. The dataset covers 6,000 sale observations of single-family residential houses between 1997 and 2009. The empirical findings are that homeowners are willing to pay a premium for new energy-efficient houses, but such premium declines in the resale market.

Walls *et al.* (2017) study energy efficiency and home prices in three US metropolitan areas (Austin, Texas; Portland, Oregon; and Research Triangle Area, North Carolina). The energy efficiency characteristics are represented by Energy Star and two local green certifications. The data sample covers 170,000 sale transactions for single-family homes during the 2005–2011 period. The analytical methods include spatial matching, propensity score matching, and hedonic regressions. They find green buildings have higher sales prices. The results indicate Energy Star certification increases sale prices of about 2% in Portland and the Triangle areas. The local green certifications have larger impact on sale prices than Energy Star in Austin (8–9%) and Portland (4%).

In the California market, Kahn and Kok (2014) examine the impact of energy efficiency or green features on the value of single-family dwellings. The sample includes 4,231 green-certified buildings and 1.6 million non-certified homes. They use the hedonic approach to analyze transaction prices. The empirical results indicate the green labels increase transaction prices by 2–4%. Additionally, the results suggest that a green label adds more value in hotter climates.

Ankamah-Yeboah and Rehdanz (2014) perform meta-analysis on 30 primary studies with 205 feasible observations. The results from the meta regressions indicate the global average of estimated premia is 7.6%. The estimates show the percentage of total variance in reported premia in primary studies that can be attributed to differences between studies is about 50%. Furthermore, the estimates show higher valuation premium in Europe, followed by the United States, with the lowest in Australia.

Shimizu (2013) employs the hedonic method to examine the new condominium market in Tokyo. The data include 82,270 asking and transaction samples during the 2005 to 2010 period. The green labels command a premium of 5.8% in asking prices and 4.7% in transaction prices. Assessing the office rental market in Tokyo, Onishi, Deng, and Shimizu (2021) employ the hedonic approach to analyze the data on Tokyo office rents from 2009 to 2019. The results show a significant positive effect of 6.5% on new contract rents. The results also show the premium varies by market segments, approximately 5.4% for medium-sized old buildings and 2.6% for large-sized new buildings.

Zhang, Liu, and Wu (2016) investigate Chinese Green Building Labels on the price premium in the residential sector in China. The dataset consists of 748 new housing projects in May 2013. Among them, 163 are official green-labeled projects and 585 are non-labeled (the control group). The results of the hedonic regressions show that green-labeled new houses have a price premium of 6.9%, compared to the non-labeled counterparts. The chapter also concludes that the official green label is a more reliable signal of greenness than a developer's self-advertised green housing in urban areas.

Table 1 provides a summary of those studies. As Table 1 shows, those research reports are based on hedonic approach, matching method, and meta-analysis. They cover different geographic regions and different samples. The presented evidence concludes that EEMs are associated with lower mortgage default risks and higher housing prices.

3. Securitization of green mortgages

Securitization of EEMs enables lenders to sell off green mortgages to free up capacity for more EEM originations. The securitization allows the lender to obtain funding quickly to make more loans. Under a green mortgage securitization, green MBS are secured by energy-efficient homes. They are created when a number of these EEMs are pooled together. That pool is then sold to Fannie Mae or Freddie Mac for use as the collateral for the new green MBS. Those green MBS are sold to investors who receive a return from the cash flows of the underlying EEMs. By aggregating the funding into a common structure, such securitization enables global institutional investors to finance individual houses. Green MBS allow investors to

Table 1. Summary of select publications on EEMs, default risks, and sale prices.

Publication	Data coverage	Impacts on mortgage default risks
Kaza, Quercia, and Tian (2013)	United States	Lower
Kaza, Quercia, and Tian (2015)	United States	Lower
Argento, Bak, and Brown (2019)	United States	Lower (for loans in high debt-to-income bracket)
Richardson and Drinkwater (2017)	European Union	Lower
Guin and Korhonen (2020)	United Kingdom	Lower
Billio *et al.* (2021)	The Netherlands	Lower
Publication	**Data coverage**	**Impacts on sale prices**
Argento, Bak, and Brown (2019)	United States	Higher
Bruegge, Carrión-Flores, and Pope (2016)	United States	Higher
Walls *et al.* (2017)	United States	Higher
Kahn and Kok (2014)	United States	Higher
Ankamah-Yeboah and Rehdanz (2014)	Global	Higher
Richardson and Drinkwater (2017)	European Union	Higher
Shimizu (2013)	Japan	Higher
Onishi, Deng, and Shimizu (2021)	Japan	Higher
Zhang, Liu, and Wu (2016)	China	Higher

gain exposure to the risks and rewards of the green and MBS markets. The supply of funds to support green finance is growing fast, as many institutional investors allocate a portion of their investments to support the low-carbon climate. The strong demand for green investments leads to some observations of green premium in the green bond market.

Different from conventional fixed-income bonds, the green MBS' (and all MBS in general) investors receive income monthly, as homeowners make mortgage payments every month. Another unique feature of green MBS is that investors' monthly income includes both interest and principal. The cash flow at the beginning is mostly from interest, and gradually more of the monthly proceeds come from principal. As such, there is no lump-sum par value when green MBS mature.

The market for green MBS is still young and has the potential to grow. It is a small segment in the overall MBS market. Fannie Mae is probably the biggest issuer of green MBS. The issuance of multifamily green MBS reached $100 billion in December 2021. Fannie Mae also launched green MBS backed by newly constructed single-family residential homes. By December 2021, Fannie Mae issued more than $600 million of green MBS backed by such single-family loans. The increasing awareness and willingness to support the environment will increase the demand for and supply of energy-efficient homes. The market for EEMs will grow and the green MBS market will increasingly gain shares in the overall MBS market.

4. Issuances of green mortgage-backed securities

In recent years, environmental issues have been rising up the political agenda as people recognize the urgency to take actions to achieve sustainability. Many governments are taking actions to reduce carbon emissions to fight the climate crisis. Green MBS are a capital market approach to provide funding to housing stock to support the environment.

In the United States, Fannie Mae is leading the industry in green MBS. Fannie Mae offers two multifamily green mortgage loan programs: Green Rewards and Green Building Certification. The Green Rewards offer incentives for borrowers to make energy efficiency improvements and the Green Building Certification is for properties with eligible green certification. Fannie Mae securitizes these loans and issues them to the market as green MBS. Fannie Mae also re-securitizes a portion of green MBS as Real Estate Mortgage Investment Conduits (REMICs). Those issues received a second opinion from CICERO and bond rating by Oekom.

Fannie Mae multifamily programs started in 2012 and the total issuance reached $100 billion by 2021. Table 2 lists the annual volume for each program and the total from 2012 to 2021. Green MBS are backed by Green Building Certification launched in 2012. The total volume reached $21.5 billion by 2021. The Green Rewards were launched several years later in 2016, with annual issuance averages of $12.88 billion during 2016–2021. The green MBS' issuances indicate more homeowners borrowed for reductions of energy use or for generation of renewable energy during the period. With the success of the multifamily programs, Fannie Mae launched single-family green MBS in 2020.

Freddie Mac developed the multifamily Green Advantage program in 2016 and single-family green MBS program in April 2021. The Green Advantage program provides financing incentives for borrowers to reduce energy and water consumption and requires borrowers to monitor and report on energy and water consumption over time. Under the single-family program, those MBS are backed by the GreenCHOICE Mortgage program. The eligible collateral includes homes with renewable energy and homes with energy efficiency rating. Eligible renewable energy sources include solar and geothermal. For homes with energy efficiency rating, the newly constructed homes

Table 2. Fannie Mae multifamily green MBS issuance ($ millions).

Year	Green rewards	Green building certification	Retired green programs	Total
2012		32.6	23.1	55.7
2013		40.8	17.4	58.2
2014			20.4	20.4
2015		111.4		111.4
2016	1,449.4	2,170.4	4.4	3,624.2
2017	19,901.6	6,463.3	1,391.2	27,756.1
2018	18,855.8	498.9	813.6	20,168.3
2019	22,153.3	626.6		22,779.9
2020	9,568.5	3,430.8		13,467.0
2021	5,334.2	3,430.7		13,467.0
Total	77,268.1	21,507.5	2,270.1	101,040.4

Note: Fannie Mae has two multifamily programs: Green Rewards and Green Building Certification.

Source: Fannie Mae.

must meet an HERS index score of 60 or less. By July 2021, Freddie Mac provided $64.3 billion in loans and issued $4.08 billion green bonds (Freddie Mac, 2021).

Green MBS contribute to improving energy efficiency in the housing sector. Fannie Mae (2021) report that, from 2012 to 2020, the annual environmental benefits are 9.5 billion kilo British Thermal Units (BTU) of source energy saved, 8.5 billion gallons of water saved, and 634,000 metric tons carbon dioxide equivalent of greenhouse gas emissions prevented. In energy bills, multifamily tenants save $184 per year per family and single-family homeowners save an estimated $843 a year. Freddie Mac (2020) states the environmental impact of its green bond issuance includes savings of 370 million gallons of water and 264 million kilo BTU of energy and a reduction of greenhouse gas emissions of 21,400 metric tons per year. As the green MBS market expands, the contributions to energy savings and emission reductions will increase.

5. Conclusion

The market for EEMs is still underserved with opportunity for growth. The environmental benefits include reductions in water and energy consumption and in emissions. Homeowners save on utility bills and enjoy increased home comfort. Mortgage lenders face lower default risks in EEMs. In terms of supply of funds to the green MBS sector, momentum is increasing in green investing as countries and companies pledge to decarbonize to address concerns over rising global temperatures and to reduce emissions in compliance with the Paris Agreement. Green MBS offer investors exposure to the green theme and the MBS asset class simultaneously.

The success of this market requires participation from all parties involved. Homeowner awareness is key to success of the market. For more homeowners to take advantage of the benefits that EEMs offer, it is helpful for governments and lenders to implement effective marketing campaigns. Some of such efforts could be as simple as television advertisements, flyers, postings, and telephone calls from bankers or mortgage brokers to bring such benefits to homeowners' attention. Homeowners are likely to take advantage of EEMs when they are aware of the contribution to environmental performance and the savings pay for the improvements.

For banks and mortgage lenders, the literature has presented evidence that EEMs lower default risks. The next logical step is to incorporate such risk reduction in mortgage underwriting. A lower mortgage rate or a larger loan amount is justified and is a prudent business practice. As the demand for EEMs increases, banks are likely to allocate additional resources and personnel to support this sustainable credit product. This will certainly contribute to the continued growth of the market.

Governments have to lead the market with policies to support EEMs, to increase homeowner awareness, and provide incentives for banks to expand this line of business. Financial incentives are essential. Many governments provide incentives for energy efficiency improvements. In the United States, Fannie Mae and Freddie Mac, for example, have established programs to fund EEMs. They also provide resources for training and tools for banks to expand and grow businesses on green mortgages. Furthermore, their securitization programs via green MBS provide a mechanism for global investors to contribute toward their environmental and social commitments. Another important step is to reduce the capital charge for EEMs. For example, Esposito *et al.* (2022) propose a method of environmental risk-weighted assets for banks to calculate capital requirements. Similarly, Richardson and Drinkwater (2017) promote reduced capital charges for banks as EEMs increase loss mitigation capacity, enhance loan-to-value, and lower probability of default. Implementation of such revised capital requirements would provide an effective incentive for banks to fund the green transition in the housing sector.

Investors play an essential role in the continued success of the market as well. There has been growing awareness about risks related to climate change. Many investors include energy and climate criteria in investment policies related to their environmental, social, and governance (ESG) goals. As such, the investment evaluation today goes beyond the traditional risk–return analysis. As proposed by Gambera, Primmer, and Finney (2021), investment decisions related to ESG take into consideration two additional factors: time and preferences. The time element relates to the duration of the ESG transition to reduce pollution in line with principles of the Paris Agreement and to fulfill sustainable goals for social responsibility and governance. The preferences element relates to the weight an investor places on sustainability in asset allocation. Investing in green MBS helps gain exposure to the green theme and is consistent with corporate social responsibility. Furthermore, investment allocation to green MBS meets the corporate objectives specified in the revised purpose of a corporation (Business Roundtable, 2019).

In summary, EEMs are a capital market solution contributing toward a low-carbon economy. Governments, investors, banks, and homeowners all recognize the benefits EEMs offer. The markets for EEMs and green MBS have started to grow. The success benefits all stakeholders and requires governments to initiate supporting policies, bank regulators to modify rules of capital requirements, banks to improve mortgage underwriting processes, homeowners to take actions to take advantage of the favorable mortgage terms, and investors to manage portfolios to meet their ESG goals.

References

Akinlusi, H. (2021). Sustainable mortgage-backed securities and retrofit financing. Industry White Chapter, Vancouver Economic Commission, Canada.

An, X. & Pivo, G. (2020). Green buildings in commercial mortgage-backed securities: The effects of Leed and energy star certification on default risk and loan terms. *Real Estate Economics*, *48*(1), 7–42.

Ankamah-Yeboah, I. & Rehdanz, K. (2014). Explaining the variation in the value of building energy efficiency certificates: A quantitative meta-analysis. Tech. Rep 1949, Kiel Working Chapter, Kiel.

Argento, R., Bak, X. F., & Brown, L. M. (2019). Energy efficiency: Value added to properties & loan performance. Freddie Mac, USA.

Billio, M., Costola, M., Pelizzon, L., & Riedel, M. (2021). Buildings' energy efficiency and the probability of mortgage default: The Dutch case. *Journal of Real Estate Finance & Economics*. https://doi.org/10.1007/s11146-021-09838-0. Accessed on 15 December 2021.

Bruegge, B., Carrión-Flores, C., & Pope, J. C. (2016). Does the housing market value energy efficient homes? Evidence from the energy star program. *Regional Science and Urban Economics*, *57*, 63–76.

Business Roundtable (2019). Statement on the purpose of a corporation. Washington, DC.

Cortellini, G. & Panetta, I. C. (2021). Green bond: A systematic literature review for future research agendas. *Journal of Risk and Financial Management*, *14*, 589. https://doi.org/10.3390/jrfm14120589.

DBRS (2019). Rating report: Sinopel 2019 B.V. DBRS Ratings Limited.

Devine, A. & McCollum, M. (2021). Advancing energy efficiency through green mortgage-backed securities. Working Chapter, York University and University of Tulsa.

Esposito, L., Mastromatteo, G., Molocchi, A., Brambilla, P. C., Carvalho, M. L., Girardi, P., Marmiroli, B., & Mela, G. (2022). Green mortgages, EU taxonomy and environment risk weigthed assets: A key link for the transition. *Sustainability, 14*, 1633. https://doi.org/10.3390/su14031633.

Eves, C. & Kippes, S. (2010). Public awareness of "green" and "energy efficient" residential property: An empirical survey based on data from New Zealand. *Property Management, 28*(3), 193–208. https://doi.org/10.1108/02637471011051327. Accessed on 18 November 2021.

Fannie Mae (2021). 2020 green bond impact report. Fannie Mae, USA.

Freddie Mac (2020). Impact bonds report. Freddie Mac, USA.

Freddie Mac (2021). Green bonds framework. Freddie Mac, USA.

Gambera, M., Primmer, R., & Finney, L. (2021). Asset allocation for an ESG world. UBS.

Green Finance Institute (2021). The way ahead for the UK's green mortgage market. Green Finance Institute, UK.

Guin, B. & Korhonen, P. (2020). Does energy efficiency predict mortgage performance? Bank of England, Staff Working Chapter No. 852.

Intermediary Mortgage Lenders Association (2020). Green mortgages. Intermediary Mortgage Lenders Association, London, United Kingdom.

Kahn, M. E. & Kok, N. (2014). The capitalization of green labels in the California housing market. *Regional Science and Urban Economics, 47*, 25–34.

Kaza, N., Quercia, R. G., & Tian, C. Y. (2013). Home energy efficiency and mortgage risks. Working Chapter, UNC Center for Community Capital, Institute for Market Transformation.

Kaza, N., Quercia, R. G., & Tian, C. Y. (2015). Energy efficiency and mortgage risks: Implications for the Northeast. Communities & Banking, Federal Reserve Bank of Boston, 22–23.

Liaw, K. T. (2020). Survey of green bond pricing and investment performance. *Journal of Risk and Financial Management, 13*(9), 193. https://doi.org/10.3390/jrfm13090193.

Onishi, J., Deng, Y., & Shimizu, C. (2021). Green premium in the Tokyo office rent market. *Sustainability, 13*, 12227. https://doi.org/10.3390/su132112227.

Richardson, S. & Drinkwater, J. (2017). Creating an EEM for Europe. Technical Report, World Green Building Council, UK.

Shimizu, C. (2013). Sustainable measures and economic value in green housing. *Open House International*, *38*, 57–63.

Walls, M., Gerarden, T., Palmer, K., & Bak, X. F. (2017). Is energy efficiency capitalized into home prices? Evidence from three U.S. cities. *Journal of Environmental Economics and Management*, *82*(C), 104–124.

Zhang, L., Liu, H., & Wu, J. (2016). The price premium for green-labelled housing: Evidence from China. *Urban Studies*. https://doi.org/10.1177/0042098016668288.

© 2024 World Scientific Publishing Europe Ltd.
https://doi.org/10.1142/9781800614451_0007

Chapter 7

Why and How to Build a World Climate Bank?

Silvio Andrae
Senior Advisor and Author, Germany
andrae@zedat.fu-berlin.de

Abstract
Climate finance mechanisms to ensure a green transition are a policy objective of the first order. Establishing a World Climate Bank (WCB) can make a significant contribution. The mandate of the WCB would be to primarily assist developing and emerging countries in transforming their economies due to climate change. Existing institutions such as the World Bank cannot provide sufficient climate change financing. Creating a new international organization (IO) can provide this confidence. The chapter justifies the need for such an institution at the macro, meso, and micro levels without overlooking the risks of institutional proliferation. The chapter concludes with policy recommendations related to establishing the new IO.

1. Introduction

Climate finance to mitigate climate change must increase three- to six-fold by 2030 to limit warming to below 2 degrees Celsius. The annual public and private funding for climate mitigation and adaptation increased by 60% between 2013 and 2020 (IPCC, 2022). However, these increases have slowed recently. This misalignment of global capital has resulted in a significant gap between current levels of climate finance and the resources needed to mitigate climate change. This gap exists across all regions and all sectors. By 2030, an estimated US$95 trillion in global investment in infrastructure (energy, transport, water, telecommunications) will be needed to address climate change. Developing countries account for about 65% of this. Recent investments in climate change mitigation, for example, need to increase by at least five times in Southeast Asia and developing countries in the Pacific, seven times in Africa, and 12 times in the Middle East by 2030 to limit warming to below 2 degrees Celsius. Across all sectors, this shortfall is most pronounced in agriculture, forestry, and other land use sectors, where current financial flows are 10 to 29 times below what is needed to meet the Paris Climate Agreement targets (IPCC, 2022).

Various measures are being discussed to achieve the goals of climate financing. Among other things, the aim is often to attract private funding. Even though the overall volume of private finance to address climate change is slowly increasing, there remains a significant investment gap. The international community and governments are expected to increase climate change subsidies, price carbon emissions, phase out public financing of fossil fuels, or adopt strong regulations mandating a low-carbon transition. All of these can help provide the certainty that the private sector needs to increase investment in climate action. Innovative financing mechanisms that allow governments to share risk with private companies can also go a long way toward mobilizing private sector finance.

The United Nations Climate Change Conference in Glasgow (COP26) has made it clear that the pledges and policy measures taken so far are insufficient. The many vulnerable countries remain dissatisfied with the progress of negotiations on climate change adaptation measures and criticize the lack of financial commitments. Developed countries first announced at COP15 in Copenhagen that they would provide US$100 billion annually from public and private sources to support developing countries. "Countries seeking support face numerous hurdles to accessing funding from a tangle of institutions charged with governing and delivering climate finance" (Pickering *et al.*, 2017, p. 2). States acted in more than 60 institutions to address climate change until the adoption of the Paris Climate Agreement in 2015 (Rowan, 2021).

This situation raises the question of whether existing institutions can finance vast amounts of investment. There are 537 development finance institutions (DFIs) today, including 40 multilateral, 441 bilateral and national, and 56 subnational DFIs (Xu *et al.*, 2019; Maradon, 2022; Suchodolski *et al.*, 2022). Two or more countries establish multilateral development banks (MDBs). They can be divided into global institutions with global members (with no distinction between regional and non-regional members) and regional institutions consisting of groups of countries from one or more regions. Unlike multilateral funds, where capital participation can vary among some countries with different levels of participation, a constitutive feature of national development banks (NDBs) is the participation of a single nation-state.

DFIs are independently managed and ensure the financial implementation of the public mission entrusted to them. Public banks have gained prominence as providers — including of green finance (Mazzucato and Semieniuk, 2018). New public banks have recently been established or planned in countries such as the United Kingdom, France, Germany, Portugal, Indonesia, Canada, and others (Marois, 2021; Xu *et al.*, 2019). The creation of these institutions is often motivated by the fact that private funding is too slow to flow into their respective projects.

The chapter hypothesizes that the capacity of existing public DFIs is insufficient to achieve the goal of adequate climate finance and close the US$5 trillion per year (by 2030) financing gap. Instead, it is necessary to establish a new public and globally active development bank — the "World Climate Bank" (WCB). This bank would specialize in climate finance. The WCB would have clear decarbonization strategies. It is not just about closing climate mitigation and adaptation financing gaps. It is also about dealing with stranded assets: current ESG financing mechanisms, such as carbon pricing, the risk of simply shifting dirty assets from developed countries to emerging economies. All of these goals are in the public interest. How the WCB could finance decarbonization is the subject of intense power struggles and class contradictions. "Finance is not politically neutral, and which activities get financed ultimately depends on investors' choices" (Semieniuk *et al.*, 2022, p. 6). Unlike existing MDBs, the

WCB would not be about taking on the financial risks of private investors to catalyze new green investments.

The focus of this chapter considers the fact that the climate issue is of central importance. This idea is not entirely new. In 2016, Broome and Foley called for a "World Climate Bank". Now the time seems ripe for a bank focused on climate finance. Focality refers to the extent to which an international organization (IO) assumes the sole and undisputed leadership role in a regime complex, even as other IOs accept its governance characteristics, collaborate with it, and learn from its expertise (Abbott *et al.*, 2015). Contrary to this focal orientation, it is claimed that no "climate project" exists independently of its social and economic impacts (Riaño *et al.*, 2022). In this respect, the different dimensions of sustainable development (environmental, social, governance) should be adequately considered. For this chapter, the institutional design of such a "solution" cannot, of course, be completely designed on the green table. Instead, only the guard rails of the business model can be designed, as follows.

The normative analysis starts at three levels: macro, meso, and micro. At the macro level, it elaborates how such a WCB is embedded in existing development bank networks. DFIs are the primary mechanisms for climate finance financial resources. They function as multilateral, bilateral, national, and subnational DFIs. Nevertheless, the funds are insufficient to meet climate change mitigation/adaptation financing needs. These individual institutions could be capitalized on; however, this is not an appropriate strategy. By establishing a WCB, economic forces will be pooled. The WCB is not intended to pursue the explicit goal of prioritizing market failures and gaps in climate finance. Instead, an alternative conceptual framework is needed. Only such an approach allows for the place- and time-bound context for the importance of public banks to be considered. Institutional functions are brought to the fore first. We should think of public banks more dynamically, and as socially constructed and reconstructed institutionalized social relations (Marois, 2021, 2022).

Today, climate finance governance is characterized by a polycentric mix of public and private capital, leveraged through financial technologies and institutions, and steered by various actors in different combinations. The establishment of an IO would provide a counterweight to the existing decentralized governance. However, the creation of an IO can undermine international cooperation. International institutions play an essential role in global politics by managing interdependence and facilitating negotiations among states. The fragmentation of global governance through multiple IOs often leads to coordination problems, redundancies, and rule conflicts. Regarding governance, it is essential to note that cooperation among states usually involves distributional conflicts. Control over institutions helps states steer multilateral negotiations toward their preferred outcome. In addition, governance should allow states to use their influence in the WCB to achieve broader geopolitical goals. At the meso level, the chapter shows how the governance of such an institution should be designed. Institutional proliferation can be interpreted as competition for bargaining power among states concerning climate finance.

On the micro level, the business model of a WCB will be detailed. In addition to the value proposition, the target groups and the infrastructure (partners, activities, resources) will be presented. The chapter concludes with policy recommendations regarding the establishment of the new IO.

2. Macro level

Given the size of the global financial system, there is sufficient capital and liquidity worldwide to fill global investment gaps. However, constraints to allocating capital to climate action exist both within and outside the global financial sector. Constraints within the financial sector include inadequate assessment of climate-related risks and investment opportunities, a regional mismatch between available capital and investment needs, home bias factors, country debt levels, economic vulnerability, and limited institutional capacity (IPCC, 2022). Middle- and low-income countries in Asia, Latin America, the Middle East, and Africa account for most of the investment needs, as they still have growing energy demand. In this respect, MDBs have a crucial role in climate finance.

2.1. *Climate finance*

Climate finance is a hot topic concerning efforts to combat the climate crisis. Energy scientist Vaclav Smil puts it in a nutshell in his latest book. Complete decarbonization of the global economy by 2050 is conceivable today only at the price of unimaginable global economic retreat or due to extraordinarily rapid change. For comparison:

> [I]n 2020, the average annual per capita energy supply of about 40% of the world's population (3.1 billion people, which includes nearly all people in sub-Saharan Africa) was no higher than the rate achieved in both Germany and France in 1860. In order to approach the threshold of a dignified standard of living, those 3.1 billion people will need at least to double — but preferably triple — their per-capita energy use and, in doing so, multiply their electricity supply, boost their food production, and build essential infrastructures. Inevitably, these demands will subject the biosphere to further degradation (Smil, 2022).

The UNFCCC (2021) explains that:

> Climate finance refers to local, national or transnational financing — drawn from public, private and alternative sources of financing — that seeks to support mitigation and adaptation actions that will address climate change.

This definition is far from the traditional notion of climate finance as concessional loans and grants, which were conceived much like official development assistance in the 1980s (Bracking and Leffel, 2021). In terms of what can be considered "climate", there is a crucial difference between measuring climate-specific financing (which only considers the portion of financing that results in climate benefits), on the one hand. On the other hand is climate-related financing (which captures the entire project cost and aims to measure the inclusion of climate considerations). The following also captures investments unrelated to climate goals but which contribute to them (hydropower, rail transport).

In climate financing, a distinction must be made between measures for climate protection and climate adaptation:

- **Climate protection**: Climate protection is about preventing or slowing down the further progress of climate change by reducing greenhouse gas emissions (e.g., through energy-saving measures and renewable energies). What falls under climate finance is somewhat simpler than climate adaptation. Fossil fuel finance continues to be the focus of criticism. According to IPCC (2022), there is a strong focus on climate mitigation in global climate finance (averaging more than 90% in 2017–2020) — particularly renewables, followed by energy efficiency and transport.

- **Climate adaptation**: Climate adaptation is the development of strategies and measures that reduce natural systems' sensitivity to the effects of climate change. Precise definitions of what is meant by adaptation and adaptation assistance are lacking. The lack of precision is epistemic: definitions are unclear not only because of divergent interests but also because states are unsure of the exact task of climate adaptation. As a result, international organizations responsible for implementing adaptation initiatives have considerable flexibility and autonomy. It provides multilateral organizations with greater autonomy to develop contextual, real-world insights into what adaptation requires in different local circumstances. As a result, it is observed that adaptation finance is heavily blended with development finance. Contributing countries provide most of their adaptation finance through bilateral channels, using funds from development assistance budgets. Finally, measuring and tracking the volume of multilateral adaptation finance remains challenging. Comprehensive reports on adaptation finance by Murphy and Parry (2020) and Buchner *et al.* (2019) state that financial flows for adaptation in developing countries amounted to an estimated US$30 billion in 2017 and 2018.

Zamarioli *et al.* (2021) point out the conflicting interpretations of "climate finance" in the Paris Climate Agreement. Under the goal of climate-compatible finance, it is required that:

- "financial flows" be mobilized by developed countries,
- be public and private,
- there is a balance between mitigation and adaptation, and
- priority is given to particularly vulnerable developing countries.

In practice, however, a second, more far-reaching interpretation has prevailed. It emphasizes the links between the broader financial system and climate change. This interpretation concerns the compatibility of national and global investments with climate goals.

Without a globally binding definition of climate finance, it is difficult to accurately forecast total climate finance needs. It is because the understanding of climate science is constantly improving, and technology costs are rapidly decreasing. In addition, there are adjustments in society. In their report, Boehm *et al.* (2021) estimate that climate finance flows will reach at least US$5 trillion annually by 2030. This level must be sustained for the 1.5 degrees Celsius by 2050 target. Boehm *et al.* (2021) state:

> Total global flows of climate finance as tracked by Climate Policy Initiative, however, are still much lower, reaching US$640 billion in 2020, an average increase of US$33.6 billion per year over the preceding five years. By comparison, total global investment in fossil fuels was estimated at US$726 billion in 2020, 13% more than the total tracked climate finance. Global climate finance would need to increase nearly eightfold to reach US$5 trillion annually by 2030, an average increase of US$436 billion a year between 2020 and 2030 (p. 271).

Boehm *et al.* (2021) identify five key indicators of how finance can get more climate action. For this chapter, public climate finance is particularly noteworthy. Increasing public funding is necessary to ensure a rapid transition to a net-zero society to achieve the goals at the required speed and scale. It includes, for example, public services and infrastructure (e.g., transportation and energy networks), research, development, and deployment of new technologies, job training, and ecosystem protection. Finally, public financing is essential to ensure equitable outcomes and transitions, which markets alone cannot guarantee. Global public climate finance must be US$1.25 trillion annually by 2030. Boehm *et al.* (2021) continue:

> Global public climate finance flows [...] amounted to US$300 billion in 2020, an average growth of US$19 billion per year between 2015 and 2020. [...] Based on available data, public climate finance would need to quadruple to reach US$1.25 trillion per year by 2030, growing at an average rate of US$95 billion per year between 2020 and 2030. This represents a 5-fold increase compared to historical growth rates (p. 172).

The Adaptation Gap Report 2020 (UNEP, 2021) notes that current efforts are insufficient to close the climate adaptation funding gap and that additional adaptation funding is needed, particularly in developing countries. COVID-19 is expected to widen the gap. The report reiterates earlier estimates that estimated adaptation costs through 2030 (2050) are US$140–300 billion (US$280–500 billion). In contrast, reported global public financial flows for adaptation in 2019/2020 were estimated at US$46 billion (Buchner *et al.*, 2021).

As falling environmental premiums do not diminish borrowers' appetite for issuing sustainable debt (Figure 1), addressing climate change will become even more difficult in an environment of rising interest rates. This is especially true for highly indebted low-income countries with limited access to international capital markets. Lower tax bases and sovereign creditworthiness limit the ability of low-income countries to engage in domestic public spending, so these countries will need international public finance to meet some of their public climate investment needs. Against this backdrop, international cooperation is more important than ever to find innovative solutions and incentives to mobilize much-needed capital for climate projects in emerging and developing countries.

In 2009, developed countries committed to mobilize US$100 billion in climate finance annually from the public, private, and

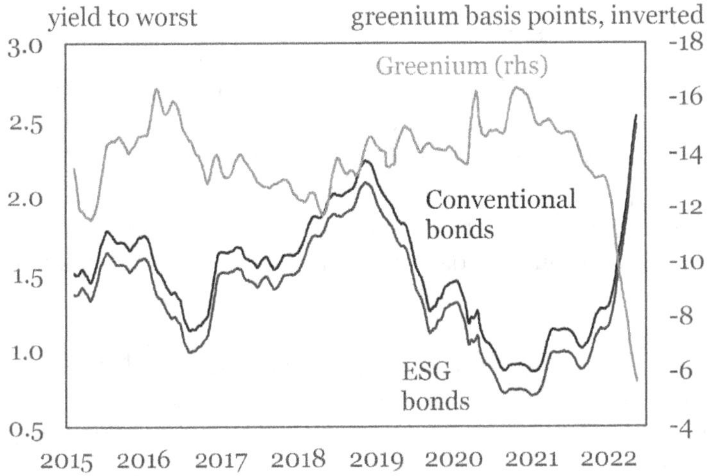

Figure 1. Rising rates have erased much of the green premium in ESG bond markets.

Source: IIF (2022, p. 2).

alternative sources for developing countries by 2020. In 2015, developed countries agreed to maintain this mobilization target until 2025 and also agreed on a new collective quantified target with a floor of US$100 billion per year.

The Organisation for Economic Co-operation and Development (OECD) estimates that public climate finance from developed to developing countries reached US$65.5 billion in 2019. It represents an average growth of US$4.3 billion annually since 2013 (OECD, 2021). In 2019, this represented one-fifth of the global public climate finance of US$343 billion. Overall, it remains the case that developing countries need sufficient public finance to make the necessary investments in climate action.

How can financing for greenhouse gas (GHG) emission reductions be strengthened? In recent years, financing GHG emission reductions through public debt has received increasing interest. It is argued that our emissions are economically unreasonable. Future people would be happy to pay for us to limit our emissions if it meant they would be less exposed to global warming. Suppose we shift the burden of technological change to future generations — a process that Broome (2017) calls "efficiency without sacrifice" (EWS). In that case, we could make them better off overall at no cost to us. Debt-financed mitigation of climate change would be one mechanism to achieve this. A new understanding of debt sustainability, including the negative impact of deferred climate investments on future GDP, has not yet taken hold. Rendall (2021) thinks: "Through long-term debt, governments could support a shift to clean technology, while compensating industries and workers that suffer in the transition, all without raising taxes" (p. 977).

Future generations will be left with both natural resources and manufactured public goods. Borrowing to finance the transition to green technology will channel some of this legacy into environmental protection.

Broome and Foley (2016) argue that debt-financed climate change mitigation will correct economic inefficiency. People pollute more than is optimal because most of the costs fall on future generations. This allocation is uneconomical because future generations would be willing to pay us to stop polluting. In principle, the present and future generations could agree to benefit everyone. Efficiency would be achieved at the point where the willingness to pay off future generations equals the desire of the present generation to pollute. Rendall (2021) presents the critics' arguments against such an EWS mechanism. It is an open question of how much of the global burden can be shifted from one generation to another (Budolfson, 2021).

There is a concern with Broome and Foley's proposals for debt financing of climate action about whether enough countries will adopt them and whether the composition of investment could change without worsening the current generation. When the economy is near capacity, government borrowing is usually assumed to drive up interest rates and "crowd out" private investment. However, this is not a shortcoming; it is part of the architecture. Government borrowing for green investment will crowd out polluting investment, changing the industrial base while maintaining the same level of consumption. People will have to consume different packages of goods. However, living standards can be maintained as long as resources are drawn from investments, according to Broome and Foley (2016).

An initiative financed by external debt would be a way for the pioneer to get the lending countries to shoulder some of the burden, which they should share in any case. On the other hand, to the extent that the effort competes with developing countries for investment capital, it would shift some of the burden to those least responsible for the problem and least able to bear it. This problem could be mitigated by using some borrowed funds from the vanguard states to help the Global South transition to green technologies.

The obstacle of limited fiscal space for economic recovery and climate action in low-income countries and some emerging economies can only be overcome in a multilateral framework. Several multilateral measures can impact the suspension of official bilateral debt payments by the G20 or the adoption of a new special drawing right allocation by the IMF. However, unconventional debt relief, debt deferral, expanded debt, and sustainable lending practices will only deliver development and climate benefits if they credibly aim to close the infrastructure gap for countries with low-carbon and climate-resilient options.

One interest of multilateral agreements is the credibility-enhancing effect that results from mutual benefits for both the donor and host countries. Guarantor countries can offset the public costs of their obligations through the tax revenues from induced exports.

Host countries would benefit from new capital inflows and the grant equivalents of reduced debt service, potentially more than US$100 billion per year (Hourcade *et al.*, 2021).

2.2. *Climate finance and MDBs*

DFIs are the primary mechanisms for Official Development Assistance (ODA) flows, including climate finance. They function as multilateral, bilateral, national, and subnational DFIs. National DFIs are government-owned development banks or specialized export–import banks authorized to partner with private companies to provide equity and debt financing (Griffith-Jones *et al.*, 2020). They generally lend funds only to companies within their jurisdiction. Bilateral DFIs, subnational DFIs, local, state/provincial, or regional investment banks, financial corporations or development agencies, and multilateral DFIs provide financing to projects and borrowers in various jurisdictions. Their legal status defines them as banks within certain national and extraterritorial jurisdictions.

Development banks are essential in financing long-term investments and correcting market failures. It is worth highlighting the financing of activities with significant externalities and the provision of public goods. The first is the case of infrastructure, where long-term financing is essential for public sector investments and relevant public–private partnerships. The second case is precisely that of climate change. Stern (2022) calls it the world's most significant market failure ever. "The *raison d'être* of public banks in this mainstream narrative is to support market-based and growth-oriented economic development by leveraging private capital" (Marois, 2021, p. 3). DFIs are acting countercyclically in global financial crises and serving as strategic actors for governments, at least according to the standard narrative (Mazzacato and Penna, 2016). Despite their global renaissance, we know little about public development banks. Apart from some large and prestigious institutions such as the World Bank, the European Investment Banks, or the Chinese development banks, DFIs are a largely unexplored field. One difficulty is to specify the common characteristics of these institutions to distinguish them from other public institutions, especially government lending programs, aid agencies, sovereign funds, or state-owned commercial banks (Xu *et al.*, 2021).

The total assets of all DFIs amount to US$18.7 trillion. The more than 500 DFIs made US$2.3 trillion in new financing in 2019. The World Bank estimates that gross capital formation — a proxy for global investment — was US$22.3 trillion in 2019. Annual DFI financing accounts for about 10% of global investment (Xu *et al.*, 2021). However, there is wide variation among DFIs in terms of size, location, geographic activity, and mandate. For nine DFIs, the individual balance exceeds US$500 billion. It is 2/3 of total assets. DFIs are spread across all regions of the world. They also occur in the least developed countries. Africa and South Asia concentrate 25% and 20% of national DFIs, respectively. National banks account for 70% of the number of DFIs worldwide; multilateral banks account for 9% (Maradon, 2022).

DFIs differ in ownership structure, geographic reach, asset size, and mandate. Overall, the business model of development banks is very different from private banks. They must factor in banking margins and risks affecting their financial balance and sustainability. They are still subject to banking laws or similar standards but must also fulfill their government mandate. They are expected to strike the right balance between operational equilibrium, risk management, and resource allocation to optimize the economic, social, and environmental impacts of their financing. This robust financial stability and investment thesis makes them specific instruments capable of playing a government-defined role distinct from commercial banks' role in all financial systems. Marois (2021) uses a variety of historical contexts to document the existence and persistence of dynamic public banks in practice. It helps to understand their functions, who benefits from them, and why.

MDBs follow two basic models. The first is the traditional division of shareholders between borrowers and non-borrowers. This model was introduced by the European Bank for Reconstruction and Development (EBRD). Many institutions have followed this model. In this model, non-borrowers provide paid-in and callable capital, which act as insurance for the institutions' portfolios. The second model can be called the "cooperative" model. In this case, all countries contribute to the capital and can also borrow from the institutions. It is the model of the European Investment Bank (EIB) and the Andean Development Corporation (CAF).

Griffith-Jones *et al.* (2018) point to the importance of development banks as an institutional tool to support the urgency of large-scale investment in sustainable development and, consequently, the need for structural change in the development model. However, apart from international financial flows focused on sustainable development, the challenge remains more significant for the planet's less developed regions. The needs are even more challenging when dealing with underdeveloped regions that face significant income disparities, high poverty rates, and climate-related vulnerabilities. In this context, the question is how to ensure that sustainable finance available on the international market is used according to the needs of local populations in less developed regions.

MDBs and bilateral aid agencies are essential in channeling public climate finance to developing countries (Buchner *et al.*, 2019; OECD, 2021). Climate change is a primary focus of developing donor strategies and portfolios (UNDP, 2021; World Bank, 2021). Meeting the Sustainable Development Goals (SDGs) has become a priority for MDBs since the launch of the SDGs in 2015. It is generally acknowledged that MDBs do not have sufficient capital to achieve the SDGs without private capital investment. In this context, the funding gap is declared to be "from billions to trillions".

In closing this gap, ways should be found to mobilize long-term private capital for infrastructure investment and green finance. This blending and mixing of public money with private capital should whet investors' appetite for climate finance and unleash otherwise reticent "animal spirits" (Marois, 2021). Existing contradictions do not occur in this view. For example, the contradiction between unlimited carbonizing growth strategies and limited decarbonizing investment commitments is difficult to resolve. Instead, such contradictions are reproduced in the SDGs. Despite a growing body of evidence questioning the efficiency of such mixed financing, it is evident.

ODA is a basic form of grant- and loan-based financial flows provided by and between states for projects at different levels. Sectors supported the development goals of health, education, trade, infrastructure, conservation, and environmental protection. In the latter case, the focus is on climate change mitigation and adaptation projects.

Finance flows from developed countries to developing countries from various climate funds and donors. Reported public climate finance in 2018 totaled US$62.2 billion (OECD, 2020).

Nevertheless, it must be noted that there are attribution problems with the methodology used to count the financial resources mobilized by the private sector through MDBs. It relates primarily to the OECD and MDB methodologies. The OECD's climate finance accounting equates loans with grants, making transparency in reporting difficult. Given these problems, the OECD calculation of climate finance is considered by many developing countries to be far too high. Bracking and Leffel (2021) note:

> Indeed, what constitutes 'climate-related' in 'climate finance,' and more broadly 'green' in green finance remain fundamentally contested between competing political interests who seek to shape how each is defined and operationalized. [...] This means that promises of finance and threats of its withdrawal are used to leverage broader debates in climate change governance, with normatively ambiguous consequences, with actors forced to make decisions on the type of activities to be pursued, and by whom, in nebulous financial scenarios (p. 13).

Weikmans and Roberts (2019) examine how the lack of internationally agreed upon modalities for accounting for climate change has led to many accounting and reporting practices. As a result, very conflicting accounts of climate accounting emerge.

The focus is on the World Bank and the three central regional development banks (IADB, ADB, and AfDB). Ocampo and Ortega (2022) note that the focus of all banks, but notably the African Development Bank (AfDB) and the Asian Development Bank (ADB), has been on infrastructure financing. Even though banks have grown, the financing provided for infrastructure is minimal. Transportation projects have the most significant weight in this area. The "financing" category includes various projects with different objectives. Of particular note is cooperation with governments to strengthen regulatory bodies and support financial inclusion programs.

Regarding climate change mitigation, MDB funding for climate change mitigation and adaptation projects has increased rapidly.

It is essential to note the low comparative level from 10 years ago. From 2011 to 2019, total commitments to support climate action in emerging and developing countries increased from US$27 billion to US$41 billion (Table 1). It should be highlighted that the EIB is also an important player but mainly supports its high-income members. Its financing for climate action in these countries reached $18 billion in 2019 (Ocampo and Ortega, 2022).

Kim and Lee (2021) examine the energy financing of MDBs (primarily the World Bank) by reviewing their sector-specific energy investments over the past 35 years (1985–2019). The authors note that

> while the amounts and share of finance for fossil fuels have decreased, those of Non-Hydro Renewable Energy (NHRE) finance has substantially increased during the last 35 years. Specifically, the annual average amounts and proportions of investments in NHRE expanded from US$61 million (1%) for the 1985–1990 period to US$996 million (16.5%) for the 2011–2019 period, but that of fossil fuels contracted from US$3.3 billion (51.8%) to US$919 million (15.2%) for the same period. It confirms that the World Bank has been greening its energy finance by shifting allocation priorities toward promoting renewable energy. In addition to NHRE, the World Bank has also increased funding for power transmission and distribution projects to improve electricity access, institutional reform, and capacity building projects to enable long-term energy transition in the recipient countries (p. 20).

Regarding the share of climate finance in total commitments, the two European banks (EIB and EBRD) have the highest shares. The other banks have seen a significant increase in this share, with the World Bank Group (WBG) and the Inter-American Development Bank (IADB) showing the most robust upward trend. Mitigation project commitments averaged about three-quarters of total climate commitments. According to the 2019 Joint Report of Multilateral Development Banks on Climate Finance, the sectors that benefited most from climate commitments were transport, renewable energy, and energy efficiency, accounting for about a quarter of commitments. The main sectors receiving adaptation finance were energy,

Table 1. Total MDB climate finance commitments with emerging and developing countries, 2011–2019 (US$ billion).

Multilateral development banks	2011	2012	2013	2014	2015	2016	2017	2018	2019
PART A: Total reported MDB climate finance commitments (USD billion)									
World Bank (WBG)	10.7	12.7	9.4	11.8	10.7	11.5	13.2	21.3	18.4
Inter-American Development Bank (IADB)	2.2	1.9	1.2	2.5	1.7	2.7	4.3	5.0	4.4
African Development Bank (AfDB)	1.6	2.2	1.2	1.9	1.4	1.1	2.3	3.3	3.6
Asian Development Bank (ADB)	3.2	3.3	3.3	2.9	2.9	4.4	5.2	4.0	7.1
European Bank for Reconstruction and Development (EBRD)	3.7	3.1	3.5	4.1	3.2	3.5	4.6	3.8	3.9
European Investment Bank (EIB)*	5.6	3.7	5.2	5.2	5.1	4.3	5.5	5.7	3.6
Total	27.0	26.9	23.8	28.4	25.0	27.5	35.1	43.1	41.0
PART B: Total reported MDB climate finance commitments as fraction of total loan commitments (%)									
World Bank (WBG)	19%	25%	19%	20%	20%	20%	24%	36%	30%
Inter-American Development Bank (IADB)	21%	17%	9%	18%	15%	24%	32%	34%	34%
African Development Bank (AfDB)	18%	34%	18%	26%	16%	10%	26%	33%	36%
Asian Development Bank (ADB)	16%	16%	16%	13%	11%	17%	16%	11%	21%
European Bank for Reconstruction and Development (EBRD)	29%	27%	31%	35%	31%	34%	42%	34%	34%
European Investment Bank (EIB)*	31%	23%	29%	23%	26%	21%	27%	29%	37%

Note: *The EIB climate finance figures included in this table do not represent EIB's total global climate finance. They include only a subset of EIB countries (emerging countries and economies in transition).

Source: Ocampo & Ortega (2022, p. 236).

transport, and infrastructure, which accounted for 26% of total commitments, followed by water and sanitation and institutional capacity support, with 20% and 14%, respectively (Ocampo and Ortega, 2022).

The central regional development banks that support emerging and developing countries have common elements on their agendas and strategies to address climate change. The three banks share goals such as reducing vulnerabilities and promoting expertise, climate resilience, capacity building, risk-sensitive land use management, climate- and disaster-resilient infrastructure design, and disaster relief. A common problem is also how to increase funding for climate finance. They have adopted mixed financing solutions to address this issue, such as first-loss guarantees, local currency debt (senior, subordinated, or contingent loans and bonds), equity, and green bond issuance.

Grants have traditionally been the main financing instrument of ODA. However, they now account for only a tiny portion of total ODA, compared to the increasing amounts of credit- or debt-based climate finance. In addition to the direct role of MDBs, support from environmental funds — the Global Environment Facility (GEF), the Green Climate Fund (GCF), and the Clean Technology Fund (CTF) — is also critical.

- **Global environment facility**: Established in 1992, the GEF has awarded more than US$20 billion in grants and mobilized more than US$107 billion in co-financing for more than 4,700 projects in 170 countries. The GEF serves as a "financial mechanism" for five conventions, including the United Nations Framework Convention on Climate Change (UNFCCC). Partner agencies include the World Bank and key regional MDBs.
- **Green climate fund**: The GCF was established by the UNFCCC in 2010 and focuses on climate change mitigation and adaptation activities in the least developed countries and Africa. Accredited entities include some MDBs and NDBs. The Fund has provided more than US$1.3 billion in funding to Africa and US$4.1 billion in co-financing commitments (WRI, 2019).
- **Clean technology fund**: The CTF invests in projects and programs that focus on transferring low-carbon technologies that help reduce greenhouse gas emissions. The beneficiary sectors

are energy, transportation, and energy efficiency. The program uses various instruments, including grants, concessional loans, and guarantees. It has provided funding from nine donor countries totaling US$5.7 billion for more than 150 projects and works closely with several MDBs.

The GEF, the World Bank-sponsored Climate Investment Fund (CIF), and the Green Climate Fund (GCF) together form the main global pillars of multilateral public finance (AF *et al.*, 2021). At the national level, National Climate Funds (NCFs) are nationally managed and owned funds that help countries collect, coordinate, combine, and account for climate finance from a variety of sources.

The role of the EIB is worth highlighting. As recently as 2019, the EIB announced its transformation into a "climate bank" in conjunction with the EU's Green Deal. It linked this to its positioning to end fossil fuel lending after 2021. Following the outbreak of coronavirus disease and the related health and economic crisis, EU decision-makers have urged the bank to support both urgent needs to combat the spread of the disease and economic recovery from the pandemic. Kavvadia (2021) provides a striking illustration of how the Bank aims to achieve this balancing act between the different objectives. She notes the following:

> It depicts that views of pursuing these two seemingly contradictory objectives of exclusively restricting the EIB's activity in green funding or boldly and urgently expanding its activity to achieve an economic rebound through a broad impact in the real economy are diverging at all fronts (p. 12).

Kavvadia examines the EIB's stakeholders in pursuing these two seemingly contradictory goals of limiting its activities exclusively to green lending and expanding its activities to achieve a broad impact on the real economy. By examining this tension, the article argues that the EIB's prioritization of restarting under the COVID-19 directive puts it at risk of deviating from its strict green commitment.

The ADB has taken a different approach. In 2019, it announced a mechanism to buy and wind down coal-fired power plants to accelerate their end-of-life. It has lowered the cost of capital for renewable energy projects while shortening the operating life of coal-fired power plants. Coal-fired power plants produce about one-fifth of global greenhouse gas emissions, making them the single largest emitter. If practical, the ADB strategy would do much more for the sustainable transition than simply phasing out these industries. This financing model also aims to encourage private investment in renewable energy.

Green bonds are an increasingly common debt-based climate finance instrument offered as part of official development assistance, particularly by large DFIs. Green bonds, for example, are part of the International Finance Corporation's loan portfolio financed through its Green Bond Program. Using a large sample of 46 countries, Mamun *et al.* (2021) show that green finance significantly reduces carbon emissions in the short and long term. This effect is due to green bonds issued to support waste management, pollution abatement, and energy efficiency improvements. It is noted that issuance activity in 2020 for green bonds occurred in only one developing country. It is critical that funds mobilized through the new global WCB complement, not replace, existing official development assistance and other priorities.

These diverse actors are often directly involved in climate finance governance as "market makers" but are more broadly interrelated by institutions responsible for environmental regulation and governance. Since the turn of the millennium, private and voluntary governance networks have become increasingly important. They include sub-state and non-state actors (Buchner, 2019, 2022). They are increasingly filling the governance gaps left by states in efforts to reduce greenhouse gas emissions. Global governance of climate change is now occurring in multiple places; climate governance is decentralized. Non-state actors operate parallelly with the legal climate regime in a "polycentric system" (see Section 3.1). This more fragmented decentralized governance model is designed to deploy public capital more effectively and increase the flow of private capital globally.

In the context of climate finance, the synergy between market logic and public sector policy has been widely recognized since the Kyoto Protocol. More recently, however, this has been reaffirmed in blended finance and green new deal discussions. Blended finance is public money pooled with private money and managed mainly by private funds targeted in different ways toward development and environmental goals. It is at the core of the "billion-to-trillion" narrative for mobilizing private finance to close the US$2.5 trillion per year "financing gap" in developing countries for the SDGs. Accordingly, current international climate governance emphasizes partnerships, synergies with private actors, blended finance, and the leverage of private funds, alongside consensus-based governance driven by "[m]arket-oriented rationalities".

2.3. *Implications for the WCB*

The question from a macro perspective is why is creating a global bank necessary? Particularly in developing countries, where access to adequate finance is a challenge and where many of the impacts of climate change will be felt most acutely, a step-change in the scale and direction of investment is needed. Whether this climate investment challenge is met will depend heavily on the availability of finance. The geographic distribution of low-carbon finance — defined as capital flows going to low-carbon actions with direct mitigation benefits — is highly uneven. Developed countries are by far the largest recipients. In contrast, developing countries — particularly Africa — receive only a tiny share (except for China and, to a lesser extent, India and some other emerging economies). The ability to mobilize finance for low-carbon investments is closely linked to local conditions (CPI, 2022).

Differences in macroeconomic conditions, business confidence, political uncertainties, and regulatory frameworks determine investment conditions. Ameli *et al.* (2021) note the following:

> Energy system transitions in developing economies require particularly high investment. However, given their underdeveloped financial markets and domestic risks, investors apply high-risk premiums to the finance they make available, making the transition more expensive than in countries with lower perceived risk. Investments are thus usually foregone, creating a climate investment trap (p. 2).

As a result, investments are usually foregone. Ameli *et al.* (2021) refer to this as the "climate investment trap". Such a trap occurs when climate-related investments remain chronically inadequate. A high perception of risk leads to high premiums that increase the cost of capital for low-carbon investments. As a result, carbon emission reductions are delayed. However, unmitigated climate change would lead to more severe impacts in these regions, affecting production systems, reducing economic output, causing unemployment and political instability, and increasing perceived risk.

Current financing frameworks present barriers to climate-related investments. On the one hand, MDBs have committed to increasing climate finance to $175 billion by 2025 (ADB *et al.*, 2019). On the other hand, MDBs have too little capital to support emerging and developing economies in climate finance and other tasks (Ocampo and Ortega, 2022). Before capitalizing on individual DFIs, forces should be combined.

The increased funding for NHRE should be allocated to the least developed countries most in need of external financial assistance. International energy and climate aid can reduce carbon emissions and the vulnerability of recipient countries to climate change by building renewable energy capacity (Ikegami and Wang, 2021). Although other studies tend to point to conditional effects depending on fossil fuel resources and other financial incentives (Mahalik *et al.*, 2021), in the end, there remains a significant need for energy investments to be financed by MDBs.

The argument in favor of a subnational approach is that combining national and subnational development policies would lead to better results. Because subnational development banks are more aware of and monitor the needs and characteristics of their regions, they would be more selective and practical, encouraging local financing and thus driving development in their areas. Finally, provincial or local public banks can increase regional welfare by preventing capital outflows from poorer to more prosperous regions by financing local projects and creditors in a more integrated economy. In particular, Suchodolski *et al.* (2022) emphasize the potential of subnational DFIs as financial and knowledge platforms that link global institutions and funds to the needs of local businesses and governments.

This means that the world has built a financial network to support climate change mitigation and adaptation. The scope is limited, however, as current pledges are still very insufficient to meet the goals of the Paris Climate Agreement.

The WCB should not have the explicit goal of prioritizing market failures and gaps in climate finance. It is not about filling funding gaps (whether global or national). The focus should be on senior loans; second-rank loans are only supplementary. Subsidized loans could be granted if government funds finance them. Risk management standards should be high.

For Marois (2021, 2022), developing an alternative conceptual framework is necessary, whose point of view I endorse. Only such a way of thinking makes it possible to consider the place- and time-bound context for the meaning of public banks. It calls for a discussion of institutional functions first, followed by a discussion of forms of ownership. We are to think of public banks as more dynamic and socially constructed and reconstructed institutionalized social relations. Marois (2022) states:

> A dynamic view then interprets these institutions from the bottom up: public banks are first theorized as institutions in the public spheres of states within global financialized capitalism. This allows us to connect the shifting strategies and interests of social forces to the institutional functions and reproduction of public banks within the confines of capitalism (p. 362).

Institutions are indeed independent entities. It is even more true for a start-up, such as the WCB. Nevertheless, they are never independent of everything else. Institutions develop and unfold within a social whole upon which they act on a more extensive and smaller scale. To be sure, the public sphere of a state offers no possible protection from the imperatives of the competitive market and capitalist accumulation. Public law, however, clearly defines the activities and responsibilities of the WCB. Legally binding mandates and requirements determine the WCB's direction and pace of work. Public guarantees and funding free the WCB from dependence on volatile global financial markets. Democratic governance and famous representative structures foster a credible ethos for serving public interests. In establishing the WCB, it is important to ensure that the WCB is not torn between competing public or private interests. Marois (2022) is all about that "public banks in public spheres in states are likewise located in and affected by (and in turn effect) this wider structural context" (p. 364).

Marois (2022) sees four dimensions of a public bank:

1. It is located in the public sphere.
2. It performs financial intermediation and banking functions without innate purpose or political orientation.
3. It can operate in public and private interests.
4. It remains a credible, proven, and evolving institution.

Some authors advocate public finance and public development banks (e.g., Mazzucato and McPherson, 2018; Marois, 2021). They call for the introduction of a global green new deal. Others emphasize the need to build the capacity and influence of public banking to counter the overwhelming power of private finance and global financialization (Brown, 2019). The functions that public banks perform shed light on the evolving meaning of the term "public bank". Creating a WCB opens up the conceptual possibility of making a public bank act in the public interest.

3. Meso level

The literature on global environmental governance (GEG) is extensive and spans several disciplines. Relatively little deal with climate finance. In the governance of climate finance, coordination among and between climate finance donors and recipient governments has a vital role. The basic idea is to improve coordination between and among climate finance donors and recipient governments, thereby overcoming what has been a very fragmented climate finance landscape (Pickering *et al.*, 2017). The coordination focus has been at the international level or between multiple countries. Analyses highlight the highly fragmented nature of the global climate governance architecture and the imbalances between different climate funds and donors (Pickering *et al.*, 2017). However, there are also very different views on what counts as climate finance (Weikmans and Roberts, 2019) (see Section 2.1).

3.1. *Governance of climate finance*

Climate finance is often seen as an integral part of the broader climate regime, not least because funding commitments by developed countries can encourage developing countries to increase their mitigation pledges and thereby achieve broader agreement on climate change. Moreover, in a world where global climate governance is dispersed among many international and national institutions, rather than being highly centralized at the multilateral level, it is not surprising that institutional arrangements for climate finance are also fragmented. Complexity and fragmentation in the context of climate finance take on particular contours, not least because climate finance institutions interact with development finance institutions. It is, therefore, worth considering climate finance as a system or subsystem in its own right (Pickering *et al.*, 2017).

A crucial structural development is the proliferation of new actors, new governance mechanisms, and new instruments such as partnerships and city networks, and intensifying the interplay between governance levels. Multistakeholder governance describes the spread of agency beyond the state and intergovernmental organizations. Multilevel governance and stakeholder partnerships, on the other hand, describe the new configurations of actors interacting at multiple levels and scales of governance. Transnational climate networks (e.g., International Cooperative Initiatives, ICI) provide an essential platform for local governments to advance their own climate change goals, engage in knowledge transfer with other cities and regions, and shape higher-level policies. The WCB needs to be part of these networks.

The UNFCCC's soft governance as coordinator and mediator within the polycentric system should be emphasized. It acts as the lead institution and coordinator in global climate policy. Soft governance technologies come in new forms of state authority, such as voluntary standards and codes. The UNFCCC represents how governance has evolved from traditional state-based regulatory systems to more heterogeneous and polycentric structures. The result is a blossoming of new voluntary initiatives, particularly in the private sector, related to green taxonomies, carbon footprinting, and climate finance disclosure.

In practice, the coordination of climate finance for developing countries involves the following:

- Improving coordination among different multilateral funds, agencies, and donors at the international level;
- Integrating climate goals into development assistance and aligning development and climate finance;
- Establishing agreements to coordinate climate finance in recipient countries.

Agreements are again made at the national and subnational levels. They are designed to ensure climate-funded programs are coordinated with other non-climate activities in related sectors and with national and subnational policies and plans. The ideal goal of coordination here is to avoid duplication, promote integration and synergies, and ensure policy coherence.

It involves not only domestic actors but often multilateral and bilateral donors as well. As donors and managers of climate finance, these actors not only participate in domestic coordination but can also promote and finance the establishment of national coordination mechanisms, potentially playing an essential role in disseminating climate finance coordination norms.

Funder and Dupuy (2022) show for an empirical case in Zambia how conflicting preferences between and among donors and state actors operate when it comes to practical institutional arrangements at the national and subnational levels. The authors state

> that the emergence of climate finance coordination in Zambia has been a highly conflictual and dynamic process with contestation centered on norm application, that is, the organizational 'how' and 'who' questions of coordination. While the World Bank has initially been successful in pursuing its preferences for climate finance coordination in Zambia, central and local government actors have over time gradually reconfigured donor-dominated coordination arrangements to match their preferences better or pursued competing coordination mechanisms. The resulting climate finance coordination arrangements are of a hybrid nature (p. 3).

Funder and Dupuy (2022) suggest

> that climate donors and governments should abandon any notion that climate finance coordination is merely an administrative process, and instead acknowledge it for the political space that it is, and as a component of climate governance. Doing so will help focus attention on ensuring that climate finance coordination processes are broadly inclusive of government and non-government actors, and that they evolve around explicit interest articulation and negotiation as per other political processes (p. 16).

Given increasing interdependence, many challenges a state faces require a coordinated global response. Typically, the opportunities and pitfalls of acting through formal IOs are emphasized (Johnson, 2014). Formal IOs are firmly rooted in codified international law; they are not the only mechanism available for global coordination, however. Less formal organizations, i.e., institutions without codification or permanent structures to which states delegate tasks, also address these challenges. Roger (2020) analyzes this informal, non-legalized approach. He shows that actors deliberately give up functionality in order to maintain informality. In this respect, the informal approach is not convincing for an adequate institutional response to climate challenges.

Classical theories of institutionalized cooperation assume that states do not create overlapping institutions to govern the same subject. Institutions that overlap in membership and scope duplicate existing functions. Consequently, this increases the complexity of institutionalized cooperation and is therefore inefficient. Regime complexity research is concerned with the increasing density of international institutions in global governance. This branch of research analyzes the constraints and opportunities that a changing institutional environment creates for strategic action and, above all, for the provision of international public goods. "Regime complexes are defined as sets of partially overlapping or nested elemental institutions that operate in a common issue area" (Lütz, 2021, p. 6). The debate mostly takes place at the macro and meso levels. The micro foundation is often missing.

The transaction costs of cooperation — which international institutions are supposed to reduce — increase in situations where actors must act across many overlapping institutions compared to situations with a single, central institution (Drezner, 2013). In contrast, it is argued that a more significant number of institutions in an issue area can facilitate cooperation. When states are members of more institutions, there are more opportunities for interaction, communication, and learning about counterparty preferences (Alter and Meunier, 2009). In addition, states can establish external institutions to strengthen cooperation on specific issues that are difficult to advance in existing forums.

Empirically, it can be observed that international cooperation is now rarely centralized in a single international organization. Instead, it is dispersed among various forums in increasingly dense institutional environments. This institutional proliferation is particularly evident in international climate policy. Institutional proliferation is the rapid increase in international institutions operating in a particular field. There is intense debate about how actors seek to shift the locus of rule-making from existing to new forums. This so-called "regime shifting" also means taking advantage of membership in different international forums where they can best enforce their specific policy preferences. The goal is to decide in favor of their interests (forum shopping). The institutional differences between the forums lead to different cost–benefit calculations for the actors. "If no external institution is available to states or non-state actors whose mandate, function and decision making rules can be changed in such a way that it competes with an already existing institution, there is still the possibility of competitively establishing a new institution" (Lütz, 2021, p. 7).

Rowan (2021) examines how states use institutional proliferation to pursue their goals in global climate policy. He identifies two competing ideas about how institutional proliferation affects international cooperation. One fears that states use institutional density to impede collective action, evade their obligations, and ultimately undermine cooperation. Others recognize the ability of states to separate governance across different forums and use overlapping institutions to support cooperation. "[T]he key to resolving these debates lies in understanding states' motivations for participating across institutions in dense institutional environments" (Rowan, 2021, p. 462).

International climate policy shows that some states are dissatisfied because cooperation under the UNFCCC is progressing too slowly. These states would prefer to cooperate at a deeper substantive level. In contrast, other states fear the sovereignty costs of stringent mitigation measures. These states would prefer to move more slowly or not at all. Rowan (2021) finds that states dissatisfied with the slow pace of cooperative progress join climate institutions that focus on building national capacity to implement ambitious climate policies. They identify electable sub-topics of the broader climate problem and marginalize them to be addressed in new climate institutions. A distinction is made between:

- **Deepeners**: States, in their efforts to advance climate policy,
- **Fragmenters**: States dissatisfied with too rapid cooperative progress.

The latter join climate institutions that focus on networking and negotiation. They question the central importance of the UNFCCC and formulate competing principles for shaping climate policy.

An implicit assumption in the discussion of competition among nation-states is that shareholders determine the behavior of MDBs and that there is little operational autonomy. However, this depends on the power relations between shareholders and MDBs. Cormier (2018) uses a theoretical approach to examine the extent to which MDBs can contribute to the SDGs, considering the external and internal constraints they face. External factors include how these IOs gain authority and legitimacy to influence the SDGs independently of shareholders. First, an IO's legitimacy is conferred by its shareholders, who provide it with a set of rules and procedures it must follow. Cormier raises the question of whether the IO has "agency" or whether it merely follows the rules. He resolves this question by arguing that institutions can gain some autonomy over time. Defining and measuring the SDGs is evidence of autonomous behavior, as the MDB can dictate what constitutes "good policy". Cormier also raises the question of whether the internal structures of the IO make it challenging to implement the SDGs. He notes that culture and internal disagreements could affect the allocation of resources among the 17 different SDGs.

In contrast, using power indices, Ray and Kamal (2019) examine the relationship between loan flows and the composition of different MDB shareholder bases. The main conclusion of the two authors is that CAF and the Islamic Development Bank (IsDB) "have successfully challenged the hegemony of traditional northern MDBs". The main argument is that they have managed to grow without ceding power to non-borrower shareholders. However, they are more capital constrained and currently use different valuation measures.

Rowan (2021) elaborates that the level of government participation in different institutions is unrelated to mitigation targets. This refutes the argument that institutions generally support or undermine cooperation. Instead, the types of institutions that states join matter. It is dissatisfaction with the cooperation that contributes to the main driver of proliferation in existing institutions.

Pratt (2021), on the other hand, argues that institutional proliferation is not a rational response to an underlying cooperation problem but is often due to competition for bargaining power among states. States seek decision-making power in IOs for several reasons. On the one hand, cooperation is about distributional conflicts. Control over institutions helps states steer multilateral negotiations toward their preferred outcome. On the other hand, states can use their influence in IOs to achieve broader geopolitical goals. In establishing IOs, member states often establish formal and informal rules, so multilateral influence affects the underlying substantive power of states. Power imbalances emerge over time as states' power shift and institutional procedures remain unchanged. Underrepresented states respond to the imbalance by demanding reforms that give them more control. Subsequent negotiations on redistributing IO influence are often complicated by credibility and information problems, which impede IO adjustment. When negotiations fail, underrepresented states build new organizations that give them greater institutional control. Overlapping of IOs is a byproduct of states' attempts to increase their influence on multilateral outcomes.

To test the relationship between power imbalance and institutional proliferation, Pratt (2021) examines the creation of multilateral development banks. This system grew from a single IO — the World — in 1944 to at least 28 overlapping institutions in 2019. The functional reason for institutionalized cooperation in development assistance is to coordinate it. Moreover, considerable proliferation has been difficult to explain on purely functional grounds. When states establish new IOs, the primary concern is for states to compete for bargaining power rather than maximize the gains from cooperation. Formal and informal IO decision-making processes are usually designed to balance multilateral influence with states' substantive power. Asymmetries between state power and multilateral influence are standard features of global governance bodies. For example, the unequal voting power granted to member states by the World Bank and IMF is subject to criticism. In each of these bodies, the distribution of institutional control does not reflect the relative power of member states.

Recently, the rise of multilateral development banks has attracted particular attention. New organizations such as the Asian Infrastructure Investment Bank (AIIB) and the New Development Bank (NDB) are challenging the primacy of established institutions. The goal of these new institutions is to mobilize resources for infrastructure or sustainable development projects. Pratt (2021) notes that a straightforward consequence of IO proliferation in development finance is a shift in power in favor of developing countries. Borrowing countries can choose from a broader range of options and should therefore have greater bargaining power. He states

> that initial imbalances in multilateral bargaining power in the World Bank encouraged states to construct new development banks. Subsequent power misalignment that emerged due to shifts in state capacity has had a similar effect, especially when misalignment persists over many years. The substantive effect of power misalignment is large in magnitude, significantly increasing the probability of institutional proliferation among disadvantaged states. Contrary to expectations, the effect of power misalignment does not depend on preference-based dissatisfaction with the existing regime (p. 106).

This result has the following implications:

1. First, newly established institutions provide leverage that gives states influence in the international financial institutions (IFIs). Therefore, to understand how states influence World Bank lending, one must know who wields power in other development banks.
2. Second, when states create a new institution to have leverage in negotiations, the interaction of institutions may be more harmonious than is commonly assumed. New institutions must be at least partly substitutes for the original IO to serve as an

external option. It means they must not be fundamentally different in their functioning from existing institutions.

What does this mean for climate finance and the thesis that the creation of a WCB is of great importance?

3.2. *Rethinking multilateralism*

The creation of a WCB embeds itself in the development of reshaping the IFIs such as the IMF and the World Bank for a new era. The mandates of the Bretton Woods institutions need to be updated, in which the most significant challenges countries face are threats to the global commons. Institutions must work closely with regional development banks and other international actors to incentivize lower-income countries and regions to invest in public goods. It is often argued that the business models of the World Bank and other multilateral development banks should also focus on risk mitigation rather than direct lending. This way, private capital should be mobilized, and global savings converted into development and climate finance. Because banks have triple-A ratings, these institutions can use risk guarantees and other credit enhancement tools. However, progress in moving away from a credit-based model has been slow. Shareholders in these institutions need to increase the grants and capital funding needed by IFIs promptly and ensure that the increased focus on global public goods does not come at the expense of spending on education, social protection, and other development priorities. Pickering *et al.* (2017) state "that the question of fragmentation in climate finance cannot be reduced to the fragmentation of the overall climate governance system; particularly, the interaction with development finance adds a distinct dimension of complexity to climate finance" (p. 12).

Wang (2021) notes that the development finance regime complex consists of various elementary regimes. Some of them cooperate and some others compete with each other. Western donor countries dominate many DFIs, but borrower countries lead some in the Global South. They share common characteristics but also have significant differences. In the bilateral arena, there are numerous national development banks and agencies. The models and norms of traditional donors and emerging market donors differ significantly.

China has taken a strategic approach to involvement in the development finance complex. Lorenzo (2021) concludes that the framework of the Belt and Road Initiative (BRI) between China and individual countries should be multilateralized. "[T]he MOUs have to be negotiated, interpreted, and applied in the context of principles and rules within and across international economic law, international environmental law, and international human rights law — so as not to frustrate the object and purpose of the treaties, to which China and many BRI-participating States are legally bound" (p. 608). Liu (2022) notes that China's engagement with the Global South is shaped by the complex logic of the national political economy and changing global geopolitics. The latter, however, are not all under China's control. In the multilateral arena, it has played a leading role in the newly formed AIIB and the NDB. So far, the AIIB has primarily reinforced the traditional World Bank-led MDB system, while the NDB has powerful features of borrower-led MDBs. China has supported cooperation among the various MDBs despite their different orientations and has used "forum linking" as its dominant strategy (Wang, 2021). Its alternative definition and operation of development assistance poses a challenge to traditional donors and provides ample opportunity for recipient countries to engage in "forum shopping".

In contrast, the emergence of regional actors within the group of Bretton Woods-inspired institutions has not yet attracted much attention. Baroncelli (2021) analyzes the dynamics of EU–World Bank interaction since the 2000s. Over time, the EU has evolved from being a follower of the World Bank and a client of World Bank-managed trust funds to a competitor by establishing new institutional instruments such as the EU–Africa Infrastructure Trust Fund to leverage loans. The newly created blended financing facilities have allowed the EU to set its lending standards, target sectors, and countries of strategic interest, and mobilize funds for infrastructure projects with regional public goods components. Baroncelli shows how the global–regional realignment has oscillated over time between competition and complementarity.

Most of the MDBs have a pure development mandate. Humphrey (2014) argues that MDBs should only be involved in projects if they can bring a better structure to a transaction than a purely private sector deal. It could be either through structural advantages due to preferred creditor status (PCS) or contractual mechanisms.

Alternatively, it is also possible that participation in a transaction brings additional benefits to the country. This benefit is referred to as "additionality" or "enabling an investment that would not otherwise have taken place" (McHugh, 2021). Proving additionality is problematic because the counterfactual can never be observed. Nevertheless, it is accepted that this is an appropriate role for an MDB, even if there is a risk of occasional crowding out of the private sector.

MDBs function similarly to commercial banks. Because of their status as supranational institutions and concessional lending, they earn a lower risk-adjusted return than private sector institutions. If an MDB or DFI were to earn returns similar to a private sector entity, the question would be "what economic purpose do they serve?" They are profitable and have historically not paid dividends, but they have retained profits as capital to enable credit expansion.

The economics of operating the larger MDBs also differ in their capital structure. They have subscribed capital but are also supported by shareholders who commit to callable capital without having to provide it. This characteristic can affect the supply and pricing of credit (Humphrey, 2014). MDB' callable capital and conservative capital structure help maintain the triple-A ratings that most institutions have and keep funding costs low (McHugh, 2021). Humphrey (2014) elaborates "that MDB shareholder composition has a major impact on loan prices, sometimes unexpected. While the backing of wealthy countries allows the World Bank and IADB to raise resources on capital markets more cheaply than the CAF, the interests of those same non-borrowing countries in using MDB net income make loan costs significantly higher at those MDBs — especially the World Bank — than they would be otherwise" (p. 611).

The 2015 Addis Ababa Action Agenda has changed the international community's approach. Now the focus is on mobilizing private sector finance to achieve the SDGs. It is crucial as it shifts the definition of development finance. Whereas previously this was reserved for MDBs, focusing on the SDGs now is something any financial institution can do. McHugh (2021) suggests:

> A more contemporary definition of development finance might therefore be the action of 'financing for development' in pursuit of the SDGs, which separates the financing from

> the type of institution that provides it. However, changing the definition of development finance seems unlikely to change the way that private capital markets function. The role, corporate identity and purpose of MDBs is different to private sector banks and should remain distinct (p. 1981).

From a financial market perspective, the two practical obstacles to mobilizing private sector resources are a lack of risk appetite for MDB projects, which affects the amount of funding available. From a capital mobilization perspective, the private sector risk appetite is lower for countries with weaker institutions. Additionally, there is the potential for a price differential between the public and private sectors due to differences in economic incentives (Gurara *et al.*, 2020).

Compared with the private sector, it is always pointed out that MDB lending is countercyclical to a significant extent. It seems to be particularly true for the World Bank. In addition, there are significant regional differences, with lending to Latin America and East Asia showing a more substantial countercyclical effect. If MDBs are countercyclical and the private sector, procyclical, this would complicate encouraging private sector co-investment in development projects (McHugh, 2021).

Humphrey (2019) examines how shareholder composition can constrain lending from the perspective of the mix of donors and recipients of voting rights. He focuses the question on the balance of power between large MDBs with donor shareholders and smaller "minilateral" development banks where the shareholder base better reflects borrowers. He sets up a case study of the African Trade and Development Bank (ATDB) and examines its lending structure. In this case, the decision to keep donor countries out of the voting shareholder base results in a much lower credit rating. The lower rating raises the cost of financing, forcing the bank to focus on shorter-term, safer loans such as trade finance rather than engaging in development projects on a larger scale. There is a clear trade-off between (i) greater organizational flexibility due to shareholder alignment with borrowers, which requires less external control, and (ii) higher development finance costs and more limited access. This appears to be further evidence that the structure of the shareholder base and the nature of the development bank significantly affect credit availability.

There is a policy problem in that the capital structures of the large MDBs rely on the presence of callable capital to maintain the AAA rating. The large MDBs with donor-dominated shareholder structures are subject to political constraints, which affect lending capacity as do capital constraints. However, also because monitoring and project evaluation must occur, it must be demonstrated that the funds are being used responsibly. It is consistent with Ray and Kamal's (2019) view that operational independence and autonomy come at a cost to recipients.

This concept is revisited in the context of organizational convergence (Humphrey, 2016). It suggests that the pursuit of the best credit rating and callable capital structure create an incentive for development banks to finance exclusively through the bond markets and retain internal capital. Given this precedent, it would be difficult for a development bank to take an alternative path, likely leading to similar business models and practices. The author uses the examples of the World Bank, the Inter-American Development Bank (IADB), and the Latin America-focused Andean Development Corporation (CAF) to show how this has already happened. A nontraditional MDB can only develop if shareholders are willing to provide equity, which can only happen if there is alignment between owners and borrowers. However, as mentioned in the case of the ATDB, this brings further complications, as creditworthiness and access to cheap, long-term financing is limited.

Yuan and Gallagher (2018) focus on government lending to support green development and environmental agenda and link it to SDG 7, "Affordable and Clean Energy." Using a dataset of lending commitments covering 11 financial institutions (MDBs, RDBs, ECAs, and state development banks), the authors use probit analysis to show that banks with solid shareholder commitment to environmental goals are the most critical lenders. And that donor preference is essential in determining where the money goes. In this respect, lending is politicized by donors' agendas. The two authors note that development banks operating in the Americas are far from playing the pivotal role they should in closing the financing gap. Given the wide range of development institutions, potential sources of difference and competition among them are also identified.

Like Humphrey and Michaelowa (2013) show, shareholder structure can also affect borrower behavior. They examine the lending behavior of the World Bank, IABD, and CAF. The authors examine the claim that borrowers seek the cheapest loan for the desired term. However, they find that the speed at which loans are approved and the approval process the borrower must go through vary widely. Similarly, external pressures to lend with "safeguards" that require monitoring may be lower at institutions with greater alignment between shareholders and borrowers.

Likewise, it can be observed that MDBs are more frequently represented in transactions with higher risk and longer maturity. It is to be expected, given the role of MDBs in penetrating areas where the private sector cannot operate.

MDBs do have similar business models. They are united in their support of the SDGs. Nevertheless, they have idiosyncrasies resulting from their different mandates, histories, shareholder profiles, and memberships. The structure of development projects influences the political risk in the countries receiving the funds. There are some trade-offs to consider, such as the strength of the local legal framework. Shareholder composition and power relations also affect the geographic distribution of loans.

Donors and domestic actors have conflicting preferences when implementing climate finance in developing countries. Funder and Dupuy (2022) note the following:

> This divergence in preferences is influenced partly by differing organizational norms and associated perceptions — such as the role and efficacy of the state in climate finance coordination, and whether climate finance should be part of the development architecture or separate from it — and partly by differing strategic interests such as opportunities for challenging or consolidating power relations between and among donors and domestic actors (p. 16).

For domestic actors, coordination difficulties can be an opportunity to overturn or consolidate existing power relations in the domestic institutional landscape. It is true not only concerning climate finance but also about the distribution of powers and mandates in the governance of sectors and resources more broadly. Norms are being reshaped according to their preferences (Funder and Dupuy, 2022).

For the WCB, it is crucial to consider the conflicting preferences between donors and domestic actors. It is essential to go beyond a simple separation between donors and recipients and keep in mind the divergent preferences and strategic orientations between different donors and domestic actors. This focus has direct implications for WDB governance.

3.3. *Implications for the WCB*

Some think that IOs play a central role in solving the problems identified by the SDGs, especially climate finance. Others assess that the effectiveness of IOs is dubious at best. They argue that large government-led initiatives such as the SDGs and related IOs cannot solve complex global problems. When establishing a WCB, one must address this criticism. The quality of a WCB's internal processes and structures are a testament to an IO's ability to enable the climate SDGs. In addition, there are the external constraints of international politics within which the WCB defines and seeks to achieve its goals. The internal and external factors do not exist in isolation but derive from and influence each other (Cormier, 2018).

The WCB is to be established as a global governor. Hofferberth and Lambach (2022) use a conceptual framework to show how such an actor emerges.[1] Theoretically, if the action arises from relationships, any entity recognized by others can become a global governor. Importantly, actors are evaluated in terms of their embeddedness in global structures and situations. WCB agency is ultimately (re)produced and exercised through practice. Therefore, we need to capture agency beyond formal, declarative action to include the everyday, small-scale practices that constitute global governance in general. These include practices of inclusion and exclusion, as well as procedures that some may not even consider "real" action. Hofferberth and Lambach interpret global governors as individuals or collectives. They act in the context of transnational social relations to influence policy.

The analysis for the ATDB highlights that borrower-led governance can lead to significant disadvantages for a regional MDB in

[1]Such an approach also corresponds to the "dynamic theory of public banks" (Marois, 2022).

accessing finance (Humphrey, 2019). Compared to the World Bank, regional MDBs have mainly developing countries as shareholders, limited equity, and a highly concentrated and risky loan portfolio. These MDBs have more difficult access to funding sources, especially capital markets. This limits their ability to provide financing on reasonable terms. This seriously impairs their very *raison d'être*.

In this respect, the members of Confederation of States should act as shareholders of the WCB. They are the pioneers in the search for cheap, clean energy. This search can be financed by borrowing. Selected states would be able to do so. Cseh's (2019) proposal for a debt-financed international climate fund that pays members in proportion to emissions reductions is an alternative proposal for how states could be motivated to participate.

Baroncelli (2021) states:

> In addition to principal-agent (PA) delegation (indirect, hierarchical) and collaboration modes (direct, horizontal), cooperation between donors (or donors and financial intermediaries) in developing countries is often mediated by third parties and socialised through ancillary organisations or institutional arrangements. In several cases, 'augmented PA models' (across long delegation chains, in which the IO is both an agent of member states and the principal of other sub-delegated agents) or 'orchestration models' (in which the IO is also the orchestrator of another IO or other intermediaries) have been employed to analyse the evolving dynamics of regime complexes (p. 81).

Orchestration involves creating, supporting, and integrating a multiactor system of indirect governance, pursuing common goals that neither the orchestrator nor the orchestrated actors could achieve individually. As such, it is used by IOs to overcome the specific limitations of the traditional hierarchical (hard and direct) and delegated (hard and indirect) modes of governance normally carried out by states. It is also used as a substitute for direct cooperation when such a modality is either less appropriate or unavailable. The WCB provides its network (e.g., regional development banks) with material incentives and rule templates. It socializes them to its practices and shares its knowledge advantage and educational resources with them. Member states do not necessarily lead the transformative dynamics of the green bank through micro institutional innovation. Rather, it can be activated primarily by the management of an IO.

Unlike the World Bank Group, which is strategically concerned with building consensus among very different actors (Abraham, 2022), the WCB should precisely describe and delineate its mandate. In this way, criticism of climate finance's potential vagueness and ambiguity is stifled (Humphrey, 2016). At the same time, it should be acknowledged that the legal status of a vague and overly broad concept such as sustainable development can help bring together different perspectives within the international community (Lorenzo, 2018). However, this benefit should not weigh too heavily for the newly minted WCB.

The WCB would voluntarily assume roles under certain multilateral environmental agreements; the Bank would not be a party to any international environmental agreement and would have no direct legal obligation. It nevertheless would occupy a position of extraordinary responsibility. The WCB would have the right and legal obligation to actively pursue climate objectives in its various lending operations in developing member countries.

The jurisdiction and scope of action of the WCB would be defined by its charter or founding document. In international law, these instruments are considered both treaties and constitutions. The purpose of the WCB is to be interpreted as a response to new needs.

While reliance on capital markets has the (questionable) advantage of limiting the political pressures exerted by shareholder countries, it also has the advantage of limiting the political pressures exerted by the public sector. Independent funding from capital markets protects from the "power of the purse" exerted on agencies dependent on direct budgetary support. Nevertheless, the case is made that much of the WCB's funding should come from budgetary resources. The governance of the WCB should be designed, so that wealthy shareholders do not use regular capital increases and increases in concessionary funds to exercise direct budgetary control and impose policy changes to their liking.

4. Micro level

The focus is on the WCB's business model. Individual aspects of the business model will be detailed below.

The following features would characterize the WCB:

- The WCB would be a separate legal entity. It could enter into contracts or take out loans in its name.
- The institution could sue and be sued.
- When it is incorporated, the WCB would have articles of incorporation.
- The WCB would hold a banking license.
- The WCB would have staff.
- The staff would be responsible for its financial performance.
- The WCB would not be established to achieve short-term and specific goals.

4.1. *Value proposition*

The value proposition describes the added value that the target group can derive from the WCB's offering compared to other MDBs. The value proposition is closely related to the positioning of the WCB. Depending on the strategic orientation, the value proposition impacts the business model. The value proposition expresses why the target group is interested in and chooses the WCB's products and services. So it is not primarily about the technology. Technology may increase the attractiveness of services and products, but not trust. In this respect, technological innovations are only ever a means to an end. The WCB must decide whether the value proposition is formulated extensively or will be more focused. However, this also makes specialization more difficult. If, on the other hand, the value proposition is very focused, it is easier to address the needs of the target group and thus also the service to be provided. The more precisely the value proposition is formulated, the more the target group will perceive its value.

The WCB should ensure that its funding initiatives prioritize activities with direct or indirect impacts on climate or nature. Innovative measures are identified and prioritized if the projects can trigger structural changes, whether on a small scale (pilot projects) or a large scale. All projects should contribute to a low-carbon economy and receive adequate funding.

Climate finance should be included in mission and vision statements and the definition of WCB strategies and policies. An important aspect that should be considered when defining strategic objectives in the WCB's multiyear plans is the assessment of market gaps, the reasons for their existence, and whether and how the WCB and its network can fill them.

The WCB would not initiate projects but finance them. It means that it would rely on the ability and motivation of project sponsors and owners to design sustainable climate projects. However, the WCB could provide technical assistance or funding to develop desirable projects or even help design key sustainable economy projects that prioritize specific investment areas.

4.2. *Target groups*

The customer segments describe the individual customer groups addressed by the products or the services. The potential customers are segmented with market analysis support to identify exact needs. The decisive question is: Who is the target group of the WCB?

The alignment of financial flows with low greenhouse gas emissions pathways is slow. A climate finance gap reflects a persistent misallocation of global capital. A WCB can be used to (partially) align finance flows with financing needs. The WCB would lower financing costs for underserved groups. Various mechanisms of the WCB could contribute to risk sharing. These include equitable financial grants, low-interest loans, guarantees, and workable business models for cross-country and cross-border access from developed to low-income countries. It also makes sense to advance access to low-carbon energy globally, especially in large low-income regions such as Africa, with accelerated financial transfers.

For the target countries, the financing needs for climate adaptation predominate. These needs are even more challenging to determine than those for climate mitigation. Mobilizing specific adaptation investments is only part of the challenge, as improving societies' adaptive capacity ultimately depends on meeting the SDGs. Bridging the investment gap in irrigation, water supply, healthcare, energy access, and quality buildings is essential to climate change adaptation. However, investment gaps have little predictive power regarding the scale of the challenge to mobilize finance. Sectors and regions offer very different financial risk–return profiles. In addition, economic costs, standardization, scalability, and replicability of investment opportunities are the basis for investment readiness. Finally, soft costs and institutional capacity provide an enabling environment. This environment is a prerequisite for eliminating financing gaps.

The WCB should act as the leading global financier of climate projects in developing countries. Here, the focus is primarily on climate adaptation projects. The WCB could also finance projects in industrialized countries — e.g., in climate protection.

4.3. *Key activities*

Typical climate finance initiatives consist of project financing. Significant investments are made in infrastructure. The quality of financial institutions, the structure of the local legal system, and the political environment strongly influence financial risk. Projects with low volatile cash flows and little need for management expertise face a higher risk of appropriation by the host government (the so-called "hold-up problem"). It should be noted that project financing significantly mitigates this risk, as high leverage and the consortium structure provide protection. High leverage increases cash flow volatility and project risk, thereby discouraging appropriation. Similarly, a large, widely dispersed consortium involving the WCB increases the reputational risk for a government to intervene. Project finance structures serve to mitigate political and legal risks.

Building a project pipeline and ensuring bankability is an essential first step in the investment cycle and a critical hurdle to further investment. It is no longer about acting only as a funder but also taking the time to develop bankable projects and an overall portfolio that provides holistic responses to climate challenges on the ground. Therefore, it would be essential to understand better the areas, communities, and countries in which the WCB would operate. The WCB should understand the real challenges and imperatives that its end customers face to be more effective and achieve a more significant impact with the products and services.

An important instrument is to carry out the climate proofing of projects. What matters is not the volume of loans extended, but the results and qualitative impact of the portfolio. What is needed are qualitative performance indicators to measure the estimated results over the life of the projects. It must be demonstrated that the various financing operations contribute to sustainable development. Assessing direct outcomes such as the number of businesses served or disbursements is insufficient. The WCB would have to translate its objectives into performance indicators, which can later be incorporated into the loan terms and monitored to verify results ex-post. In addition, impact evaluation methods and indicators would be applied. This requires consistent information and appropriate capacity for follow-up. Overall, systematic integration of monitoring and evaluation components occurs in the early phases of project preparation. Finally, the WCB should standardize its indicators and evaluation systems and other operational-level procedures to facilitate the development of a comprehensive assessment of its contribution to the implementation of climate goals.

The loan is the leading financial product preferred. The bank should be less conservative in granting loans; it has a broad scope to mobilize new resources and increase the loan volume. Part of the loan portfolio pays to finance infrastructure projects, especially sustainable infrastructure (projects aimed at climate change mitigation or adaptation). Infrastructure financing plays a significant role in developing economies.

In addition, structuring activities maximize the potential of guarantees, bonds, or direct capital injections (Figure 2).

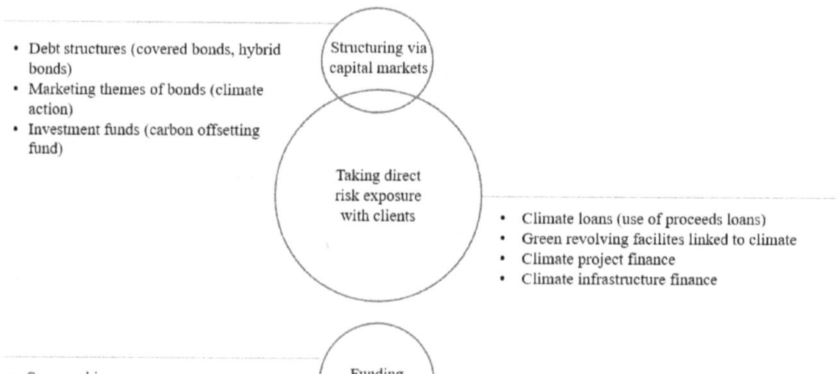

Figure 2. How WCB can channel capital into the low-carbon economy.
Source: Own representation.

Since the WCB would primarily rely on public funds, private financing guarantees would play a minor role. Governments could also act as sovereign guarantors for the WCB, helping it expand its lending, become more innovative, and undertake transactions with higher financial additionality. Guarantors require good liability management and large reserves to maintain financial indicators. Selection processes are needed to identify cases where guarantees represent the best risk–benefit option.

The WCB would not be able to avoid attracting private funding. However, this should not be the highest priority. The most common financial instrument is mixed financing to facilitate the mobilization of private funds. Private investment is subsidized through grants or low-interest loans. Other typical schemes rely on trust funds or ad hoc mechanisms such as first-loss guarantees (e.g., for mezzanine financing). To be effective, the WCB must establish precise rules to prevent blended financing from distorting competition or, more importantly, creating moral hazards by creating unfair advantages for private actors. In the case of the WCB, bond buyers should not provide the core financing (only the additional financing). Only this ensures that investors also have an interest in the specifics of each debtor country. The more dependent the WCB becomes on others, the more likely it is to change its activities to meet external requirements and standards. The WCB would have to balance two sets of "principals": the prominent political and financial owners of the WCB (government shareholders) and the less apparent suppliers of liquidity essential to MDB operations (e.g., bond buyers).

It should be noted that the latter are not necessarily concerned with climate goals — the stated purpose for which governments establish the WCB. Instead, they are concerned with the security of their investments. This risk can be mitigated if the bonds are designed as green bonds according to international standards.

Humphrey (2016) notes that financial pressures pushed the existing MDBs in operational directions not anticipated by their founders. They were governments unwilling to commit large amounts of budgetary resources. It forced MDBs to rely increasingly on private capital markets to raise funds. In any case, the reliance on bond markets proved to be much greater than initially intended. Accordingly, MDBs were forced to significantly change their operational procedures — lending policies, financial management, country risks — and even the basic shareholder structure from the founders' original plans. Humphrey (2016) states:

> The degree of dependence on bond markets turned out to be much higher than originally intended in each case, and pushed the MDBs to modify their operational procedures — loan policies, financial management, country risk — and even basic shareholding structure substantially from the original intentions of founders (p. 107).

In light of these experiences, the WCB must ensure that governments provide many budgetary resources. Experience shows that an MDB need not be subject to the whims of bondholders as long as it has strong financial support from one or more governments. Generous contributions of concessional funds could enable the WCB to take a radically different approach to climate lending, with lending more closely aligned with borrowing countries' priorities. Regardless of the composition of shareholders — the United States, developed countries, or borrowing countries — refinancing can be established only with substantial budgetary support from one or more wealthy nations. Without such support, the WCB would have to rely on private financial markets to raise funds necessary to operate effectively. The WCB would then have to keep a very close eye on the perceptions of private capital markets in shaping its operational and financial policies. Whether this reliance on capital markets and the attendant operational pressures are "good" for climate goals is a complex question that cannot be answered systematically here.

Finally, the WCB's business model includes buying stranded assets and working toward a sustainable transition of dirty, emissions-intensive industries from within. Stranded assets, assets that have been converted into liabilities due to sudden or unforeseen devaluations, are a growing concern in the age of climate change. In addition to harmful environmental impacts, the volume of stranded assets could pose catastrophic risks to the financial system if not addressed. Trillions of dollars in stranded assets are expected to become worthless over the next 15 years. "Stranded fossil fuel assets of between US$7 trillion and US$11 trillion arise" (Mercure *et al.*, 2021, p. 1139). While other financial institutions fear a downgrade in their credit ratings if they engage in this form of active ownership, the WCB's mandate and status would make it particularly well-suited to absorb the stranded assets that are eventually jettisoned by the financial sector.

4.4. *Key resources*

Because of their knowledge of the economic realities of each sector, their experience from various operations, and their close relationships with governments, development banks are the financial actors best positioned to drive this climate finance. Creating a green, multilateral development bank solves the problem of making substantial financial commitments. The balance sheet structure needs to be built in line with the objectives that align with the shareholders.

In order to fulfill its mission, the WCB must have a level of capital commensurate with its risk-bearing capacity vis-à-vis its business partners. At the same time, it must ensure that long-term funds cover its liabilities. It needs a balanced liability structure and sufficient collateralization of its activities.

Without a market value, the fair "purchase price" for an environmental benefit is difficult to determine. Therefore, assessing the appropriate level of a subsidy or a subsidized rate remains complex. When it comes to subsidizing an environmental externality, one must also be able to determine a "price" for what can be offset by the subsidy. Currently, very few quantitative methods have the necessary elements to calculate the correct level of subsidy. An essential and valuable exception is the use of the shadow price of carbon to value projects, as the European Investment Bank does. This practice should be applied to the WCB.

The WCB would operate in countries or contexts where public institutions are still weak and lack clear guidance on government priorities; internal staff have some, but not all, of the skills or qualifications to catalyze climate-specific development priorities.

Responsibility for the ambitious climate targets must come from within the bank. In other words, it must be part of the bank's DNA. Climate targets are used as a cornerstone for action from the top down — from high-level directives to those who plan, review, and approve loans. To integrate climate goals into all bank actions and processes, they must be firmly embedded in the organizational culture, supported by appropriate incentives and (institutional) capacity building (Domorenok *et al.*, 2021).

Ongoing funding for the WCB should be based on pre-agreed contributions from all countries, similar to the way countries regularly provide new funding to the International Development Association. When distributed on a fair and equitable basis among many countries, contributions amount to barely 0.02% of GDP for most countries or less than 0.1% of annual national budgets.

4.5. *Key partners*

The concept of the WCB is embedded in multilevel governance (vertical networks from neighborhood to national and international levels and horizontal networks of non-state and subnational actors at different levels). When multiple actors — national, regional, and city decision-makers, as well as non-state actors and civil society — work together, to seize the opportunities, it leads to the most impactful mitigation gains.

The WCB would work closely with other multilateral, regional, and national DFIs. Their brokering activities are systematically used to provide national DFIs with easier access to local markets and concessional financing, provided that this brings climate benefits. They also need to share their expertise so that these national development banks can act as effective intermediaries in implementing the main agreements signed between governments.

The WCB would actively participate in the emergence of partnerships focused on climate finance. Harnessing the potential of partnerships paves the way to achieve practical results and catalyze sustainable changes in development. Interesting practices in this area include (i) joining forces to develop standard methodologies and standardize existing approaches; (ii) fostering alliances that would allow the WCB to learn how its partners are adapting to the Global Agenda; and (iii) building partnerships that aim to obtain technical and financial support from other actors that also want to contribute to climate goals.

The WCB would be a component of the Sustainable Development Cooperation Framework (SDCF). Such transnational cooperation mechanisms are needed to harness resources and capabilities from various sources, such as sustainable finance, technology and know-how, policy expertise and data, and other capacities. According to Horan (2021), there are a variety of collaborative arrangements that can support sustainable transformations. These include, for example, multistakeholder partnerships, public–private partnerships, geopolitical partnerships, peace agreements, social partnerships, informal diaspora alliances, and sponsorship by philanthropists.

It is widely recognized in UN circles that donor governments prioritize certain bilateral relationships with agencies, countries, and ministries. One problem with this approach is that it can lead to isolated and uncoordinated implementation. In this respect, the WCB can also be seen as a mechanism for pooling such funding and making it available for transformative collaborative frameworks.

The WCB would create an inventory of existing partnerships. This way, missing key partnerships can be identified to create a targeted partnership portfolio in each country. The WCB is for developing collaboration platforms that bring together different stakeholders. It is recognized that such platforms can mobilize stakeholders for joint projects.

5. Policy recommendations

Climate finance should focus policy attention on global equity issues. Climate finance supporting a just transition is likely key to a successful global low-carbon transition. Because this process is about equity within and across generations, difficult political trade-offs are required. The implications for a just transition in climate finance are clear: expanding equitable and better access to climate finance for vulnerable countries, communities, and sectors, not just the most profitable private investment opportunities, and a more significant role for public finance in meeting existing financing commitments. Instead of unilateralism, the answer may lie in a globally collaborative policy approach.

While limited pipelines, limited absorptive capacity, and limited institutional capacity of developing countries are often cited as challenges to accelerating finance, the question remains as to what role international public climate finance plays in addressing this gap. It is also a question of whether there is a substantial funding gap for patient institutional capacity building. While current short-term, mainly project-based capacity building often does not meet needs, alternative, well-structured patient interventions and funding through the WCB could play an important role.

Another priority is to accelerate the implementation of the climate finance pledges made in the Copenhagen Accord (and repeated since) of US$100 billion per year (and likely more in light of growing financing gaps) from developed to developing countries. Add to this the pledge made at COP26 in Glasgow to provide US$40 billion annually in adaptation finance from 2025. There should be rapid agreement on crucial definitions. Moving to a grant-equivalent definition of net inflows for climate finance would eliminate many uncertainties: disbursing climate finance flows based on grant equivalents that are comparable across institutions, instruments, and countries and more accurately measuring the effective transfer of resources.

Activities mobilized for adaptation and resilience are often not marketable. Their funding will continue to come from the public sector (Murphy and Parry, 2020). At the international level, it will consist of grants based on technical assistance, budget support, basket funding for large projects/programs, sector-wide approaches, or multilateral financing. The WCB can be an active component here.

The UNFCCC is at the heart of climate change's global, transnational governance node. It acts as a coordinator and a facilitator within this dispersed network. The newly established WCB would take over the financing side of the UNFCCC. In this way, how the WCB integrates the GEF into its business model can be ensured. The network to partner agencies, including the World Bank and the main regional MDBs, will be ensured (see Section 2.2).

The analysis leads to the following key policy recommendations.

5.1. *Centralization versus decentralization*

Stakeholders value the expertise, prestige, size, and resources of globally established institutions. Global institutions are questioned, supplemented, but rarely replaced. Fragmented structures have become the "new normal", but that does not necessarily mean instability. Actors take advantage of fragmentation by forum shopping or creating new, decentralized institutions that serve their national or regional strategic interests. Materially enormous powers often drive integration into a regime complex by linking forums. They seek to gain first-mover advantages by spreading their regulatory models across different levels. Policymakers should therefore be aware that dominant solutions reflect inherent power asymmetries. Emerging market demands for excellent representation on IMF and World Bank governing bodies have become more insistent over the past 10 years. The more incremental reforms in a vote and quota shares triggered a search for regional alternatives. Regional actors prefer decentralized, regional, or bilateral arrangements for strategic reasons related to national or regional needs. Decentralized arrangements can give materially weaker actors a stronger voice in decision-making processes. However, actors such as the EU have also followed in the footsteps of the World Bank. They have created hybrid development finance institutions characterized by collaboration between public and private actors. For climate finance, the creation of a multilateral development bank is beneficial. The advantages of centralization and joining forces outweigh the disadvantages.

5.2. *Specialization*

When global and regional organizations specialize and focus on their comparative advantages, duplication of effort is avoided, even when formal mandates overlap significantly. By specializing individual institutions, a decentralized regime complex allows local experimentation with institutional alternatives that other forums and institutions can adopt. It can promote the integration of a regime complex by disseminating best practices based on synergy and cognitive interaction. Path dependency will likely reinforce the focal institution as the sole and undisputed leader of a field. In this way, the coherence of a regime complex is increased. Existing institutions can reduce the transaction costs of creating new institutions, as actors can mimic the design of a focal institution. The specialization strategy applies to both global and regional actors. It is also important to note that the WCB should not be an implementing agency on the ground. Instead, the WCB should act as an integrator rather than becoming a new silo that only reinforces fragmentation.

5.3. *Weights of votes*

The system of equal weights and the consensus rule are unprecedented in the history of multilateral financial institutions. The World Bank, the IMF, and the Asian Development Bank use weighted voting systems and majority voting rules. Among other things, this system results in few new members joining; therefore, the WCB should clarify its rules for allocating shares and voting weights to members. The rules on voting weights differ in the founding case and when new members join. In any case, the WCB should not adopt the equal weighting system. Luo and Yang (2021) discuss different models (including the NDB and AIIB).

5.4. *Voice*

The normative guardrails of the Bretton Woods institutions (e.g., liberalization, individual property rights, or good governance) are necessarily shared by emerging powers or materially weaker actors. In development finance, they often clash with the principles of non-interference in domestic affairs and unconditionality that shape traditional patterns of South–South cooperation. Disintegration, however, can give materially weaker actors a stronger voice in decision-making in regional governance arrangements. Moreover, lack of integration is thought to allow for flexibility, experimentation, and innovation. Similar to the World Bank (Abraham, 2022), it is, on the one hand, about describing the issue of climate finance in its complexity and involving stakeholders as an effective solution. As a result, entirely new practices are emerging. On the other hand, stakeholders thereby articulate themselves as a new political subject.

5.5. *Standards*

The establishment of the WCB would create an IO that itself becomes an international legislator. It must equally enable other non-state actors to also participate in international legislation. The interests of the people affected by the projects must be made transparent. Mechanisms exist to hold them accountable in the event of misconduct. The bank should operate using basic minimum standards established at the multilateral level. For example, the rules and procedures used by IFs to assess equivalence and acceptability — such as a Safeguards Diagnostic Review — serve as a guide. Activities will be consistent with obligations and commitments under international business, environmental, and human rights laws. These standards are derived from the MDBs' environmental and social safeguards. In line with a multistakeholder approach, the technical expertise of IOs is combined with the views and interests of states and various non-state actors. Multistakeholder governance is linked to the idea of a "bottom-up" approach. It means that policy-making and coordination require the input, deliberation, and consensus of people directly involved in operations and decision-making. Similarly, initiatives and proposals can come from any participant, and there are defined procedures for developing collective agreements on policies.

5.6. *Cooperation*

The new WCB must embed itself in the network of development banks. Cooperation among MDBs in these areas is critical, as is networking with NDBs. Complementarity among MDBs' activities is essential given the diversity of regional priorities. In general, competition among them can help improve the programs they support. However, climate finance should be prioritized by the new WCB. Finally, smooth cooperation between MDBs and international funds that finance climate change programs should be sought. The global–regional interface arrangement should seek to take advantage of centralized and decentralized solutions. Global nodes provide members of a regime complex with expertise and resources; they promote harmonization to prevent inefficient duplication or regulatory arbitrage. Decentralized or regional institutions provide solutions with more excellent representation of more minor powers and allow flexibility and experimentation. They serve regional strategic interests and provide specialized solutions and regional public goods. Managing global–regional linkages in a regime complex would require an intelligent combination of positive and negative coordination. Positive coordination seeks to explore and leverage the options of all stakeholders for common strategies to maximize overall policy effectiveness and efficiency. Negative coordination seeks to ensure that new initiatives by specialized actors or subunits do not conflict with the established strategies and interests of other affected entities.

In our context, positive coordination would occur at multi-, plurilateral, bilateral, and regional levels, relying on coordination committees or working groups. Here, "hub facilitators" could facilitate the management of global–regional interfaces and help separate consensual from contentious issues. Negative coordination would aim to prevent the negative externalities of decentralized institutions. Rules inspired by the principle of subsidiarity could define possible divisions of labor between central and decentralized entities in a regime complex based on specialized knowledge and comparative advantage.

6. Conclusion

Based on the assumption that global problems require global solutions, this chapter argues for creating a WCB. In creating a new institution such as the WCB, the principals should be aware of the dense institutional environment. The founding idea of a WCB is not obsolete because sub-state and non-state actors have now taken on significant functions in global climate policy. The establishment of the WCB should not be based on the assumption that it will act autonomously in the area of climate finance. Instead, the WCB should be designed to function within a regime complex. Institutional conflict is predictable. Thus, the WCB must have a robust capacity to engage other institutions (e.g., other multilateral development banks). The success of the WCB depends on its ability to adapt to the emergence of such partners flexibly.

Certain types of fragmented governance of climate finance are harmful. For example, conflicts over norms could undermine the equitable distribution of funding. With multiple institutional arrangements, the effectiveness could be compromised, not least by the administrative burden on recipient countries seeking access to funds. However, compliance with various social and financial safeguards is critical in the fragmented landscape. Funding through many institutions with different accounting standards and decision-making mechanisms hinders transparency and accountability. Established institutions may be favored where developed countries have significant influence.

However, a fragmented climate finance system can offer advantages, including speed, flexibility, and innovation. For example, using established institutions (such as bilateral or multilateral funds) could increase the speed of financing. Some redundancy or duplication may also help the system cope with external shocks. Some advocates emphasize that fragmentation can promote experimentation and learning. For example, initiatives not possible under the consensus-based UNFCCC can take place in other institutions.

Increased participation of non-state actors in climate finance could help improve the democratic legitimacy of climate finance. It requires some degree of vertical fragmentation of governance arrangements (Pickering *et al.*, 2017).

There is a large gap between the public climate finance provided to date and the resources required. Estimated financing needs for climate action as a percentage of current GDP (US$2,015) are about 2–4% for developed countries and about 5–10% for developing countries. Climate finance flows need to increase by a factor of 4–8 in developing countries and 2–5 in developed countries. This discrepancy becomes even more remarkable when adaptation, infrastructure, and SDG-related investment needs are considered (Hourcade *et al.*, 2021). However, the differences among developing countries are significant. China dominates flows to East Asia, whose average flows of US$269 billion (more than 95% of total mitigation flows to East Asia) would need to increase by 2 to 4, a level comparable to developed countries.

With the help of establishing a global climate bank presented here, a contribution can be made to ensure that developing countries, particularly, can access the necessary financial resources. "Rather, the problem resides in granting otherwise normative and contestable aspirations (which are indeed an indispensable part of being a social and political being!) a timeless status that seemingly bestows fundamental meaning on a bank by being 'public'. Far from catalyzing positive change this can overly constrain possibilities, obscure pitfalls, and undermine meaningful democratization" (Marois, 2022, p. 366). There are enough public functions to summarize what a democratized climate public bank can and should look like.

Smil (2022) notes:

> The reality is that any sufficiently effective step will be decidedly non-magical, gradual, and costly. We have been transforming the environment on increasing scales and with rising intensity for millennia, and we have derived many benefits from these changes — but, inevitably, the biosphere has suffered. There are ways to reduce those impacts, but the resolve to deploy them at required scales has been lacking, and if we start acting in a sufficiently effective manner on a global scale, we will have to pay a

> considerable economic and social price. Will we act deliberately, with foresight, or will we act only when forced by deteriorating conditions?

The creation and establishment of a WCB are embedded in recent developments around global governance; it is a vital component in the discourse around polycentrism, fragmentation, and gridlock in world politics. *Per aspera ad astra*: Our aspirations take us to the stars.

References

Abbott, K., *et al.* (2015). Orchestration: Global governance through intermediaries. In K. Abbott *et al.* (Eds.), International organizations as orchestrators (pp. 3–36). Cambridge: Cambridge University Press.

Abraham, K. J. (2022). Modeling institutional change and subject-production: The World Bank's turn to stakeholder participation. *International Studies Quarterly, 66*(3), 1–13.

ADB, *et al.* (2019). High level MDB statement. September 23, 2019.

Adaptation Fund (AF), *et al.* (2021). The climate funds are committed to working together. Joint Statement.

Alter, K. & Meunier, S. (2009). The politics of international regime complexity. *Perspectives on Politics, 7*(1), 13–24.

Ameli, N., *et al.* (2021). Higher cost of finance exacerbates a climate investment trap in developing economies. *Nature Communications, 12*, 4046.

Baroncelli, E. (2021). Cooperating through competition: EU challenge and support to the World Bank focality in multilateral development finance. *Global Policy, 12*(4), 80–89.

Boehm, S., *et al.* (2021). State of climate action 2021: Systems transformations required to limit global warming to 1.5°C. World Resources Institute, Washington, DC.

Bracking, S. & Leffel, B. (2021). Climate finance governance: Fit for purpose? *WIREs Climate Change, 12*, e709.

Broome, J. (2017). Do not ask for morality. In A. Walsh, S. Hormio, & D. Purves (Eds.), *The Ethical Underpinnings of Climate Economics* (pp. 9–21). London: Routledge.

Broome, J. & Foley, D. (2016). A World Climate Bank. In I. González-Ricoy & A. Gosseries (Eds.), *Institutions for Future Generation* (pp. 156–169). Oxford: Oxford University Press.

Brown, E. (2019). Banking on the people: Democratizing money in the digital age. The Democracy Collaborative, Washington, DC.

Buchner, B., *et al.* (2019). Global landscape of climate finance 2019. November 11, 2019.

Buchner, B., *et al.* (2021). Global landscape of climate finance 2021. Climate Policy Initiative, December 2021.

Budolfson, M. (2021). Political realism, feasibility wedges, and opportunities for collective action on climate change. In M. Budolfson, T. McPherson, & D. Plunkett (Eds.), *Philosophy and Climate Change* (pp. 323–345). Oxford: Oxford University Press.

Climate Policy Initiative (CPI) (2022). The state of climate finance in Africa: Climate finance needs of African countries. June 2022.

Cormier, B. (2018). Analyzing if and how international organizations contribute to the sustainable development goals: Combining power and behavior. *Journal of Organizational Behavior*, *39*(5), 545–558.

Cseh, A. (2019). Aligning climate action with the self-interest and short-term dominated priorities of decision-makers. *Climate Policy*, *19*(2), 139–146.

Domorenok, E., Graziano, P., & Polverari, L. (2021). Policy integration and institutional capacity: Theoretical, conceptual and empirical challenges. *Policy and Society*, *40*(4), 1–18.

Drezner, D. (2013). The tragedy of the global institutional commons. In M. Finnemore & J. Goldstein (Eds.), *Back to Basics: State Power in a Contemporary World* (pp. 281–311). Oxford: Oxford University Press.

Funder, M. & Dupuy, K. (2022). Climate finance coordination from the global to the local: Norm localization and the politics of climate finance coordination in Zambia. *The Journal of Development Studies*, *58*(10), 1899–1916.

Griffith-Jones, S., *et al.* (2018). The future of national development banks. In S. Griffith-Jones & J. A. Ocampo (Eds.), *The Future of National Development Banks* (pp. 1–36). Cambridge: Cambridge University Press.

Griffith-Jones, S., Attridge, S., & Gouett, M. (2020). Securing climate finance through national development banks. ODI Report, Overseas Development Institute.

Gurara, D., Presbitero, A., & Sarmiento, M. (2020). Borrowing costs and the role of multilateral development banks: Evidence from cross-border syndicated bank lending. *Journal of International Money and Finance*, *100*, 102090.

Hofferberth, M. & Lambach, D. (2022). Becoming global governors: Self-agentification, recognition, and delegation in world politics. *Global Studies Quarterly*, *2*(3), 1–12.

Horan, D. (2022). Towards a portfolio approach: Partnerships for sustainable transformations. *Global Policy, 13*(1), 160–170.

Hourcade, J.-C., Dasgupta, D., & Ghersi, F. (2021). Accelerating the speed and scale of climate finance in the post-pandemic context. *Climate Policy, 21*, 1–15.

Humphrey, C. (2014). The politics of loan pricing in multilateral development banks. *Review of International Political Economy, 21*(3), 611–639.

Humphrey, C. (2016). The invisible hand: Financial pressures and organisational convergence in multilateral development banks. *The Journal of Development Studies, 52*(1), 92–112.

Humphrey, C. (2019). 'Minilateral' development banks: What the rise of Africa's trade and development bank says about multilateral governance. *Development and Change, 50*(1), 164–190.

Humphrey, C. & Michaelowa, K. (2013). Shopping for development: Multilateral lending, shareholder composition and borrower preferences. *World Development, 44*, 142–155.

Ikegami, M. & Wang, Z. (2021). Does energy aid reduce CO_2 emission intensities in developing countries? *Journal of Environmental Economics and Policy, 10*(4), 343–358.

Institute of International Finance (IIF) (2022). IIF Weekly Insight: Climate collaboration in a polarized world. May 26, 2022.

Intergovernmental Panel on Climate Change (IPCC) (2022). Climate change 2022: Mitigation of climate change, Chapter 15.

Johnson, T. (2014). *Organizational Progeny: Why Governments are Losing Control Over the Proliferating Structures of Global Governance.* Oxford: Oxford University Press.

Kavvadia, H. (2021). Restrictive or expansive? European Investment Bank's challenge to equipoise climate finance with post-pandemic boost. *Fulbright Review of Economics and Policy, 1*(2), 170–185.

Kim, J. W. & Lee, J.-S. (2021). Greening energy finance of multilateral development banks: Review of the World Bank's energy project investment (1985–2019). *Energies, 14*(9), 2648.

Liu, H. (2022). China engages the Global South: From bandung to the Belt and Road Initiative. *Global Policy, 13*(S1), 11–22.

Lorenzo, J. A. P. (2018). "Development" versus "sustainable development"? (Re-)Constructing the International Bank for Sustainable Development. *Vanderbilt Journal of Transnational Law, 51*(2), 399–476.

Lorenzo, J. A. P. (2021). A path toward sustainable development along the Belt and Road. *Journal of International Economic Law, 24*, 591–608.

Lütz, S. (2021). Global–regional realignments in trade, finance and development: Introduction to the special issue. *Global Policy, 12*(S4), 5–13.

Luo, H. & Yang, L. (2021). Equality and equity in emerging multilateral financial institutions: The case of the BRICS institutions. *Global Policy, 12*(4), 482–508.

Mahalik, M. K., *et al.* (2021). Assessing the effectiveness of total foreign aid and foreign energy aid inflows on environmental quality in India. *Energy Policy, 149*, 112015.

Mamun, M. A., Boubaker, S., & Nguyen, D. K. (2022). Green finance and decarbonization: Evidence from around the world. *Finance Research Letters, 46*(B), 102807.

Marodon, R. (2022). Can development banks step up to the challenge of sustainable development? *Review of Political Economy, 34*(2), 268–285.

Marois, T. (2021). *Public Banks: Decarbonisation, Definancialisation, and Democratisation.* Cambridge: Cambridge University Press.

Marois, T. (2022). A dynamic theory of public banks (and why it matters). *Review of Political Economy, 34*(2), 356–371.

Mazzucato, M. & McPherson, M. (2018). The Green New Deal: A bold mission-oriented approach. IIPP Policy Brief. London: Institute for Innovation and Public Purpose.

Mazzucato, M. & Penna, C. C. R. (2016). Beyond market failures: The market creating and shaping roles of state investment banks. *Journal of Economic Policy Reform, 19*(4), 305–326.

Mazzucato, M. & Semieniuk, G. (2018). Financing renewable energy: Who is financing what and why it matters. *Technological Forecasting & Social Change, 127*, 8–22.

McHugh, C. A. (2021). Mobilising private funding of development finance. *The Journal of Development Studies, 57*(12), 1979–2001.

Mercure, J.-F., *et al.* (2021). Reframing incentives for climate policy action. *Nature Energy, 6*, 1133–1143.

Murphy, D. & Parry, J.-E. (2020). Filling the gap: A review of multilateral development banks' efforts to scale up financing of climate adaptation. International Institute for Sustainable Development.

Ocampo, J. A. & Ortega, V. (2022). The global development banks' architecture. *Review of Political Economy, 34*(2), 224–248.

OECD (2020). Climate finance provided and mobilised by developed countries in 2013–18. Paris: OECD.

OECD (2021). Climate finance provided and mobilised by developed countries: Aggregate trends updated with 2019 data.

Pickering, J., Betzold, C., & Skovgaard, J. (2017). Managing fragmentation and complexity in the emerging system of international climate finance. *International Environmental Agreements: Politics, Law and Economics, 17*, 1–16.

Pratt, T. (2021). Angling for influence: Institutional proliferation in development banking. *International Studies Quarterly, 65*(1), 95–108.

Ray, R. & Kamal, R. (2019). Can south–south cooperation compete? The Development Bank of Latin America and the Islamic Development Bank. *Development and Change, 50*(1), 191–220.

Rendall, M. (2021). Public debt and intergenerational ethics: How to fund a clean technology 'Apollo Program'? *Climate Policy, 21*(7), 976–982.

Riaño, M. A., *et al.* (2022). Scaling up public development banks' transformative alignment with the 2030 agenda for sustainable development. *Review of Political Economy, 34*(2), 286–317.

Roger, C. B. (2020). *The Origins of Informality: Why the Legal Foundations of Global Governance are Shifting, and Why It Matters.* Oxford: Oxford University Press.

Rowan, S. S. (2021). Does institutional proliferation undermine cooperation? Theory and evidence from climate change. *International Studies Quarterly, 65*(2), 461–475.

Semieniuk, G., *et al.* (2022). Stranded fossil-fuel assets translate to major losses for investors in advanced economies. *Nature Climate Change, 12*, 532–538.

Smil, V. (2022). *How the World Really Works: The Science behind How We Got Here and Where We're Going.* New York: Viking/Penguin.

Stern, N. (2022). A time for action on climate change and a time for change in economics. *Economic Journal, 132*, 1259–1289.

Suchodolski, S. G., *et al.* (2022). From global to local: Subnational development banks in the era of sustainable development goals. *Review of Political Economy, 34*(2), 318–339.

UNDP (2021). The gathering storm — Adapting to climate change in a post-pandemic world. Adaptation Gap Report 2021. Nairobi, United Nations Environment Programme.

UNEP (2021). Adaptation gap report 2020. Nairobi.

UNFCCC (2014). Biennial Assessment and Overview of Climate Finance Flows Report. UNFCCC Standing Committee on Finance. Bonn.

UNFCCC (2021). Introduction to climate finance.

Wang, H. (2021). Regime complexity and complex foreign policy: China in international development finance governance. *Global Policy, 12*(4), 69–79.

Weikmans, R. & Roberts, J. T. (2019). The international climate finance accounting muddle: Is there hope on the horizon? *Climate and Development, 11*(2), 97–111.

World Bank (2021). World Bank Group climate change action plan 2021–2025: Supporting green, resilient, and inclusive development. World Bank, Washington, DC.

World Resource Institute (WRI) (2019). Key policy issues in the Green Climate Fund: A guide for the perplexed. Washington, DC.

Xu, J., Ren, X., & Wu, X. (2019). Mapping development finance institutions worldwide: Definitions, rationales, and varieties. NSE Development Financing Research Report No. 1.

Xu, J., *et al.* (2021). What are public development banks and development financing institutions? — Qualification criteria, stylized facts and development trends. *China Economic Quarterly International, 1*(4), 271–294.

Yuan, F. & Gallagher, K. P. (2018). Greening development lending in the Americas: Trends and determinants. *Ecological Economics, 154*, 189–200.

Zamarioli, L. H., *et al.* (2021). The climate consistency goal and the transformation of global finance. *Nature Climate Change, 11*, 578–583.

© 2024 World Scientific Publishing Europe Ltd.
https://doi.org/10.1142/9781800614451_0008

Chapter 8

Equity Capital as a Driver of Sustainable Transition

Jonathan Taglialatela[*,†,§], **Roberto Barontini**[‡,¶], **and Francesco Testa**[‡,||]

[†]*School of Management, Politecnico di Milano, Milan, Italy*
[‡]*Institute of Management, Sant'Anna School of Advanced Studies, Pisa, Italy*
[§]*jonathan.taglialatela@polimi.it*
[¶]*roberto.barontini@santannapisa.it*
[||]*francesco.testa@santannapisa.it*

Abstract

This chapter provides exploratory evidence on the importance of equity capital as a determinant of the performance of environmental, social, and governance (ESG) factors. We suggest that more evidence is needed on the drivers of ESG performance, and we investigate the role of lagged equity capital as its determinant. We argue that due to the long-term payoff structure and cash flow volatility of ESG investments as well as the incentives to direct resources toward existing bondholders, equity capital is better suited to support the implementation of ESG practices compared to traditional debt. We test this hypothesis by analyzing the ESG performance dimensions of an international sample of 6,638 firms and find that firms with a higher equity-to-asset ratio exhibit a significantly higher ESG performance. These results hold on the aggregated ESG score and on the pillar scores. The empirical evidence provided is useful to asset managers and decision makers who must screen firms for their ESG potential and choose the better financial resources in the perspective of firm sustainability aims.

---

[*]Corresponding author.

1. Introduction

This chapter investigates the relationship between a firm's share of equity financing and Environmental, Social, and Governance (ESG) performance. All parties involved in the sustainable transition are making huge efforts to identify successful strategies to speed up the adoption of ethical social and governance practices, to achieve decarbonization, and to support the adoption of environmentally friendly business practices. In such a dynamic context, firms must gather relevant amounts of new financial resources. The instruments used to raise this capital, i.e., the firm's financing mix, might be significantly associated with their ESG performance.

We provide new evidence on the financing strategies that result in a better performance in environmental, social, and governance characteristics (Gillan *et al.*, 2021). Previous literature has explored the link between sustainability-related efforts and firm financing mix, suggesting that sustainable practices have a negative correlation with the use of leverage, since firms with a better ESG performance are more likely to be financed with equity (Pijourlet, 2013). In addition, evidence supports the existence of a negative relationship between the use of debt and fair employee treatment (Verwijmeren and Derwall, 2010; Bae, Kang, and Wang, 2011). However, our study discusses the opposite temporal and causal perspective, analyzing whether a firm's share of equity financing is significantly associated with the subsequent ESG performance. Indeed, ESG investments are recognized as expensive in the short term and tend to provide returns in the long term (Starks, Venkat, and Zhu, 2020). Therefore, this payoff structure might be suboptimal when finance is raised by debt instruments, which require immediate cash flows to repay interests and capital. Conversely, equity capital might be a more feasible choice due to increased flexibility from a temporal perspective. Consequently, managers of firms that are mostly financed by equity capital could be more likely to implement sustainable practices, resulting in these firms being better performers from an ESG perspective.

We investigate if this is the case with an empirical analysis of Refinitiv's ESG data. Our results suggest that equity financing is positively associated with ESG performance. From the environmental perspective, additional equity financing is associated with lower emissions of pollutants in the atmosphere and higher efficiency in using natural resources. The results on the social dimension suggest a similar trend, highlighting that firms with more equity resources tend to have a higher commitment toward the community, human rights, and the well-being of their work force. The governance scores are higher for equity financed firms, suggesting that equity intensive firms do better in the implementation of good governance practices and on adopting CSR policies.

Therefore, our evidence supports the view that equity financing is associated with better ESG performance. Recent worldwide developments, especially the need to tackle the climate change issue, have called for a change in the corporate sector's attitude toward the adoption of sustainable policies, supporting the shift to a long-term perspective in taking investment decisions. Our study provides evidence that the implementation of sustainable practices, which imply a long-term orientation, seems better supported by equity financing. These results could be useful in designing effective policies to speed up the sustainable transition. In addition, managers that are interested in improving their firms' ESG performances can take this evidence into account when deciding which financing instruments are more appropriate to the task.

The remainder of this chapter is structured as follows: the next section summarizes existing literature and develops a hypothesis. Section 3 describes the data and the methodology; Section 4 introduces econometric estimates and discussion; and Section 5 describes conclusions along with the limitations and future research directions.

2. Leverage and ESG performance

The relationship between equity financing and ESG performance has been subject to substantial scrutiny by academic researchers. A large literature investigates if the implementation of ESG practices affects the importance of debt in the firm financing mix, with the aim to justify a causal effect from ESG measures toward capital structure choices. According to existing findings, firms with a better ESG performance have a lower cost of equity (El Ghoul *et al.*, 2011; Breuer *et al.*, 2018), a lower cost of debt (Raimo *et al.*, 2021; Mariani *et al.*, 2021), and better credit ratings (Jiraporn *et al.*, 2014). Other authors show that firms investing more in sustainable practices are more likely to receive equity financing (Pijourlet, 2013) and find that fair employee treatment is negatively associated with debt usage (Bae, Kang, and Wang, 2011). The results of these studies suggest that whether a firm implements sustainable practices is a relevant determinant of its subsequent capital structure choices, and that such practices contribute to lower information asymmetries, in turn affecting financing choices — for a comprehensive review see Benlemlih (2017). All existing studies adopt a perspective that investigates the impact of ESG practices on several dimensions related to financing decisions. This evidence has helped to inform managers of the most likely consequences of implementing sustainable business strategies.

Nevertheless, in the most recent years we have observed a change in the attitude toward ESG practices in the corporate world. Indeed, since 2015 we have witnessed the United Nations approving the 2030 Agenda for Sustainable Development, the European Union setting up a Sustainable Finance Action Plan, and even leading asset managers claiming that firms should embrace a sustainable approach to doing business (Fink, 2022). Clearly, these developments stress the need to identify the factors that can increase firms' sustainable performance and speed up the sustainable transition. Therefore, in this chapter we reverse the approach adopted by the previous literature, discussing the role of the equity versus debt financing as a means to finance the implementation of ESG practices. Then, we try to answer the following question: *are firms with higher shares of equity financing able to obtain a better ESG performance?*

According to both academics and practitioners, sustainable investment seems to be profitable in the long term rather than in the short term (Starks, Venkat, and Zhu, 2020; McKinsey, 2019). Starks, Venkat, and Zhu (2020) highlight that ESG-related investments are able to improve environmental, social, and governance performance but seem costly in the short term and are more valued by long-term investors. On the one hand, a firm financed with equity capital might have the flexibility to tolerate short-term losses and the ability to wait the time that is necessary for sustainable practices to create value. On the other hand, firms that rely heavily on debt capital must be ready to direct cash flows toward interest payments. In addition, the payments on interest expenses start immediately after contracting the debt and missing these payments can increase the bankruptcy risk. As a result, more indebted firms have a lower ability to invest in projects with less predictable cash flows or where the value creation happens too far in the future.

The relationship between cash flow volatility of Corporate Social Responsibility (CSR) intensive firms is, therefore, a relevant issue to take into consideration when investigating if equity-intensive firms are better drivers to speed up the sustainable transition. A recent study by Sun and Ding (2020) finds that the relationship between ESG practices and the volatility of firms' cash flow is well explained by a U-shaped curve. According to the authors, additional ESG practices will first increase the firms' moral capital, reassuring stakeholders that the firm is effectively safeguarding their interests. However, after a certain threshold, the financial burden associated with ESG practices and the competition that they have with other uses of funds contribute to increase the cash flow volatility. We argue that firm managers ruling over a firm financing policy are aware that substantial amounts of equity investments can stand the potential short-term losses and the increase in volatility of cash flows that are related to ESG practices and therefore might decide to implement them to capture long-term value opportunities and the benefits with stakeholder relations. However, the same is not applicable for highly indebted firms. Indeed, cash flow volatility is negatively correlated with debt financing (Keefe and Yaghoubi, 2016), because firms with increasingly volatile cash flow might find it substantially difficult to repay their debt on time. Consequently, managers of indebted firms are aware of these increased risks and might avoid implementing ESG practices, to direct their available cash flows toward investments that are able to provide short-term and less volatile value, in turn ensuring that debt can be repaid. Then, firms with a higher share of equity financing might be better equipped to catch the opportunities offered by ESG investments.

At last, inspired by the work of Bae, Kang, and Wang (2011) that links leverage and fair employee treatment, additional support to our theoretical framework comes from the capital structure model developed by Maksimovic and Titman (1991). This model shows that the incentives for a firm to honor its implicit contracts with stakeholders actually affect their willingness to do business with the firm. Indeed, their model demonstrates that indebted firms have an incentive to reduce product quality in order to increase current cash flows and satisfy existing bondholders, and this incentive is stronger if these changes cannot be identified immediately by the stakeholders. We argue that the relationship between equity levels and ESG practices can be viewed through this perspective. ESG enhancing measures can be seen as an implicit contract between the firm and its stakeholders, as suggested by the stakeholder theory (Coase, 1937; Freeman, 1984; Freeman *et al.*, 2004). In addition, as demonstrated by the existence of greenwashing practices (Bowen and Aragon-Correa, 2014; Delmas and Burbano, 2011; Testa *et al.*, 2018), the quality of ESG measures implemented might be disguised by managers and the actual measures implemented might be recognized only years later. Therefore, for indebted firms there is, after contracting the debt, an incentive to reduce or avoid ESG enhancing practices in order to direct those resources toward bondholders claims.

This theoretical reasoning suggests that firms that are more equity-intensive will be more attracted toward ESG enhancing projects, whereas higher levels of debt might lead managers to avoid or reduce their efforts in terms of ESG practices with the aim to free up available cash flows that can be used to repay the debt. Accordingly, our hypothesis states the following:

Hypothesis 1 The equity-to-asset ratio is positively correlated to ESG performance and to individual scores.

3. Data and methodology

The data used for this analysis are gathered from Refinitiv's Asset4 database. Refinitiv, which owns Thomson Reuters data platform, is one of the most important providers of sustainability-related and financial data. We use the Asset4 database, which is integrated in the EIKON-Datastream platform and covers around 8,500 firms globally, representing 70% of the global market capitalization.

The framework of Refinitiv's ESG ratings is summarized in Figure 1. For each of the firms included in the database, Asset4's content research analysts gather documental proofs to justify more than 450 datapoints. Among these datapoints, 186 comparable measures are used in the ESG scoring process. These data are grouped in 10 category scores, which represent several dimensions of the environmental, social, and governance concepts. To calculate the category scores, a percentile ranking methodology is adopted, which aims to

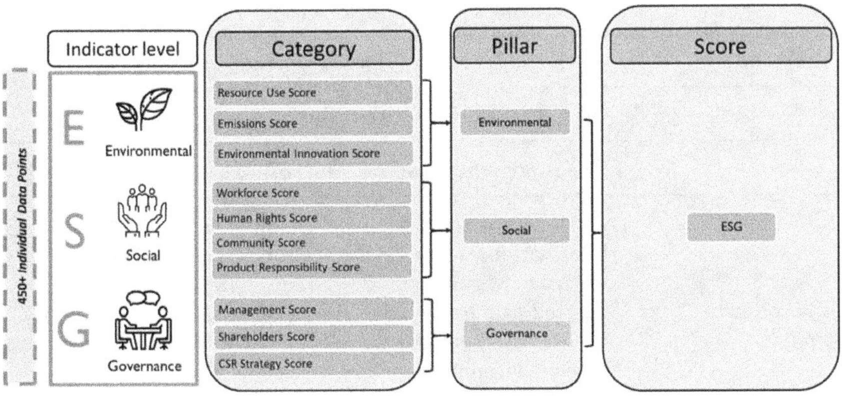

Figure 1. Structure of Refinitiv ESG indicators.

assign scores that are based on the performance of other firms in the same industry.

The category scores are then rolled up into three pillar scores, which correspond to the main ESG dimensions. To consider the importance of the ESG themes in different industries, a proprietary ESG Magnitude Matrix is implemented in the form of category weights. Similarly, the pillar scores are weighted together to originate the aggregated ESG score, which provides a general indication of the ESG performance of the firm (Refinitiv, 2021).

To perform the analysis, we downloaded the full set of ESG scores, pillars, and category scores for all firms included in the Asset4 database. At the time of data downloading (May 2020), the entire database included 8,512 firms. After excluding firms belonging to the financial services sector, we created a panel dataset for 6,638 firms for 15 years (2003–2018). Our empirical analysis includes the firms' ESG scores, the pillar scores, and each category score. The independent variable is the ratio of Total Equity to Total Asset. Table 1 exhibits the list of variables that we include in our models and descriptive statistics for the sample are reported in Table 2.

We start the analysis of our sample by creating a dummy variable that equals 1 if in a given year the equity/asset ratio is below the sample median. Table 3 exhibits a series of t-tests on all the dependent variables that indicate ESG performance, comparing the subsample with higher equity ratio to the subsample with lower equity ratio,

Table 1. Variable list.

Variable	Description
	Dependent variables
	ESG aggregated score and pillars
ESG score	Overall company score based on the self-reported information in the environmental, social, and corporate governance pillars.
Environment pillar	Weighted average relative rating of a company based on the reported environmental information and the resulting three environmental category scores.
Social pillar	Weighted average relative rating of a company based on the reported social information and the resulting four social category scores.
Governance pillar	Weighted average relative rating of a company based on the reported governance information and the resulting three governance category scores.
	Environmental
Emission	A company's commitment and effectiveness toward reducing environmental emission in the production and operational processes.
Environmental innovation	A company's capacity to reduce the environmental costs and burdens for its customers, thereby creating new market opportunities through new environmental technologies and processes or eco-designed products.
Resource use	A company's performance and capacity to reduce the use of materials, energy, or water, and to find more eco-efficient solutions by improving supply chain management.
	Social
Community	The company's commitment toward being a good citizen, protecting public health, and respecting business ethics.
Human rights	A company's effectiveness toward respecting the fundamental human rights conventions.
Product responsibility	A company's capacity to produce quality goods and services integrating the customer's health and safety, integrity, and data privacy.
Workforce	A company's effectiveness in ensuring job satisfaction, creating a healthy and safe workplace, maintaining diversity and equal opportunities, and developing opportunities for its workforce.

Table 1. *(Continued)*

Variable	Description
	Dependent variables
	Governance
Management	Measures a company's commitment and effectiveness toward following best practice corporate governance principles.
Shareholders	A company's effectiveness toward equal treatment of shareholders and the use of anti-takeover devices.
CSR strategy	A company's practices to communicate that it integrates the economic (financial), social, and environmental dimensions into its day-to-day decision-making processes.
	Control variables
Equity on total assets	Total equity on total assets.
Capital intensity	Total assets on revenues.
Log of total assets	Logarithm of firm's total assets.
Sales growth	Year-on-year turnover growth.
EBITDA on total assets	Earnings before interest, taxes, depreciation, and amortization divided total asset.

with all equity ratios one year lagged to reduce the risk of confoundedness. As suggested by the results, all ESG performance indicators seem significantly lower in the case of firms with lower share of equity financing. In order to investigate this further, we run pooled ordinary least squares (OLS) regressions with clustered standard errors on firms, estimating the following equation:

$$Y_{it} = \beta_0 + \beta_1 \text{ Equity\_int}_i + \beta_2 \text{X}_\text{i} + \varepsilon_{it}$$

where Y_{it} represents the different dimensions of ESG performance that we consider, Equity_int$_i$ is the independent variable representing the share of equity resources on the total assets, and X_i represents a vector of control variables including firm size (logarithm of total asset), year, sector, country, sales growth, and profitability.

Table 2. Descriptive statistics.

Descriptive statistics	Mean	Std. dev.	Median	Min.	Max.
ESG score	40.020	20.457	37.530	0.120	95.070
Environment pillar score	31.877	28.146	26.800	0.000	99.060
Social pillar score	39.921	23.447	36.450	0.050	98.640
Governance pillar score	47.749	22.619	47.750	0.150	99.330
Emissions score	35.986	33.243	30.460	0.000	99.820
Environmental innovation score	21.094	29.702	0.000	0.000	99.810
Resource use score	35.886	33.219	30.360	0.000	99.830
Community score	49.779	28.901	49.640	0.000	99.870
Human rights score	22.118	31.295	0.000	0.000	99.480
Product responsibility score	38.607	32.165	33.820	0.000	99.850
Workforce score	50.164	28.841	50.000	0.140	99.870
CSR strategy score	31.947	33.237	20.910	0.000	99.870
Management score	50.173	28.515	50.000	0.020	99.980
Shareholder score	50.313	28.839	50.000	0.050	99.980
Leverage (equity/total asset)	0.691	0.239	0.695	0.245	1.000
Log total assets	14.062	1.964	14.170	0.000	20.745
Sales growth	0.104	0.262	0.077	−0.534	1.023
EBITDA on total assets	0.112	0.106	0.115	−0.163	0.305
Observations	87,979				

4. Econometric results

The econometric analysis presented in this chapter starts with the analysis of the ESG score and of the environmental, social, and governance pillars. Table 4 exhibits OLS pooled regression with standard errors clustered on the individual firms. Model 1 shows that the ESG score is positively correlated to the ratio of equity resources on total assets. We observe a similar and strongly significant positive relationship also for Environmental, Social, and Governance pillars'

Table 3. ***T*-tests on ESG performance of the firms comparing firms with an equity/asset ratio, lower than the sample median (calculated on a yearly level) to firms with an equity/asset ratio higher than the sample median.**

	***T*-test**	***t*-stat**
ESG score	-5.514^{***}	(−29.55)
Environment pillar score	-8.815^{***}	(−34.38)
Social pillar score	-4.983^{***}	(−23.18)
Governance pillar score	-3.766^{***}	(−18.16)
Emissions score	-9.619^{***}	(−31.72)
Environmental innovation score	-6.971^{***}	(−25.12)
Resource use score	-8.543^{***}	(−28.12)
Community score	-6.002^{***}	(−22.64)
Human rights score	-4.999^{***}	(−17.36)
Product responsibility score	-5.205^{***}	(−17.62)
Workforce score	-4.728^{***}	(−17.85)
CSR strategy score	-8.508^{***}	(−28.03)
Management score	-3.426^{***}	(−13.09)
Shareholder score	-1.788^{***}	(−6.74)
Observations	47,634	

Note: The equity/asset ratio is one year lagged. t statistics are in parentheses, $^{***}p < 0.01$.

scores, providing an initial support for our hypothesis. Size and profitability are significantly and positively related to ESG performance, suggesting that larger, more profitable firms exhibit a better ESG performance. On the other hand, we find that sales growth is negatively associated with ESG performance, suggesting that a higher growth rate might result in a lower ability to implement sustainable practices, which might be due to the managers' focus on handling the firms' expansion. We drill down in this analysis by focusing on the specific indicators that compose each specific score, in order to understand if equity intensity is specifically relevant for certain dimensions.

Table 5 digs deeper on the environmental dimension, providing OLS regression for Emission scores (model 1), Environmental Innovation scores (model 2), and Resource Use scores (model 3). Equity financing is positively correlated to the scores achieved in

Table 4. Pooled OLS regression of ESG performance indicators on equity/total asset.

	(1) ESG	(2) Environment pillar	(3) Social pillar	(4) Governance pillar
Equity/ total asset	4.188***	4.041***	5.171***	3.529***
	(0.871)	(1.170)	(1.008)	(1.045)
Log total assets	8.181***	10.601***	8.361***	5.533***
	(0.143)	(0.189)	(0.166)	(0.177)
Sales growth	−6.274***	−7.290***	−5.702***	−5.964***
	(0.385)	(0.496)	(0.452)	(0.514)
EBITDA/ total assets	18.274***	17.359***	18.947***	18.180***
	(1.674)	(2.264)	(1.980)	(2.040)
Nation	Y	Y	Y	Y
Sector	Y	Y	Y	Y
N	43917	43836	43836	43917
R-squared	0.425	0.456	0.404	0.144

Note: All independent variables are lagged by one year. Standard errors are in parentheses. Significance level: $^{***}p < 0.01$.

the emission, in line with recent evidence on the link of carbon emission and financial structure (Yao and Tang, 2021). Similarly, a more equity-intensive firm shows a higher performance in efficient use of natural resources and in adoption of eco-efficient solutions along its supply chain. These results are expected and in line with our theoretical framework. Surprisingly, the lagged financial structure does not seem to be a significant determinant of firms' environmental innovation efforts, in contrast to previous evidence that suggests that additional equity financing is positively associated with green innovation (Yang *et al.*, 2020; Xiang *et al.*, 2022). However, existing evidence is mainly focused on green patenting and R&D efforts, which suffer from high levels of asymmetric information that specifically suits them to be financed with equity capital. Refinitiv's Environmental Innovation scores, which can be defined as the firms capacity to implement new environmental technologies and processes or eco-designed products, is based on a wide set of indicators that are aimed at measuring the company's capacity to reduce environmental costs,

Table 5. Pooled OLS regression of environmental performance indicators on equity/total asset.

	(1) Emissions	(2) Environmental innovation	(3) Resource use
Equity/ total assets	6.926***	0.542	6.866***
	(1.386)	(1.305)	(1.418)
Log total assets	12.335***	6.441***	12.086***
	(0.224)	(0.249)	(0.224)
Sales growth	−8.277***	−4.217***	−8.865***
	(0.594)	(0.558)	(0.622)
EBITDA/ total assets	21.874***	2.122	25.050***
	(2.651)	(2.561)	(2.763)
Nation	Y	Y	Y
Sector	Y	Y	Y
N	43,833	42,502	43,833
R-squared	0.437	0.303	0.400

Note: All independent variables are lagged by one year. Standard errors are in parentheses. Significance level: $^{***}p < 0.01$.

such as introduction of products with positive effects on the environment or as the application of screening criteria to its asset under management, a set of measures that might be less sensitive to the financing source employed.

Table 6 provides regression models on the social score components, suggesting that firms with a higher share of equity financing are better in serving the community (model 1) and in respecting the rights of humanity (model 2) and of their workforce (model 4). These results are in line with our expectations, suggesting a positive effect of equity financing on the firms social efforts, and are in agreement with findings in the literature that suggest that firms introducing CSR measures are financed with shareholders' equity rather than long-term debt (Benlemlih, 2017). However, we do not find a positive and significant effect of the financing sources on the product responsibility score (model 3). This suggests that the ability of the companies to introduce health, safety, and data privacy measures in their products is not determined by their level of equity financing. In that case, the existing public policies and regulations play a pivotal

Table 6. Pooled OLS of social performance indicators on equity/total asset.

	(1) Community	(2) Human rights	(3) Product responsibility	(4) Workforce
Equity/ total assets	3.390***	6.535***	0.963	6.945***
	(1.195)	(1.318)	(1.488)	(1.224)
Log total assets	8.416***	8.774***	6.913***	8.975***
	(0.191)	(0.243)	(0.258)	(0.194)
Sales growth	−6.401***	−5.236***	−7.095***	−5.613***
	(0.566)	(0.581)	(0.660)	(0.597)
EBITDA/ total assets	14.405***	22.515***	19.115***	26.361***
	(2.366)	(2.621)	(2.924)	(2.431)
Nation	Y	Y	Y	Y
Sector	Y	Y	Y	Y
N	43,833	43,833	43,833	43,833
R-squared	0.354	0.345	0.216	0.362

Note: All independent variables are lagged by one year. Standard errors are in parentheses. Significance level: $^{***}p < 0.01$.

role in pushing firms to adopt those initiatives by probably making the role of financing resources irrelevant.

At last, Table 7 shows pooled OLS regressions for the determinants of the governance score. The econometric results suggest that a positive relationship exists between the share of equity financing and the adoption of a CSR strategy (model 1) and the implementation of best practices in corporate governance (model 2), results that are in line with our expectations. Surprisingly, we do not observe a significant relationship between the share of equity financing and the shareholder score, which tries to measure the effectiveness of the company in the equal treatment of shareholders and in using anti-takeover devices, including several datapoints that are focused on controversies and shareholder protection. Despite the fact that better quality of shareholder protection policies and enforcement leads to lower agency costs and therefore lower leverage (Gungoraydinoglu and Öztekin, 2011), the opposite might not always be the case. Indeed, differently than other measures analyzed, such practices

Table 7. Pooled OLS regression of governance performance indicators on equity/total asset.

	(1) CSR strategy	(2) Management	(3) Shareholder
Equity/total assets	7.117***	3.770***	0.349
	(1.380)	(1.323)	(1.386)
Log total assets	12.056***	5.233***	2.297***
	(0.234)	(0.221)	(0.246)
Sales growth	−7.068***	−7.144***	−1.248*
	(0.632)	(0.669)	(0.717)
EBITDA/total assets	19.208***	21.527***	5.413**
	(2.712)	(2.636)	(2.758)
Nation	Y	Y	Y
Sector	Y	Y	Y
N	43,918	43,960	43,960
R-squared	0.379	0.088	0.030

Note: Standard errors are in parentheses. Significance levels: $^{*}p < 0.1$, $^{**}p < 0.05$, $^{***}p < 0.01$.

might be less impactful on the future expected cash flows. As a result, managers will not necessarily be driven by equity/asset ratio when deciding whether to implement these measures, but rather by other factors, such as the ownership structure, including the existence of controlling shareholders or of takeover threats.

4.1. *Robustness analyses*

According to existing literature, the investigation of firm capital structure should take into account that common leverage measures are often imperfect (Keefe and Yaghoubi, 2016; Welch, 2011). In order to corroborate our results, we repeat the estimations employing alternative specifications to our equity/total asset ratio. First, we include the Net financial position (Net Debt) divided by the firm's earnings before interests, taxes, depreciation, and amortization (EBITDA). Then, as an alternative, we also use firms' Total Debt divided by its Total Equity. In both variables, the occurrence of a negative denominator (either negative equity or negative EBITDA) resulted in extreme values where extremely leveraged firms exhibited a negative leverage. To correct for these deviations, we applied the following procedure: first, we calculated the leverage proxy; then we removed from the sample the firms whose denominator was negative; subsequently, we calculated a measure of the variation around the median value as median ±2* interquartile range of the leverage indicator, obtaining an upper and a lower bound of the distribution. Then, we winsorized the extreme values within the upper and lower bounds of the distribution. At last, we reintroduced the firms with negative value assigning the upper bound as default value for the leverage ratio. When included in the analysis, both alternative specifications support the results of the main analyses.

5. Conclusion and limitations

This chapter investigates the role of equity capital as a driver of ESG performance. A rich literature has investigated the effect of implementing ESG measures on the capital structure and financing choices of firms. However, evidence on the type of financing structures that are associated with future implementation of ESG practices is still scant.

In this chapter, we provide an exploratory analysis of this relationship. We start by observing that several studies hint that ESG practices cause a lower cost of capital, better credit ratings, and lower information asymmetry (Breuer *et al.*, 2018; El Ghoul *et al.*, 2011; Mariani *et al.*, 2021; Raimo *et al.*, 2021; Jiraporn *et al.*, 2014). Firms implementing ESG practices are also more likely to receive equity financing and to treat their employees fairly (Pijourlet, 2013; Bae, Kang, and Wang, 2011). However, we argue that we need more evidence from the opposite perspective, that is, showing how a given financial structure might influence the implementation of ESG performance.

Therefore, we collect ESG and financial data for all the firms covered in the Refinitiv Asset4 database. We focus on the aggregated ESG scores, on the Environmental, Social, and Governance pillars, and on the 10 category scores on which the latter are based. We divide the sample in two, comparing the firms with an equity/asset ratio higher than the median to the other half of the sample. Through a battery of t-tests, we find that the aggregated ESG score, the pillars, and the category scores are all higher for firms that are in the higher equity/asset ratio, suggesting that additional investigation is needed. Then, we implement pooled OLS regressions for each of these dependent variables, linking the ratio equity/total asset one year lagged to each ESG performance indicator.

The results on the ESG score and the pillars are unanimous in supporting our hypothesis, suggesting that firms that have a higher share of equity capital are significantly better performers in terms of implementation of ESG practices. Then, we drill down on each specific category score. We find that more equity capital is associated with lower emissions and better eco-efficiency, but that it is not a significant determinant of a firm's capacity to invest in new environmental technologies and processes or eco-designed products. When exploring the determinants of the social performance, results suggest that less indebted firms are better in serving the community, and in respecting human rights and their workforce, in line with previous findings in the literature. However, the implementation of product responsibility measures such as health, safety, and data privacy characteristics is not driven by the level of equity capital. At last, we focus on governance category scores, and we find that equity capital is positively related to the implementation of a CSR strategy and of managerial best practices. However, approving shareholder protection measures and anti-takeover provisions seems not to be determined by the level of equity financing.

Overall, this chapter provides a first exploratory analysis of the role of capital structure as a determinant of ESG performance. We argue that recent global changes in the attitude toward ESG practices and investments have created a need to identify the most promising firms in terms of ESG potential, rather than investigating the consequences of implementing ESG practices.

We have only scratched the surface of this issue, providing an overall indication of the association between lagged equity/asset ratio and the subsequent several dimensions of ESG performance. Indeed, the results presented suffer from several limitations. The most relevant is certainly that the methodology that we implemented does not allow us to test and claim a causal relationship between equity/asset ratio and sustainable performance. Future research might implement causal inference methodologies that allow certain estimation of not only the direction but also the magnitude of the effect of additional equity financing on firms' ESG performances.

In addition, as highlighted previously, we only relate the leverage levels in a certain point in time with ESG performance indicators. However, an interesting perspective might focus on isolating the trends in capital structure dynamics to better establish the persistence between certain financing choices and subsequent changes in ESG performance. Moreover, future scholars may explore which organizational dynamics are triggered by different financing structures, which can explain different ESG performances.

All in all, after considering the limitations of the study, our results should open up a debate in the academic community, which so far has often neglected the role of leverage in determining ESG performance. At last, these results should be useful to asset managers and decision makers who have to identify and screen firms that are most promising from an ESG performance perspective. The actual level of equity/asset seems to be a relevant predictor of the future sustainable performance and should therefore be taken into account in the decision processes.

Acknowledgment

We are grateful to FondoFSI for the support received for this research. An intermediate version of this chapter appeared in the report by Scuola Superiore Sant'Anna and FondoFSI titled "The role of finance in a sustainable transition".

References

Bae, K. H., Kang, J. K., & Wang, J. (2011). Employee treatment and firm leverage: A test of the stakeholder theory of capital structure. *Journal of Financial Economics*, *100*, 130–153.

Benlemlih, M. (2017). Corporate social responsibility and firm financing decisions: A literature review. *Journal of Multinational Financial Management*, *42–43*, 1–10.

Bowen, F. & Aragon-Correa, J. A. (2014). Greenwashing in corporate environmentalism research and practice: The importance of what we say and do. *Organization and Environment*, *27*, 107–112.

Breuer, W., Muller, T., Rosenbach, D., & Salzmann, A. (2018). Corporate social responsibility, investor protection, and cost of equity: A cross-country comparison. *Journal of Banking & Finance, 96*, 34–55.

Coase, R. H. (1937). The nature of the firm. *Economica, 4*, 386–405.

Delmas, M. A. & Burbano, V. C. (2011). The drivers of greenwashing. *California Management Review, 54*, 64–87.

El Ghoul, S., Guedhami, O., Kwok, C. C. Y., & Mishra, D. R. (2011). Does corporate social responsibility affect the cost of capital? *Journal of Banking & Finance, 35*, 2388–2406.

Fink, L. (2022). Annual Letter to CEO, Blackrock. Retrieved from https://www.blackrock.com/corporate/investor-relations/larry-fink-ceo-letter.

Freeman, R. E. (1984). *Strategic Management: A Stakeholder Approach.* Boston: Pitman.

Freeman, R. E., Wicks, A. C., & Parmar, B. (2004). Stakeholder theory and "the corporate objective revisited". *Organization Science, 15*, 364–369.

Gillan, S. L., Koch, A., & Starks, L. T. (2021). Firms and social responsibility: A review of ESG and CSR research in corporate finance. *Journal of Corporate Finance, 66*, 101889.

Gungoraydinoglu, A. & Öztekin, Ö. (2011). Firm- and country-level determinants of corporate leverage: Some new international evidence. *Journal of Corporate Finance, 17*, 1457–1474.

Jiraporn, P., Jiraporn, N., Boeprasert, A., & Chang, K. (2014). Does corporate social responsibility (CSR) improve credit ratings? Evidence from geographic identification. *Financial Management, 43*, 505–531.

Keefe, M. O. & Yaghoubi, M. (2016). The influence of cash flow volatility on capital structure and the use of debt of different maturities. *Journal of Corporate Finance, 38*, 18–36.

Maksimovic, V. & Titman, S. (1991). Financial policy and reputation for product quality. *Review of Financial Studies, 4*, 175–200.

Mariani, M., Pizzutilo, F., Caragnano, A., & Zito, M. (2021). Does it pay to be environmentally responsible? Investigating the effect on the weighted average cost of capital. *Corporate Social Responsibility and Environmental Management, 28*, 1854–1869.

McKinsey (2019). Five ways that ESG creates value. In *McKinsey Quarterly* (pp. 1–12). McKinsey & Company.

Pijourlet, G. (2013). Corporate social responsibility and financial decisions. In European Financial Management Association (Eds.), *European Financial Management Association Annual Meeting.* Reading: EFMA.

Raimo, N., Caragnano, A., Zito, M., Vitolla, F., & Mariani, M. (2021). Extending the benefits of ESG disclosure: The effect on the cost of debt financing. *Corporate Social Responsibility and Environmental Management, 28*, 1412–1421.

Refinitiv (2021). Environmental, social and governance (ESG) scores from Refinitiv. Retrieved from https://www.refinitiv.com/content/dam/marketing/en_us/documents/methodology/refinitiv-esg-scores-methodology.pdf.

Starks, L. T., Venkat, P., & Zhu, Q. (2020). Corporate ESG profiles and investor horizons. *SSRN Electronic Journal.* Working Paper.

Sun, W. B. & Ding, Y. (2020). Corporate social responsibility and cash flow volatility: The curvilinear moderation of marketing capability. *Journal of Business Research, 116*, 48–59.

Testa, F., Miroshnychenko, I., Barontini, R., & Frey, M. (2018). Does it pay to be a greenwasher or a brownwasher? *Business Strategy and the Environment, 27*, 1104–1116.

Verwijmeren, P. & Derwall, J. (2010). Employee well-being, firm leverage, and bankruptcy risk. *Journal of Banking & Finance, 34*, 956–964.

Welch, I. V. O. (2011). Two common problems in capital structure research: The financial-debt-to-asset ratio and issuing activity versus leverage changes. *International Review of Finance, 11*, 1–17.

Xiang, X., Liu, C., & Yang, M. (2022). Who is financing corporate green innovation? *International Review of Economics & Finance, 78*, 321–337.

Yang, B., Chou, H.-I., & Zhao, J. (2020). Innovation or dividend payout: Evidence from China. *International Review of Economics & Finance, 68*, 180–203.

Yao, X. & Tang, X. (2021). Does financial structure affect CO_2 emissions? Evidence from G20 countries. *Finance Research Letters, 41*, 101791.

© 2024 World Scientific Publishing Europe Ltd.
https://doi.org/10.1142/9781800614451_0009

Chapter 9

Can Central Banks Go Green? The Interaction Between Monetary Policy and Climate Change

Xuan-Hoa Nghiem[†,¶], **Hai Hong Trinh**[*,‡,‖], **and Ikram Ullah Khan**[§,**]

[†]*Faculty of Economics and Management, International School, Vietnam National University, Hanoi, Vietnam*
[‡]*School of Economics and Finance, Massey University, Palmerston North, New Zealand*
[§]*Institute of Management Sciences, University of Science and Technology Bannu, Khyber Pakhtunkhwa (KP), Pakistan*
[¶]*hoanx@vnuis.edu.vn, xuanhoanghiem@gmail.com*
[‖]*h.h.trinh@massey.ac.nz*
[**]*ikram.bnu@gmail.com*

Abstract

Since the 2030 Agenda for Sustainable Development was adopted by the United Nations in 2015 and combating climate change with urgent action is the 13th Sustainable Development Goal (SDG), the roles of financial sectors including central banking systems in facilitating sustainable finance have been documented (Dikau and Volz, 2019, 2021). Since the responsibility for financial and macroeconomic uncertainties is a part of the functionality of central banking systems as well as their regulatory control over credit, monetary, and financial systems, the allocations of

[*]Corresponding author.

green-oriented capital investments rely on their functionality and public financial governance policies. This chapter provides a literature review on central banking systems and their roles in fostering sustainable finance to mitigate climate change risk toward green growth.

1. Introduction

While the focus of the world over the last two years has been on the COVID-19 pandemic, there are still lingering problems that occupy the minds of policymakers, scholars, and ordinary people alike. Among them, probably one issue of utmost importance is climate change. Climate change appears to be an endemic problem that has not been properly and fully addressed. The effects of climate change are deep, devastating, and disastrous. The consequences of climate change risks include greenhouse gas (GHG) emissions, global warming, rising temperatures, more frequent natural calamities, and other inverse impacts on the world.

To mitigate the severe consequences of climate change, numerous measures have been proposed at different levels, including global, regional, national, and individual. However, the roles of the financial sector including banking institutions in mitigating the climate change risk have become more prominent and attracted more attention from international scholars in recent years (Bolton *et al.*, 2020; Bowman, 2010; Caby, Ziane, and Lamarque, 2020; Campiglio *et al.*, 2018; Chen *et al.*, 2021; Gonzalez, 2021; Grippa, Schmittmann, and Suntheim, 2019; Mackintosh, 2019; Svartzman *et al.*, 2021). Even though this is a relatively new emerging area, the fields of environmental and green finance have attracted increasing attention through their huge potential to help economies obtain the target of zero-emission and assist businesses in reducing their carbon-emitting activities. The financial sector and the banking industry in particular play a crucial leading role in allocating and managing investments in environmentally friendly projects to mitigate the effects of climate change worldwide, such as renewable energy, energy-saving activities, and vehicles including the use of solar power, electric motors, cars as well as clean energy usage and production projects (Grippa, Schmittmann, and Suntheim, 2019; HSBC, 2020). Among the major stakeholders in the field of green finance, banks are expected to make significant contributions to mitigating the consequences of climate change. However, despite its importance, studies on the roles of banking institutions in climate risk adaptation are limited in terms of the number of studies, scale, and scope. Since climate change action is the 13th priority among the 17 Sustainable Development Goals (SDGs)[1] proposed by the United Nations to combat the global climate change risk and its impacts, the involvement of the central banking systems through their regulatory monitoring in the credit, money, and financial systems in order to facilitate the development of green finance and to impose an appropriate carbon pricing approach to be followed by financial institutions toward sustainable development has been increasingly important in recent years (Dikau and Volz, 2019; Macaire and Naef, 2021; McConnell, Yanovski, and Lessmann, 2022). For a more detailed investigation of how "central banks" can go green, there is a need to synthesize the previous studies of central banks and their involvement in climate change action in recent years toward the 2030 Agenda for Sustainable Development adopted by the General Assembly of the United Nations in 2015.[2]

Motivated by the reasons mentioned above, this chapter contributes to the existing literature in the following ways. First and foremost, it provides a systemic literature review of the existing studies on the involvement of the central banks in climate change adaptation and their activities in designing, proposing, and implementing policies as well as allocating investments in green-oriented projects for mitigating the impacts of climate change risk worldwide. Second, this chapter proposes and describes two critical concepts including (1) green central bank and (2) central bank for green. The aim is to arrive at a better understanding of the differences between those two concepts and their clarification for readers, policymakers, and scholars on how monetary policies can generate different impacts as well as on their roles in combating climate change risk.

[1]For the full description of the UN's SDGs, please visit https://sdgs.un.org/goals.

[2]For the 2030 Agenda for Sustainable Development, please visit https://sdgs.un.org/2030agenda.

The arguments and analysis from the chapter put forward the two closely related concepts. While the "green central banking" approach views central banks as trouble-makers due to their "brown" activities, the "central banking for green" views central banks as having the potential and responsibility to make their activities and the financial system greener. The chapter also makes clear that if left unchecked and uncontained, climate change and its associated extreme weather events may inflict severe consequences on society in general and on the objectives of monetary policy in particular.

The remainder of this chapter is organized as follows: Section 2 provides an overview of climate change and related studies; Section 3 provides detailed discussions and a systemic literature review on the potential of monetary policies in tackling climate change effects; Section 4 elaborates in more detail on the effects of climate change risk and their associations with monetary policies adopted by central banking systems; and Section 5 concludes the main findings and important policy implications.

2. Climate change: An overview of its causes and consequences

The world today is facing serious issues in terms of global warming and other environmental concerns. The dire impacts of climate change are worsening and being felt everywhere while its future projections present a gloomy picture. For future survival, it is imperative to take notice and adapt to emerging needs to address climate changes. Climatic changes are evident from the fact that the Earth's climate displays abnormal patterns that may last for a long time. The changing environment hazards the lives of mankind. Many aspects of this degradation have severe adverse effects on human lives and other living beings. There are several causes of the depravation of the environment, like emissions of greenhouse gases that pollute the environment.

Climate changes have negative impacts on human lives such as spreading infectious diseases and other issues that are very harmful to society (Batten *et al.*, 2016). Previous literature shed light on how central banks can play a role in mitigating climate change concerns.

Many climate risks exist in today's industrialized society and both the industrial and financial sectors have to cope with the challenges of climate risks and devise policies to mitigate the harmful impacts of climate change (Dikau and Volz, 2021). The key factor of climate change is the explosion of CO_2 that is released into the environment mainly by human activities. Central banks are primarily responsible for setting monetary policies, which control the flow of demand and supply of money smoothly, and affect exchange rate stability. Several central banks are now committed to checking the implications of climate change and pro-environmental roles of banks as a result of national and international financial regulations (Campiglio *et al.*, 2018). Central banks can contribute to the understanding of climatic changes and their relationships by devising the framework for monetary policies. Carney (2015) describes two types of risks faced by financial institutions that are the outcomes of climate change; i.e., physical risks and transition risks.

The climatic change-related risks (like severe heatwaves, storms, and flood surges) can physically affect lives and finances of the insurers who now have to cover against them. The lender banks may face many losses in case such claims were not insured. To minimize such losses, carbon and a climate-friendly economy are necessary, which could cost in other ways like grounding the oil and gas reservoirs (Meinshausen *et al.*, 2009). These types of measures bring about significant changes in the central banks' mandates based on the extent to which they are concerned with addressing the climate-related issues. Physical risks, from improved frequency and severity of deadly weather events including hurricanes, also pose problems in the financial system. Similarly, transition risks, such as sudden tightening of policies concerning carbon emission, could also have adverse macroeconomic supply shock. Especially, the central banks' measures and instructions for other commercial banks to go online, promoting green banking, lesser use of fossil oil, focusing on utilizing renewable energy, and other environment-friendly practices have substantially grown to the desired level to curb environmental degradation. Climatic risks have a direct influence on agriculture and food products because of the seasonal price volatility. Similarly, energy-related products get a sharp increase in prices due to adverse climatic conditions. All such costs are affecting the inflationary pressures in an economy (de France, 2019).

3. The role of a central bank in the fight against climate change: A systemic literature review

3.1. *The central bank as a problem and as a solution*[3]

3.1.1. *Central bank as a problem (green central bank)*

A central bank, through the conduct of its monetary policy, can impact the climate change problem. If it wants to boost growth, its policy will be expansionary, thus encouraging businesses to expand their production, which in turn can increase pollution and worsen environmental issues. Therefore, central banks should consider environmental issues when designing and implementing monetary policies as well as performing other functions.

In the "central bank as a problem" (green central bank) approach, we hold that central banks may, either intentionally or unintentionally, cause environmental consequences. Therefore, central banks should be given the mandates to support the environment as well as other sustainable development goals.

One example of the detrimental impact of central banks on the environment is the fact that central banks may invest in companies that are carbon-intensive or do more harm than good to the environment in other ways. In other words, central banks may support brown financial flows — support fossil fuel companies. We explicitly mention three of these central banks, namely, the Swiss National Bank (SNB — the central bank of Switzerland), the European Central Bank (ECB), and the Bank of England (BoE — the central bank of England).

The first example, the SNB, has been infamous for its investments in firms in carbon-intensive industries (fossil fuel, automobile) (van 't Klooster and Fontan, 2020). Meanwhile, the ECB, in spite of being mandated to support sustainable development and protect the environment, has been criticized for ignoring environmental criteria. For example, terms, conditions, and criteria of the Corporate Sector

[3]We propose these concepts based on the idea of "green IT" (which views that the adoption of IT will result in environmental problems such as higher energy consumption, higher CO_2 emission) and "IT for green" (which sees IT as an important instrument in protecting the environment). For a detailed discussion, see Cai, Chen, and Bose (2013).

Purchase Program (CSPP) implemented by the ECB require firms to have a high credit rating, which in turn favors manufacturing, oil, and electricity companies with expensive equipment and reserves of natural resources serving as collateral, while firms engaging in renewable energy are denied the access.

Another example of the central bank's activities that do more harm than good to the environment is the establishment of the COVID Corporate Financing Facility (CCFF) by the Bank of England and the Treasury in March 2020. Despite the fact that the UK government pledged to "build back better" to make the UK economy fairer, greener, and more resilient, the CCFF's conditions are regarded as too easy and favorable for larger firms rather than the small and medium-sized enterprises (SMEs). Barmer, Kazi, and Youel (2020) estimate that more than 50% of loans provided by CCFF went to carbon-intensive firms such as car producers, oil and gas companies, and firms in the aviation industry. At a regional level, the European Central Bank (ECB) Quantitative Easing (QE) program has also been criticized for its bias toward carbon-intensive firms and discrimination against low-carbon firms, thus making it difficult for the decarbonization of economies (Dafermos *et al.*, 2020).

van 't Klooster and Fontan (2020) also posit that unconventional monetary policies carried out in European countries also worsen the environmental problem as central banks involved are given broader discretion without corresponding accountability. Furthermore, in the pursuit of market neutrality, programs implemented by central banks and commercial banks are often insensitive to environmental issues.

The above-mentioned analysis implies that several central banks have been engaged in activities detrimental to the environment. Therefore, central banks may pose serious problems and challenges to the fight against climate change as well as efforts to protect the environment and decarbonize economies. In this approach, we view central banks as problem-makers and relevant authorities have to take measures to make them become greener. This is the "central banks as a problem" or "green central banks" approach that we propose.[4]

[4]In this context, "green" implies (1) lower energy and water usage; (2) reduction of waste and pollution; (3) natural resources' conservation; and (4) reuse and recycling of materials (Hart, 1995; Cai, Chen, and Bose, 2013).

3.1.2. *Central bank as a solution (central bank for green)*

As Dikau and Volz (2021) argue, a central bank overlooking and ignoring climate-related risks is considered failing to fulfill its job. Therefore, it is not an overstatement to say that central banks have an important role to play and strong potential to realize in the fight against climate change.

For example, central banks can carry out measures aimed at reducing energy consumption, promoting energy saving as well as other sustainable activities. Central banks may also require commercial banks to give priority to projects that are environment-oriented. Another example of how central banks can help is to impose some measures aimed at scaling back the financing of fossil fuels (brown financial flows). Central banks are also expected to regularly disclose and communicate their climate track and alignments of their activities with climate commitments.

In spite of its crucial importance, the role played by central banks in the fight against climate change is not unambiguous and uncontroversial. Koumbarakis (2021) argues that in order to reap the full benefits of monetary policy, central banks should take into consideration environmental issues when designing their monetary policy. Because central banks can inject money into or withdraw money from circulation, where this money goes to does matter. If these flows of funds are "brown" (go to fossil fuel companies), it would do more harm than good to sustainable development. In contrast, if they are "green" (invested in green projects), they will support and accelerate sustainable development (Koumbarakis, 2021).

Worse still, central banks even put forward two arguments to support their pursuit of market neutrality and, therefore, insensitivity to environmental issues (Koumbarakis, 2021). The first argument is that allowing financial markets to decide on risk premia will lead to efficient resource allocation. However, supporting arguments for this claim are weak as monetary policy is implemented mainly due to the fact that prices in financial markets do not stay at the level necessary to obtain macroeconomic objectives. Koumbarakis (2021) posits that if markets are efficient, no asset buying programs would be needed. They also argue that making monetary policy become green also contributes to making financial markets more efficient.

The second argument is that when taking the environment into account, central banks will have to make political choices, thus politicizing monetary policy. However, as Koumbarakis (2021) argues, the design and implementation of unconventional monetary policies (such as quantitative easing) involve making political choices. Therefore, these choices should be considered.

3.1.3. *The tools of central banks in the fight against climate change: A review*

Climate change has been a lingering phenomenon and challenge in the world. Primarily, the fight against global warming falls on the shoulders of governments that are signatories to the Paris Agreement on climate change. To apply relevant policies, many coordinated efforts are obligatory by governments and central banks to mobilize the financial system, thereby ensuring coping with the climatic risks and motivating green finance. Along with individual and national efforts to address the climate-related crises, other groups, like investors and insurance companies, have joined hands with the environmentalists to work on carbon-neutral portfolios and sustainable development. Other notable players in the fight against environmental hazards are the central banks and other financial institutions. The role of central banks is very important in considering and dealing with climate-related financial risks. The foremost vital aspect of covering climate changes is awareness of the climatic hazards. This holds that the financial regulatory bodies like central banks and other economic agents have to take the lead in proliferating the idea of climatic risks and their mitigation through economic and financial mechanisms (Aufauvre and Bourgey, 2019). Central banks are now more concerned with tackling the issue of environmentalism by inducing other commercial banks to follow the financial norms that are at par with sustainable development goals. Central banks, acting as financial supervisors, have a crucial role in shaping the responses to climatic changes. Many central banks are considering incorporating climate-related risks and green finance across their operations as well as across their supervisee banks. To fulfill their mandates for monetary stability, central banks need to upkeep their measures and actions at par with the Paris Agreement on climate change (Dikau, Robins, and Volz, 2020). Numerous instruments that are already in practice by central banks can be adjusted so as to account for climate-related financial risks and/or help achieve the banking roles for climate and sustainability goals.

The central banks' role in tackling climate-related risk may be formed in two ways. First, the physical risks, that are more visible and immediate, are caused by the creation of extreme weather moments like storms, hurricanes, floods, self-generated wildfires, increasingly rising levels of water, and their resulting losses that insurance companies need to cover. Secondly, the transition risks, which are not more visible and are long-term oriented, can be addressed by several measures, including the measures associated with the public authority as well as the private initiatives that are targeted to achieve a model using low-carbon production (Banque de France, 2019). In this regard, France aims to gradually phase out vehicles having internal combustion engines by 2040.

Central banks possess some potentially powerful tools to contain climate change. Green Central Banking (2018) posits that central banks can support the fight against climate change in general and the transition toward a low-carbon economy in particular. First, central banks may adopt green macroprudential regulations: the use of green-supporting factors (lowering capital requirements for green projects and/or investments) or the application of so-called "brown penalizing factor" (raising capital requirements for projects/investments posing risks to the environment).

Second, central banks can also implement a green monetary policy under which they will increase the purchase of bonds from climate-friendly companies while decreasing that of fossil fuel firms.

4. The consequences of climate change (and its related effects) on monetary policy and financial stability: A systemic literature review

While central banks are believed and expected to play a larger role in combating climate change, it is widely held that the latter may exert a significant impact on the former. In other words, climate-related risks can be seen as financial risks (Bingler, Colesanti Senni, and Monnin, 2020). This view has been widely accepted and acknowledged not only by academics (Battiston, Mandel, and Monasterolo, 2019; Bretschger and Karydas, 2019; Caldecott *et al.*, 2016; Gros *et al.*, 2016; Roncoroni *et al.*, 2021; Stolbova, Monasterolo, and Battiston, 2018) but also practitioners (Bolton *et al.*, 2020) for central banks and financial regulators. Therefore, climate risks can impact the conduct of monetary policy (Oustry *et al.*, 2020). More generally, climate changes (and the associated consequences) pose a great and imminent risk to the global economy in general and for central banks in particular. Climate risk differs from other types of risks due to its irreversible nature, possible nonlinearities, and tipping points (European Central Bank, 2021).

The effects of climate change (and natural disasters) on objectives of monetary policy (and to a larger extent, the whole economy) are usually regarded as an indirect impact of climate change/natural disasters (Cavallo and Noy, 2010). The study provides a literature review on the economics of natural disasters with their (in)direct effects on economic development. For example, after an event happens, infrastructures may be destroyed, causing relevant authorities to use resources to reconstruct them, thus depriving production of necessary capacities. On the other hand, damages to capital, inventories, fixed assets, mortality, and morbidity are regarded as direct impacts (Cavallo and Noy, 2010).

Theoretically, climate change and its associated consequences such as global warming and other extreme weather events, may inflict severe, far-reaching consequences not only on the financial sector but also the macroeconomy (and therefore, objectives of central banks) as a whole. Even consequences of the current COVID-19 pandemic are considered a small part of the possible negative effects caused by climate change, rising global temperature, and associated events (Anwar *et al.*, 2020; Koumbarakis, 2021).

It is widely agreed that climate change presents two major types of risks, namely, transition risks and physical risks (Dafermos *et al.*, 2020; European Central Bank, 2021). The first type of risk, transition risks, arises from measures to fight against climate change as well as to protect the environment. For example, governments around the world are committed to restricting global warming to less than 2°C. To reach that goal, countries need to undergo a transition toward zero-carbon emissions. While this transition progress is expected to make significant contributions to tackling global warming, it can also pose serious challenges to governments and policymakers.

Transition risks are often defined as economic and/or financial risks resulting from a disorderly transition toward a low-carbon economy, that is the carbon mitigation process. Transition risks also stem from the revaluation of assets such as the replacement of traditional power generation processes/methods with advanced and low-cost renewable energy technologies or banks subject to reputational risks due to their divestment efforts (Green Central Banking, 2018). Dollman *et al.* (2020) even warn of the Minsky moment caused by a disorderly transition, which in turn may invite the sudden collapse of asset prices.

Meanwhile, Green Central Banking (2018) defines physical risks as negative and severe consequences of climate-related events (floods, storms, cyclones, earthquakes, and other natural disasters) on the economy. For example, these events may disrupt the supply chain, induce food and product scarcity, and adversely affect industries, sectors, and the economy as a whole. In addition to the detrimental effects on the financial positions of households and firms, physical risks can also inflict substantial damage on the insurance sector and the larger financial sector. van Oorschot, van Toor, and Schellekens (2020) elaborate more on this point. According to them, physical risks may threaten business continuity, lower business value as well as deprive businesses of the ability to make profits and repay their debts. These difficulties are likely to translate into credit and market risks confronting financial institutions. Market and credit risks may cause reputational damage and higher non-performing loans, thus also leading to operational risks. These risks, in turn, may leave financial institutions vulnerable to liquidity risks and might result in economic hardship and a slowdown.

Worse still, Green Central Banking (2018) also argues that while these effects are severe, they are tangible and much smaller compared with the total costs induced by climate-related events. These costs include output loss resulting from lower productive capital and reconstruction of damaged assets (Green Central Banking, 2018). According to the European System of Financial Supervisors' (ESFS) report in 2020, the estimated costs of physical risks may amount to 10% to 20% of global output at the end of this century.

van Oorschot, van Toor, and Schellekens (2020) even posit that these types of risks can interact with and reinforce each other. On the one hand, greater physical risks make it necessary to effect a transition that has inherent transition risks. On the other hand, hesitation to bring about a transition is likely to cause higher physical risks, which in turn may lead to a more abrupt and sudden transition period as well as other transition risks.

While there are more than a few theoretical papers on the impact and implications of climate change on monetary policy, their empirical counterparts are quite limited and can be divided into studies of the short-run and long-run effects of climatic events. Despite the fact that the first short-run study was conducted in 1993 by Albala-Bertrand (1993), the empirical literature on the impact of climate change/natural disasters on monetary policy (and, to a larger extent, macroeconomic) objectives came to prominence in the 2000s. Skidmore and Toya (2002) document a positive short-run effect of natural disasters on growth, while C. Raddatz (2007) employs the panel vector autoregressive model (panel VAR) to conclude that natural disasters exert significant short-run adverse effects on output. Building on this study, Loayza *et al.* (2012), Noy and Vu (2010), and C. E. Raddatz (2009) document the negative effects of natural disasters on macroeconomic objectives. They also find that while large and high-income countries are well-positioned to withstand the impact of climate change/natural disasters, smaller and poorer countries are more vulnerable.

In addition to studies employing panel country-level data, other researchers also examine the impact of climatic events on the economy using state-level data or individual country-level data. For example, Strobl (2011) documents the negative impact of hurricanes on US coastal counties. Noy and Vu (2010) find that natural disasters can have contradictory effects on output growth.

Apart from macroeconomic objectives, researchers also investigate the effects of natural disasters on other variables. Rodriguez-Oreggia (2010) discover that disaster-hit areas in Mexico will experience higher poverty and lower human development indices. Meanwhile, Mechler (2009) confirms the significant impact of natural disasters on household consumption, which in turn may adversely affect economic growth. Finally, by employing data on European firms, Leiter *et al.* (2009) record mixed effects of natural disasters on firms' capital stock, negative effects on firms' productivity, and positive effects on firms' employment.

In addition to short-run effects, scholars also evaluate the long-run impacts of climate change/natural disasters on macroeconomic outcomes. While Toya and Skidmore (2007) document expansionary effects of natural disasters, Noy and Nualsri (2007) record the opposite. Later findings from C. E. Raddatz (2009) and Jaramillo (2009) lend support to Noy and Nualsri (2007). Inspired by the seemingly counterintuitive findings of Skidmore and Toya (2002), which the authors attribute to the Schumpeterian creative destruction hypothesis, other scholars evaluate the feasibility of this hypothesis. While Crespo Cuaresma, Hlouskova, and Obersteiner (2008) conclude that this hypothesis is likely to be correct for high-income countries only, Hallegatte and Dumas (2009) posit that natural disasters are likely to do more harm than good to economies. Similarly, Cavallo *et al.* (2013) argue that unless natural disasters bring about a radical political revolution, the impacts of these extreme weather events on growth will be mostly negative.

More recently, researchers have also focused on the impact of climatic events on inflation and the banking sector. For example, Beirne *et al.* (2021) document the significant impact of natural disasters on overall headline inflation in European countries with prices of food and beverages increasing while prices of other items decrease in response to more natural disasters. Meanwhile, Faccia, Parker, and Stracca (2021) evaluate the impact of temperature shocks on GDP deflators in 33 advanced economies and 15 emerging and developing economies from 1990 to 2018. They conclude that the effects of rising temperature on inflation are non-negligible, and therefore, climate change does matter for the goal of price stability.

Bayangos, Cachuela, and Prado (2021) present the impact of extreme weather episodes on the Philippine banking sector. Evidence using branch-level supervisory data find that extreme weather episodes can cause loan growth of bank branches to deteriorate and non-performing loans to increase.

5. Conclusion and future research

The above-mentioned review and analysis clearly indicate that climate change (and its associated extreme weather events) can exert profound, catastrophic effects on the economy as a whole, especially on the objectives of the banking sector (central bank and commercial banks alike). Therefore, banks, especially central banks, are expected to make significant contributions to contain climate change and reduce its possible negative consequences.

However, current practices of central banks around the world (even those of central banks in advanced economies) seem not to live up to expectations. On the contrary, their operations even, whether intentionally or not, provide favorable conditions for brown financial flows, thus worsening the emission and climate change problems. Therefore, central banks should be mandated to make greater contributions to greening their operations and the financial system. Future research can focus on working out solutions for central banks to make their activities become greener. Another potential line of research should further investigate the effects of climate change and its associated extreme weather events not only from a macro-perspective but also from a micro one. Findings from these studies are expected to help policymakers and researchers enhance the awareness of firms and people regarding the consequences of climate change and figure out possible solutions.

References

Albala-Bertrand, J. M. (1993). Political economy of large natural disasters: With special reference to developing countries. *OUP Catalogue*. Oxford University Press.

Anwar, R. S., Mohamed, M., Hamzan, S. M., Malek, N. S. A., Zain, M. H. M., Jaafar, M. H., Sani, S., Brazil-De Vera, R. M., Desquitado, M. C. T., Praneeprachachon, V., Wong, D., Lim, B. A., Goh, G., Tan, W., & Hong, J. (2020). Report on The Roles of ASEAN Central Banks in Managing Climate and Environment-related Risks. Kuala Lumpur. Retrieved from https://www.bnm.gov.my/-/report-on-the-roles-of-asean-central-banks-in-managing-climate-and-environment-related-risks.

Aufauvre, N. & Bourgey, C. (2019). The role of central banks and supervisory authorities in stimulating consideration for long-term issues: The case of climate change. Paper presented at the *Annales Des Mines-Réalités Industrielles.*

Barmer, D., Kazi, D., & Youel, S. (2020). The COVID corporate financing facility. Where are the conditions for the billion£ bailouts? *Positive Money*. https://positivemoney.org/publications/ccff.

Batten, S., Sowerbutts, R., & Tanaka, M. (2020). *Climate Change: Macroeconomic Impact and Implications for Monetary Policy.* In: Walker, T., Gramlich, D., Bitar, M., & Fardnia, P. (eds) *Ecological, Societal, and Technological Risks and the Financial Sector.* Palgrave Studies in Sustainable Business In Association with Future Earth. Palgrave Macmillan, Cham. https://doi.org/10.1007/978-3-030-38858-4_2.

Battiston, S., Mandel, A., & Monasterolo, I. (2019). CLIMAFIN handbook: Pricing forward-looking climate risks under uncertainty. Available at SSRN 3476586.

Bayangos, V. B., Cachuela, R. A. D., & Prado, F. L. E. D. (2021). Impact of extreme weather episodes on the Philippine banking sector — Evidence using branch-level supervisory data. *Latin American Journal of Central Banking, 2*(1), 100023. https://doi.org/10.1016/j.latcb.2021.100023.

Beirne, J., Dafermos, Y., Kriwoluzky, A., Renzhi, N., Volz, U., & Wittich, J. (2021). The effects of natural disasters on price stability in the Euro area.

Bingler, J. A., Colesanti Senni, C., & Monnin, P. (2020). Climate financial risks: Assessing convergence, exploring diversity. CEP Discussion Notes, 6.

Bolton, P., Després, M., Pereira da Silva, L., Samama, F., & Svartzman, R. (2020). 'Green Swans': Central banks in the age of climate-related risks. *Banque de France Bulletin, 229*(8), 1–15.

Bowman, M. (2010). The role of the banking industry in facilitating climate change mitigation and the transition to a low-carbon global economy. *Environment and Planning Law Journal, 27*, 448.

Bretschger, L. & Karydas, C. (2019). Economics of climate change: Introducing the Basic Climate Economic (BCE) model. *Environment and Development Economics, 24*(6), 560–582. https://doi.org/10.1017/S1355770X19000184.

Caby, J., Ziane, Y., & Lamarque, E. (2020). The determinants of voluntary climate change disclosure commitment and quality in the banking industry. *Technological Forecasting and Social Change, 161*, 120282. https://doi.org/10.1016/j.techfore.2020.120282.

Cai, S., Chen, X., & Bose, I. (2013). Exploring the role of IT for environmental sustainability in China: An empirical analysis. *International Journal of Production Economics, 146*(2), 491–500. https://doi.org/10.1016/j.ijpe.2013.01.030.

Caldecott, B., Harnett, E., Cojoianu, T., Kok, I., & Pfeiffer, A. (2016). *Stranded Assets: A Climate Risk Challenge.* Washington, DC: Inter-American Development Bank.

Campiglio, E., Dafermos, Y., Monnin, P., Ryan-Collins, J., Schotten, G., & Tanaka, M. (2018). Climate change challenges for central banks and financial regulators. *Nature Climate Change*, *8*(6), 462–468. https://doi.org/10.1038/s41558-018-0175-0.

Carney, M. (2015). Breaking the tragedy of the horizon–climate change and financial stability. Speech given at Lloyd's of London, *29*, 220–230.

Cavallo, E., Galiani, S., Noy, I., & Pantano, J. (2013). Catastrophic natural disasters and economic growth. *The Review of Economics and Statistics*, *95*(5), 1549–1561. https://doi.org/10.1162/REST_a_00413.

Cavallo, E. & Noy, I. (2010). *The Economics of Natural Disasters: A Survey.* IDB WP Series No. IDB-WP-124, Inter-American Development Bank.

Chen, C., Pan, D., Huang, Z., & Bleischwitz, R. (2021). Engaging central banks in climate change? The mix of monetary and climate policy. *Energy Economics*, *103*, 105531. https://doi.org/10.1016/j.eneco.2021.105531.

Crespo Cuaresma, J., Hlouskova, J., & Obersteiner, M. (2008). Natural disasters as creative destruction? Evidence from developing countries. *Economic Inquiry*, *46*(2), 214–226. https://doi.org/10.1111/j.1465-7295.2007.00063.x.

Dafermos, Y., Gabor, D., Nikolaidi, M., Pawloff, A., & van Lerven, F. (2020). Decarbonising is easy.

de France, B. (2019). Greening the financial system: The new frontier. *Financial Stability Review.* Banque de France.

Dikau, S., Robins, N., & Volz, U. (2020). A toolbox for sustainable crisis response measures for central banks and supervisors. London: Grantham Research Institue on Climate Change and the Environment, London School of Economics and Political Science and SOAS centre for Sustainable Finance.

Dikau, S. & Volz, U. (2019). Central banking, climate change, and green finance. In J. D. Sachs, W. T. Woo, N. Yoshino, & F. Taghizadeh-Hesary (Eds.), *Handbook of Green Finance: Energy Security and Sustainable Development* (pp. 81–102). Singapore: Springer.

Dikau, S. & Volz, U. (2021). Central bank mandates, sustainability objectives and the promotion of green finance. *Ecological Economics*, *184*, 107022. https://doi.org/10.1016/j.ecolecon.2021.107022.

Dollman *et al.* (2020). *Low-Carbon Transitions and Systemic Risk.* Retrieved from https://www.vivideconomics.com/wp-content/uploads/2020/10/Low-Carbon-Transitions-and-Systemic-Risk-Final-1.pdf.

European Central Bank (2021). Climate change and monetary policy in the Euro area. https://doi.org/10.2866/101932.

Faccia, D., Parker, M., & Stracca, L. (2021). Feeling the heat: Extreme temperatures and price stability (December 1, 2021). ECB Working Paper No. 2021/2626, Available at SSRN: https://ssrn.com/abstract=3981219 http://dx.doi.org/10.2139/ssrn.3981219.

Gonzalez, C. I. (2021). The role of central banks in combating climate change and developing sustainable finance. *Banco de Espana Article*, *31*, 21.

Green Central Banking (2018). A green Bank of England: Central banking for a low-carbon economy. Retrieved from https://greencentralbanking.com/research/bank-of-england-central-banking-low-carbon-economy/.

Grippa, P., Schmittmann, J., & Suntheim, F. (2019). Climate change and financial risk: Central banks and financial regulators are starting to factor in climate change. *Finance & Development*, *56*(4). Retrieved from https://www.imf.org/en/Publications/fandd/issues/2019/12/climate-change-central-banks-and-financial-risk-grippa.

Gros, D., Lane, P. R., Langfield, S., Matikainen, S., Pagano, M., Schoenmaker, D., & Suarez, J. (2016). Too late, too sudden: Transition to a low-carbon economy and systemic risk. Reports of the Advisory Scientific Committee.

Hallegatte, S. & Dumas, P. (2009). Can natural disasters have positive consequences? Investigating the role of embodied technical change. *Ecological Economics*, *68*(3), 777–786. https://doi.org/10.1016/j.ecolecon.2008.06.011.

Hart, S. L. (1995). A natural-resource-based view of the firm. *The Academy of Management Review*, *20*(4), 986–1014. https://doi.org/10.2307/258963.

HSBC (2020). Sustainable financing and investment survey 2020: Pandemic intensifies awareness of environment and society. Retrieved from https://www.sustainablefinance.hsbc.com/mobilising-finance/sustainable-financing-and-investment-survey-2020.

Jaramillo, C. R. (2009). Do natural disasters have long-term effects on growth? Documento CEDE(2009-24).

Koumbarakis, A. (2021). The greenness of central banking: Rethinking the macroprudential framework. Available at SSRN 3821041.

Leiter, A. M., Oberhofer, H., & Raschky, P. A. (2009). Creative disasters? Flooding effects on capital, labour and productivity within European firms. *Environ Resource Econ.*, *43*, 333–350. https://doi.org/10.1007/s10640-009-9273-9.

Loayza, N. V., Olaberría, E., Rigolini, J., & Christiaensen, L. (2012). Natural disasters and growth: Going beyond the averages. *World Development*, *40*(7), 1317–1336. https://doi.org/10.1016/j.worlddev.2012.03.002.

Macaire, C. & Naef, A. (2021). Impact of green central bank collateral policy: Evidence from the People's Bank of China.

Mackintosh, S. P. (2019). Central banking and climate change. *World Economics, 20*(4), 25–42.

McConnell, A., Yanovski, B., & Lessmann, K. (2022). Central bank collateral as a green monetary policy instrument. *Climate Policy, 22*(3), 339–355. https://doi.org/10.1080/14693062.2021.2012112.

Mechler, R. (2009). Disasters and economic welfare: Can national savings help explain post-disaster changes in consumption? World Bank Policy Research Working Paper (4988).

Meinshausen, M., Meinshausen, N., Hare, W., Raper, S. C. B., Frieler, K., Knutti, R., ... Allen, M. R. (2009). Greenhouse-gas emission targets for limiting global warming to 2°C. *Nature, 458*(7242), 1158–1162. https://doi.org/10.1038/nature08017.

Noy, I. & Nualsri, A. (2007). What do exogenous shocks tell us about growth theories? Working Paper.

Noy, I. & Vu, T. B. (2010). The economics of natural disasters in a developing country: The case of Vietnam. *Journal of Asian Economics, 21*(4), 345–354. https://doi.org/10.1016/j.asieco.2010.03.002.

Oustry, A., Erkan, B., Svartzman, R., & Weber, P.-F. (2020). Climate-related risks and central banks' collateral policy: A methodological experiment.

Raddatz, C. (2007). Are external shocks responsible for the instability of output in low-income countries? *Journal of Development Economics, 84*(1), 155–187. https://doi.org/10.1016/j.jdeveco.2006.11.001.

Raddatz, C. E. (2009). The wrath of God: Macroeconomic costs of natural disasters. World Bank Policy Research Working Paper (5039).

Rodriguez-Oreggia, E. (2010). The impact of natural disasters on human development and poverty at the municipal level in Mexico. CID Research Fellow and Graduate Student Working Paper Series.

Roncoroni, A., Battiston, S., Escobar-Farfán, L. O. L., & Martinez-Jaramillo, S. (2021). Climate risk and financial stability in the network of banks and investment funds. *Journal of Financial Stability, 54*, 100870. https://doi.org/10.1016/j.jfs.2021.100870.

Skidmore, M. & Toya, H. (2002). Do natural disasters promote long-run growth? *Economic Inquiry, 40*(4), 664–687. https://doi.org/10.1093/ei/40.4.664.

Stolbova, V., Monasterolo, I., & Battiston, S. (2018). A financial macro-network approach to climate policy evaluation. *Ecological Economics, 149*, 239–253. https://doi.org/10.1016/j.ecolecon.2018.03.013.

Strobl, E. (2011). The economic growth impact of hurricanes: Evidence from U.S. coastal counties. *The Review of Economics and Statistics, 93*(2), 575–589. https://doi.org/10.1162/REST_a_00082.

Svartzman, R., Bolton, P., Despres, M., Pereira Da Silva, L. A., & Samama, F. (2021). Central banks, financial stability and policy coordination in the age of climate uncertainty: A three-layered analytical and operational framework. *Climate Policy, 21*(4), 563–580. https://doi.org/10.1080/14693062.2020.1862743.

van Oorschot, M., van Toor, J., & Schellekens, G. (2020). Indebted to nature, exploring biodiversity risks for the Dutch financial sector.

van 't Klooster, J. & Fontan, C. (2020). The myth of market neutrality: A comparative study of the European Central Bank's and the Swiss National Bank's corporate security purchases. *New Political Economy, 25*(6), 865–879. https://doi.org/10.1080/13563467.2019.1657077.

Part III
Green Finance in Europe

© 2024 World Scientific Publishing Europe Ltd.
https://doi.org/10.1142/9781800614451_0010

Chapter 10

Impact Investments Through the Expansion of Renewable Energies — Macro Simulation Analyses and Overview of Green Finance Landscape of Austria

Sebastian Goers[*,†,§], **Friedrich Schneider**[†,‡,¶], **Mario Reisinger**[†,‖], **and Robert Tichler**[†,**]

[†]*Energieinstitut at the Johannes Kepler University Linz, Linz, Austria*

[‡]*Research Institute for Banking and Finance, Johannes Kepler University Linz, Linz, Austria*

[§]*goers@energieinstitut-linz.at*

[¶]*friedrich.schneider@jku.at*

[‖]*reisinger@energieinstitut-linz.at*

[**]*tichler@energieinstitut-linz.at*

Abstract

Mitigation of climate change on the Austrian level requires efforts to reduce greenhouse gas emissions via the increased use and expansion of renewable energies. In this regard, we quantify via simulation analyses the macroeconomic effects of expanding renewable energy use in electricity and heat production in Austria. The results clearly show that these measures to combat climate change in the long term can also generate positive short- and medium-term economic effects in the form of additional economic and employment growth. The timing of these results is

[*]Corresponding author.

highly relevant given the past economic downturn due to the COVID-19 pandemic and the crisis in Ukraine. After evaluating the Austrian Green Finance sector, it becomes clear that, on the one hand, risk exposure of investors rises when financial portfolios reflect high greenhouse gas emissions and, on the other hand, Green Finance portfolios yield similar returns on investment. Credible domestic climate policies and legislation can potentially support the financing of the necessary investments.

1. Introduction

In the discussion on the transition of the Austrian energy system, reference is made to the reduction of greenhouse gas (GHG) emissions and the resulting reduction in damage caused by climate change (Steininger *et al.*, 2015, 2020). However, a further significant positive effect is neglected: the positive impact on the level of employment as well as on the growth of the domestic economy in the case of an even stronger change in the energy system to renewable energy sources (RES). The simulation analyses we present in this chapter show which concrete investments would be necessary and what macroeconomic benefits may arise. Using Austria as an example, we quantify the impacts of RES expansion and discuss the role of green finance.

By signing the Paris Agreement, Austria has committed itself to contributing toward limiting global warming to well below 2°C, and if possible to below 1.5°C, and has set the goal of being climate neutral by 2040 at the latest. In this context, Kirchengast and Steininger (2020) evaluate that if Austria is to achieve the goal of climate neutrality in 2040 and make its fair contribution to global climate goals, a drastic reduction of GHG emissions is necessary. It must not emit more than 700 million tons of CO_2e by 2040 and no more than 550 million tons of CO_2e by 2030. This means reducing emissions by 4.5 million tons of CO_2e each year and by 3.4 million tons of CO_2e after 2030. Data from the Environment Agency Austria reveal that GHG emissions in Austria increased by 1.5% from 2018 to 2019, amounting to 79.7 million tons of CO_2e in 2019 (Umweltbundesamt, 2021). In Austria, no significant GHG emission reduction can be realized compared to 1990 since the country has already approached its 1990 levels Umweltbundesamt (2021, 2022) in 2019 and 2020 (78.4 and 73.6 million tons of CO_2e, respectively). The measures taken against the COVID-19 pandemic for 2020 had a significant impact on national emissions. Austria's emissions in

2021 rose again around 2% and were expected to rise in 2022 to around 4% compared to the corresponding time in the previous year (Sommer *et al.*, 2021). Hence, far-reaching transformation steps to mitigate GHG emissions via the reduction of the use of fossil energy are required to meet future climate targets. In addition to increasing energy efficiency, the increased use of RES is one of the two most important strategies for achieving this goal.

The Austrian Federal Ministry for Climate Action, Environment, Energy, Mobility, Innovation, and Technology (BMK) highlights that in 2019 the most important RES in Austria's total electricity generation of around 71 terawatt-hours (TWh) is hydropower, which contributes more than half of the electricity generated (BMK, 2021a). It is followed by wind power with slightly above 10%. Photovoltaics (PV), with a share of around 2%, have so far played only a minor role in electricity supply. Total renewable electricity (excluding pumped storage) covered 62% of electricity consumption in 2019. The Renewable Energy Expansion Act (EAG) was established in Austria in 2021. It aims to increase the annual electricity generation from renewable sources by 27 TWh by 2030 while ensuring the security of supply (Republic Austria Parliament, 2021). Thus, 100% electricity from RES should be achieved by 2030, with an addition of PV of 11 TWh, wind of 10 TWh, hydropower of 5 TWh, biomass of 1 TWh, and green gas of 5 TWh. According to Statistik Austria data, with regard to heat, 55 TWh of energy were used for space heating in households in 2020, with 44% covered by fossil energy (oil and gas). The direct use of RES for heat generation in the building sector is mainly in the form of biomass, solar thermal, and geothermal energy, as well as the use of heat pumps. RES are also used directly in the industry sector to generate heat for industrial processes.

Simultaneously, Austria's economic performance has been facing challenging developments since the end of 2019 and after the start of the COVID-19 pandemic. Following macroeconomic reports of the Austrian Institute of Economic Research (Baumgartner *et al.*, 2021; Schiman, 2021), real gross domestic product (GDP) fell by approximately 7% in 2020, and unemployment rose by a third despite the use of COVID-19 short-time work. After the COVID-19 recession diminished, a strong recovery of the international economy started in spring 2021, pulling the Austrian economy along as well. However, renewed regulatory restrictions to contain the COVID-19 pandemic, persistent supply-chain issues, and high raw material prices all dampened the recovery in the second half of the year. Baumgartner *et al.* (2021) put real economic growth at 4.4%, equivalent to nominal GDP of 403 billion € in 2021. For 2022, a recovery in domestic economic output was expected due to the strong international economy and fiscal policy measures. According to Baumgartner *et al.* (2021), this will cause GDP to grow by 2.6% per year in the period 2022–2026, significantly faster than in the interim crisis period 2010/2019 (1.5% per year). However, the current Ukraine war and Russian sanctions are massively dampening these expectations. According to Köppl-Turyna *et al.* (2022), a downward correction in GDP growth of around 1.3% was expected. This negative impact on growth is expected to increase in 2023 but diminish by 2026. The developments are driven by the direct links of domestic companies in Russia and Ukraine, the increase in energy prices — driven primarily by the price of gas — and the associated sharp rise in inflation.

Summing up, in view of these developments, the economic recession caused by the COVID-19 pandemic, and current developments in the context of the Ukraine crisis, Austria is faced with the challenge of taking effective and efficient measures to create jobs and increase economic growth in the short, mid, and long term. At the same time, the expansion of renewable energy will be essential for Austria to achieve its climate and energy policy goals (see Figure 1).

In response to the economic recessions caused by the COVID-19 pandemic, there is a demand for a green recovery. The idea is that

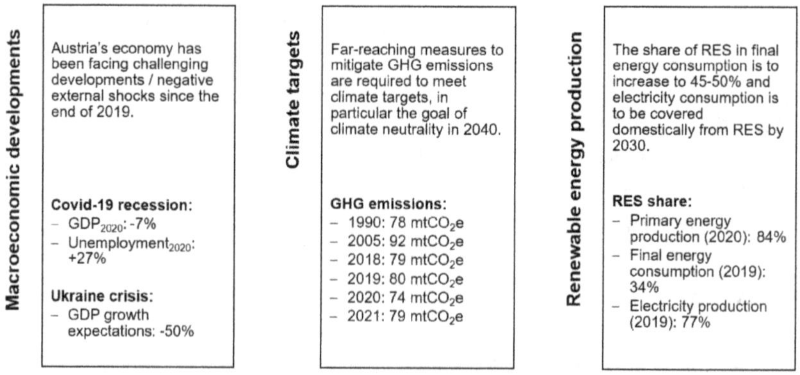

Figure 1. Overview: Macroeconomic developments, climate targets, and the role of RES in Austria.

economic (policy) decisions must have a positive impact on the climate, and future measures must support the decarbonization of the economy (Hammer and Hallegatte, 2020). Thus, renewable energy plays a crucial role in this green recovery (Hepburn *et al.*, 2020; IRENA, 2020). For Austria, a first macroeconomic quantification of the impacts of RES was carried out by Bointner *et al.* (2013). It was shown that from 2001 to 2011 significant positive effects were created in the form of an increase in GDP by an average of 0.1%. Further, macroeconomic impact assessments of energy transitions in Austria, which are triggered and financed by an eco-social tax reform, were concurrently analyzed specifically for Austria in Kirchner *et al.* (2019) and Goers and Schneider (2019a, b). They show that GHG reductions can be achieved through taxation, and particularly recycling tax revenues can potentially mitigate tax burden, potential regressive impacts, competitiveness issues for industries as well as negative macroeconomic impacts. In addition, Goers and Scneider (2019a,b) show that taxing GHG emissions and fossil energy consumption can, on the one hand, create positive environmental effects and, on the other hand, generate revenues that positively stimulate the domestic economy in the context of investments (e.g., in H_2 and e-mobility, building renovation) that drive the energy transition.

We extend these macroeconomic impact assessment analyses on the energy transition in Austria and add to the existing literature with regard to the role of investments in RES as a way out of short-term recessions (COVID-19 recession) and currently expected macroeconomic negative developments as a result of the Ukraine crisis. Our analyses are suitable to show how a small open economy can respond to external negative shocks in a relatively timely manner and at the same time prevent climate change damages in the long run by increasing the share of RES.

The central question of green finance is how the investments for the achievement of the climate and energy transition and economic growth can be successfully financed. The increasing importance of environmentally and socially sustainable financial products is also reflected in Austria (Codagnone *et al.*, 2020). Further, Breitenfellner *et al.* (2020) qualitatively find that the Austrian green finance market is still underdeveloped and conclude that policy instruments such as GHG pricing promote sustainable investment. Therefore, investments in green finance can be a chance to redirect financial flows from portfolios with high emission exposure to sustainable low-carbon funds. Further, it gives incentives for sectors with significant carbon footprints for their transformation to low-carbon business models.

The results of our macroeconomic simulation analyses show that positive effects for the Austrian economy can be realized by 2030 by focusing on increasing the share of RES in electricity and heat production. Investment in the expansion and the continuous substitution of imported fossil fuels can create economic growth and employment. The decisive factors for the intensity of the effects are the total investment amounts, the sectoral effectiveness, and the specific import quotas of the respective technologies. Moreover, investments in RES have also shown to reduce risks for investors, such as transition risks (loss of value caused by regulations) of companies with a high carbon footprint. In addition, research projects show that sustainable funds yield comparable financial performance while having a significant lower risk profile compared to conventional funds.

In the following, Section 2 describes the methodological approach. Subsequently, Section 3 is dedicated to the presentation of the macroeconomic simulation analyses' results. Based on this, the role of green finance and the instruments and approaches available in Austria are discussed in Section 4. A conclusion accounting for policy recommendations is offered in Section 5.

2. Data and methodological approaches

In our analysis, we proceed in a 3-step process covering quantitative and qualitative approaches. First, we process the data collected on the expansion of RES in Austria, which includes the specific energetic amounts of expansion and the necessary investments. These data are then used as input for macroeconomic simulation analyses to quantify impacts on the Austrian economy. Finally, the results are discussed in the context of Austria's green finance framework qualitatively.

2.1. *Collection and processing of Austria-specific data on the expansion of RES*

In order to have a profound data basis for the simulations of GDP and employment effects through the expansion of renewable energy in Austria, data and information were collected from experts and stakeholders from Austrian associations of renewable energy technologies (see Table 1) in the form of a survey questionnaire (Goers *et al.*, 2020). The data collection was carried out for biogas, biomass CHP, geothermal energy (near-surface, deep), hydropower, photovoltaics, solar thermal energy, and wind power. These data were collected until the end of 2020, so the survey ran simultaneously to the development and public discussion of the EAG.

The questionnaire collected data on technology-specific expansion paths and necessary additional investments. Based on the information provided by the associations, the expansion paths up to 2030 (Figure 2 and Table 2) were derived. For renewable electricity, an additional expansion of 30.2 TWh in total was predicted by 2030,

Table 1. Analyzed RES technologies and sources of data and information on expansion paths (Goers *et al.*, 2020).

Technology	Association that provided data on the expansion
Biogas	Kompost & Biogas Verband Österreich
Biomass CHP	IG Holzkraft
Geothermal energy — near-surface	Geothermie für Österreich
Geothermal energy — deep	Geothermie für Österreich
Hydropower	Kleinwasserkraft Österreich
Photovoltaics	PV Austria
Solar thermal energy	Austria Solar
Wind power	IG Windkraft

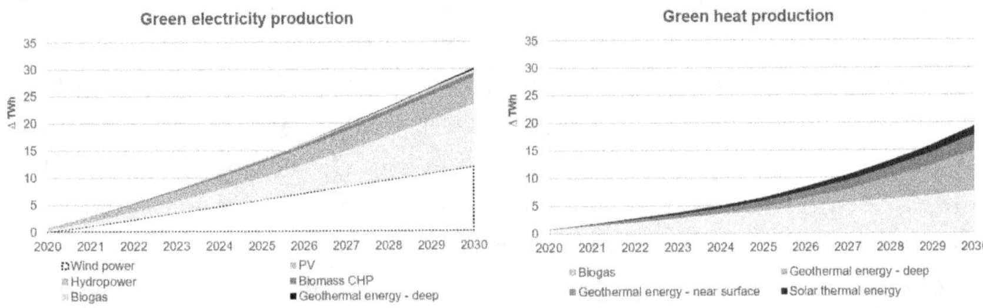

Figure 2. Cumulative additional RES for production of electricity and heat in Austria until 2030 (Goers *et al.*, 2020).

Table 2. RES technologies' *status quo* and additional expansion for electricity and heat production in Austria until 2030 (BMK, 2021a; Goers *et al.*, 2020).

Electricity production		
RES technology	2019	$\sum$ additional expansion in 2030
Hydropower	29.8	+5.0
Wind power	7.5	+11.9
Bioenergy	4.8	+1.5
PV	1.7	+11.4
Geothermal energy — deep	0	+0.3
Heat production		
RES technology	2019	$\sum$ additional expansion in 2030
Bioenergy	11.3	+7.5
Solar thermal energy	2.1	+1.5
Ambient heat	0.3	+10.3

with PV and wind each generating about 40% of this. These figures are only slightly above the targets actually implemented in 2021 for the expansion of renewable electricity production by the EAG. For the heat sector, an additional 19.3 TWh can be provided by renewables by 2030, according to the associations' data. This would be achieved via additional capacity for biogas and deep geothermal energy, to about 40% each.

In addition to determining specific expansion paths, the information provided by the associations also includes quantifying the technology-specific investments required to achieve these expansion paths. Data on necessary additional investment volumes, as well as their sectoral effectiveness and import quotas, were collected and are listed in Table 3.

For the simulation of macroeconomic impacts, the sector in which the investment takes effect plays a decisive role. Sectors such as manufacturing have strong interdependencies with other sectors, so that investments in these sectors can have a strong impact on other sectors or on the economy as a whole. Likewise, the import quotas of the materials and services required in the expansion process are valuable information. By taking the import quota into account, the domestic effects of the investments can be represented more accurately. All these data are used as input parameters for the simulations in

Table 3. Necessary investments through expansion of renewable energy technologies in Austria (Goers *et al.*, 2020).

	∑ Expansion in TWh	Investments in bn € per TWh	Sector	Import quota
Biogas	+8.1	+0.3	Manufacturing: 27%	20%
			Construction: 53%	20%
			Services: 20%	20%
Biomass CHP	+1.0	+1.0	Manufacturing: 85%	31%
			Construction: 14%	1%
			Services: 1%	1%
Geothermal — near-surface	+2.9	+0.8	Manufacturing: 50%	30%
			Construction: 25%	0%
			Services: 25%	0%
Geothermal — deep	+2.1	+0.2	Manufacturing: 30%	50%
			Construction: 60%	50%
			Services: 10%	20%
Hydropower	+5.0	+0.9	Manufacturing: 45%	5%
			Construction: 40%	0%
			Services: 15%	0%
Photovoltaics	+11.4	+1.3	Manufacturing: 70%	50%
			Construction: 29%	30%
			Services: 1%	0%
Solar thermal	+1.5	+2.3	Manufacturing: 31%	30%
			Construction: 32%	30%
			Services: 37%	30%
Wind power	+11.9	+0.6	Manufacturing: 75%	80%
			Construction: 15%	15%
			Services: 10%	10%

Section 3. In the segment of electricity production by RES until 2030, the highest necessary investments are expected for PV with 1.3 billion € per TWh, followed by hydropower with 0.9 billion € per TWh. For heat supply by RES, the highest average costs per year of 2.3 billion € per TWh are incurred for solar thermal technology.

2.2. *Macroeconomic ex-ante simulation analyses*

The simulation model MOVE2 (Goers *et al.*, 2015) was used to determine the effects of the expansion of RES technologies. This is a macroeconometric tool for impact assessment of energy and climate policy measures on the Austrian level. A major advantage of the model is the representation of the links between the economy and energy (production and consumption). The time series-based model consists of a large number of stochastic equations and identities that represent the economic activities of different economic sectors and private households as well as the resulting flows of 24 different energy sources. For each of the 12 economic sectors considered, key variables such as investment, gross value added, employment, wages, and energy consumption are estimated by systems of equations using historical data based on macroeconomic and energy data from Statistik Austria and Eurostat. Private households are presented as an aggregate in terms of their energy and non-energy consumption. The model is based on the GDP measurement concept via the expenditure method, so that GDP is calculated from the sum of investment, consumption, government spending, and net exports (= exports minus imports).

Each simulation involves the calculation of two different paths of the Austrian economy. The first path calculates the future development and may be referred to as the business-as-usual scenario. The second path, the simulation scenario, calculates the future development of all endogenous variables resulting from a change in a certain parameter (here: sectoral investments and energy production data). The difference between the two scenarios displays the effect of the change of the parameters. The simulations are based on the RES expansion data presented in Section 2.1 and were conducted for the period 2022–2030. In contrast to Goers *et al.* (2020), current developments in the COVID-19 recession have been taken into account for the model's business-as-usual scenario.

2.3. *Qualitative assessment of Austria's green finance sector*

The qualitative assessment follows a literature review of Green Finance and particularly focuses on the Austrian market and its recent development in research and governance. In 2020, a research project called Risk Fin Porto examined the finance sector in Austria with respect to the transition to a low-carbon economy and society. The main findings of this research project are summarized in

Section 4 and formed the basis for the development of the Green Finance Plan of the Ministry of Finance and Ministry of Climate in Austria. The goals of the Green Finance Plan aim to reduce climate risks, foster transparency, and incentivize climate friendly investments. From this, the Green Finance Alliance (GF Alliance) emerged and its main objectives and governance structure are analyzed.

3. Simulation analyses results

Our simulation analyses' results show that investments in the expansion of renewable energies for electricity and heat supply can have significant positive effects on the Austrian economy. In total, the investments trigger an additional nominal GDP in 2030 of 16 billion € as well as an increase in employment of 210,000 employees. Compared to the business-as-usual scenario, nominal GDP grows on average by 9.0 billion € per year and employment increases by more than 100,000 employees annually. In relative terms, this means an average increase of 2.1% in GDP and 2.7% in employment (Table 4).

The most decisive drivers for these overall positive macroeconomic trends are investment impulses in new electricity and heat production plants and heating systems based on renewable energy sources, as well as positive trade balance effects due to lower energy imports. The expansion of renewable energies has direct and indirect effects due to investments in plants and the necessary extension of the grids. A special feature is the permanent expenditure for operation and maintenance, which perpetuates the investment impulses. The use of fossil fuels, which are largely imported in Austria, is declining. Hence, foreign trade plays an important role in the net effects.

Table 4. Additional GDP and employment effects in Austria through investments in the expansion of RES in electricity and heat production until 2030.

		2025	2030	$Ø_{2022–2030}$
Δ GDP	bn €	+9.7	+16.0	+9.0
Δ GDP	%	+2.3	+3.5	+2.1
Δ Employment	#employees	+130,000	+210,000	+105,000
Δ Employment	%	+3.3	+5.3	+2.7

Reduced imports of fossil fuels and increased exports of renewable energy generation plants have a positive effect on the trade balance, while increased imports of these plants have a negative effect on the overall economy. Given the high global expansion dynamics, the associated growing export opportunities and the rapid decline in technology costs via global learning curves play an important role in the long-term development of macroeconomic effects. In addition, there are induced effects resulting from changes in the incomes of households and companies. If there is increased employment and income in industries producing renewable energies, income flows to the additional employees, among others, will be spent according to their propensity to consume. Thus, creating multiplier effects that will be felt throughout the Austrian economy and above all service providers.

The intensity of the positive macroeconomic effects is mainly determined by the total volumes of investment and the import ratios of the components, materials, and services used. For electricity production by RES, this means that the strongest GDP and employment effects are generated by the expansion of PV, hydropower, and wind (see Figure 3). On the one hand, these technologies have the highest absolute investment volumes. On the other hand, most of the investments flow into the sectors of material goods production and construction, which trigger high macroeconomic multiplier effects due to their interdependencies with other domestic sectors. The import quotas for PV and wind power technologies are high, which means that domestic production of the required components would make the positive effects even stronger.

However, the expansion of renewables also leads to a decline in investment in conventional plants, especially when there is overcapacity and their economic viability is low. Power plants that are no longer needed are shut down temporarily or permanently and have to be decommissioned ahead of schedule.

Analogously, for heat production through RES (see Figure 4), the positive effects are somewhat weaker. This is due to lower total investment volumes, as well as to the fact that a small amount flows into the sector of material goods production and a higher share of the investments is effective in the sector of construction. In this segment, near-surface geothermal energy and solar thermal energy show the highest positive effects in 2030.

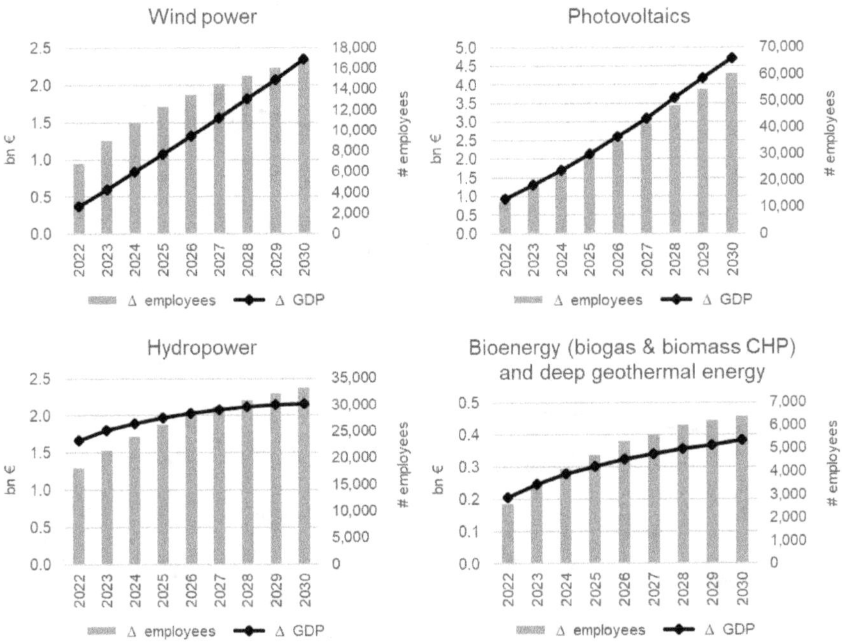

Figure 3. Additional GDP and employment through the expansion of RES for electricity production in Austria until 2030.

The substitution of fossil energy sources by renewable energy also results in effects that are not quantified by the GDP measurement method used here. External effects due to CO_2 emissions and the resulting climate change would decrease through the increased use of renewables, so that from an environmental economic perspective, one can speak of a double dividend (Kirchner *et al.*, 2019; Goers and Schneider, 2019a, b). On the one hand, investments in the expansion of renewables in the context of an energy transition result in economic growth and additional employment; on the other hand, there is a clear environmental benefit because of mitigating GHG emissions, as shown in Figure 5.

It should be noted that the economic effects of a simultaneous expansion of different technologies may be lower due to possible overlaps and interactions. Further, it should also be noted that changes in energy tax revenues for the public sector and in the investment behavior of companies due to the conversion of the energy system are not taken into account in the simulations.

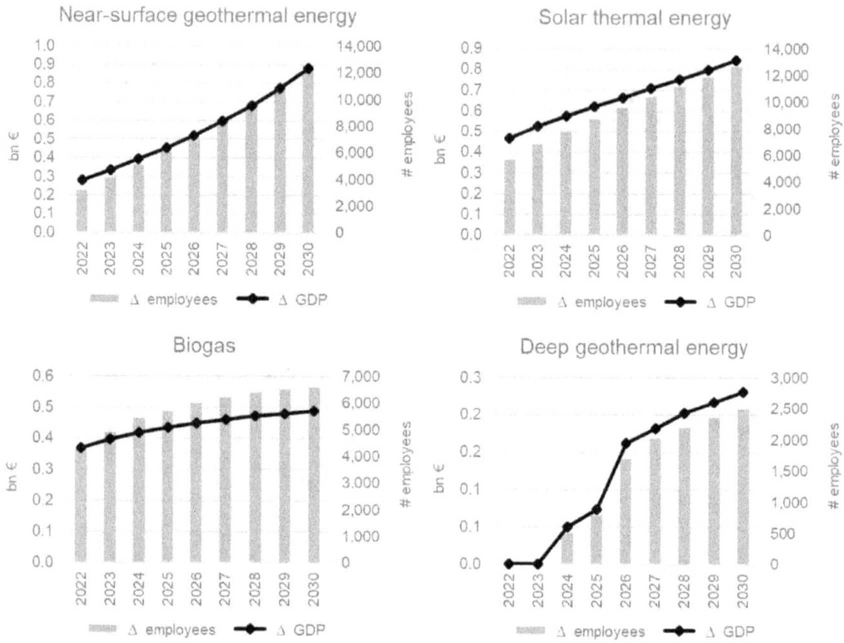

Figure 4. Additional GDP and employment through the expansion of RES for heat production in Austria until 2030.

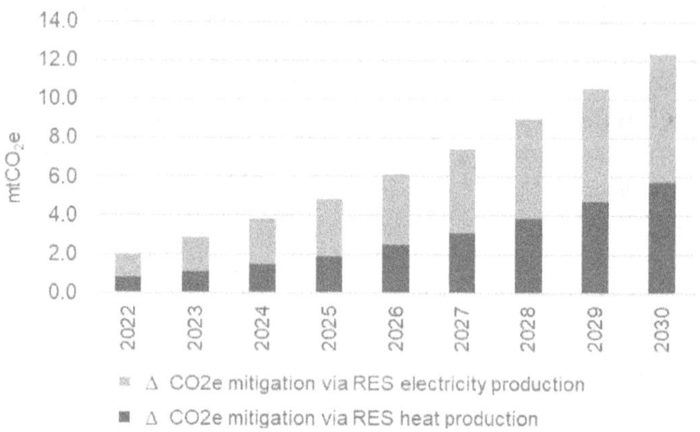

Figure 5. Mitigation of GHG emissions through the expansion of RES for electricity and heat production in Austria until 2030.

In order to provide incentives for the expansion of renewable energies and thus create additional GDP and employment, subsidies and their regulatory framework are essential. A combination of an increase in the volume of subsidies for renewable energies and market-based incentives could trigger investment and consumption impulses from companies and households and represents a cornerstone for linking the economy and the climate toward climate neutrality. The derivation of a detailed promotion or financing strategy could not be undertaken within the scope of the present study, but represents a significant issue for future analyses. However, to take a qualitative look at this significant issue, Section 4 examines the current Austrian green finance landscape and relates it to the simulation analyses.

4. Green finance in Austria

The research project Risk Fin Porto examines the finance sector in Austria in respect to the transition to a low-carbon economy and society (Umweltbundesamt, 2020). It was funded by the Austrian Climate Research Programme (ACRP) and formed the basis for the development of the Green Finance Plan of the Ministry of Finance and the Ministry of Climate. The goals of the Green Finance Plan aim to reduce climate risks, foster transparency, and incentivize climate friendly investments. In 2020, several stakeholders (Austrian National Bank, Financial Market Authority, research consortium Risk Fin Porto) published guidelines for sustainability risks in the finance sector. The findings from about 200 interviews of participants of different sectors, focus groups, and workshop discussions were that the financial sector plays a key role in climate crisis mitigation and that Austrian equity funds are strongly invested in high GHG emission sectors, which cause the biggest carbon footprint among the participants.

Dörig *et al.* (2020) showed that European companies followed by Asian companies have the highest disclosure rate on emissions, whereas American companies have the lowest ones. Austrian equity funds managed by Austrian Asset managers (equity funds AT–AM) represent in their portfolio disclosure rates of about 43% of Austrian compared to 53% of European companies (in total 55% of Europe,

30% of Asia, and 19% of North America disclose their emissions). Further, Austrian equity funds (equity funds AT) also show lower disclosure rates of Austrian companies compared to their European counterparts (including them) with 55% and 69%, respectively. The carbon footprint of the aforementioned Austrian funds (an aggregate of the underlying companies' GHG emissions) is the highest among the European, the Global, and the low-carbon benchmark. The Austrian equity funds AT–AM have a greenhouse gas intensity of more than 254 tCO_2e per million € turnover, whereas the global benchmark situates around 230 tCO_2e/million € turnover, the European benchmark **166** tCO_2e/million € turnover and the low-carbon benchmark shows less than **50** tCO_2e/million. For all funds, the economic sectors energy, utilities, and materials represent the major carbon footprint. These risks of emission exposure (loss of value caused by climate friendly regulations, costs of business transformation to achieve a low-carbon economy) can be allocated to the investors directly (Dörig *et al.*, 2020).

Moreover, the research group found that the Austrian Traded Index (ATX) is exposed to stronger climate risks by the transformation of the economic system because of the country's +6°C temperature pathway. Sustainable funds in contrast yield comparable gains and conventional funds are exposed to significant higher risks. Nevertheless, sustainable funds are still a niche for investments and the share of financial institutions managing climate risks systematically is small (Umweltbundesamt, 2020).

The national energy and climate protection plans (NECPs) require investments of around 17 billion € per year until the year 2030 in climate protection measures. For this, private capital is needed to reach the climate goals on national and international levels. As mentioned before, risks caused by climate change are increasing and becoming more costly. The target of the Green Finance Alliance is to support companies and society to build a stronger and more resilient future as a result of investments in sustainable business cases. Already initiated in 2019 and supported by the former Ministry of Sustainability and Tourism and the Ministry of Finance, a stakeholder process tipped the starting point of this project. In consequence, Austria's Green Finance Agenda developed. The report of the BMK (2021b) states the following: "The core component of

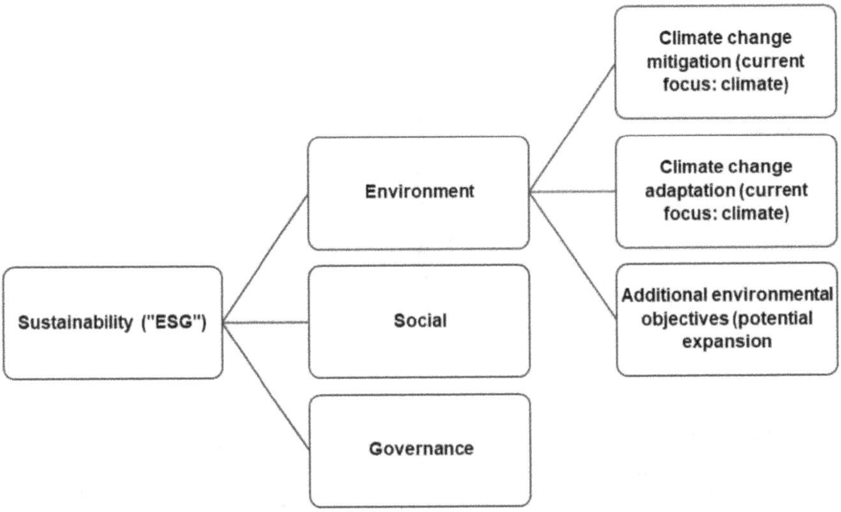

Figure 6. Objectives of the GF Alliance (BMK, 2021b).

this initiative is tó integrate climate into core business as a target dimension in combination with science-based targets."

BMK (2021b) states that the Green Finance Alliance voluntarily align their portfolio with the 1.5°C target, and the goal of the European Union in the long term is to become climate neutral by 2050 as in Figure 6. Every financial company registered in Austria can join the Green Finance Alliance and serve as a role model, aligning core business activities with climate goals. In consequence, pension funds, banks, insurance companies, and corporate provision funds are invited to join the alliance.

All members of the Green Finance Alliance have to take measures for their core business to comply with the target dimensions of a 1.5°C alignment, GHG neutrality by 2050, expansion of green activities, managing climate risks, and encouraging resilience and climate governance and mainstreaming. These measures can be split into general measures and action-area-specific measures in the core business. The governance structure of the GF Alliance is shown in Figure 7. Department VI/3 (Green Finance and Sustainable Economy) at the BMK is responsible for the strategic management of the alliance and the steering committee, for the assessment of evaluation results from

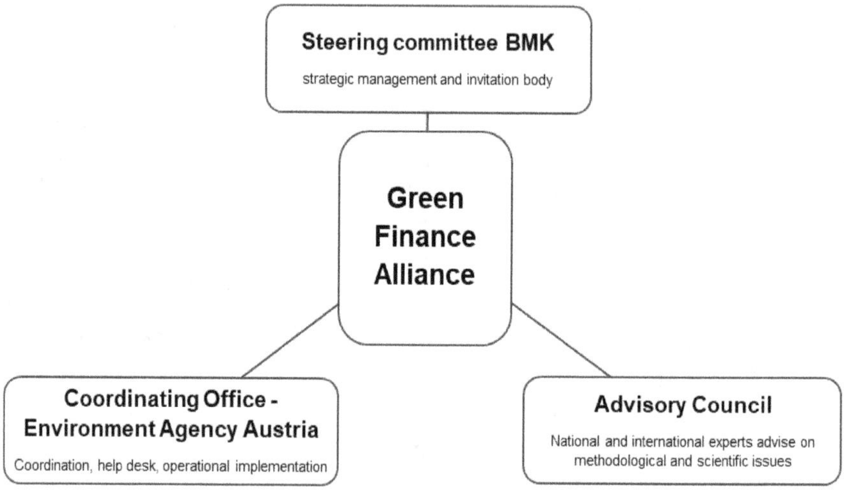

Figure 7. Governance structure of the GF Alliance (BMK, 2021b).

the annual monitoring process, acceptance of new members, and the composition of the advisory council. The Environment Agency Austria is the coordinating office and provides operational implementation, coordination, and support. The advisory council consists of international and Austrian experts in the field of Green Finance and assists with "substantive and science-based development of the Green Finance Alliance".

In 2016, the European Commission installed the High-Level Expert Group on Sustainable Finance. The experts reported in 2018 that annually around 180 billion € are necessary for investments in renewable energy, sustainable transport, and energy efficiency in buildings. The Green Finance Alliance stems from the European initiative to reach national goals. The regulation (EU) 2020/852 published in 2020 classifies sustainable activities in the European Union (Sustainable finance taxonomy) and a draft on a European Green Bond Standard was published by the European Commission in 2021.

These initiatives on the national and European levels will redirect substantial investments in green portfolios and therefore in renewable energy generation. The divestment of fossil fuel-based business models and investment in green sustainable business models will decrease risk exposure of businesses and foster economic growth as shown in the macroeconomic simulation in the case of Austria. Green Finance and investment in renewable energy will have significant positive impacts on economic growth and the excess of growth of the current macroeconomic simulation will be determined by the shift of financial volumes from conventional funds to sustainable green funds.

5. Conclusion

On the macroeconomic level, Austria has been and is currently struggling with difficult developments as a result of the COVID-19 recession and uncertainties caused by the Ukraine crisis. With regard to climate policy goals in the future and, in particular, net carbon neutrality by 2040, Austria faces major tasks, whereby renewable energies can play an even stronger role in energy production. In view of these developments, this chapter presented an attempt to quantify the macroeconomic impacts of investments in the additional expansion of RES in electricity and heat production and presented the role of green finance in Austria in this context.

Our simulation results clearly show that positive impacts — increase in GDP and employment — are created in the context of energy production expansion via RES. The key drivers are investment impulses, which also — depending on import ratios of the required materials and services — trigger indirect and induced effects in other sectors of the economy. In addition, there are positive effects on the current account balance through the avoidance of fossil energy imports. At the same time, GHG emissions are mitigated significantly.

The targeted consideration or promotion of the financing of this transformation via green finance can play an important accompanying role. This can succeed if targeted government measures help overcome investment barriers. For example, government subsidies of the financing costs can increase the attractiveness of climate-friendly projects, for example, through preferential credits or interest rate subsidies (Steckel and Jakob, 2018). Other measures may reduce financing costs by mitigating the risk expressed in financing costs. One concrete instrument in this sense is government guarantees for climate-friendly credits. If credit guarantees apply specifically to climate-friendly investments, they become more attractive compared to fossil-based alternatives (Steckel and Jakob, 2018). Credit guarantees proved their worth as a tool to support the economy during the COVID-19 crisis, leading to higher borrowing and lower financing rates for participating firms (ECB, 2020a).

Both strong and credible climate policies and legislation are potential policy solutions that could lead to a shift in investment away from carbon-intensive assets. Le *et al.* (2020) find that a developed and well-functioning financial sector is substantial for the deployment of renewable energy. They recommend that policymakers should offer policies that facilitate financing for RE firms. Further, the findings of Kempa *et al.* (2021) suggest that ambitious and credible environmental policy targets increase investors' confidence in the long-term profitability of green firms' and technologies' business models. In this context, environmental policies not only have a positive effect on expected corporate profits, but can also have an important risk-reducing effect. This suggests that a consistent environmental policy — regardless of its direct impact on profitability — sends a valuable signal to investors. The introduction of CO_2 pricing in Austria (Köppl *et al.*, 2021) in July 2022 is expected to be a step in this direction, although the medium-term CO_2 price development will be decisive for the intensity.

Finally, we would like to state that by no means do we see our research as completed. We agree with the view of Breitenfellner *et al.* (2020), and state that Austria's green finance sector is not yet fully mature. It should be noted, however, that green and sustainable finance is about to arrive in the financial sector. Regulatory and environmental policies such as CO_2 pricing and EAG support this development, and their impact on green finance in Austria needs to be evaluated continuously. With respect to the simulation results presented here, sensitivity analyses with respect to energy prices (based on current market developments) and investment volumes (change in the context of technological progress) will certainly have to be carried out in the future. Rising energy import prices can increase the positive macroeconomic effects by the expansion of RES production.

References

Baumgartner, J., Kaniovski, S., Fink, M., Pitlik, H., & Rocha-Akis, S. (2021). Starker privater Konsum treibt das Wirtschaftswachstum. Mittelfristige Prognose 2022 bis 2026 unter Berücksichtigung der Steuerreform 2022/2024. WIFO-Monatsberichte, *94*, 711–736 (in German).

BMK (2021a). Energie in Österreich - Zahlen, Daten, Fakten. Bundesministerium für Klimaschutz, Umwelt, Energie, Mobilität, Innovation und Technologie, Vienna (in German).

BMK (2021b). Green Finance Alliance. An initiative of the Austrian Green Finance Agenda. Executive Summary. Bundesministerium für Klimaschutz, Umwelt, Energie, Mobilität, Innovation und Technologie, Vienna (in German).

Bointner, R., Biermayr, P., Goers, S., Streit-Maier, J., & Tichler, R. (2013). Wirtschaftskraft Erneuerbarer Energie in Österreich und Erneuerbare Energie in Zahlen. Blue Globe Report #1/2013. Austrian Climate and Energy Fund, Vienna (in German).

Breitenfellner, A., Hasenhüttl, Lehmann, G., & Tschulik, A. (2020). Green finance — Opportunities for the financial sector. Financial Stability Report *40*, 45–61.

Codagnone, R., Wagner, J., & Zhan, J.C. (2020). Nachhaltige Investmentzertifikate und Anleihen in Österreich. In Statistiken — Daten und Analysen Q2/20. OeNB, 47–55 (in German).

Dörig, P., Lutz, V., Rattay, W., Stadelmann, M., Jorisch, D., Kunesch, S., & Glas, N. (2020). Kohlenstoffrisiken für den österreichischen Finanzmarkt (Carbon exposure. The Austrian state of the market). RiskFinPorto — Working Paper No. 4 (in German).

ECB (2020). Economic and Monetary Developments. European Central Bank. Economic Bulletin Issue 6/2020.

Goers, S. & Schneider, F. (2019a). Austria's path to a climate-friendly society and economy-contributions of an environmental tax reform. *Modern Economy, 10*, 1369–1384.

Goers, S. & Schneider, F. (2019b). Economic, ecological and social benefits through redistributing revenues from increased mineral oil taxation in Austria: A triple dividend. *Green Finance, 1*, 442–456.

Goers, S., Baresch, M., Tichler, R., & Schneider, F. (2015). MOVE2: Simulation model of the (upper) Austrian economy with a special focus on energy including the socio-economic module MOVE2Social-integration of income, age and gender. Energieinstitut at the Johannes Kepler University, Linz.

Goers, S., Schneider, F., Steinmüller, H., & Tichler, R. (2020). Wirtschaftswachstum und Beschäftigung durch Investitionen in Erneuerbare Energien. Energieinsititut an der JKU Linz (in German).

Hammer, S. & Hallegatte, S. (2020). Planning for the economic recovery from COVID-19: A sustainability checklist for policymakers. World Bank blog on Development and a Changing Climate.

Hepburn, C., O'Callaghan, B., Stern, N., Stiglitz, J., & Zenghelis, D. (2020). Will COVID-19 fiscal recovery packages accelerate or retard progress on climate change? *Oxford Review of Economic Policy, 36*, 1–48.

IRENA (2020). Post-COVID Recovery. International Renewable Energy Agency.

Kempa, K., Moslener, U., & Schenker, O. (2021). The cost of debt of renewable and non-renewable energy firms. *Nature Energy, 6*, 135–142.

Kirchengast, G. & Steininger, K. (2020). Treibhausgasbudget für Österreich auf dem Weg zur Klimaneutralität 2040. Wegener Center for Climate and Global Change, University of Graz (in German).

Kirchner, M., Sommer, M., Kratena, K., Kletzan-Slamanig, D., & Kettner-Marx, C. (2019). CO_2 taxes, equity and the double dividend: Macroeconomic model simulations for Austria. *Energy Policy, 126*, 295–314.

Köppl, A., Schleicher, S., & Schratzenstaller, M. (2021). CO_2-Bepreisung in der Steuerreform 2022/2024. WIFO Research Briefs, 13 (in German).

Köppl-Turyna, M., Strohner, L., & Berger, J. (2022). Ukraine-Russland-Krise und ihre Folgen — Ermittlung auf Basis von Erdgaspreisentwicklungen und Exportstopps. EcoAustria — Institut für Wirtschaftsforschung, Vienna (in German).

Le, T.-H., Nguyen, C. P., & Park, D. (2020). Financing renewable energy development: Insights from 55 countries. *Energy Research & Social Science, 68*, 101537.

Republic Austria Parliament (2020). Erneuerbaren-Ausbau-Gesetz — EAG; Erneuerbaren-Ausbau-Gesetzespaket — EAG-Paket (58/ME) (in German).

Schiman, S. (2021). Vierte COVID 19-Welle bremst kräftigen Aufschwung. Prognose für 2021 (Fourth COVID 19 Wave Slows Strong Upswing. Economic Outlook for 2021). WIFO-Monatsberichte, *94*, 695–709 (in German).

Sommer, M., Sinabell, F., & Streicher, G. (2021). Ein Ausblick auf die Treibhausgasemissionen in Österreich 2021 und 2022 (An Outlook on Greenhouse Gas Emissions in Austria in 2021 and 2022). WIFO Working Papers, 628 (in German).

Steckel, J. C. & Jakob, M. (2018). The role of financing cost and de-risking strategies for clean energy investment. *International Economics, 155*, 19–28.

Steininger, K. W., Bednar-Friedl, B., Knittel, N., Kirchengast, G., Nabernegg, S., Williges, K., Mestel, R., Hutter, H.-P., & Kenner, L. (2020). Klimapolitik in Österreich: Innovationschance Coronakrise und die Kosten des Nicht-Handelns, Wegener Center Research Briefs 1-2020, Wegener Center Verlag, Universität Graz, Austria (in German).

Steininger, K. W., König, M., Bednar-Friedl, B., Kranzl, L., Loibl, W., & Prettenthaler, F. (2015). *Economic Evaluation of Climate Change Impacts: Development of a Cross-sectoral Framework and Results for Austria*. Springer International Publishing, Switzerland.

Umweltbundesamt (2020). Risk Fin Porto.

Umweltbundesamt (2021). Austria's informative inventory report 2021 — Submission under the UNECE Convention on Long-range Transboundary Air Pollution and Directive (EU) 2016/2284 on the reduction of national emissions of certain atmospheric pollutants. REP-0762, Vienna.

Umweltbundesamt (2022). Treibhausgas-Bilanz Österreichs (2020) (in German).

© 2024 World Scientific Publishing Europe Ltd.
https://doi.org/10.1142/9781800614451_0011

Chapter 11

ESG Performance and Board of Directors Compensation: A European Perspective

Alfred Wong[*,†] **and Alain Neher**[‡]

School of Business, Charles Sturt University,
Bathurst, NSW, Australia
[†]*awong@csu.edu.au*
[‡]*aneher@csu.edu.au*

Abstract

While the literature has previously investigated CEO compensation, board of director compensation has recently gained attention in scholarly works. Yet, board compensation and ESG performance have not been considered. Therefore, the purpose of this chapter is to explore whether there is an association between ESG performance and the compensation of the board of directors. Data from a sample of 2,499 listed European corporations have been statistically analyzed. The results show evidence that ESG performance is associated with board compensation. Firms with higher ESG performance tend to exhibit higher compensation for their board of directors. Following the stakeholder theory, this study highlights the importance of incorporating ESG metrics in the board members' compensation plans and responsibilities to ensure sustainable long-term wealth for all stakeholders. At the same time, the corporation's board compensation package must be carefully designed and incorporated into the corporate policy under the premise of reasonableness.

[*]Corresponding author.

> Corporate social performance (CSP) is found to be positively associated with prior financial performance, supporting the theory that slack resource availability and CSP are positively related. CSP is also found to be positively associated with future financial performance, supporting the theory that good management and CSP are positively related (Waddock and Graves, 1997, p. 303).

> Around the globe, a third of all professionally managed assets, or roughly $30 trillion, are now subject to ESG criteria (Howad-Grenville, 2021, para. 1). Robust ESG and impact measures can help us keep score, and, when necessary, make course corrections. Ultimately, however, no matter how and what we measure, we need to act our way into greater understanding, insight, and even purpose (para. 23).

1. Introduction

This chapter analyzes the relationship between Environmental, Social, and Governmental (ESG) performance and board of directors' (BoD) compensation. Specifically, the study investigates whether the individual environmental, social, or governance performance and the corporation's collective ESG score are related to its BoD compensation.

Recently, practitioners and policymakers have given increased attention to sustainability issues and acknowledge that ESG activities contribute to corporations and benefit all stakeholders (e.g., Business Roundtable, 2019; Harrison *et al.*, 2020; McKinsey and Company, 2020; UN SSE, 2015). Research into ESG has attracted growing attention with studies of its relationship with corporate financial performance, stock returns, or other financial aspects of the corporation (Lisin *et al.*, 2022; Waddock and Graves, 1997). One of these aspects is executive compensation (e.g., Bebchuk and Tallarita, 2022; Cavaco *et al.*, 2020). That is, what are a corporation's ESG metrics and its CEO remuneration. However, there is a lack of research examining the impact of ESG performance on the compensation of the corporation's BoD. Adopting an ESG orientation or eco-orientation is a strategic business decision with a corporation's BoD ultimately responsible (Miles and Munilla, 1993). Therefore it is important to include the BoD's influence on ESG performance.

Compensation plays an essential role in communicating corporate priorities. This chapter contributes to both scholarly literature and practice. The present study examines the relationships between the compensation of the corporation's BoD and its ESG scores in a sample of 2,499 listed European corporations. Differences between the individual scores are emphasized, with differences in ESG scores found between Western, Eastern, Northern, and Southern European regions. Policymakers and corporations should consider this study's results when embedding and further developing ESG and designing their BoD compensation to align with the business model and value drivers. As such, ESG-based compensation and incentives signal the importance to stakeholders of an ESG orientation and its impact on strategy, culture, and investment.

Using firm-level data from the four major regions of Europe, our results provide clear evidence that board compensation is associated with ESG performance. Board compensation differs significantly between the high ESG performing group and the low performing group. Overall, firms with higher ESG performance tend to exhibit higher compensation for their board of directors.

The methodological approach illustrates the methods used to analyze the data and outlines the scope of the analyses, defines the key variables, describes the sample demographics, and illustrates descriptive statistics. The remainder of this chapter provides the context of both ESG and board compensation and outlines the proposition of the study. The chapter concludes with implications, limitations, and further avenues for research.

2. Context and relevance of ESG

2.1. *Environmental, social, and governance*

In recent years, attention given to sustainability issues has substantially increased, and practitioners have taken the perspective that ESG activities contribute economically to both corporations and their shareholders. For example, in a survey of more than 1,000 corporate CEOs, 93% considered sustainability critical to the success of their business in the future (UN SSE, 2015). Similarly, McKinsey's 2019 Global Survey on valuing ESG programs reports that CEOs and investment professionals agree that ESG activities create shareholder value (McKinsey and Company, 2020). In 2019, a group of prominent American CEOs (Business Roundtable) issued a new "Statement on the Purpose of a Corporation" committing to lead their companies for the benefit of all their stakeholders, that is, employees, customers, suppliers, community, and shareholders (Business Roundtable, 2019). This step is seen as a strong signal that "the tide has shifted, replacing shareholder primacy with a multistakeholder purpose for corporations" (Harrison *et al.*, 2020, p. 1225) and outlines a new standard for corporate responsibility (Business Roundtable, 2019). Meanwhile, governments are increasingly emphasizing the importance of corporate ESG and The United Nations Sustainable Stock Exchanges (SSE) Initiative recommends that large businesses report their ESG practices by the year 2030 (UN SSE, 2015). Similarly, the European Commission set up an action plan to finance sustainable growth, including measures to enhance ESG transparency (Financial Stability, 2020).

ESG activities contribute to shareholder value while simultaneously achieving environmental, social, and governance objectives. A recent review reveals that a dominant theoretical basis of ESG research is stakeholder theory (Li *et al.*, 2021). One emerging perspective is that socially responsible behavior guides ESG activities to enhance shareholder welfare by "doing well by doing good" (Albuquerque *et al.*, 2020, p. 594). This view is based on stakeholder theory made popular by Freeman's (1984) seminal work stating that corporations have a broader responsibility to society and should be accountable to all stakeholders. The opposite view of the stakeholder theory and ESG activities is generally attributed to Friedman (1970), who sees such activities as a manifestation of managerial agency issues between managers and shareholders by benefiting stakeholders generally and not exclusively shareholders.

ESG is a framework system defined as a corporation's responsibility to improve social welfare and equitable and sustainable long-term wealth for stakeholders (Jamali *et al.*, 2017; Turban and Greening, 1997). It provides insight into an organization's aptitude to sustain its Corporate Social Responsibility (CSR) (Lisin *et al.*, 2022). ESG-oriented firms tend to exhibit effective and efficient governance, fewer environmental regulatory problems, less earnings volatility, and have access to funds at a lower cost of capital (Kumar, 2020; Lisin *et al.*, 2022; Raimo *et al.*, 2021). Furthermore, corporations that integrate an ESG strategy are likely to be better positioned for long-term success, profitability, and ultimately create value that benefits shareholders (Eccles and Klimenko, 2019). Studies have also shown that integrating ESG into a corporation's valuation model improves its non-financial indicators, for instance, consumer satisfaction, market acceptance, and the societal values the corporation brings to its stakeholders (Mohammad and Wasiuzzaman, 2021).

2.2. *ESG score — Concept of ESG performance and data source*

The ESG score is an innovative method to evaluate a corporation's activities and consists of an aggregate of three different aspects: the environmental, social, and governance pillars. The score does not focus on financial reporting but on statements of a corporation's influence on the three pillars of the score. Rating agencies use ESG data to evaluate the corporation's level of ESG performance. Hence, the ESG score concept recognizes corporations who practice CSR, provides investors with appropriate tools and evaluations to carry out ethical and socially responsible investing, and enhances CSR-related disclosure and reporting from corporations (Lisin *et al.*, 2022). Corporations that adopt an ESG orientation lie on a continuum *from compliance* to the integration of ESG principles into culture, values, strategy, and compensation plan, on the other end (Koors *et al.*, 2019; Munilla and Miles, 2005). Koors and colleagues argue that where a firm lands on the continuum may be partly driven by the organizational size or its associated industry, or both.

Refinitiv (formerly Thomson Reuters Eikon) provided the data. Overall, Refinitv offers one of the most comprehensive ESG databases in the industry, covering corporations representing over 70% of the global market capitalization across more than 500 different ESG metrics from 2002 (Refinitiv, 2021a). Refinitv ESG scores are based on self-reported measures of a corporation's relative ESG performance, commitment, and effectiveness (Refinitiv, 2021a). The ESG scores measure the corporation's (1) resource use, (2) emissions, (3) product innovation, (4) workforce, (5) human rights, (6) community development, (7) product responsibility, (8) management, (9) shareholders, and (10) CSR strategy.

Refinitiv ESG scores are well-acknowledged in scholarly literature and have been used numerously in prior studies (e.g., Albuquerque *et al.*, 2020; Ding *et al.*, 2021; Dyck *et al.*, 2019; Li *et al.*, 2021).

Table 1. Definition of Refinitiv's scores.

Score range	Grade	Description	
0 to 25	D–/D/D+	"D" scores indicate poor relative ESG performance and an insufficient degree of transparency in reporting material ESG data publicly.	ESG laggards
>25 to 50	C–/C/C+	"C" scores within this range indicate satisfactory relative ESG performance and a moderate degree of transparency in reporting material ESG data publicly.	
>50 to 75	B–/B/B+	"B" scores indicate good relative ESG performance and an above-average degree of transparency in reporting material ESG data publicly.	
>75 to 100	A–/A/A+	"A" scores indicate excellent relative ESG performance and a high degree of transparency in reporting material ESG data publicly.	ESG leaders

Sources: Adapted from Refinitiv (2021a,b).

Refinitiv categorizes its score range into a letter grade, as shown in Table 1. These letter grades (from D– to A+) will be used in this study as *ESG performance* for the different analyses.

3. ESG performance and board compensation

3.1. *Board of directors' compensation*

While the literature has previously paid more attention to investigating CEO compensation (Elnahass *et al.*, 2022), director compensation issues have only recently gained consideration in scholarly works (Almarayeh, 2021). This development makes sense given that "the board is the highest decision-making body at the firm with power to hire and fire management, set executive compensation, and ultimately guide the strategic direction of the firm" (Boivie *et al.*, 2015, p. 1581). Board compensation is considered a central incentive mechanism in shaping directors' behavior and monitoring effectiveness (Ang *et al.*, 2002) besides stimulating them to work toward better corporate performance (e.g., Andreas *et al.*, 2012; Lemma *et al.*,

2020) and wealth maximization (Brick *et al.*, 2006). On the policy level, in their "Study on directors' duties and sustainable corporate governance", the European Commission discusses the integration of sustainability competencies into the board of directors, which may impact the composition and compensation of the board of directors (European Commission, 2020).

However, there is uncertainty around the appropriate amount of board compensation. It is argued that it should be sufficiently high to attract high-caliber individuals and reward them for their responsibilities (Magnan *et al.*, 2010). Yet, remuneration should not be so high as to potentially weak the directors' objectivity, judgment, and independence (Almarayeh, 2021).

Institutional shareholders are increasingly observing board compensation, and thus shareholders attempt to install mechanisms that align the interests of the agents and the principals (Almarayeh, 2021). Jensen and Meckling (1976) indicated that management compensation plans are designed to ensure that all corporate parties act toward maximizing the organization's value while reducing agency costs. Later, Jensen (2002) emphasized that a firm cannot maximize value if it ignores the interests of *any* of its stakeholders. This reflects Freeman's (1984) stakeholder theory, which views the corporate environment as an ecosystem of related parties who need to be considered and treated respectfully to keep the firm profitable and successful, including benefiting its shareholders.

3.2. *ESG performance and board compensation*

Over the last decade or so, the ESG literature body has increased, for example, investigating relationships between ESG performance and corporate financial performance (e.g., Nekhili *et al.*, 2021; Velte, 2017, 2020), ESG performance and share market returns (e.g., Albuquerque *et al.*, 2020; Wheatley, 2022), ESG disclosure and board compensation (e.g., Suttipun, 2021), CSR and CEO compensation (e.g., Cai *et al.*, 2011; Callan and Thomas, 2011), and ESG ratings and board composition (Waterstraat *et al.*, 2021). Most recently, Bebchuk and Tallarita (2022) used ESG metrics in executive pay. However, the link between ESG performance and board of directors' compensation has not been empirically researched. Therefore, this chapter aims to contribute to the ESG performance and board remuneration literature by addressing this gap.

While mixed empirical results are apparent between ESG performance and firm performance, the literature overall suggests a positive relationship (Lisin *et al.*, 2022; Velte, 2020). Similar evidence appears for ESG performance and equity market returns, indicating that higher ESG performance is more resilient in times of crises such as the COVID-19 pandemic (Wheatley, 2022). Further literature on similar aspects reveals that ESG disclosure impacts board compensation, CSR affects CEO compensation, and board compensation links to firm performance (e.g., Callan and Thomas, 2011; Handa, 2018; Lemma *et al.*, 2020; Suttipun, 2021). In contrast, Bebchuk and Tallarita (2022), question the benefits of ESG-based CEO compensation. They conclude that encouraging and expanding ESG-based compensation at the executive level might give self-interested CEOs a powerful tool to increase their payoffs without creating meaningful stakeholder value. Hence, as a primary internal corporate governance mechanism, the board of directors must monitor the executive management effectively and drive value enhancement for shareholders (Merendino and Melville, 2019) while paying full attention to its stakeholders. For those boards that strongly believe in moving their firms along the continuum and toward deeper embedding of ESG factors into the organization, incentives may be a catalyst (Koors *et al.*, 2019). Koors and colleagues thus suggest that board compensation can be a powerful tool for advancing business strategies. In turn, ESG integrated into the business strategy will likely contribute to sustainable corporate success and value creation (Eccles and Klimenko, 2019).

Hence, this investigation considers today's societal and organizational importance of ESG and the highest organizational compensation level, directly reporting to the firms' shareholders, proposing a link between ESG performance and board compensation.

4. Data and methodology

Member States of the European Union (EU) have been leading the way for sustainable development, evidenced by a steady increase in the SDG Index score from 2005 to 2020 (Lafortune *et al.*, 2021).

Furthermore, the Directive 2014/95/EU legislated by the European Parliament and Council (2014) highlighted the need to improve social and environmental information disclosure by large corporations within the EU. More broadly, the governance of sustainability has become increasingly important and forms a vital part of a firm's corporate strategy. Indeed, there has been a greater emphasis on the role of the board of directors in fostering sustainability targets as part of a firm's corporate strategy (Khoo *et al.*, 2021; Pucheta-Martínez and Gallego-Álvarez, 2019).

Three selection criteria are used to find the most suitable sample for the study. First, firms located in the European regions are chosen to provide focus on European companies. To this end, companies listed on European stock exchanges are included to ensure the quality of data and availability of financial information. Second, for a company to be included in the sample, each firm must have consecutive annual board compensation from filed annual reports for at least two years between 2016 and 2020. Third, firms with missing ESG data are excluded over the entire sample period. After applying these criteria, a list of 2,499 publicly listed European firms emerged for the period 2016 to 2020.

The selected companies are categorized using the Global Industry Classification Standard (GICS) into 11 sectors, further broken down into 68 subsectors. In addition, each company is uniquely identified using the Reuters Instrument Code (RIC), and net sales reported calculated over the sample period are sourced from the Thomson Reuters database. This variable is used as a proxy for firm size following Albuquerque *et al.* (2020). It provides a better understanding of the amount dedicated to board compensation by firms as a percentage of revenue.

For each of the selected companies, the compensation of the board members is collected from Refinitiv's Officers and Directors database. The compensation amount represents the board's total yearly compensation, including base salary, cash bonus, share-based awards, option-based awards, fees, and other compensation plans. The firms' data categorized by country and region are collected to allow grouping of the variables of interest by four main European regions. Accordingly, the ESG data are obtained from the Refinitiv ESG universe for companies that are headquartered in Northern Europe (NE), Western Europe (WE), Southern Europe (SE), and

Eastern Europe (EE). This resulted in 8,304 data points with ESG information rated between A+ to D–. Table A.1 in the Appendix tabulates the breakdown of ESG rating grouped by region and country of headquarters.

The Thomson Reuters ASSET4 database was used to obtain ESG data for the selected firms. The overall ESG score was constructed using three main pillars, namely: (1) Environmental (E) captures information relating to emission, innovation, and resource use; (2) Social (S) attempts to measure issues concerning human rights, product responsibility, workforce, and community issues; and (3) Governance (G) focuses on the effects of management, shareholders, and CSR strategy. Ten different proportional weights for the subcategories of E, S, and G scores are added to obtain the overall ESG score. The information available from corporate websites, stock exchange filings, financial reports, by-laws, and other news sources are used to determine the scores.

Data cleaning is carried out before analyzing the data using statistical analysis to identify observations with missing or extreme values. There were instances where ESG ranking or total board compensation were not available, and these firms were excluded from the analysis. In addition, board compensation data that were above or below the standardized z-score threshold of ±3.29 (Tabachnick and Fidell, 2013, 2019) were also excluded, resulting in the deletion of 17 observations for the total board compensation variable. The final sample available for analysis consisted of 7,425 observations across all four European regions.

The ESG and firm-level data obtained from the secondary database were subsequently analyzed using descriptive statistics, bivariate analysis of differences between groups across categories, nonparametric statistical analysis of differences between groups, and comparison of medians between groups. Specifically, analyses between subgroups were conducted using the contingency table approach to allow comparison of results between subgroups and analyze the association between variables. Furthermore, bivariate tests of differences concerning regions, sizes, and rating groups were used to analyze the dataset.

Figure 1 depicts the means and medians of board compensation categorized by 12 rating groups (A+ to D–), while Figure 2 uses four rating groups (A to D) to plot the bar graph. The latter is constructed

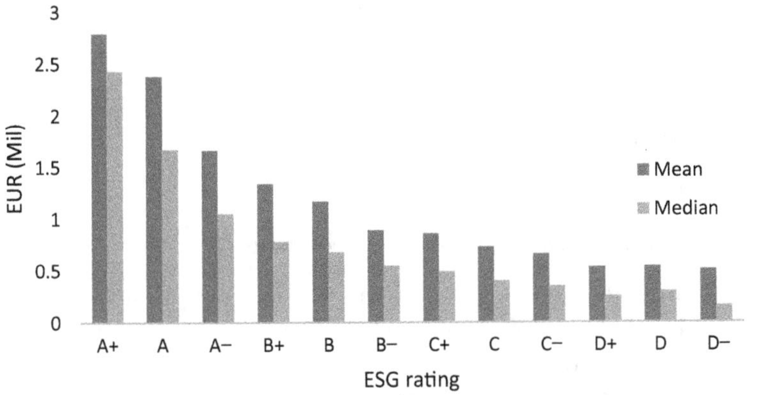

Figure 1. Board compensation and ESG ratings (A+ to D–).

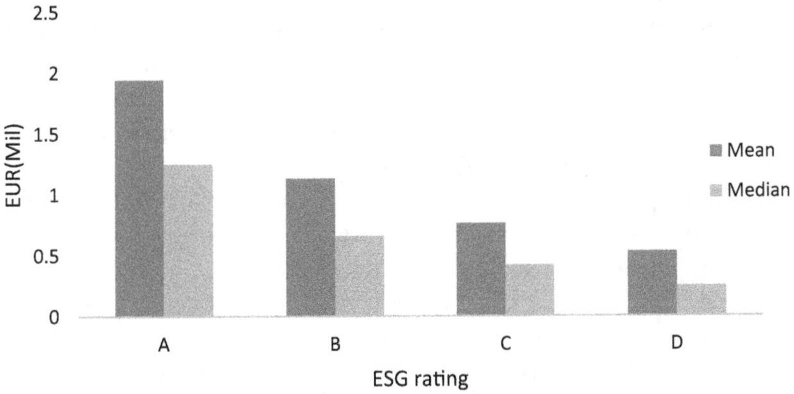

Figure 2. Board compensation and ESG ratings (A to D).

by merging the intermediate ratings into four main groups: A(A+, A, A–); B(B+, B, B–); C(C+, C, C–); and D(D+, D, D–).

The figures provide a clear picture of the relationship between the size of board compensation and ESG performance. Notably, as the performance of the ESG rating declines, the size of board compensation decreases steadily. In Figure 1, a company rated A+ has a median compensation of around EUR2.4 million. This contrasts sharply with a company rated D–, which has a median of EUR0.2 million ($\Delta = -92.7\%$). Similarly, in Figure 2, group A has a median of around EUR1.25 million, while group D has a much lower median of EUR0.25 million ($\Delta = -80\%$).

5. Analysis and results of ESG performance and board compensation

5.1. *Board compensation and revenue*

Table 2 provides an overview of the preliminary data by European regions. In the far-right column, "% Comp" represents the total board compensation as a percentage of net sales. This is calculated by dividing total board compensation (denoted as Comp in Column 3) by the number of companies and then dividing by the average net sales reported in Column 4.

As shown in Column 2, the sample consisted of firms mainly located in the northern (52%) and western regions (34%) of Europe. Although EE has the lowest number of firms, each firm in this region has an annual revenue of nearly EUR500 million, substantially larger than the remaining three regions with annual revenues between EUR6 to EUR7 million per year.

At first glance, the results indicate some variations in total board compensation across the regions. On average, yearly total board compensation for SE amounts to EUR1.13 million for each firm (= 279.57/247). WE followed, with board compensation of around EUR0.93 million, while NE and EE showed compensation of EUR0.56 million in the same financial year. However, taking revenue size into account shows a notable difference across the regions. For instance, 17.85% of the net sales for firms located in SE are invested in board compensation (= (279.57/247)/6.34). This result contrasts sharply with the % Comp of 0.11% reported for EE. Focusing on companies located in this region suggests that large non-EU corporations dominate EE. Firms in this region allocated less than 1% of revenue to board compensation despite the revenue size.

5.2. *Summary statistics*

As a preliminary analysis, Table 3 summarizes the basic characteristics of the main variables. The median scores reported for ESG, S, and G are above 50, suggesting, on the whole, the sampled firms

Table 2. Selected companies by European regions.

Regions	# Companies	Comp (€m)	Ave net sales (€m)	% Comp
NE	1,296	724.52	7.43	7.52
WE	853	791.02	7.80	11.89
SE	247	279.57	6.34	17.85
EE	103	57.55	496.05*	0.11

Note: "Comp" is calculated as the sum of total board compensation for all selected firms. "% Comp" is the total board compensation expressed as a percentage of net sales. "Ave Net Sales" is calculated using the mean net sales reported for the period 2015–2020. *This is largely due to very large firms located in this region.

Table 3. Descriptive statistics of board compensation and ratings.

Variable	N	Mean	Median	Std. dev.	Skewness	Kurtosis	K–S stat
Comp	7,425	1.06	0.58	7.15	70.47	5,603.51	0.254***
ESG	8,304	50.91	52.12	21.28	−0.19	−0.77	0.041***
E	8,290	44.69	44.78	28.49	0.01	−1.17	0.055***
S	8,290	55.11	56.72	23.78	−0.27	−0.81	0.051***
G	8,305	49.59	50.05	23.44	−0.05	−0.98	0.044***

Note: Test of normality using the Kolmogorov–Smirnova (K–S) statistic is rejected at the 1% level of statistical significance (***).

exhibit good relative performance (>50 to 75/100) with an above-average degree of transparency in ESG reporting to the public (Thomson Reuters, 2022). The median for the E score shows satisfactory (>25 to 50/100) relative performance with a moderate degree of transparency in data reporting.

Total board compensation is represented by the variable "Comp", which has a highly skewed and kurtotic distribution even after omitting the outliers. Furthermore, the mean value for Comp is much higher than its median, indicating a non-symmetrical distribution. The remaining variables exhibit a low degree of skewness and kurtosis, showing a minor difference between their means and medians. However, for all variables listed in Table 3, the null hypothesis of the normal distribution is strongly rejected at the 1% level of statistical significance using the Kolmogorov–Smirnova test statistic.

Accordingly, the Mann–Whitney test was used to test group differences, which does not require a strong assumption about the population distribution. The chi-square distribution was used as a means for testing the statistical significance.

5.3. *Comparison of key variables across European regions*

Given the evidence of non-normality of the variables, the aforementioned Mann–Whitney test was carried out to test for differences in the overall distribution across the European regions. Such a non-parametric approach alleviates analytical error resulting from the assumption that a population is normally distributed when such an assumption is empirically violated (Zikmund, 2003). Furthermore, the test statistic is more robust to outliers since the values are ranked. The test compares the sum of the ranks in the paired European regions as listed in Table 4 (Panels A to F). For each paired region, the Mann–Whitney U test statistic is used to decide whether the difference in mean ranks is significant.

Comparing the mean ranks for the NE and WE pair, Panel A of Table 4 provides evidence of significant differences in mean ranks between these regions. Firms in WE exhibit a larger mean rank (3,657) for the Comp variable and thus suggest they tend to pay higher compensation to their board of directors relative to firms located in NE; the corresponding Mann–Whitney U test statistic is highly significant ($U = 3{,}995{,}985, p < 0.01$, 2-tailed). Similarly, mean ranks are significantly higher for the ESG, E, and S scores, with mean ranks of 3,763, 3,824, and 3,825, respectively. However, for the G score, the mean rank for WE is only marginally larger than EE, and the difference is not statistically significant. Results for the NE and SE pair in Panel B reveal a very similar pattern, suggesting mean ranks for firms in NE are significantly larger for the selected variables, except for the G score. However, for the NE and EE pair in Panel C, differences in mean ranks for EE firms are only significantly larger for Comp (2,099) and S score (2,241). Firms located in NE generally achieved higher mean ranks for ESG and G, but the difference in mean ranks is not significant for these variables when compared with EE firms.

Table 4. Nonparametric comparison of mean ranks.

	Paired region	N	Mean rank	Mann–Whitney U	Z-stats
Panel A (NE & WE)					
Comp	NE	3,812	2,955	3,995,985	−14.87***
	WE	2,676	3,657		
ESG	NE	4,003	3,231	4,919,498	−10.94***
	WE	2,905	3,763		
E	NE	3,993	3,173	4,696,803	−13.41***
	WE	2,900	3,824		
S	NE	3,993	3,172	4,692,758	−13.45***
	WE	2,900	3,825		
G	NE	4,003	3,452	5,804,943	−0.12
	WE	2,905	3,458		
Panel B (NE & SE)					
Comp	NE	3,812	2,070	624,861	−17.94***
	SE	601	3,073		
ESG	NE	4,003	2,359	1,430,257	−11.89***
	SE	950	2,973		
E	NE	3,993	2,346	1,392,669	−12.8***
	SE	951	3,005		
S	NE	3,993	2,320	1,288,432	−15.43***
	SE	951	3,114		
G	NE	4,003	2,486	1,869,267	−0.86
	SE	951	2,442		
Panel C (NE & EE)					
Comp	NE	3,812	2,099	547,925	−4.40***
	EE	336	1,799		
ESG	NE	4,003	2,232	865,562	−1.05
	EE	446	2,164		
E	NE	3,993	2,213	864,069	−1.03
	EE	446	2,279		
S	NE	3,993	2,241	807,349	−3.24***
	EE	446	2,034		
G	NE	4,003	2,228	882,368	−0.41
	EE	446	2,202		

(*Continued*)

Table 4. (*Continued*)

	Paired region	N	Mean rank	Mann–Whitney U	Z-stats
Panel D (WE & SE)					
Comp	WE	2,676	1,565	605,727	−9.46***
	SE	601	1,969		
ESG	WE	2,905	1,888	1,262,287	−3.95***
	SE	950	2,052		
E	WE	2,900	1,892	1,280,602	−3.31***
	SE	951	2,029		
S	WE	2,900	1,865	1,203,374	−5.90***
	SE	951	2,111		
G	WE	2,905	1,938	1,354,027	−0.92
	SE	951	1,900		
Panel E (WE & EE)					
Comp	WE	2,676	1,556	317,543	−8.78***
	EE	336	1,114		
ESG	WE	2,905	1,721	517,978	−6.83***
	EE	446	1,385		
E	WE	2,900	1,715	526,652	−6.32***
	EE	446	1,404		
S	WE	2,900	1,735	467,770	−9.42***
	EE	446	1,272		
G	WE	2,905	1,679	638,258	−0.502
	EE	446	1,655		
Panel F (SE & EE)					
Comp	SE	601	547	53,892	−11.85***
	EE	336	329		
ESG	SE	950	766	147,279	−9.19***
	EE	446	554		
E	SE	951	760	154,014	−8.26***
	EE	446	569		
S	SE	951	790	125,848	−12.27***
	EE	446	506		
G	SE	951	697	210,640	−0.204
	EE	446	702		

Note: *** indicates the null hypothesis of no difference in mean ranks is rejected at the 1% level of statistical significance.

The results for the WE and SE pair, as presented in Panel D, indicate that firms located in SE have significantly higher mean ranks for board compensation, ESG, E, and S scores. Similar results can be seen in Panel F when SE is compared with EE. The comparison of mean ranks between WE and EE in Panel E suggests that mean ranks for the same four variables have higher values for firms located in WE. However, across all six panels, mean ranks for the governance score (G) are not statistically significant in any paired groups. Overall, the findings from Tables 2 and 4, taken together, suggest that firms located in SE have the highest scores for ESG, E, and S and have allocated the largest amount of their revenues toward board compensation. By comparison, firms located in EE have the least impressive ESG performance while paying a negligible amount of board compensation as a percentage of their revenues.

5.4. *Comparison of rating categories across regions*

The following section provides closer scrutiny of the ESG data by region. Attention is given to the analysis of ESG performance by four rating groups (A to D) previously defined. The first goal is to test for any association between the regions and ESG performance, and the second is to examine the proportions of rating groups by region. The analysis is grouped by overall ESG rating and three main pillars (E, S, and G). Test results are displayed in Panels A to D in Table 5.

The test of association between the European regions and ESG groups has a chi-square statistic of 248.24(df $= 9$, 2-tailed), and the null hypothesis of independence can be rejected at the 1% level. Thus, there is an association between ESG rating and companies located across various European regions. A similar conclusion can be reached for three pillars, as shown in Panels B to D.

The comparison of column proportions is conducted by using a z-test. For each significant pair (at the 5% level), the region of the smaller proportion (in parentheses) is reported below the region with the larger proportion. For instance, Panel A shows that for firms that are located in NE, 11.6% are classified as group A (−A, A, A+), 35.6%, as group B (−B, B, B+), 36.9%, as group C (−C, C, C+), and finally, 15.9% belong to group D (−D, D, D+). Across the regions, firms in SE have the highest proportion of group A (20.5%), and this proportion size is significantly larger than those reported for NE (11.6%) and EE (5.2%). EE has the largest proportion of group C firms (43.9%), significantly larger than those found for NE, SE, and WE.

For the Environmental pillar shown in Panel B, the proportions of firms belonging to groups C and D are significantly larger than firms

Table 5. Comparison of rating categories in the European regions.

	Regions							
	NE		WE		SE		EE	
	%	*N*	%	*N*	%	*N*	%	*N*
Panel A: ESG group (chi-square stat. = 248.25***, df = 9)								
A	11.6	463	18.3	531	20.5	195	5.2	23
	[EE]		[EE, NE]		[EE, NE]			
B	35.6	1426	40.8	1,185	47.2	448	39.5	176
			[NE]		[EE, NE, WE]			
C	36.9	1,476	28.3	821	23.5	223	43.9	196
	[SE, WE]		[SE]				[NE, SE, WE]	
D	15.9	638	12.6	368	8.8	84	11.4	51
	[EE, SE, WE]		[SE]					
Panel B: E group (chi-square stat. = 306.89***, df = 9)								
A	14.9	596	24.3	702	26.7	254	7.8	35
	[EE]		[EE, NE]		[EE, NE]			
B	22	877	28.1	816	31.7	301	30.3	135
			[EE]		[NE]		[NE]	
C	27.4	1,093	23.2	674	21.3	203	31.0	138
	[SE, WE]						[SE, WE]	
D	35.7	1,427	24.4	708	20.3	193	30.9	138
	[SE, WE]						[SE, WE]	
Panel C: S group (chi-square stat. = 362.95***, df = 9)								
A	17.5	699	30.4	880	38.5	366	13	58
			[EE, NE]		[EE, NE, WE]			
B	35.6	1,420	34.3	995	36.2	344	32.5	145
C	32.7	1,307	23.6	685	16.6	158	36.1	161
	[SE, WE]		[SE]				[SE, WE]	
D	14.2	567	11.7	340	8.7	83	18.4	82
	[SE, WE]						[SE, WE]	
Panel D: G group (chi-square stat. = 26.89***, df = 9)								
A	17.4	694	16.9	490	14.4	137	12.3	55
	[EE]							
B	33	1,317	33.7	977	33.4	318	37.7	168
C	30.5	1,219	31.9	925	35.1	334	35.2	157
					[NE]			
D	19.1	763	17.5	507	17.1	162	14.8	66

Note: *** indicates the null hypothesis of no association between EU regions and rating groups is rejected at the 1% level of statistical significance.

in SE and WE. Similarly, for the Social pillar reported in Panel C, firms in EE also have larger shares of groups C and D. In contrast, the results in Panel D show no evidence of a significant difference in proportions across the region, except for SE, which records a significantly larger proportion of C group firms compared with NE.

5.5. *Comparison of rating group by compensation size*

The next analysis considers the association between compensation size and ESG performance by rating groups. This will help verify if ESG performance is linked to the size of board compensation, as one might reasonably expect that firms with an ESG focus are more likely to pay more to attract members with socio-environmental-governance expertise and experience to the board of directors.

Comp variable is used to create three ranked groups of approximately equal observations in each group. The first group (g1) has a mean board compensation of EUR0.22 million, while group 2 (g2) and group 3 (g3) have means of EUR0.59 million and EUR2.37 million, respectively. A comparison of column proportions is conducted using a z-test, and for each significant pair (at the 5% level), the percentile group of the smaller proportion (in parentheses) is reported below the percentile group with the larger proportion.

Panel A of Table 6 indicates that the test of association between the Comp percentile groups and ESG groups has a chi-square statistic of 1,491.54 (df = 6, 2-tailed), and the null hypothesis of independence can be rejected at the 1% level. Similar results can be observed in the remaining panels. Thus, there is a strong association between the size of board compensation and ESG ratings.

In Table 6, comparing proportions across ranking groups and compensation sizes reveals some interesting results. In Panel A, firms in g3 have significantly larger proportions of firms with group A (31.2%) and group B (43.8%) ratings compared with g1 and g2. In contrast, firms in the lowest percentile group of g1 exhibit significantly larger proportions of firms with group C and D ratings when compared with those reported for g2 and g3. These results can be consistently observed across all four panels. In summary, the evidence presented in Table 6 shows that in g1, there is a significantly larger proportion of companies with low ESG ratings (C and D) compared with

Table 6. Comparison of ratings by compensation size.

	Percentile group of board compensation					
	g1		**g2**		**g3**	
	%	*N*	%	*N*	%	*N*
Panel A: ESG group (chi-square stat. = 1,491.54***, df = 6)						
A	2.5	63	13.2 [g1]	326	31.2 [g1,g2]	772
B	28.2	699	47.6 [g1,g3]	1,177	43.8 [gp1]	1,085
C	45.4 [g2,g3]	1,124	31.8 [g3]	786	21	520
D	23.9 [g2,g3]	589	7.4 [g3]	186	4	98
Panel B: E group (chi-square stat. = 1,032.15***, df = 6)						
A	7	172	17.8 [g1]	441	34.7 [g1,g2]	859
B	18.5	458	30.1 [g1]	746	29.9 [g1]	739
C	29.2 [g3]	722	27.9 [g3]	691	20	496
D	45.3 [g2,g3]	1,120	24.2 [g3]	597	15.4	381
Panel C: S group (chi-square stat. = 1,168.74***, df = 6)						
A	8.8	218	23.4 [g1]	578	43.1 [g1,g2]	1,067
B	30.5	754	42.1 [g1,g3]	1,041	34.3 [g1]	849
C	40 [g2,g3]	989	25.6 [g3]	633	18.7	464
D	20.7 [g2,g3]	511	9 [g3]	223	3.9	95
Panel D: G group (chi-square stat. = 921.27***, df = 6)						
A	6.8	168	19 [g1]	470	28.5 [g1,g2]	705
B	25.6	632	39.3 [g1]	972	40.2 [g1]	995
C	39.2 [g2,g3]	968	31.2 [g3]	773	23.8	588
D	28.4 [g2,g3]	703	10.5 [g3]	260	7.5	187

Note: *** indicates the null hypothesis of no association between board compensation sizes and rating groups is rejected at the 1% level of statistical significance.

g2 and g3. In contrast, g3, which includes firms that pay the largest board compensation, has a significantly larger proportion of high ESG rating groups (A and B) than those with lower board compensations (g1 and g2).

The following analysis involves a further breakdown of the rating groups by European regions. The results are presented in Table 7. In all cases, the null hypothesis of independence between compensation size and European regions (by ranking group) can be rejected at the 1% level using a 2-tailed test. Thus, there is evidence of a significant association between the size of board compensation and European regions when classified according to ranking groups. Notably, across all panels, large firms in percentile group g3 have significantly larger proportions of firms belonging to each of the ranking groups. Firms that pay the highest board compensation (in g3) are from WE (47.50%) and SE (17.10%), with proportions significantly higher than firms in g1 and g2, respectively. Overall, the findings reported in Table 6 remain largely unchanged even after controlling for regional effects.

5.6. *Board compensation by firm size and industry*

In this section, attention is given to exploring the relationship between ESG performance and board compensation by considering firm size and industry effect. Firm size is proxied by average net sales previously discussed. Ranking by average net sales, from the smallest to the largest values, was performed to create three ranked groups. Each group contains one-third of the total number of firms that are labeled as "small", "medium", and "large". Firms are identified according to three main industry groups: Banks, Capital Markets, and Software & IT to capture the industry effect. The remaining firms are classified as "Others".

In Figures 3 and 4, bar plots visually depict the mean and median of board compensation by ESG ranking groups and firm size. In both figures, compensation size decreases with ESG performance, more prominently noted for large firms. The numerical results are displayed in the top panels of Table 8.

Panel C of Table 8 tabulates the results for each paired ranking group. Due to highly skewed distributions in the dataset, the median test is used to test for any statistical difference in medians between

Table 7. Comparison of board compensation by ESG rating and regions.

	Percentile group of board compensation					
	g1		g2		g3	
	%	*N*	%	*N*	%	*N*
Panel A: ESG group A (chi-square stat. = 62.61***, df = 6)						
NE	47.60 [g3]	30	51.20 [g3]	167	34.10	263
WE	38.10	24	39.30	128	47.50 [g2]	367
SE	4.80	3	8.30	27	17.10 [g1,g2]	132
EE	9.50 [g2,g3]	6	1.20	4	1.30	10
Panel B: ESG group B (chi-square stat. = 173.07***, df = 6)						
NE	44.30 [g3]	310	58.10 [g1,g3]	684	36.80	400
WE	41.10 [g2]	287	31.70	373	44.00 [g2]	477
SE	5.40	38	7.30	86	15.30 [g1,g2]	166
EE	9.20 [g3]	64B	2.90	34	3.90	42
Panel C: ESG group C (chi-square stat. = 123.88***, df = 6)						
NE	64.30 [g2,g3]	723	59.80 [g3]	470	41.90	218
WE	25.90	291	32.70 [g1]	257	41.00 [g1,g2]	213
SE	2.40	27	3.70	29	10.80 [g1,g2]	56
EE	7.40 [g2,g3]	83	3.80	30	6.30 [g2]	33
Panel D: ESG group D (chi-square stat. = 96.22***, df = 6)						
NE	72.30 [g2,g3]	426	47.30 [g3]	88	33.70	33
WE	21.60	127	41.40 [g1]	77	56.10 [g1,g2]	55
SE	2.20	13	7.50 [g1]	14	10.20 [g1]	10
EE	3.90	23	3.80	7	0.00	1

Note: *** indicates the null hypothesis of no association between board compensation sizes and EU regions is rejected at the 1% level of statistical significance.

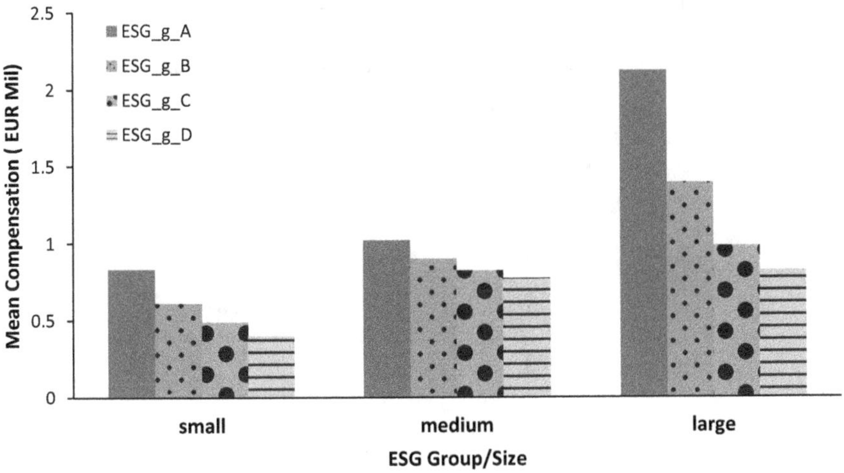

Figure 3. Mean compensation by ESG rating and firm size.

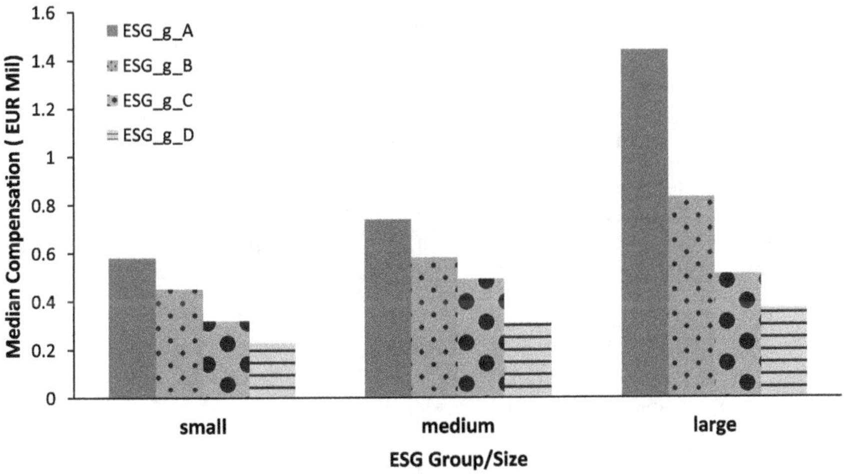

Figure 4. Median compensation by ESG rating and firm size.

the rating groups. The median test is performed using a 2-tailed test with the null hypothesis of equal median between the ranking groups. The chi-square test statistic is highly significant (at the 1% level) across all four paired ranking groups (A and B, A and C, and A and D). Thus, there is strong evidence to support the notion that the size of board compensation differs significantly when comparisons

Table 8. Comparison of ratings by firm size.

Board compensation (EUR'Mil) by firm size			
	Small	**Medium**	**Large**
Panel A: Mean for ESG group			
A	0.83	1.02	2.12
B	0.61	0.90	1.39
C	0.49	0.82	0.98
D	0.41	0.77	0.82
Panel B: Median ESG group			
A	0.58	0.74	1.44
B	0.45	0.58	0.83
C	0.32	0.49	0.51
D	0.23	0.31	0.37
Panel C: Test for equality of medians			
Between ESG groups			
A and B	128.95***	57.68***	339.20***
A and C	13.54***	30.76***	325.67***
A and D	106.2***	58.04***	267.69***
Between E groups			
A and B	87.89***	15.61***	212.83***
A and C	34.70***	15.50***	179.48***
A and D	77.24***	19.24***	206.11***
Between S groups			
A and B	70.26***	35.85***	250.21***
A and C	25.97***	31.52***	231.30***
A and D	52.49***	48.47***	201.98***
Between G groups			
A and B	114.9***	76.55***	171.22***
A and C	58.49***	37.64***	134.31***
A and D	141.07***	60.55***	116.63***
N	1,685	2,476	3,264

Note: *** indicates the null hypothesis of equal median between the rating groups is rejected at the 1% level of statistical significance.

are made between the highest ESG performing group (A) and the lower performing groups (B and below).

Finally, Table 9 also provides evidence that the size of board compensation decreases with ESG performance when the analysis is performed by industry group. Again, the difference in medians between group A and group D can be seen across all three main industries, particularly in the capital markets group, where firms in group A have a median of EUR5.46 million and firms in group D have a median of EUR0.22. Panel B shows that the null hypothesis of equal medians across all paired ranking groups can be rejected, mostly at the 1% level of statistical significance.

6. Conclusion, implications, limitations, and future research avenues

6.1. *Conclusion*

This chapter has aimed to explore the association between the performance of ESG and the compensation of the board of directors for listed companies within the European region. It considers ESG performance data collected between 2016 to 2020, providing an overview of sustainability management as reflected in the ESG rating of European firms, which usually lead the way in integrating sustainability into their corporate strategy.

The main result presented in this chapter suggests clear evidence that board compensation is associated with ESG performance across four different European regions. The analysis suggests that firms with higher ESG performance tend to pay higher BoD compensation even after accounting for firm size and industry effect.

Except for firms located in Eastern Europe, most large firms (64.60%) from the Western and Southern regions are generally more willing to invest in high ESG performance. Firms located in Southern Europe have the highest ESG performance and invested the most in board compensation as a percentage of sales revenue. This region also exhibits the largest share of firms rated between −B and A+. A possible explanation for this result may be that a relatively large proportion of firms in this region are member states of the European Union since 87.26% of SE firms are located in Italy, Spain, and Greece.

Table 9. Comparison of ratings by industry group.

	Board compensation (EUR'Mil) by industry group			
	Banks	Capital markets	Software & IT	Others
	Median	Median	Median	Median
Panel A: By ESG and individual groups				
ESG group				
A	2.57	5.46	1.35	1.21
B	0.93	0.74	0.59	0.65
C	0.80	0.31	0.34	0.43
D	0.41	0.22	0.17	0.26
E group				
A	1.30	2.13	0.97	0.96
B	0.86	0.53	0.49	0.68
C	0.98	0.42	0.40	0.53
D	0.72	0.26	0.28	0.38
S group				
A	2.02	1.87	0.73	1.01
B	0.86	0.43	0.42	0.59
C	0.79	0.27	0.32	0.44
D	0.43	0.30	0.19	0.31
G group				
A	1.62	1.59	0.75	0.88
B	1.08	0.60	0.48	0.68
C	0.79	0.34	0.36	0.46
D	0.49	0.22	0.27	0.32
Panel B: Test for equality of medians				
Between ESG groups				
A and B	42.92***	126.56***	34.34***	765.96***
A and C	37.97***	24.71***	8.06**	571.34***
A and D	49.73***	84.48***	29.25***	642.59***
Between E groups				
A and B	35.07***	68.74***	17.06***	548.53***
A and C	34.94***	40.25***	11.15***	366.65***
A and D	40.17***	72.41***	21.36***	498.59***
Between S groups				
A and B	37.82***	38.32***	31.51***	658.18***
A and C	35.42***	25.68***	24.38***	542.09***
A and D	45.60***	14.17***	31.01***	639.98***
Between G groups				
A and B	37.43***	113.53***	15.73***	401.28***
A and C	24.76***	49.59***	6.61**	247.02***
A and D	25.16***	131.46***	17.92***	334.15***
N	343	570	285	6,227

Note: *** (**) indicates the null hypothesis of equal median between the rating groups is rejected at the 1% (5%) level of statistical significance.

Consistent with the stakeholder theory, this study highlights the importance of incorporating ESG metrics in the board members' compensation plans and responsibilities. Furthermore, it reinforces a corporation's responsibility to ensure sustainable long-term wealth for all stakeholders.

6.2. *Implications for practice*

This study demonstrates a strong relationship between ESG performance and BoD compensation. Koors *et al.* (2019) suggested that incentives, such as board remuneration, may be a catalyst for operationalizing ESG factors. However, where exactly on the continuum an organization aims to land depends on how it approaches ESG and integrates it into its business strategy. Each organization has to find the best way to do this keeping in perspective the business model and the organizational culture as well as its ability to obtain resources. As this study has shown, larger corporations tend to have a higher ESG score than smaller ones. It is, therefore, important that corporations conduct a value-driver analysis to understand which of the three ESG factors most impacts the business in the short term and the longer term (Koors *et al.*, 2019).

Stakeholders not only consider financial performance when assessing the appropriateness of pay and compensation, but non-financial factors, predominantly ESG performance, as well (Tharp and Freeman, 2021). Consequently, the design of the remuneration programs should align with these value drivers and, ultimately, with the ESG performance. Reasonableness of the remuneration is key — for example, how does it compare to a similar-sized corporation, in the same industry, in terms of performance goals, both financial and non-financial? The reasonableness of BoD compensation is also an important message to communicate to stakeholders to increase the likelihood of acceptance. Compensation can also be a strategic instrument to communicate business priorities (Koors *et al.*, 2019). For example, investors become aware that the corporation is committed to ESG and sustainable business conduct and ethical reporting. Incentive-based ESG signals to management and employees its importance to the corporation alluding to embedding and operationalizing ESG into the business and corporate culture and values

(Koors *et al.*, 2019). Also, a misalignment between corporate performance and board compensation, for example, through a decline in profitability and increase in remuneration, would alert employees as such behavior would go against ESG principles. Such conflicting messages communicated to staff would also go against a culture of fairness most corporations highlight in their values and mission statements (Tharp and Freeman, 2021) and thus would infringe on organizational authenticity (Neher *et al.*, 2021). In conclusion, under the premises of reasonableness, a corporation's board compensation package must be carefully designed and incorporated into the corporate policy and transparently communicated.

6.3. *Limitations*

While the results of this research are based on a substantive sample of listed European companies, results are limited to those and need to be interpreted within this context, particularly as Europe is considered among the most advanced regions regarding sustainability and ESG. According to the 2021 Global Sustainability Rankings (Solability, 2022), only two countries in the top 20 are not European (Japan and New Zealand).

Also, sustainability and ESG are increasingly appreciated by corporate leaders, investors, policymakers, and scholars, however, there is no standardized, accurate, and audited information available yet, providing transparency and allowing comparability. Besides the widely acknowledged Refinitiv data source, other recognized providers also offer ESG data and scores using different ESG rating methodologies.

The present study investigated how board compensation and ESG performance may relate to each other. It does not consider causal factors that may impact the key variables of interest and thus cannot predict the relationship between them.

Despite its limitations, the study certainly adds to the theoretical understanding of the relationship between ESG scores and board compensation and its implication to practice.

6.4. *Future research avenues*

Further studies may consider additional ESG rating data providers, such as Morningstar (Sustainalytics), Bloomberg, and S&P, given the different ESG rating methodologies for data triangulation. This study has shown that there are noteworthy differences between the European regions. As digging deeper to find out the reasons for these differences was outside the scope of the investigation, further exploration, such as country-specific policy requirements, would complement this study. Conversely, given the focus on the European regions, it would additionally be interesting to replicate this study with other larger regions globally, such as Northern America, East Asia, or Oceania, and to compare and contrast the differences to gain a more complete picture of ESG scores and BoD compensation. What learnings can be drawn from the differences? By extending the findings of this chapter, a further avenue of research could explore the relationship between the amount of the board compensation and ESG performance using a multivariate analysis approach that accounts for other firm characteristics such as risk appetite and financial performance indicators, for example, return on equity (ROE) and net sales. By adding financial performance dimensions, the reasonableness of the board compensation undergoes scrutiny and hence may require remuneration adjustments or can be justified.

Lastly, it is particularly important to further discuss these empirical results from moral and ethical standpoints. For example, should board members be paid more for better ESG outcomes or is it a fundamental expectation as part of their responsibilities? A critical discussion is needed on what these results mean for practice and the potential for immoral and unethical behavior, which links back to the premises of reasonableness when defining the board compensation packages.

Appendix

Table A.1. Proportion of ESG rating by European regions.

		ESG rating											
		A+	A	A–	B+	B	B–	C+	C	C–	D+	D	D–
Region/EU	Country of HQ	%	%	%	%	%	%	%	%	%	%	%	%
NE	Denmark	0.0	0.2	2.7	2.5	2.9	3.3	3.5	3.1	2.4	1.2	1.3	2.4
($n = 4{,}003$)	Faroe Islands	0.0	0.0	0.0	0.0	0.1	0.1	0.1	0.0	0.1	0.0	0.0	0.0
	Finland	5.1	3.5	3.2	3.6	3.7	2.7	1.5	1.8	1.5	2.0	0.5	2.4
	Guernsey	0.0	0.0	0.1	0.5	0.4	0.6	1.5	1.9	3.1	2.7	2.4	1.8
	Iceland	0.0	0.0	0.0	0.0	0.1	0.2	0.2	0.1	0.3	0.0	0.0	0.6
	Rep. of Ireland	0.0	1.5	2.9	2.3	2.1	1.8	3.1	4.2	3.9	2.5	1.1	2.4
	Isle of Man	0.0	0.0	0.1	0.2	0.2	0.2	0.4	0.3	0.1	0.2	0.0	0.0
	Jersey	0.0	0.0	0.0	0.1	0.5	0.2	0.3	0.7	1.7	2.0	0.5	0.0
	Norway	0.0	2.0	1.6	3.6	2.7	3.3	3.1	3.5	2.7	3.0	1.6	0.6
	Sweden	2.6	6.0	9.7	7.4	7.3	7.5	10.2	9.3	9.9	10.4	11.7	24.6
	United Kingdom	20.5	17.9	22.0	19.9	24.0	27.9	28.7	29.5	31.1	37.5	31.1	14.4
WE	Austria	0.0	0.2	1.2	2.0	3.4	2.0	2.6	1.9	0.1	0.5	0.3	0.0
($n = 2{,}905$)	Belgium	0.0	0.5	1.4	3.6	3.0	3.9	2.2	2.7	2.0	1.3	2.1	1.2
	France	12.8	15.4	17.0	12.2	9.1	7.6	4.1	3.2	3.6	2.2	4.3	4.2
	Germany	30.8	15.4	10.6	11.1	7.3	8.8	10.7	8.4	10.3	10.4	10.9	12.6
	Liechtenstein	0.0	0.0	0.0	0.0	0.0	0.2	0.2	0.1	0.0	0.0	0.0	0.0
	Luxembourg	0.0	1.5	1.2	1.0	1.3	1.9	1.7	1.9	0.9	1.3	2.1	1.2
	Monaco	0.0	0.0	0.0	0.0	0.0	0.0	0.2	0.0	0.7	0.7	1.9	0.0
	Netherlands	5.1	4.7	3.4	5.3	5.7	2.8	3.0	3.3	3.2	1.5	1.3	1.8
	Switzerland	20.5	10.9	5.2	5.7	6.9	5.8	7.1	8.8	7.3	10.0	13.0	18.6

SE	Cyprus	0.0	0.0	0.0	0.0	0.0	0.0	0.5	0.9	0.9	0.7	0.0	0.0
($n = 950$)	Gibraltar	0.0	0.0	0.0	0.0	0.0	0.1	0.2	0.2	0.0	0.0	0.0	0.0
	Greece	0.0	0.7	2.2	1.3	1.0	1.0	1.5	1.5	1.3	1.0	3.5	4.8
	Italy	2.6	8.0	4.4	5.9	6.7	7.0	3.4	3.0	2.9	2.3	2.6	1.6
	Malta	0.0	0.0	0.0	0.0	0.0	0.4	0.1	0.5	0.4	0.3	0.8	0.6
	Portugal	0.0	0.5	1.9	1.4	0.9	1.0	0.3	0.2	0.1	0.5	0.8	0.0
	Russia	0.0	0.5	0.3	0.1	0.0	0.0	0.0	0.0	0.0	0.0	0.0	0.0
	Slovenia	0.0	0.0	0.0	0.0	0.1	0.2	0.0	0.0	0.0	0.0	0.0	0.0
	Spain	0.0	9.5	6.4	6.8	4.4	3.2	2.7	1.7	1.9	1.0	1.9	0.6
EE	Cyprus	0.0	0.0	0.0	0.0	0.0	0.0	0.0	0.0	0.0	0.0	0.3	0.0
($n = 446$)	Czech Republic	0.0	0.0	0.0	0.3	0.2	0.3	0.4	0.2	0.8	0.0	0.0	0.0
	Hungary	0.0	0.0	0.4	0.5	0.4	0.2	0.4	0.0	0.1	0.3	0.3	0.0
	Poland	0.0	1.1	0.6	1.5	2.4	2.6	2.7	3.4	2.5	2.3	2.9	1.2
	Romania	0.0	0.0	0.1	0.1	0.1	0.1	0.3	0.2	0.0	0.0	0.0	0.0
	Russia	0.0	0.0	1.4	1.1	3.0	3.0	3.0	3.3	4.1	2.2	0.8	2.4
	Ukraine	0.0	0.0	0.0	0.0	0.1	0.1	0.1	0.2	0.1	0.0	0.0	0.0
European Union													
($n = 8{,}304$)	EU (57.9%)	59.0	69.0	69.0	69.0	62.0	58.0	55.0	51.0	49.0	42.0	49.0	62.0
	Non-EU (42.1%)	41.0	31.0	31.0	31.0	38.0	42.0	45.0	49.0	51.0	58.0	51.0	38.0

Note: Five companies located in Russia and one in Cyprus were included in the SE region. We reclassified all 6 companies into the EE group and repeated all of our analyses. The results remain unchanged in terms of statistical significance. For NE, 79.56% of the sample consisted of companies from Sweden, the UK, and Norway. For WE, 72.9% are companies from Germany, Switzerland, and France, while SE has 87.26% of companies from Italy, Spain, and Greece. Finally, for EE, 92.92% of the companies are from Russia, Poland, and Hungary.

References

Albuquerque, R., Koskinen, Y., Yang, S., & Zhang, C. (2020). Resiliency of environmental and social stocks: An analysis of the exogenous COVID-19 market crash. *The Review of Corporate Finance Studies, 9*(3), 593–621. https://doi.org/10.1093/rcfs/cfaa011.

Almarayeh, T. (2021). Board gender diversity, board compensation and firm performance: Evidence from Jordan. *Journal of Financial Reporting and Accounting* (ahead-of-print). https://doi.org/10.1108/JFRA-05-2021-0138.

Andreas, J. M., Rapp, M. S., & Wolff, M. (2012). Determinants of director compensation in two-tier systems: Evidence from German panel data. *Review of Managerial Science, 6*(1), 33–79. https://doi.org/10.1007/s11846-010-0048-z.

Ang, J., Lauterbach, B., & Schreiber, B. Z. (2002). Pay at the executive suite: How do US banks compensate their top management teams? *Journal of Banking & Finance, 26*(6), 1143–1163. https://doi.org/10.1016/S0378-4266(01)00165-0.

Bebchuk, L. A. & Tallarita, R. (2022). The perils and questionable promise of ESG-based compensation. SSRN. https://doi.org/10.2139/ssrn.4048003.

Boivie, S., Bednar, M. K., & Barker, S. B. (2015). Social comparison and reciprocity in director compensation. *Journal of Management, 41*(6), 1578–1603. https://doi.org/10.1177/0149206312460680.

Brick, I. E., Palmon, O., & Wald, J. K. (2006). CEO compensation, director compensation, and firm performance: Evidence of cronyism? *Journal of Corporate Finance, 12*(3), 403–423. https://doi.org/10.1016/j.jcorpfin.2005.08.005.

Business Roundtable (2019). Business Roundtable redefines the purpose of a corporation to promote 'an economy that serves all Americans'. Retrieved 20 March from https://www.businessroundtable.org/business-roundtable-redefines-the-purpose-of-a-corporation-to-promote-an-economy-that-serves-all-americans.

Cai, Y., Jo, H., & Pan, C. (2011). Vice or virtue? The impact of corporate social responsibility on executive compensation. *Journal of Business Ethics, 104*(2), 159–173. https://doi.org/10.1007/s10551-011-0909-7.

Callan, S. J. & Thomas, J. M. (2011). Executive compensation, corporate social responsibility, and corporate financial performance: A multi-equation framework. *Corporate Social Responsibility and Environmental Management, 18*(6), 332–351. https://doi.org/10.1002/csr.249.

Cavaco, S., Crifo, P., & Guidoux, A. (2020). Corporate social responsibility and governance: The role of executive compensation. *Industrial Relations: A Journal of Economy and Society*, *59*(2), 240–274. https://doi.org/10.1111/irel.12254.

Ding, W., Levine, R., Lin, C., & Xie, W. (2021). Corporate immunity to the COVID-19 pandemic. *Journal of Financial Economics*, *141*(2), 802–830. https://doi.org/10.1016/j.jfineco.2021.03.005.

Dyck, A., Lins, K. V., Roth, L., & Wagner, H. F. (2019). Do institutional investors drive corporate social responsibility? International evidence. *Journal of Financial Economics*, *131*(3), 693–714. https://doi.org/10.1016/j.jfineco.2018.08.013.

Eccles, R. G. & Klimenko, S. (2019). The investor revolution: Shareholders are getting serious about sustainability. *Harvard Business Review* (May–June). https://hbr.org/2019/2005/the-investor-revolution.

Elnahass, M., Salama, A., & Trinh, V. Q. (2022). Firm valuations and board compensation: Evidence from alternative banking models. *Global Finance Journal*, *51*, 100553. https://doi.org/10.1016/j.gfj.2020.100553.

European Commission (2020). Study on directors' duties and sustainable corporate governance: Final report. Directorate-General for Justice and Consumers. https://doi.org/doi/10.2838/472901.

European Parliament and Council (2014). Directive 2014/95/EU of the European Parliament and of the Council: Amending Directive 2013/34/EU as regards disclosure of non-financial and diversity information by certain large undertakings and groups. *Official Journal of the European Union*, *L 330*, 1–9.

Financial Stability-Financial Services and Capital Markets Union (2020). Renewed sustainable finance strategy and implementation of the action plan on financing sustainable growth. European Commission. https://ec.europa.eu/info/publications/sustainabl-finance-renewed-strategy_en.

Freeman, R. E. (1984). *Strategic Management: A Stakeholder Approach*. Pitman, Boston.

Friedman, M. (1970). The social responsibility of business is to increase its profits. *New York Times Magazine*, September 13.

Handa, R. (2018). Does corporate governance affect financial performance: A study of select Indian banks. *Asian Economic and Financial Review*, *8*(4), 478–486. https://doi.org/10.18488/journal.aefr.2018.84.478.486.

Harrison, J. S., Phillips, R. A., & Freeman, R. E. (2020). On the 2019 Business Roundtable "Statement on the purpose of a corporation". *Journal of Management*, *46*(7), 1223–1237. https://doi.org/10.1177/0149206319892669.

Howad-Grenville, J. (2021). ESG impact is hard to measure — But it's not impossible. *Harvard Business Review* (January). Retrieved from https://hbr.org/2021/2001/esg-impact-is-hard-to-measure-but-its-not-impossible.

Jamali, D., Karam, C., Yin, J., & Soundararajan, V. (2017). CSR logics in developing countries: Translation, adaptation and stalled development. *Journal of World Business, 52*(3), 343–359. https://doi.org/10.1016/j.jwb.2017.02.001.

Jensen, M. C. (2002). Value maximization, stakeholder theory, and the corporate objective function. *Business Ethics Quarterly, 12*(2), 235–256. https://doi.org/10.2307/3857812.

Jensen, M. C. & Meckling, W. H. (1976). Theory of the firm: Managerial behavior, agency costs and ownership structure. *Journal of Financial Economics, 3*(4), 305–360. https://doi.org/10.1016/0304-405X(76)90026-X.

Khoo, E. S., Lim, Y., Lu, L. Y., & Monroe, G. S. (2021). Corporate social responsibility performance and the reputational incentives of independent directors. *Journal of Business Finance & Accounting, 49*, 841–881. https://doi.org/10.1111/jbfa.12569.

Koors, J., Meyer, P., & Partners LLC. (2019). Executive Compensation and ESG. *Harvard Law School Forum on Corporate Governance*, 1–4. Retrieved from https://corpgov.law.harvard.edu/2019/2009/2010/executive-compensation-and-esg/.

Kumar, P. C. (2020). ESG compliant companies provide superior returns. https://www.thestar.com.my/business/business-news/2020/02/29/esg-compliant-companies-provide-superior-returns.

Lafortune, G., Cortés Puch, M., Mosnier, A., Fuller, G., Diaz, M., Riccaboni, A., Kloke-Lesch, A., Zachariadis, T., Carli, E., & Oger, A. (2021). Europe sustainable development report 2021: Transforming the European Union to achieve the sustainable development goals. https://s3.amazonaws.com/sustainabledevelopment.report/2021/Europe+Sustainable +Development+Report+2021.pdf.

Lemma, T. T., Mlilo, M., & Gwatidzo, T. (2020). Board remuneration, directors' ownership and corporate performance: The South African evidence. *International Review of Applied Economics, 34*(4), 491–511. https://doi.org/10.1080/02692171.2020.1773654.

Li, T.-T., Wang, K., Sueyoshi, T., & Wang, D. D. (2021). ESG: Research progress and future prospects. *Sustainability, 13*(21), 11663. https://doi.org/10.3390/su132111663.

Lisin, A., Kushnir, A., Koryakov, A. G., Fomenko, N., & Shchukina, T. (2022). Financial stability in companies with high ESG scores: Evidence from North America using the Ohlson O-score. *Sustainability, 14*(1), 479. https://doi.org/10.3390/su14010479.

Magnan, M., St-Onge, S., & Gélinas, P. (2010). Director compensation and firm value: A research synthesis. *International Journal of Disclosure and Governance, 7*(1), 28–41. https://doi.org/10.1057/jdg.2009.13.

McKinsey and Company (2020). The ESG premium: New perspectives on value and performance (survey). McKinsey & Company. https://www.mckinsey.com/business-functions/sustainability/our-insights/the-esg-premium-new-perspectives-on-value-and-performance.

Merendino, A. & Melville, R. (2019). The board of directors and firm performance: Empirical evidence from listed companies. *Corporate Governance: The International Journal of Business in Society, 19*(3), 508–551. https://doi.org/10.1108/CG-06-2018-0211.

Miles, M. P. & Munilla, L. S. (1993). The Eco-orientation: An emerging business philosophy? *Journal of Marketing Theory and Practice, 1*(2), 43–51.

Mohammad, W. M. W. & Wasiuzzaman, S. (2021). Environmental, Social and Governance (ESG) disclosure, competitive advantage and performance of firms in Malaysia. *Cleaner Environmental Systems, 2*, 100015. https://doi.org/10.1016/j.cesys.2021.100015.

Munilla, L. & Miles, M. (2005). The corporate social responsibility continuum as a component of stakeholder theory. *Business and Society Review, 110*(4), 371–387.

Neher, A., Wong, A., & Miles, M. P. (2021). The relationship between the level of a corporation's public disclosure of its managerial values and its level of organizational authenticity. *European Business Review*(ahead-of-print). https://doi.org/10.1108/EBR-06-2020-0150.

Nekhili, M., Boukadhaba, A., & Nagati, H. (2021). The ESG–financial performance relationship: Does the type of employee board representation matter? *Corporate Governance: An International Review, 29*(2), 134–161. https://doi.org/10.1111/corg.12345.

Pucheta-Martínez, M. C. & Gallego-Álvarez, I. (2019). An international approach of the relationship between board attributes and the disclosure of corporate social responsibility issues. *Corporate Social Responsibility and Environmental Management, 26*(3), 612–627. https://doi.org/10.1002/csr.1707.

Raimo, N., Caragnano, A., Zito, M., Vitolla, F., & Mariani, M. (2021). Extending the benefits of ESG disclosure: The effect on the cost of debt financing. *Corporate Social Responsibility and Environmental Management, 28*(4), 1412–1421. https://doi.org/10.1002/csr.2134.

Refinitiv (2021a). Environmental, social and governance (ESG) scores from Refinitiv. Refinitiv.

Refinitiv (2021b). Refinitiv ESG company scores. Retrieved 3 March from https://www.refinitiv.com/en/sustainable-finance/esg-scores#score-range.

Solability Sustainable Intelligence (2022). *The GSCI Global Sustainability Competitiveness Index*. Retrieved 27 March from https://solability.com/the-global-sustainable-competitiveness-index/the-index.

Suttipun, M. (2021). The influence of board composition on environmental, social and governance (ESG) disclosure of Thai listed companies. *International Journal of Disclosure and Governance, 18*(4), 391–402. https://doi.org/10.1057/s41310-021-00120-6.

Tabachnick, B. G. & Fidell, L. S. (2013). *Using Multivariate Statistics* (6th ed.). Pearson, Boston.

Tabachnick, B. G. & Fidell, L. S. (2019). *Using Multivariate Statistics* (7th ed.). Pearson, Boston.

Tharp, C. & Freeman, K. (2021). Executive compensation is a powerful communication to stakeholders. *People & Strategy, 44*(4), 36–41. Retrieved from https://www.bu.edu/hrpi/files/2021/2010/PSJ-Fall-2021-feature-tharp-freeman.pdf.

Thomson Reuters (2022). Thomson Reuters ESG scores. Retrieved 4 February from https://www.refinitiv.com/content/dam/marketing/en_us/documents/methodology/esg-scores-methodology.pdf.

Turban, D. B. & Greening, D. W. (1997). Corporate social performance and organizational attractiveness to prospective employees. *Academy of Management Journal, 40*(3), 658–672. https://doi.org/10.5465/257057.

UN SSE United Nations Sustainable Stock Exchange Initiative (2015). Model guidance on reporting ESG information to investors: A voluntary tool for stock exchanges to guide issuers. https://sseinitiative.org/wp-content/uploads/2015/09/SSE-Model-Guidance-on-Reporting-ESG.pdf.

Velte, P. (2017). Does ESG performance have an impact on financial performance? Evidence from Germany. *Journal of Global Responsibility, 8*(2), 169–178. https://doi.org/10.1108/JGR-11-2016-0029.

Velte, P. (2020). Does CEO power moderate the link between ESG performance and financial performance? *Management Research Review, 43*(5), 497–520. https://doi.org/10.1108/MRR-04-2019-0182.

Waddock, S. A. & Graves, S. B. (1997). The corporate social performance–financial performance link. *Strategic Management Journal, 18*(4), 303–319. https://doi.org/10.1002/(SICI)1097-0266(199704)18:4⟨303::AID-SMJ869⟩3.0.CO;2-G.

Waterstraat, S., Kustner, C., & Koch, M. (2021). Does board composition taking account of sustainability expertise influence ESG ratings? An exploratory study of European banks. In A. Gerber & K. Hinkelmann (Eds.), *Society 5.0* (pp. 129–138). Springer International Publishing, Cham. https://doi.org/10.1007/978-3-030-86761-4_11.

Wheatley, J. (2022). Sustainability & resilience: The value of strong environmental, social and corporate governance (ESG) during the COVID-19 pandemic [Charles Sturt University]. Bathurst.

Zikmund, W. G. (2003). *Business Research Methods* (7th ed.). Thomson/ South-Western, Oklahoma.

© 2024 World Scientific Publishing Europe Ltd.
https://doi.org/10.1142/9781800614451_0012

Chapter 12

Regulating Sustainable Finance and the Green Transition in the EU

Vasja Rant
School of Economics and Business, University of Ljubljana, Ljubljana, Slovenia
vasja.rant@ef.uni-lj.si

Abstract
Sustainable finance developed according to market-based logic first, driven by risk and return considerations. However, rising social costs of sustainability problems and international sustainability commitments, particularly with respect to climate change, coupled with market failures of mainstream finance, point to a more regulated approach in the future. The European Union (EU) is at the forefront of these regulatory efforts. In the past few years, the EU developed a comprehensive sustainable finance framework in the context of a broader European Green Deal strategy. Its objective is to redirect private capital flows to finance the EU green transition using three building blocks: a science-based EU classification system (taxonomy) of sustainable economic activities, sustainability disclosure rules for non-financial and financial companies, and sustainability tools for designing financial products. Implementation of the EU sustainable finance framework will have substantial implications for the financial industry, policymakers, and research and may help shape international sustainability standards.

1. Introduction

The world is facing profound environmental, social, and economic challenges. The latest reports of the Intergovernmental Panel on

Climate Change (IPCC) (2021, 2022a, and 2022b) underscore the gravity of the situation with respect to climate change, its causal relationship with human activity, and its dire implications for the society. The loss of biodiversity, pollution, and waste threaten the ecosystems upon which a thriving society and economic activity depend. Using the concept of planetary boundaries, scientists increasingly understand how environmental problems are interrelated and why the Earth system equilibrium of the last 10,000 years, which has facilitated the rise and progress of civilization, is in danger of becoming destabilized (Rockström *et al.*, 2009a; Rockström *et al.*, 2009b; Steffen *et al.*, 2015; Lade *et al.*, 2020; Persson *et al.*, 2022). Climate and environmental challenges can exacerbate social inequality problems, which are often attributed to globalization and technology and their interactions with national policies, institutions, market power, and financialization (Burke, Hsiang, and Miguel, 2015; Islam and Winkel, 2017; Ravallion, 2018; Van Reenen, 2018; Nolan, Richiardi, and Valenzuela, 2019; Autor *et al.*, 2020; Admati, 2021).[1] Inequality may in turn contribute to political polarization, which can hamper global governance at a time when we urgently need it to tackle common sustainability problems (Lockwood, 2018; Pástor and Veronesi, 2021).

Today's sustainability problems are related to the design of our economic systems, which have until recently been focused on short-term shareholder profits, linear production methods, resource depletion, and fossil fuels as the main energy source. To address them, a paradigm shift toward a long-term stakeholder view and a circular economy, independent of fossil fuels, is required (European Commission, 2019; Rant, 2021). Finance lies at the nexus of these efforts. Through its ability to mobilize financial resources and allocate them to the most productive uses, it is uniquely placed to help steer the paradigm shift. For this purpose, finance itself must become sustainable. Sustainable finance is built on the premise that environmental and social factors should be considered

[1] In contrast with evidence of rising inequalities *within* countries, inequalities *between* countries have decreased over the past three decades. Both trends roughly correspond with the period of intensive globalization, rising standards of living in many developing countries, and a stagnating middle class in developed countries. See Bourguignon (2015) and Milanovic (2016).

alongside financial variables in financing and investment decisions because they co-determine long-run profitability and financial stability (Schoenmaker and Schramade, 2018). Over the last decade, sustainable finance has seen a global surge and is projected to grow further (Toole, 2022). This growth has been partly organic due to changing perceptions of financial and non-financial companies about sustainability risks, but it has also been imposed by policy choices and regulation (Ahlström and Monciardini, 2021). The latter is particularly true for the European Union (EU), where a new and comprehensive green transition and sustainable finance framework has taken shape over the last few years (European Commission, 2019).

Regulatory codification of sustainable finance in the EU is an inflection point that opens up several questions: should sustainable finance be guided by regulation or should it be left to the market? What are the motives behind sustainable finance regulation? How are these motives reflected in the EU sustainable finance framework and the broader sustainability agenda of the European Green Deal? What do the changes in the EU regulatory framework imply for market players and policymakers? And, finally, what do they imply for academic research? The objective of this chapter is to address these questions by reviewing the recent academic literature, EU policies, and regulation on the subject. In doing so, the chapter makes two contributions. First, it provides economic rationale behind the sustainable transformation of finance with a specific focus on comparing the arguments in favor of a regulated as opposed to a market-based approach. Second, it reviews the evolving EU framework for sustainable finance and places it in the broader context of the European Green Deal, highlighting reinforcements and complementarities between different policy instruments, and their broader implications for different stakeholders.

The chapter shows that the EU regulatory push into sustainable finance is driven by policy needs to substantially redirect private capital flows toward sustainable investments in order to close the EU green financing gap and deliver the ambitious climate and other environmental objectives of the European Green Deal. It is also economically justified by market failures of regular finance, in particular, short-termism, failure to capture social (as opposed to private) costs and benefits, systemic risk associated with the green transition, and sustainability-related information asymmetries. The EU sustainable finance framework will fundamentally reshape sustainability disclosures of non-financial enterprises and the financial industry in the EU and will likely play an important role in defining the international sustainable finance standards. By doing so, it may succeed in triggering a broader transformation of finance, channeling capital flows to sustainability objectives.

The rest of this chapter is structured as follows: Section 2 looks at sustainable finance from an academic perspective by confronting economic arguments between a market-based and a regulation-based approach, building a case for the latter. Section 3 explains the European Green Deal as a broader context of the EU sustainable finance framework, highlighting key instruments relevant for implementation of the European Green Deal and their relationship with sustainable finance. Section 4 focuses on the EU sustainable finance framework by explaining its overall strategy and describing in detail its three key components, namely, the EU taxonomy, sustainability disclosures of financial and non-financial enterprises, and sustainability tools. Section 5 discusses the implications of the EU sustainable finance framework for the financial industry, for monetary, financial, and economic policies, and for academic research. Section 6 summarizes the key points of this chapter.

2. Should sustainable finance be regulated?

The market for sustainable finance has experienced meteoric rise over the last decade. From its humble beginnings with the first green bonds issued as recently as 2007 by the European Investment Bank (European Investment Bank, 2022) and 2008 by the World Bank (World Bank, 2018), the market surpassed a trillion dollars in 2021. Sustainable bond issuance is now more than 20 times the size of 2015, accounts for 10% of global debt capital markets, and has broadened to include social and sustainability bonds in addition to green bonds. Sustainable lending has also taken off and reached more than 700 billion dollars in 2021, a 300% increase relative to 2020. Additionally, the nascent sustainable equity market is growing fast, driven partly by a surge in mergers and acquisitions (M&A) activity among sustainable companies (Toole, 2022).

These fast moving trends necessitate a deeper understanding of the underlying forces and incentives of players behind the sustainable finance market development. To warrant government intervention through regulation, they also require identification of possible market failures from the perspective of the broader sustainability objectives.

2.1. *Arguments behind a market-based approach to sustainable finance*

To rationalize the recent market drive toward sustainable finance from a business standpoint, it is important to distinguish the motives of key market participants. This includes financial institutions as providers of sustainable financial products and services, investors as buyers of these products, and non-financial actors (primarily corporate, but also government at different levels) as issuers and borrowers seeking funds for sustainable investment projects. Additionally, regulators and policymakers as well as other non-state actors[2] have stakes in the market because they see it as an instrument to deliver sustainability policy objectives or otherwise contribute to the policy-making and information-building processes.

Non-financial actors' motives to engage in environmental, social, and governance (ESG) projects primarily stem from perceived advantages of such engagement for economic performance and competitive position (Hockerts, 2015). The main advantages come in terms of operational benefits (risk reduction and efficiency gains) and market opportunities (brand building and new market[3] creation), with risk and efficiency benefits being the most widely considered advantages so far (Hockerts, 2015; Bengo, Boni, and Sancino, 2022). Risk preoccupation is understandable, given that the largest single sustainability challenge for companies is climate change, which entails substantial physical and transition risks (Sanderson *et al.*, 2019). Physical risks refer to impairments of assets, supply chain disruptions, or shifts in supply and demand as a result of climate change. They may be acute due to increased frequency of extreme weather events (such as storms, floods, droughts, or fires) or chronic due to

[2]Such as industry and non-governmental organizations, civil society groups, and academia.

[3]This implies both responding to new customer demands or segments and attracting human talent to develop new ideas.

long-term trends (such as rising sea levels or changing precipitation and temperature patterns). Transition risks, on the other hand, refer to sweeping technological and organizational changes required to reach the carbon neutrality objective (Krueger, Sautner, and Starks, 2020). In addition to uncertainties about technology, this risk also includes regulatory and reputational risk, making proper timing of the carbon transition on the company level a delicate balancing act that could result in stranded assets, damaged reputation, or even regulatory non-compliance, if not managed properly (Stroebel and Wurgler, 2021). Climate change risks are substantial. Dietz *et al.* (2016) estimated that up to 30% of global assets under management could be at risk from climate change as a result of asset and productivity losses. Battiston *et al.* (2017) found that direct and indirect exposures to climate-policy-relevant sectors represent a large portion of investors' equity portfolios, whereas the portion of banks' loan portfolios exposed to these sectors is comparable to banks' capital. General awareness about sustainability risks has been increasing, which implies a growing demand for sustainability-themed investment projects (Gadenne, Kennedy, and McKeiver, 2009). However, there is also evidence that corporate sector responses to these risks are slow and inadequate (Goldstein *et al.*, 2019).

Investors' ESG incentives are closely tied to the fortunes of the non-financial actors they invest in. Their role, however, is not only reactive to the demand for sustainable finance coming from non-financial actors, but also proactive because sustainability risks can affect future cash flows and values of financial assets. A growing number of recent studies are finding asset pricing effects of climate change risk in various market segments, including in equity markets, bond markets, housing markets, and bank credit markets (Jung, Herbohn, and Clarkson, 2018; Bernstein, Gustafson, and Lewis, 2019; Delis, De Greiff, and Ongena, 2019; Baldauf, Garlappi, and Yannelis, 2020; Giglio, Kelly, and Stroebel, 2021; Venturini, 2022). However, there is also evidence that markets could be under-pricing this risk (see, for example, Krueger, Sautner, and Starks, 2020 or Venturini, 2022). Increased market attention to environmental risks can lead to portfolio realignments away from companies that are heavily exposed to such risks, like companies in carbon-intensive industries or companies close to environmental disaster zones (Choi, Gao, and Jiang, 2020; Alok, Kumar, and Wermers, 2020). On the other hand, it can also lead to active investor engagement as a way to influence corporate behavior and promote sustainable transformation of invested companies, particularly in the case of long-term investments (Krueger, Sautner, and Starks, 2020). Some ESG investors are also motivated by ethical concerns. However, non-pecuniary motives are largely subservient to investment performance (Amel-Zadeh and Serafeim, 2018). Several proactive approaches are used by investors under the term sustainable and responsible investing (SRI), including sustainability-themed investments, best-in-class investment selection, exclusions/negative screening, norms-based screening, ESG integration, engagement, voting as well as impact investing (Deloitte, 2020). Proactive role of investors means that additional demand for sustainable finance is generated within the financial sector itself and that the financial industry is helping to shape the transition into a carbon-neutral, sustainable economy.

Financial institutions as providers of sustainable financial products and services require relevant information about sustainability risks and impacts on entity and investment levels to design such products. Similarly, investors and other users (clients, customers, policymakers, non-governmental organizations, and civil society) require this information for analysis and decision-making. As a result, the rapid growth of sustainable finance has been accompanied by increasing demand for disclosures of non-financial, ESG information, catering to the needs of diverse stakeholders. Over the past several years, this has led to proliferation of ESG reporting frameworks and standards, developed by a network of industry standard setters, non-governmental organizations, and international bodies (Bracking and Leffel, 2021).[4] Some standards, such as the Task Force on Climate-related Financial Disclosures (TCFD) recommendations and the Greenhouse Gas (GHG) Protocol, provide guiding principles and accounting standards for climate reporting. Others either cater to the broader public interest of disclosing the impact of economic activities

[4]Including(but not limited to) the Task Force on Climate-related Financial Disclosures (TCFD), the Greenhouse Gas (GHG) Protocol, the Global Reporting Initiative (GRI) developed by the Global Sustainability Standards Board (GSSB), Sustainability Accounting Standards Board (SASB), Climate Disclosure Standards Board (CDSB), CDP (formerly Carbon Disclosure Project), and International Integrated Reporting Council (IIRC).

on sustainable development, such as the Global Reporting Initiative (GRI) Standards and the CDP (formerly Carbon Disclosure Project) Questionnaire, or focus more narrowly on sustainability information that is material for company value creation, such as the Sustainability Accounting Standards Board (SASB) standards and the Climate Disclosure Standards Board (CDSB) Framework. Some standard setters integrate sustainability reporting into a broader concept of management of financial and other types of capital for value creation, such as the International Integrated Reporting Council (IIRC) <IR>Framework, whereas others, such as the CDP, also provide data repository platforms (CDP *et al.*, 2020). ESG standards and frameworks furthermore underpin the development of ESG metrics, benchmark indices, and ratings, which are often used for marketing purposes and product development (Consolandi *et al.*, 2009; Mori and Christodoulou, 2012; Cash, 2018).

This overlapping ecosystem has been subject to criticism, because companies are often unsure of which standard to follow and because the system is prone to greenwashing due to its largely voluntary and qualitative nature. As a result, there has been a strong push toward convergence of ESG standards and frameworks recently. Several key standard setters agreed to work together toward the development of global sustainability reporting standards in 2020, culminating in the establishment of the International Sustainability Standards Board in 2021 (ISSB) under the auspices of the International Financial Reporting Standards (IFRS) Foundation (CDP *et al.*, 2020). Furthermore, the IFRS Foundation and the GRI have announced they intend to coordinate the work programs and activities of their standard-setting boards, the ISSB and the Global Sustainability Standards Board (GSSB) (IFRS, 2022). These initiatives envisage a two-pillar global approach to sustainability reporting: a first pillar of investor-focused standards to be developed by the IFRS/ISSB for use in capital markets and a second pillar of multi-stakeholder-oriented standards set by the GRI/GSSB. The key standard setters specifically recognized the crucial role of the EU in developing common global standards due to its leading position and technical expertise in devising a mandatory sustainable finance framework in the EU (CDP *et al.*, 2020).

Although the arguments presented above have shown that market-based logic has been a strong *pull* factor behind the development of sustainable finance, it is important not to underestimate the relevance of non-market *push* factors, in particular global policy commitments embodied by the sustainable development goals (SDGs) and the Paris Agreement (United Nations, 2015a, b). Global policymakers are increasingly eyeing sustainable finance as a key instrument to deliver climate and other sustainability objectives (Ahlström and Monciardini, 2021). The Paris Agreement outlines an explicit goal of "making finance flows consistent with a pathway toward low greenhouse gas emissions and climate-resilient development" and calls on the signatories to "continue to take the lead in mobilizing climate finance". Similarly, initiatives such as "Billions to Trillions" and "Maximizing Finance for Development" by the World Bank, the International Monetary Fund, and Multilateral Development Banks indicate a shift in the mindset toward financialization of sustainable finance and increasing use of blended finance. These approaches commit public resources to bear the risk of sustainable development in order to attract private capital (Gabor, 2021). While this new "Wall Street Consensus" may be beneficial for leveraging the sustainable finance market, it also carries the risk of subordinating public fiscal space to private capital interests and inducing structural changes in the financial and government sectors without a clear line of sight of the ultimate benefits in terms of progress toward sustainability objectives (Gabor, 2021; Tan, 2022). Considering financial industry excesses from the past, a level of caution about excessive financialization of sustainability is warranted.

2.2. *Arguments behind a regulated approach to sustainable finance*

The case for a regulated approach to sustainable finance rests on finding evidence of market failures with respect to sustainability objectives. From the economic perspective, sustainability challenges amount to negative externalities of existing production and consumption patterns. Hardin (1968) speaks about the *Tragedy of the Commons*, where isolated individuals bring ruin to all by overconsumption of common resources (such as clean air or water) in the absence of information, communication, and rules governing the use of such resources. In reality, information is available, communication is possible, rules can evolve along societal norms, and trust can be built to find solutions to common pool problems (Ostrom, 2010; Frischmann *et al.*, 2019). This process is now underway in the growing sustainable finance market: non-financial and financial actors are increasingly taking into account risks associated with climate change and other sustainability challenges because of widespread information, effective communication, and changing norms about sustainability. The proper market failure question is therefore not whether the market will deliver sustainable transformation of finance and the economy on its own, but whether this transformation will be fast and broad enough in the absence of government intervention to prevent excessive social costs due to unresolved sustainability challenges.

There is reason to believe that organic growth of sustainable finance will not be fast enough. Climate change, which dominates sustainability debates, is not just global in nature but entails a strong inter-temporal element with potentially catastrophic costs in the long run and relatively low mitigation benefits in the short run. In other words, future generations will bear the brunt of the impact of climate change whereas current mitigation actions will take time to produce discernible effects on the climate. Although finance by nature makes inter-temporal decisions, climate-related costs and benefits are typically taken into account only insofar as they fall within the investment horizon of the financial industry. To emphasize this problem, Carney (2015) characterized the climate crisis as the *Tragedy of the Horizon*: beyond the business and political cycles and beyond the horizon of technocratic policymakers, such as central banks and financial supervisors. Short-termism of finance implies that the private inter-temporal discount factor is typically higher than the desired social discount factor, resulting in a low emphasis on distant events in present valuations and consequently slow adjustments of behavior (Schoenmaker, 2017).

However, fast changes of behavior in response to the climate crisis are of the essence. If pledges of the Paris Agreement to limit global warming to well below 2 and preferably to 1.5°C compared to pre-industrial levels are to be met, humanity is literally running out of time. The IPCC (2021) estimates that the remaining global carbon budget after 2020 that is consistent with the 1.5°C goal stands at 400 $GtCO_2$ at a 67% degree of certainty (the higher the probability, the lower the remaining carbon budget). For the 2.0°C goal, the respective figure is 1,150 $GtCO_2$. At the current annual rate of global emissions of roughly 50 $GtCO_2$ (2018 estimate), these remaining budgets would be exhausted in 10–25 years. Given the fact that global emissions are again on the rise after a temporary decline due to the

COVID-19 pandemic, time may be even shorter (Liu *et al.*, 2022). Overshooting the Paris Agreement targets risks opening the path to high-temperature climate scenarios with substantially increased frequency of extreme weather events, shifts in climate patterns, and rising sea levels, which may be incompatible with stable human societies (Richards *et al.*, 2021). The message of natural sciences is therefore clear: the paradigm shift to a carbon-neutral economy has to be accelerated and completed in the relatively near future. In this context, regulating sustainable finance to accelerate the green transition is validated by short-termism of finance that may lead to excessive social costs.

Another factor weighing in on the need to bring finance fully on board of sustainability is the sheer scale of the green transition challenge, especially in relation to climate change. The European Commission estimates that in order to reach the EU's internal goal of carbon-neutrality by 2050 and the intermediate objective of a 55% reduction of GHG emissions by 2030, total supply and demand side investments in the energy system across the EU will amount to EUR 1,051 billion per year in the 2021–2030 period and to EUR 1,195 billion per year in the subsequent period of 2031–2050 (European Commission, 2020a; European Commission, 2021a). Relative to the level of investment in the energy system in the 2011–2020 period, which stood at EUR 660 billion, this amounts to an increase of EUR 392 billion and EUR 535 billion per year, respectively. Public resources will not be sufficient to finance these estimated needs, even when taking into account public financial institutions, such as development banks. Unregulated market for sustainable finance will also not be able to meet the challenge because private financial players only take into account private and not social costs and benefits of climate change (Schoenmaker, 2017). A regulated approach to sustainable finance is therefore justified by the need to shift the incentives of private financial players to increase their participation in financing of the green transition.

The required speed and scale of the green transition also imply systemic implications for the economy and the financial system (Battiston, Dafermos, and Monasterolo, 2021). This transition requires nothing less than a complete rethinking of technological solutions and business models across many sectors, with direct implications for their competitiveness and ultimately for financial and price stability. Conversely, reneging on climate and sustainability action would also inevitably lead to adverse systemic effects. Climate change and the required transformation of the economic system also carry social and employment implications in the affected sectors. It is therefore no wonder that sustainability is fast becoming a focal point of financial supervision and monetary policy, on the one hand, and environmental, social, and employment policies, on the other hand. The use of sustainability criteria by central banks, financial supervisors, and governments provides a further argument in favor of a more common, regulated approach toward sustainable finance.

In the end, a certain level of regulation of sustainable finance may also be in the best interest of private financial players because it reduces information asymmetries that are inherent in the market quest for sustainability. This may help to mitigate an underproduction of standardized high-quality information needed by investors (Troeger and Steuer, 2021; Rogge and Ohnesorge, 2021). As already discussed, the recent proliferation of ESG standards and ratings has generated a substantial problem of greenwashing, where the primary objective of companies is to look but not act green. As a result, there is a lot of hype about green investments that may not live up to scrutiny. For example, Kishan (2022) reports that the ESG fund industry is ripe for a shakeout due to widespread greenwashing. Regulation that helps to define sustainable principles and activities therefore brings some much-needed clarity to the field that could help spur further growth of sustainable finance.

However, there are two important caveats to the above arguments. The first one relates to the increased costs of regulatory compliance. The traditional financial sector is already one of the most heavily regulated sectors of the economy. Adding another layer of sustainable finance regulation could have negative implications for the competitiveness of the sector at a time when it is facing substantial challenges from new competition (fintech, including bigtech) after a prolonged period of unfavorable market conditions (low interest rates) that is only now coming to an end (Claessens, Coleman, and Donnelly, 2018; Stulz, 2019). Since sustainable finance regulation is ultimately about disclosures of sustainability risks and impacts of economic activities, the burden is also passed on to non-financial actors, who have to provide the ultimate data inputs. This could have detrimental effects on smaller players in both financial and non-financial sectors who may find it difficult to cope with increased regulatory burden, leading to further market consolidation and concentration, unless regulation is sensitive to company size. If left unchecked, such market dynamics could disproportionately affect financial systems and economies of smaller countries.

The second caveat is in terms of the well-known risks of government failure (Furton and Martin, 2019). One such failure may be the naïve belief that the government knows the right solutions to sustainability problems. While the end goals of decarbonization and broader sustainability are clear, there are "many roads that lead to Rome". By committing to regulation, the government is choosing to select some roads over the others. In the case of the EU approach, a typical example of such self-constraining mentality was reluctance to include nuclear energy as a sustainable activity in the initial version of the EU taxonomy, despite its advantage as a non-carbon energy source. Another government failure problem could be inefficiencies and losses that may yet result from a sudden triggering of massive public and private capital flows to sustainability causes by regulation, especially under blended finance approaches, which guarantee returns to private investors and shift risks to public balance sheets.

Despite these drawbacks, the balance of arguments seems to be in favor of a regulated approach to sustainable finance due to the sheer size of social costs associated with unabated climate and other environmental problems, which outweigh aforementioned considerations. Nevertheless, policymakers and regulators should be acutely aware of potential downside risks of sustainable finance regulation and try to minimize them.

3. Planning and regulating the green transition in the EU

The EU approach to sustainable finance is embedded in the European Green Deal (EGD). Adopted in 2019, the EGD is the EU green and digital growth strategy for the future with the goal to transform the EU into a sustainable, climate-neutral economy over the coming years and decades (European Commission, 2019).

3.1. *The European Green Deal*

The headline objectives of the EGD are to reach zero net GHG emissions by 2050 and decouple economic growth from resource use by transitioning from a linear to a circular economy. Additionally, the EGD is also concerned with the preservation and restoration of biodiversity, improving human health and well-being, and ensuring a socially just and inclusive transition with a promise "to leave no one behind". These objectives follow on the footsteps of previously fragmented EU environmental, climate, and energy policies. The EGD aligns the EU sustainability objectives with the Paris Agreement targets and the United Nations' SDGs and integrates them horizontally across all major policy areas through a process called sustainability mainstreaming. This is also how the EU sustainable finance policy was integrated into the EGD framework.

Implementation of the EGD rests upon a comprehensive set of instruments. The first such instrument would be the EU strategies and action plans, developed to provide guiding principles and objectives within specific policy areas, such as climate, industrial, or agricultural policy, often with concrete timelines to deliver the objectives. The second instrument relates to national strategies, such as the National Energy and Climate Plans, the Recovery and Resilience Plans, or the Common Agricultural Policy Strategic Plans, which have to be aligned with the EGD. National strategies further specify member state policies to reach the EGD objectives. The third instrument is regulation. The EGD envisages substantive changes to the EU regulatory framework both in terms of existing and new regulations to deliver the EGD objectives. The final instrument is financial resources. The EGD combines sustainability policies with investment planning and funding. This is achieved both by blending budgetary and market funding and by stimulating further growth of sustainable finance through regulation.

3.2. *Addressing climate objectives*

Two elements of the EGD bear specific relevance for acceleration of the EU's climate change mitigation efforts with important implications for sustainable finance. The first element includes the substantially increased medium-term climate targets. The second one concerns effective regulation of carbon pricing and member states' GHG emissions reductions with the aim to deliver the more ambitious climate targets.

Even before the EGD, the EU already planned to cut GHG emissions by 40% by 2030 relative to 1990 levels. The EGD raised this target to 55%. By 2019, the EU (without the UK) managed to decrease GHG emissions, including transport, by 25% relative to 1990 (European Environmental Agency, 2022). Increased 2030 ambitions therefore mean that the EU will now have to redouble the last three decades of GHG emissions reductions in the space of only 10 years, which is clearly a very ambitious objective. Moreover, the new 2030 target as well as the 2050 climate neutrality goal are now enshrined in the European Climate Law (2021/1119), making them legally binding for the member states.

In order to deliver climate policy targets, the EU relies on three key instruments, the Emissions Trading System Directive (2003/87/EC, as amended by 2018/410), the Effort Sharing Regulation (2018/842), and the Land Use, Land Use Change, and Forestry Regulation (2018/841), which together cover all EU GHG emissions and removals. The European Commission proposed to revise each of these instruments in its "Fit for 55" legislative package on 14 July 2021 to reflect increased climate ambitions (European Commission, 2021b).

The Emissions Trading System (ETS) Directive covers emissions of the power sector, energy-intensive industry, and a part of commercial aviation, accounting for approximately 40% of EU emissions. It follows a cap-and-trade principle where the amount of emissions covered by the system, corresponding to the amount of allowances, is capped. Companies under the EU ETS must submit sufficient allowances corresponding to their emission output at the end of year or face fines. Under the system, they can either buy, receive, or trade allowances with each other. The EU ETS cap is reduced each year to ensure a decreasing profile of emissions. The idea is that a decreasing cap will put upward pressure on the market price of allowances and drive up the cost of carbon-intensive technologies, encouraging investment into low- or zero-carbon alternatives. The "Fit for 55" legislative package expands the scope of the EU ETS to the maritime shipping sector and envisages a separate ETS for road transport and building sectors. It also significantly increases the pace of emissions reductions by lowering the overall emissions cap and increasing its annual rate of reduction from 2.2 to 4.2%, on the back of a much lower 1.74% reduction rate before 2021. Whereas the EU ETS has had its share of start-up problems, including excessive supply of allowances in its early phases and subdued demand for allowances during the global and Euro area financial and economic crises, the system seems to have reached maturity with the price of allowances consistently growing over the last four years, including through the COVID-19 period.

Next, the Effort Sharing Regulation sets binding emissions reduction targets for member states in sectors not covered by the EU ETS, such as transport, buildings, small industries, agriculture, and waste, accounting for the remaining 60% of EU emissions. In these sectors, the "Fit for 55" proposal raises EU-level targets from 29 to 40% by 2030, on the back of a 10% target for 2020. National targets are differentiated according to relative prosperity, with less developed member states having less demanding targets. Implementations of national targets rest upon national climate policies, in particular National Energy and Climate Plans.

Finally, the Land Use, Land Use Change, and Forestry Regulation sets a binding commitment for each member state to ensure that emissions from land use are completely compensated by CO_2 removals from the atmosphere within the sector (no debit rule). The "Fit for 55" proposal additionally sets a new overall EU target for carbon removals by natural sinks (such as forests) in the sector, equivalent to 310 million tonnes of CO_2 emissions by 2030.

These key instruments for climate change mitigation are further supported by sectoral legislation and standards in the areas of energy efficiency, renewable energy, CO_2 emissions standards for cars, sustainable fuels, and energy taxation, all of which are also being revised by the "Fit for 55" proposal to increase their level of stringency. Notably, the proposed revisions imply a complete phasing out of newly produced cars with internal combustion engine in the EU by 2035 and expansion of charging capacity for electricity- and hydrogen-powered vehicles. They also include increased EU-level targets for the minimum share of renewables and the minimum rate of increase in energy efficiency by 2030 as well as less favorable taxation of fossil fuels relative to green energy. To prevent carbon leakage through production offshoring to countries with lower climate standards, which could occur in the face of increasing upward pressure on EU carbon prices, the Commission is also proposing a new Carbon Border Adjustment Mechanism, effectively placing a carbon tax on imports. To address social concerns, a new Social Climate Fund is proposed to help EU citizens finance investments in energy efficiency, new heating and cooling systems, and cleaner mobility.

Whereas the "Fit for 55" proposals are politically contentious and have been subject to challenging negotiations under the EU legislative procedure,[5] their implications for the carbon market are clear: the EU drive toward carbon neutrality will place increasing costs on carbon-based technologies. This could have substantial financial impact on companies' profit margins, turnover, and capital expenditure plans in the affected sectors as well as social impact in terms of higher traditional (fossil fuels-based) energy prices for end-consumers. The EU is therefore using climate regulation to create price incentives for market participants to transition toward low- and zero-carbon technologies. Changes in behavior of companies and individuals induced by the ambitious EU sustainability agenda also put pressure on the financial industry to develop its own transition plans from traditional to sustainable finance to maintain long-term profitability and preserve financial stability.

Complementary to well-defined mitigation instruments, a new EU climate change adaptation strategy was also adopted in 2021 (European Commission, 2021c). This strategy focuses on three key objectives: smarter adaptation by improving scientific understanding of climate change impacts, faster adaptation by accelerating development and rollout of climate adaptation solutions, and systemic adaptation by improving and integrating adaptation strategies and plans across government and policy levels. The need to adapt to the risks of a changing climate will also create additional financial pressures on companies and individuals and provide further motivation for the financial industry to monitor such risks and adaptation efforts.

3.3. *Addressing other sustainability objectives*

Apart from climate policy, other sustainability objectives of the EGD are delivered through a wide range of policy initiatives. These include

[5]By 2023 key elements of "Fit for 55" proposals have already been adopted into EU law.

supplying clean, affordable, and safe energy, transforming industry to become sustainable using the concept of a circular economy, promoting energy- and resource-efficient construction and renovation of buildings, accelerating the shift to sustainable and smart mobility, designing sustainable food and agriculture systems, preserving and restoring ecosystems and biodiversity, and eliminating pollution.

To implement these initiatives, the European Commission adopted several EU-wide strategies and action plans in 2020 and 2021. The list of strategic documents is long and includes European industrial strategy, circular economy action plan, "farm to fork strategy", biodiversity strategy, blue economy strategy, chemicals strategy, strategy for energy system integration, hydrogen strategy, methane strategy, offshore renewable energy strategy, renovation wave strategy, zero pollution action plan, and organic action plan (European Commission, 2022a).[6]

Although a detailed discussion of each of these strategies and action plans is beyond the scope of this chapter, several key themes can nonetheless be observed. The first and most significant one is broad industrial transformation in heavy industry, transport, manufacturing, and construction. The main envisaged drivers of this transformation are decarbonization, modernization (including renovation in the case of buildings), and promotion of circular production processes that emphasize recycling and reusability of energy, materials, and products, to reduce waste. The second theme is promotion of zero-carbon or low-carbon energy sources, including renewables, where the EU plans to develop the untapped potential of offshore wind energy, and alternative fuels, such as clean hydrogen and biofuels. The third theme is increasing EU's technological, industrial, energy, and strategic autonomy due to geopolitical tensions and supply chain problems. This is to be achieved by reforming competition and intellectual property rules, preventing market distortions due to subsidized foreign competitors, reshoring strategic parts of supply chains, and, in the case of energy autonomy, which became an

[6]As a response to recent external challenges, including the war in Ukraine and the U.S. Inflation Reduction Act, the European Commission also launched two new initiatives in 2022 and 2023, related to the EGD, namely the REPowerEU and the Green Deal Industrial Plan, which aim to increase domestic development, production and deployment of clean energy technologies.

overriding priority since the start of the war in Ukraine, by accelerating the transition to clean energy and diversifying supplies. The themes of industry, energy, and autonomy are also reflected in the formation of industry-wide ecosystems and alliances. These include alliances in clean hydrogen, renewables, and low-carbon fuel value chains, batteries, processor and semiconductor technologies, industrial clouds and platforms, circular plastics, and raw materials. The next theme is development of a sustainable food and agriculture system by reducing the use of chemicals, pesticides, and antimicrobials in agriculture, promoting organic farming as well as healthy, plant-based foods, thereby reducing food waste and overall environmental footprint of agriculture. This is also closely related to the protection of EU natural capital as the next theme, which aims to restore damaged ecosystems in oceans, rivers, and forests, improve the health of EU-protected habitats and species, as well as improve environmental conditions in urban and cultivated environments. Finally, the last theme covered by EU horizontal and sectoral strategies is elimination of waste and pollution, targeting toxic chemicals and pollutants to improve the quality of air, soil, and water.

3.4. *Green transition investment and financing*

To finance economic and industrial transformation envisaged by the EGD agenda, the EU adopted the EGD Investment Plan (EGDIP) in early 2020 with three specific objectives. First, to mobilize substantial public and private funding for sustainable investments on top of available EU budget resources in the 2021–2030 period. The second objective was to provide an enabling framework for private investors and the public sector to properly identify sustainable investments, based upon the evolving EU framework for sustainable finance, and the integration of sustainability into fiscal and economic policy coordination at the EU level (the so-called European Semester). The final objective was to provide support in planning and executing sustainable investment projects (European Commission, 2020b).

The logic of the EGDIP rests upon leveraging green expenditures of the EU budget to attract additional resources through national co-financing and blended finance. The original EGDIP figures extrapolated climate and environment-related expenditures available in the 7-year EU budget plan for 2021–2027 (the multiannual financial framework) over a 10-year period (2021–2030), yielding EUR 503 billion. This was in turn supposed to mobilize EUR 561 billion in public and private funding, mostly through member state budgets (EUR 114 billion), the European Investment Bank's implementation of the InvestEU programme (EUR 279 billion), and a new Just Transition Mechanism, providing transition finance to the less developed carbon-intensive EU regions (EUR 143 billion). This brought total available financial resources of the EGDIP in the 2021–2030 period to EUR 1,064 billion, implying a leveraging factor of 2.12 relative to the EU budget resources.

The original EGDIP figures have to be adjusted, however, because they were based on the 2018 proposal of the 2021–2027 multiannual financial framework by the European Commission and not on the final deal agreed by the European Council on 21 July 2020. The final deal deviated substantially from the initial Commission proposal in two important ways. First, to address significant challenges of the post-pandemic recovery in the face of green and digital transitions, a new EUR 750 billion EU Recovery Instrument, the NextGenerationEU, was adopted besides the traditional, EUR 1,074 billion, multiannual financial framework. Second, the target share of climate-related expenditures in the EU budget in the 2021–2027 period was raised from 25% in the Commission proposal to 30% in the final deal, on the back of a lower 20% target in the 2014–2020 period The (European Commission, 2021d). Both changes substantially increased green EU budget expenditures available for leveraging within the EGDIP. Reflecting this, the draft EU budget for 2022 estimated 2021–2027 climate-related expenditures at EUR 626 billion, biodiversity-related expenditures at EUR 102 billion, and other environmental expenditures at EUR 44 billion, implying a total of EUR 772 billion of available green EU budget expenditures in the 2021–2027 period (European Commission, 2022b). A 10-year extrapolation of these figures would therefore yield EUR 1,102 billion in EU budget funding for climate and environmental objectives, a substantial increase from the original EGDIP estimate of EUR 503 billion. Considering the EGDIP leveraging factor of 2.12, this implies an EU green finance potential of EUR 2,332 billion in the 2021–2030 period instead of the originally advertised EUR 1,064 billion.

Not all this EU green finance potential is new, however. As indicated above, EU budget expenditures already addressed climate and environmental objectives in the 2014–2020 period. The European

Commission (2022b) estimated that the EU budget spent EUR 216 billion on climate, EUR 85 billion on biodiversity, and EUR 52 billion on other environmental objectives in the 2014–2020 period, implying pre-existing green EU budget expenditures of EUR 353 billion. This means that only EUR 419 billion out of the available EUR 772 billion of green EU budget expenditures in the 2021–2027 period is actually *additional* to the 2014–2020 levels. Extrapolating this lower figure to 10 years and considering the EGDIP leveraging factor yields EUR 598 billion of *additional* green EU budget expenditures and EUR 1,265 billion of *additional* EU green finance potential in the 2021–2030 period (EUR 60 billion and EUR 126 billion per year, respectively). Pre-existing and planned climate and environmental expenditures of the EU budget and adjusted EGDIP estimates are shown in Table 1.

The additional EU green finance potential in the 2021–2030 period has to be reconciled with the additional EU green investment needs (the EU green investment gap). The climate part of this investment gap was presented in Section 2.2 and amounts to additional investment needs of EUR 392 billion per year in 2021–2030, rising to EUR 535 billion per year in 2031–2050, on top of climate investment levels in the 2011–2020 period. Addressing the remaining environmental objectives of the EGD will require more resources. The European Commission (2020c) estimated that a further EUR 130 billion of additional investments per year are needed in the 2021–2030 period to address objectives in the areas such as biodiversity, circular economy, and pollution prevention and control, bringing the total EU green investment gap in the 2021–2030 period to EUR 522 billion per year. These figures should be considered as low estimates of total implementation costs of the EGD, since they only relate to climate and environmental objectives of the EGD, whereas the EGD also has a notable social component, stemming from the pledge "to leave no one behind".[7] Pre-existing and estimated future green investment needs as well as the implied EU green investment gaps are shown in Table 2.

---

[7]For example, the European Commission (2020c) also estimated that as much as EUR 192 billion of additional investments per year may be needed in social infrastructure in areas such as education and life-long learning, health, long-term care, and affordable housing.

Table 1. EU green finance potential based on EU budget, EGDIP, and EIB funding.

EUR billions	Pre-existing			Planned			Additional
Source of EU green finance	Reference period (a)	Amount per period (b)	Amount per year (c)	Reference period (d)	Amount per period (e)	Amount per year (f)	Amount per year (f) − (c)
EU budget (1)	2014–2020	353	50	2021–2027	772	110	60*
Climate	2014–2020	216	31	2021–2027	626	89	59
Biodiversity	2014–2020	85	12	2021–2027	102	15	2
Other environmental objectives	2014–2020	52	7	2021–2027	44	6	−1
EGDIP (2)	—	—	—	2021–2030	2,332	233	126
Funded by EU budget	—	—	—	2021–2030	1,102	110	60*
Leveraged by EGDIP	—	—	—	2021–2030	1,229	123	67
EIB Climate Bank (3)	2012–2019	150	19	2021–2030	1,000	100	81

Notes: EGDIP figures are adjusted to reflect the final European Council agreement on the multiannual financial framework 2021–2027 and the NextGenerationEU as follows. First, a leveraging factor of total EGDIP resources relative to EU budget resources is calculated from the original figures in the Communication on the European Green Deal Investment Plan. This yields a leveraging factor of EUR 1,064 bn/EUR 503 bn = 2.1153. Second, the estimated climate and environmental mainstreaming figures for the period 2021–2027 from the draft EU budget 2022 are extrapolated to 10 years, yielding EUR 772 bn × 10/7 = EUR 1,102 bn. Third, the leveraging factor from the first step is applied to the extrapolated 10-year budget figures, resulting in 2.1153 × EUR 1,102 bn = EUR 2,332 bn. The additional EGDIP resources per year (on top of pre-existing) are estimated by applying the same leveraging factor to the additional annual EU budget resources per year for climate and environmental objectives, that is 2.1153 × EUR 60 bn = EUR 126 bn. Funds leveraged by EGDIP are calculated as the difference between the total EGDIP figure and the EU budget figure. *Table 1 double-reports available EU budget resources under EU budget and EGDIP. To calculate the total of additional annual EU green finance resources, the EU budget figure should only be considered once. The total is therefore EUR 60 bn + EUR 67 bn + EUR 81 bn = EUR 208 bn.

Sources: (1) European Commission (2022b); (2) European Commission (2020b); (3) European Investment Bank (2020).

Table 2. EU green investment needs.

EUR billions per year	EU green investments 2011–2020 (a)	EU green investment needs 2021–2030 (b)	EU green investment needs 2031–2050 (c)	EU green investment gap 2021–2030 (b) − (a)	EU green investment gap 2031–2050 (c) − (a)
Climate objectives (1)	660	1,051	1,195	392	535
Supply side	47	103	197	56	150
Power grid	13	44	81	31	68
Power plants, boilers, and new fuels	34	59	116	25	82
Demand side	613	948	998	336	385
Industrial sector	10	25	14	15	4
Residential sector	88	180	174	92	87
Tertiary sector	40	94	81	54	41
Transport sector	474	649	728	175	254
Other environmental objectives (2)	—	—	—	130	—
Protection of biodiversity and ecosystems	—	—	—	7	—
Circular economy and resource efficiency	—	—	—	35	—
Pollution prevention and control	—	—	—	46	—
Water protection and management	—	—	—	36	—
Research and development	—	—	—	7	—

Sources: (1) European Commission (2020a) for 2031–2050 and European Commission (2021a) for 2021–2030; (2) European Commission (2020c).

Comparing the additional EU green finance potential (EUR 126 billion per year) with the EU green investment gap (EUR 522 billion per year) shows that only a quarter of the estimated investment gap is funded by the EU budget and EGDIP framework. This highlights an urgent need to secure additional financial resources for climate, environmental, and other sustainability objectives. The European Investment Bank (EIB) has already responded to this call by declaring its intent to become the EU climate bank and pledging to allocate EUR 1,000 billion (EUR 100 billion per year) to the financing of climate objectives in 2021–2030 (European Investment Bank, 2020). Since the EIB has already allocated EUR 150 billion (EUR 19 billion per year) to climate objectives in 2012–2019, the climate bank pledge translates to additional EUR 81 billion per year.[8] EIB figures are reported in Table 1.

Adding the EIB climate bank pledge (EUR 81 billion per year) to the available funding based on the EU budget and EGDIP framework (EUR 126 billion per year) raises the total additional EU green finance potential in the 2021–2030 period to EUR 208 billion per year. This is still far below the estimated EU green investment gap over the same period (EUR 522 billion per year), which implies that as much as 60% of additional green financing needs in the 2021–2030 period or EUR 314 billion per year will have to be covered by yet unaccounted for additional funding. This substantial funding gap, shown in Figure 1, is the driving force behind the EU push into sustainable finance.

4. Planning and regulating sustainable finance in the EU

The EU involvement in sustainable finance predates the EGD and EGDIP. The EU adopted the first elements of non-financial (sustainability-related) reporting for large companies in 2014 with follow-up non-binding guidelines for such reporting in 2017 and additional specific guidelines for reporting climate-related information in 2019. Parallel to these ad hoc beginnings, a new sustainable finance

[8]This assumes that the EIB climate bank pledge is fully additional to the EIB participation in the EGDIP framework.

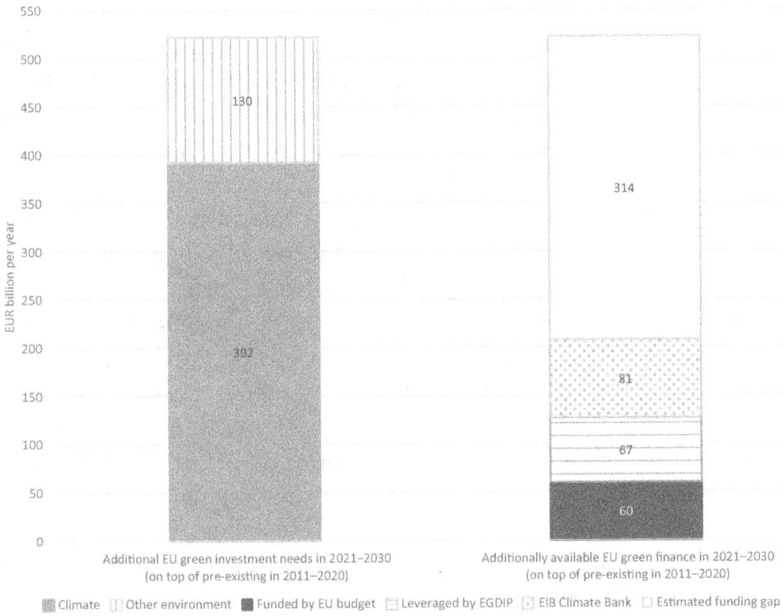

Figure 1. EU green funding gap in the 2021–2030 period.
Sources: Additional EU green investment needs per year from Table 1, additionally available EU green finance per year from Table 2.

strategy was adopted in 2018. This opened the space for a systematic development of the EU sustainable finance framework that we see today.

4.1. *Sustainable finance strategy*

The current EU framework for sustainable finance can be traced to the 2018 Sustainable Finance Action Plan, which is based on recommendations of the High-Level Expert Group on Sustainable Finance, established in 2016. Two key recommendations of the expert group were increasing long-term orientation of finance to focus on societies' long-term needs and promoting long-term financial stability by incorporating ESG factors into investment decisions and financial risk management (European Commission, 2018).

Based on these guidelines, the Sustainable Finance Action Plan proposed 10 specific actions to support the transition from traditional to sustainable finance. The first and most fundamental of them was to establish an EU classification system of sustainable activities, the so-called EU taxonomy, as a necessary precondition and complementary instrument for the other actions. The other proposals were to (1) establish EU standards and labels for sustainable financial products, such as green bonds, (2) reinforce advisory capacity for planning and executing sustainable investment projects, (3) incorporate sustainability into financial advice for clients, (4) develop sustainability benchmarks for investors to track and measure performance, (5) integrate sustainability into credit ratings and marketing research, (6) clarify fiduciary duty of institutional investors and asset managers with respect to sustainability, (7) incorporate sustainability into prudential requirements for financial institutions, (8) strengthen disclosure and accounting rules on sustainability, and (9) promote sustainable, long-term oriented corporate governance to avoid undue short-termism.

Drawing on the work already under progress based on the Sustainable Finance Action Plan and the changed circumstances after the adoption of the EGD, the multiannual financial framework, and the NextGenerationEU, the European Commission published a renewed sustainable finance strategy on 6 July 2021 (European Commission, 2021e). The renewed strategy identified four main areas where further action is needed beyond the proposals included in the Sustainable Finance Action Plan.

The first area is *increased emphasis on sustainability transition process, not just the end goal.* This requires recognition of intermediary activities on the pathway toward sustainability that reduce harmful climate and environmental impacts but are not considered fully sustainable in an orthodox sense. Among such activities, the Commission specifically referred to keeping nuclear energy and natural gas options open.

The second area is *greater inclusiveness of the sustainable finance framework*, in particular for small and medium-sized enterprises and households (as retail investors and consumers). This requires better access to sustainable retail financial products, such as green loans or mortgages, advisory services about sustainability, insurance protection against climate risks, and putting more emphasis on the social (not just environmental) component of sustainability.

The third area is *strengthening the financial sector's link to sustainability* through a double-materiality approach. On the one hand, this approach rests upon understanding and improving resilience of individual financial institutions and the financial system to financially material sustainability risks through actions by financial institutions and through microprudential and macroprudential supervision. The other side of double-materiality is related to the transposition of EU sustainability objectives and transition planning into long-term financing strategies and decision-making processes of financial institutions and into the monitoring toolkit of competent supervisory authorities, thereby increasing the financial system's positive impact on sustainability.

The last area is *EU contribution to global sustainable finance efforts*, building on its domestic experience and internationally recognized sustainability leadership. For this, the EU is actively advocating key elements of an international sustainable finance architecture, such as common principles of taxonomies, disclosure frameworks, and double-materiality, in relevant international forums. These include the G20 Sustainable Finance Working Group, the International Platform on Sustainable Finance, the Task Force on Climate-related Financial Risks in the Basel Committee on Banking Supervision, the International Association of Insurance Supervisors, the Financial Stability Board, as well as standard-setters, such as the IFRS Foundation.

Taking into account the above-described EU sustainable finance strategy, as well as the broader context of the EGD and EGDIP, the current state of the EU sustainable finance framework is based on three building blocks that will evolve further in the future in line with the actions envisaged by the strategic documents. These building blocks are (1) EU taxonomy, (2) disclosure regimes for non-financial and financial companies, and (3) sustainable finance tools.

4.2. *EU taxonomy*

The EU taxonomy is a classification system establishing a science-based list of environmentally sustainable economic activities as a prerequisite for informed decision-making by companies, investors, and policymakers. The idea behind it is to help scale up sustainable investment and prevent greenwashing. Its envisaged application is broad and includes both mandatory and voluntary uses, such as disclosures of taxonomy-aligned activities by non-financial and financial enterprises, the development of standards and labels for sustainable financial products, identification of sustainable investment opportunities, or the preparation of green transition strategies and plans by companies. Moreover, it is highly likely that other areas of EU or national policies will gradually become taxonomy-aligned. Notably, this may include member states' fiscal and economic policy coordination in the context of the European Semester, prudential requirements under banking supervision, or even the conduct of monetary policy (in particular, asset purchase programs).

The Taxonomy Regulation (2020/852) is focused around six environmental objectives that are aligned with the objectives of the EGD: (1) climate change mitigation, (2) climate change adaptation, (3) sustainable use and protection of water and marine resources, (4) transition to a circular economy, (5) pollution prevention and control, and (6) protection and restoration of biodiversity and ecosystems. The regulation defines sustainable activities as those that meet three specific criteria. First, they should *substantially contribute* to one or more of the six listed objectives (SC criterion). Next, they should do so without harming any of the remaining objectives, which is referred to as the *do no significant harm* principle (DNSH criterion). Finally, they must also comply with the *minimum safeguards* related to responsible business conduct and human rights (MS criterion). These safeguards are based on internationally recognized principles, in particular the UN Guiding Principles on Business and Human Rights (United Nations, 2011) and the OECD Guidelines for Multinational Enterprises (OECD, 2011).

The Taxonomy Regulation covers three types of activities, namely, activities that make a significant contribution to environmental objectives based on their own performance, enabling activities, which directly facilitate other activities to make a substantial contribution, and transition activities, which do not yet have technologically and economically feasible low-carbon alternatives. Transitional activities are only relevant for climate change mitigation and are restricted by additional criteria, including best-in-class performance with respect to GHG emissions, non-hindrance of low-carbon alternatives, and avoidance of long-term lock-ins of carbon-intensive assets.

In practice, compliance of individual activities with SC and DNSH criteria is checked against technical screening criteria established through delegated acts under the Taxonomy Regulation for the six taxonomy objectives. The European Commission has so far adopted one such act, the Taxonomy Climate Delegated Act (2021/2139), covering the first two taxonomy objectives (climate change mitigation and climate change adaptation) and has put forward a separate delegated act, addressing the remaining four objectives, for notification to the Council and the European Parliament in June 2023. These acts are envisaged to be "living" documents reviewed and updated according to the pace of technological and scientific progress. One such review of the Taxonomy Climate Delegated Act has been completed with the inclusion of nuclear energy and natural gas as transitional activities. The European Commission adopted the complementary delegated act for this purpose in March 2022.

Activities on the EU taxonomy list are labeled as taxonomy-eligible. If they also meet the SC, DNSH, and MS criteria, they are labeled as taxonomy-aligned. This distinction is relevant, because companies under the scope of EU sustainability disclosure rules will have to report both categories of activities in the future (European Banking Federation & UNEP Finance Initiative, 2022). In order to enable users to check which activities are included on the taxonomy list and view the technical screening criteria, the Commission has also launched the EU Taxonomy Compass, which displays a matrix of relevant activities per environmental objective and sector.

The development of technical screening criteria for the purpose of delegated acts and further extensions of the EU taxonomy are entrusted to the Platform on Sustainable Finance, consisting of public and private sector experts. These include the European Environmental Agency, the European Supervisory Authorities,[9] the European Investment Bank, the European Union Agency for Fundamental Rights, financial and non-financial market participants, accounting experts, and representatives of relevant industries and civil society. The Platform on Sustainable Finance replaced the earlier Technical Expert Group on Sustainable Finance, which advised

[9]The European Banking Authority (EBA), the European Insurance and Occupational Pensions Authority (EIOPA), and the European Securities and Markets Authority (ESMA).

the European Commission in the run-up to the Taxonomy Regulation. Before adopting delegated acts, the European Commission also consults the Member State Expert Group on Sustainable Finance regarding the appropriateness of the technical screening criteria and the approach taken by the Platform.

Whereas the EU taxonomy currently only covers environmental aspects of sustainability, work is underway to develop a parallel taxonomy of socially sustainable activities and extend the environmental taxonomy to include significantly harmful, intermediate (amber), and low environmental impact economic activities (Platform on Sustainable Finance, 2022a,b). This would expand the EU sustainable finance framework to the full range of sustainability goals under the EGD and the SDGs and provide additional clarity with respect to those activities that do not significantly contribute to sustainability objectives.

4.3. *Sustainability disclosures*

Corporate sustainability disclosure requirements primarily concern large non-financial and financial companies with the aim to establish a continuous stream of reliable and comparable qualitative and quantitative information about sustainability aspects of business that can feed into corporate strategy, risk management, investment decisions, product and service design, as well as supervisory practices. In the EU, they are governed by two separate legislative acts: the Non-Financial Reporting Directive (2014/95/EU) and the Sustainable Finance Disclosures Regulation (2019/2088). Furthermore, the Taxonomy Regulation created additional reporting requirements for companies covered by the Non-Financial Reporting Directive (Article 8 of the Taxonomy Regulation) and for companies covered by the Sustainable Finance Disclosures Regulation (Articles 5–7 of the Taxonomy Regulation). Separately, sustainability disclosures have also become integrated into the EU banking prudential framework under Article 449a of the Capital Requirements Regulation II (2019/876), which requires large institutions to provide qualitative and quantitative disclosures, with an emphasis on climate-related reporting.

4.3.1. *Non-financial reporting directive (NFRD)*

The NFRD requires large public-interest companies with more than 500 employees, including listed companies, banks, insurance companies, and other companies designated to be in the public interest by national authorities (around 11,000 companies in total), to report sustainability information on an annual basis. Sustainability disclosures relate to climate, other environment, social, and employee-related matters, respect for human rights, anti-corruption, and anti-bribery matters as well as board diversity. Reporting follows the "double-materiality" principle, meaning that companies have to report about sustainability risks to their business and about their own social and environmental impact. Pursuant to the NFRD, the Commission published non-binding guidelines for companies in 2017 to improve consistency of their disclosures. These guidelines were supplemented in 2019 to include reporting of climate-related information. Nevertheless, reliability and comparability of reporting under the NFRD remains an acute problem. Coupled with increasing demand for credible sustainability data due to the fast development of green financial markets, EGD policies, and sustainable finance regulation (in particular, the Sustainable Finance Disclosure Regulation), this prompted the Commission to propose a revision of sustainability reporting requirements under the NFRD on 21 April 2021 with a new Corporate Sustainability Reporting Directive (CSRD). The CSRD directive has been adopted in 2022 (2022/2464).

The CSRD extends the scope of existing sustainability reporting requirements to all large companies and all companies listed on regulated markets, including listed small and medium-sized enterprises (SMEs) (except micro-enterprises), which increases the coverage to approximately 50,000 companies. It also introduces more detailed reporting and mandatory auditing of sustainability disclosures to increase their reliability. Furthermore, to address comparability concerns, the proposal envisages the development of mandatory EU sustainability reporting standards. These standards have been developed by the European Financial Reporting Advisory Group (EFRAG) and adopted by the Commission after consultation with the Member State Expert Group on Sustainable Finance, the European Securities and Markets Authority, and other relevant advisory bodies and institutions. To decrease compliance costs for listed SMEs, the Commission proposed the development of separate, scaled-down standards for SMEs, which could also be used by non-listed SMEs on a voluntary basis. In addition to standardization, the CSRD also requires digitalization of sustainability reporting to increase its usability in financial markets.

In its technical recommendations for the development of EU sustainability reporting standards, EFRAG specifically emphasized the need for convergence of the many moving parts in the EU sustainable finance framework. In particular, EFRAG noted that EU sustainability reporting standards should be consistent with the Taxonomy Regulation as well as with the Sustainable Finance Disclosure Regulation demands (European Financial Reporting Advisory Group, 2021). This is a sensible approach, since Article 8 of the Taxonomy Regulation specifically requires that all companies under the scope of NFRD (in the future, CSRD) report their taxonomy-aligned economic activities.

To further specify the contents and presentation of taxonomy-based reporting requirements under the NFRD/CSRD, the European Commission adopted the Disclosures Delegated Regulation (2021/2178) on 6 July 2021, which defines several key performance indicators (KPIs) and reporting templates to be used by non-financial and financial companies. Large non-financial companies will have to report three KPIs, namely, the proportion of turnover, capital expenditures (CapEx), and operating expenditures (OpEx), aligned with the EU taxonomy. Additional KPIs are envisaged for financial undertakings. Credit institutions (banks) will be required to disclose a green asset ratio (GAR), which shows the proportion of all taxonomy-aligned on-balance-sheet exposures (loans and advances, debt securities, equities, and repossessed collaterals) relative to total covered assets. Several GAR breakdowns by types of exposure counterparties and activities, environmental objectives, and existing versus new exposures (stock versus flow GAR) are also envisaged. Other financial institutions, including asset managers, investment firms, insurance and reinsurance companies, have their own KPIs, which are either investment-based or service-based and follow a logic similar to GAR. For investments, the KPI is based on the proportion of weighted average value of taxonomy-aligned investments relative to total investments, whereas for services, it is based on the proportion of revenue from taxonomy-aligned services relative to total revenue. As in the case of GAR, several breakdowns of investment-based and service-based KPIs apply.

4.3.2. *Sustainable finance disclosures regulation (SFDR)*

The SFDR complements corporate sustainability disclosures by creating a comprehensive reporting framework specifically for the financial industry, including banks (acting in portfolio management capacity), insurance companies, investment and pension funds, and financial advisory firms. The regulation requires financial market participants and financial advisors to disclose sustainability-related data and policies to their customers at entity and product (service) level following the "double-materiality" approach.

At entity level, financial companies under the scope of the SFDR will have to regularly publish information on their websites about their policies on integration of sustainability risks in the investment decision-making process (the "outside-in" part of double-materiality) and consideration of principle adverse impacts of their investment decisions on sustainability indicators (the "inside-out" part of double-materiality). Additionally, they will also be required to disclose information about the consistency of remuneration and sustainability policies.

At financial product (service) level, a similar double-materiality logic applies. Financial companies will have to disclose information in pre-contractual disclosures about the integration of sustainability risks into investment decisions, including their likely impacts on product returns (the "outside-in" part), and information about product impact on sustainability factors (the "inside-out" part). The SFDR gives specific recognition to financial products with positive externalities on sustainability. Two categories of such products are considered: (1) products that promote environmental or social characteristics (or a combination thereof) and (2) products that have sustainable investment as their objective. For these products, financial companies will have to provide specific information in pre-contractual disclosures, on their websites and in annual reports, about how the product's contribution to sustainability is achieved, including by using designated quantitative measures, such as sustainability indices and benchmarks, where available.

Furthermore, SFDR disclosures were supplemented by the Taxonomy Regulation, which aligned the climate and environmental part of SFDR disclosure requirements at product level with taxonomy-based definitions and compliance criteria. Specifically, financial companies under the scope of the SFDR will have to include information in pre-contractual disclosures and in periodic reports about how and to what extent environmentally sustainable investments underlying their financial products are taxonomy-aligned and to which taxonomy-based environmental objective they contribute. Additionally, they will also have to provide a clear statement about the extent to which environmentally sustainable investments underlying their financial products do not follow taxonomy-based objectives and criteria.

The SFDR mandated the Joint Committee of European Supervisory Authorities (ESAs)[10] to develop regulatory technical standards (RTSs) in order to specify the content, methodologies, and presentation of sustainability disclosures by financial companies. The Joint Committee published the initial draft of seven RTSs on 2 February 2021. The additional SFDR disclosure requirements with respect to climate and environmental objectives, created by the Taxonomy Regulation, required further specifications on how to include this additional information in pre-contractual disclosures. In turn, the Joint Committee amended its initial draft by six additional RTSs to cover taxonomy-aligned disclosures, including compliance with the DNSH principle. The final draft of RTSs was published on 22 October 2021 and aims to streamline reporting requirements to avoid duplication and to establish a single rulebook for sustainability disclosures under the SFDR and the Taxonomy Regulation (Joint Committee of the European Supervisory Authorities, 2021a, b). The European Commission adopted the proposed RTSs as a single delegated act on 6 April 2022. They apply from 1 January 2023.

4.4. *Sustainability tools*

The third building block of the EU sustainable finance framework is a set of investment tools, including financial product benchmarks, standards, and labels. Benchmarks, such as specially constructed indices, are increasingly used by investors as a yardstick to measure performance of investment portfolios and financial products.

[10]The Joint Committee is a cooperation forum between the European Supervisory Authorities (EBA, EIOPA, and ESMA).

In recent years, a wide variety of low-carbon and other green indices with varying degrees of ambition and divergent methodologies have emerged from the financial industry to help align investment strategies with climate and environmental objectives. Such a situation is conducive to information asymmetries and market fragmentation that impede capital flows and may encourage greenwashing. To increase transparency, the EU is developing minimum standards for low-carbon benchmarks. Standardization in turn allows the creation of reliable green labels for products that can be used for marketing purposes.

Two types of low-carbon benchmarks were adopted by the EU: the "EU Climate Transition Benchmark" and the "EU Paris-aligned Benchmark". In order to be labeled as "EU Climate Transition", the benchmark portfolio has to be on a decarbonization trajectory, whereas in order to be labeled "EU Paris-aligned", the benchmark portfolio's carbon emissions have to be aligned with the objectives of the Paris Agreement, which is a stricter condition. On 17 July 2021, the Commission adopted further minimum technical requirements for EU Climate Benchmarks as well as a number of ESG disclosure requirements for benchmark administrators.

In addition to the climate benchmarks, the European Commission is also developing standards for green financial products. The first one in the making is the EU Green Bonds Standards, proposed by the Commission on 6 July 2021. Its aim is to become a gold standard for green bonds that would enable easy access to large-scale financing of climate and environmentally friendly investments to issuers, while protecting investors from greenwashing. The standard is intended to be voluntary and inclusive (open to all EU and non-EU, public and private issuers) and fully compliant with the definitions of climate and environmentally sustainable economic activities according to the EU taxonomy. External reviews of the use of bond proceeds are envisaged in the pre-issuance, mid-life, and post-issuance phases to ensure taxonomy alignment. Furthermore, to encourage green retail lending, the Commission also intends to explore definitions and possible supporting tools for green retail loans and green mortgages in 2022. Finally, the Commission is planning to extend the widely recognized EU Ecolabel to retail financial products with criteria being developed in collaboration with the EU Joint Research Centre.

5. Implications of the EU approach to sustainable finance

The implications of the EU sustainable finance framework for the financial industry are profound. Financial market participants, including banks, insurance companies, pension and investment funds, will have to adjust their strategies and business models to take into account EU sustainable finance regulations as well as the broader transition to sustainability, stemming from the EGD. Given its central relevance to the framework, the EU green taxonomy will become the key standard for climate and environmentally sustainable investment decisions and reporting in the EU in the coming years and will likely have a strong influence on the development of global sustainability reporting standards. In time, it may be complemented by an equivalent EU social taxonomy and an extended EU environmental taxonomy that includes a list of significantly harmful activities. Furthermore, sustainability disclosures at entity, product, and service levels will become mandatory for financial market participants and will have to follow harmonized reporting standards as well as adhere to taxonomy principles in the case of environmental sustainability. When adjusting to these changes, financial market participants will be aided by an increasing stream of reliable (audited) and comparable (standardized) sustainability data and taxonomy-based KPIs, required from both non-financial and financial companies, as well as credible EU standards for sustainability benchmarks, indices, and green financial products.

A sustainable finance framework also has important implications for monetary, financial, and fiscal policies. In its renewed monetary policy strategy, published on 8 July 2021, the ECB noted that implications of climate change and carbon transition will be taken into account in the conduct of monetary policy and central banking. Specifically, the ECB intends to adapt the design of its monetary policy operational framework in relation to disclosures, risk assessment, corporate sector asset purchases, and the collateral framework (European Central Bank, 2021). Although academic merits of central bank environmentalism are uncertain at this point, the EU Treaty provisions allow the ECB to go beyond the primary objective of price stability to address other EU objectives, including environmental, when price stability is not at stake. Beyond monetary policy, financial policy will also be affected. In November 2020, the ECB published a report, which finds that banks are lagging behind significantly on their climate and environmental risk disclosures (European Central Bank, 2020). As a result, the ECB carried out a full supervisory review of banks' practices with respect to climate change risks and conducted climate-related stress tests in 2022. The next step could be to give greater weight to climate-related and environmental risks in bank capital requirements. Finally, the need to find a balance between the sustainable post-pandemic fiscal policies and the necessary public investments in carbon transition also trend highly in the ongoing review of the EU fiscal and economic governance rules. These developments in other policy areas will take account of the EU sustainable finance framework, in particular in relation to taxonomy and disclosures.

The increased stream of quantitative sustainability data based on the EU sustainable finance framework also has important implications for financial research. Based on this data, it will be possible to study relationships between firm-level sustainability characteristics and other firm-, industry-, or economy-level characteristics, such as financial statement variables, asset prices, competitiveness, credit risk or cost, and access to finance. Furthermore, such data would in time also allow to conduct dynamic analyses of the green transition at firm, industry, and economy levels, since an important purpose of the sustainable finance framework is not just to differentiate between sustainability characteristics of firms in the cross-section, but to help them transition to a more sustainable state over time. Aggregated sustainability data based on the EU sustainable finance framework would also enable macroeconomic and systemic analyses as well as cross-country comparisons within the EU. These and other research uses of EU sustainability data that may help to inform decision-makers highlight the need for an open policy of sustainability data sharing for the purposes of academic research.

In the end, while the EU sustainable finance framework is still a work in the making, many of the pieces of the puzzle are now beginning to fit together and we can envisage their further convergence in the future, as outlined in strategic documents. This allows us to paint a bigger picture of the relevance of the framework. First, it is clear that the end goal of the framework is to redirect capital flows to finance the transition to a sustainable, climate-neutral economy. Furthermore, it is now clear that the common EU taxonomy and harmonized disclosure standards are at the core of the sustainable finance strategy and will likely permeate the remaining parts of the framework as well as other policy fields. Finally, it is clear that the EU has broader ambitions with its regulatory approach and is pushing to shape international sustainable finance standards in its own image. What is not clear at this point is how the market dynamics of the application of the framework will play out inside the EU. Transition from traditional to sustainable finance could create significant problems for the financial industry and non-financial enterprises. If not implemented systematically by the relevant actors and monitored carefully by the competent supervisory authorities, it could lead to profitability losses due to increased compliance costs or eventual capital shortfalls due to slow or superficial adjustments of business models and asset devaluations, which could act as preludes to further consolidation of the sector. This highlights the need for all relevant financial and non-financial players to plan and prepare for the expected change brought about by the EU sustainable finance framework.

6. Conclusion

This chapter presented arguments from academic and regulatory perspectives which show that we may be about to witness a fundamental transformation of finance in the EU toward sustainability objectives. While sustainable finance largely followed a market-based, unregulated growth as an attractive industry niche in the past, academic arguments speak in favor of a more regulated and harmonized approach going forward in order to accelerate and broaden the development of sustainable finance and to reduce sustainability-related information asymmetries. These arguments primarily stem from the need to substantially accelerate decarbonization of our societies to mitigate climate change, but also to address other environmental and social objectives, which necessitates massive additional investments into our energy and economic systems for years to come. Public (budgetary) resources will not be sufficient to cover these additional investment needs. Hence, the EU has been building a sustainable finance framework that aims to incentivize private players in the financial industry to redirect capital flows into the green transition.

The EU sustainable finance framework has to be considered in the context of the broader EU green and digital transition strategy, the European Green Deal. It rests upon three interconnected pillars. The first pillar is an EU taxonomy that defines environmentally sustainable economic activities according to science-based criteria. The second one relates to sustainability disclosure regimes for non-financial and financial enterprises aimed at providing a reliable and comparable stream of sustainability data for the financial industry and other stakeholders. The third one consists of a set of sustainability tools, including standards for sustainable financial products and sustainability benchmark indices. The sustainable finance framework is set to fundamentally transform the financial industry and non-financial enterprises in terms of raising the profile of sustainability as a key element of corporate strategic, investment, and financing decisions, which should help to deliver the green transition.

References

Admati, A. R. (2021). Capitalism, laws, and the need for trustworthy institutions. *Oxford Review of Economic Policy*, *37*(4), 678–689.

Ahlström, H. & Monciardini, D. (2021). The regulatory dynamics of sustainable finance: Paradoxical success and limitations of EU reforms. *Journal of Business Ethics*, *177*(1), 193–212. https://link.springer.com/article/10.1007/s10551-021-04763-x#citeas

Alok, S., Kumar, N., & Wermers, R. (2020). Do fund managers misestimate climatic disaster risk. *The Review of Financial Studies*, *33*(3), 1146–1183.

Amel-Zadeh, A. & Serafeim, G. (2018). Why and how investors use ESG information: Evidence from a global survey. *Financial Analysts Journal*, *74*(3), 87–103.

Autor, D., Dorn, D., Katz, L. F., Patterson, C., & Van Reenen, J. (2020). The fall of the labor share and the rise of superstar firms. *The Quarterly Journal of Economics*, *135*(2), 645–709.

Baldauf, M., Garlappi, L., & Yannelis, C. (2020). Does climate change affect real estate prices? Only if you believe in it. *The Review of Financial Studies*, *33*(3), 1256–1295.

Battiston, S., Dafermos, Y., & Monasterolo, I. (2021). Climate risks and financial stability. *Journal of Financial Stability, 54*, 100867.

Battiston, S., Mandel, A., Monasterolo, I., Schütze, F., & Visentin, G. (2017). A climate stress-test of the financial system. *Nature Climate Change, 7*(4), 283–288.

Bengo, I., Boni, L., & Sancino, A. (2022). EU financial regulations and social impact measurement practices: A comprehensive framework on finance for sustainable development. *Corporate Social Responsibility and Environmental Management, 29*(4), 809–819. https://onlinelibrary.wiley.com/doi/full/10.1002/csr.2235

Bernstein, A., Gustafson, M. T., & Lewis, R. (2019). Disaster on the horizon: The price effect of sea level rise. *Journal of Financial Economics, 134*(2), 253–272.

Bourguignon, F. (2015). The globalization of inequality. Princeton: Princeton University Press, 224 pp.

Bracking, S. & Leffel, B. (2021). Climate finance governance: Fit for purpose? *Wiley Interdisciplinary Reviews: Climate Change, 12*(4), e709.

Burke, M., Hsiang, S. M., & Miguel, E. (2015). Global non-linear effect of temperature on economic production. *Nature, 527*(7577), 235–239.

Carney, M. (2015). Breaking the tragedy of the horizon–climate change and financial stability. Speech given by Mark Carney, Governor of the Bank of England and Chairman of the Financial Stability Board at Lloyd's of London on 29 September 2015.

Cash, D. (2018). Sustainable finance ratings as the latest symptom of 'rating addiction'. *Journal of Sustainable Finance & Investment, 8*(3), 242–258.

CDP, CDSB, GRI, IIRC and SASB (2020). Statement of Intent to Work Together Towards Comprehensive Corporate Reporting. Summary of alignment discussions among leading sustainability and integrated reporting organisations CDP, CDSB, GRI, IIRC and SASB. https://29kjwb3armds2g3gi4lq2sx1-wpengine.netdna-ssl.com/wp-content/uploads/Statement-of-Intent-to-Work-Together-Towards-Comprehensive-Corporate-Reporting.pdf.

Choi, D., Gao, Z., & Jiang, W. (2020). Attention to global warming. *The Review of Financial Studies, 33*(3), 1112–1145.

Claessens, S., Coleman, N., & Donnelly, M. (2018). "Low-For-Long" interest rates and banks' interest margins and profitability: Cross-country evidence. *Journal of Financial Intermediation, 35*, 1–16.

Consolandi, C., Jaiswal-Dale, A., Poggiani, E., & Vercelli, A. (2009). Global standards and ethical stock indexes: The case of the Dow Jones Sustainability Stoxx Index. *Journal of Business Ethics, 87*(1), 185–197.

Delegated Regulation (EU) 2021/2139. Establishing the technical screening criteria for determining the conditions under which an economic activity qualifies as contributing substantially to climate change mitigation or climate change adaptation and for determining whether that economic activity causes no significant harm to any of the other environmental objectives. European Commission. https://eur-lex.europa.eu/legal-content/EN/TXT/?uri=CELEX%3A32021R2139.

Delegated Regulation (EU) (2021/2178). Specifying the content and presentation of information to be disclosed by undertakings concerning environmentally sustainable economic activities, and specifying the methodology to comply with that disclosure obligation. European Commission. https://eur-lex.europa.eu/legal-content/EN/TXT/?uri=uriserv:OJ.L_.2021.443.01.0009.01.ENG.

Delis, M. D., De Greiff, K., & Ongena, S. (2019). Being stranded with fossil fuel reserves? Climate policy risk and the pricing of bank loans. Climate Policy Risk and the Pricing of Bank loans (September 10, 2019). EBRD Working Paper (231).

Deloitte (2020). Sustainable Finance Disclosure Regulation: Is the financial industry ready for the Big One, An international overview. https://www2.deloitte.com/content/dam/Deloitte/lu/Documents/sustainable-dev/lu-sustainable-finance-disclosure-regulation.pdf.

Dietz, S., Bowen, A., Dixon, C., & Gradwell, P. (2016). 'Climate value at risk' of global financial assets. *Nature Climate Change*, *6*(7), 676–679.

Directive (EU) 2018/410. To enhance cost-effective emission reductions and low-carbon investments. European Parliament, Council of the EU. https://eur-lex.europa.eu/legal-content/EN/TXT/?uri=celex%3A32018L0410.

Directive 2003/87/EC. Consolidated text: Establishing a scheme for greenhouse gas emission allowance trading within the Community. European Parliament, Council of the EU. https://eur-lex.europa.eu/legal-content/EN/TXT/?uri=CELEX%3A02003L0087-20210101.

Directive 2014/95/EU. Disclosure of non-financial and diversity information by certain large undertakings and groups. European Parliament, Council of the EU. https://eur-lex.europa.eu/legal-content/EN/TXT/?uri=CELEX%3A32014L0095.

European Banking Federation and UNEP Finance Initiative (2022). Practical approaches to applying the EU Taxonomy to bank lending.

European Central Bank (2020). ECB report on institutions' climate-related and environmental risk disclosures. Frankfurt am Main, November 2020. https://www.bankingsupervision.europa.eu/ecb/pub/pdf/ssm.ecbreportinstitutionsclimaterelatedenvironmentalriskdisclosures202011~e8e2ad20f6.en.pdf.

European Central Bank (2021). An overview of the ECB's monetary policy strategy. Frankfurt am Main, July 2021. https://www.ecb.europa.

eu/home/search/review/pdf/ecb.strategyreview_monpol_strategy_overview.en.pdf.

European Commission (2018). Action Plan: Financing Sustainable Growth. COM(2018) 97 final. Brussels, 8.3.2018. https://eur-lex.europa.eu/legal-content/EN/TXT/?uri=CELEX:52018DC0097.

European Commission (2019). The European Green Deal. COM(2019) 640 final. Brussels, 11.12.2019. https://eur-lex.europa.eu/legal-content/EN/TXT/?qid=1576150542719&uri=COM%3A2019%3A640%3AFIN.

European Commission (2020a). Impact assessment accompanying the document stepping up Europe's 2030 climate ambition, investing in a climate-neutral future for the benefit of our people. SWD(2020) 176 final. Brussels, 17.9.2020. https://eur-lex.europa.eu/legal-content/EN/TXT/?uri=CELEX%3A52020SC0176.

European Commission (2020b). Sustainable Europe Investment Plan (European Green Deal Investment Plan). COM(2020) 21 final. Brussels, 14.1.2020. https://eur-lex.europa.eu/legal-content/EN/TXT/?uri=CELEX%3A52020DC0021.

European Commission (2020c). Identifying Europe's recovery needs. SWD(2020) 98 final. Brussels, 27.5.2020. https://eur-lex.europa.eu/legal-content/EN/TXT/?uri=SWD:2020:98:FIN.

European Commission (2021a). Impact Assessment Report Accompanying the Proposal for a Directive as regards the promotion of energy from renewable sources. SWD(2021) 621 final. Brussels, 14.7.2021. https://eur-lex.europa.eu/legal-content/EN/ALL/?uri=SWD:2021:621:FIN.

European Commission (2021b). 'Fit for 55': delivering the EU's 2030 Climate Target on the way to climate neutrality. COM(2021) 550 final. Brussels, 14.7.2021. https://eur-lex.europa.eu/legal-content/EN/TXT/?uri=CELEX:52021DC0550.

European Commission (2021c). Forging a climate-resilient Europe — the new EU Strategy on Adaptation to Climate Change. COM(2021) 82 final. Brussels, 24.2.2021. https://eur-lex.europa.eu/legal-content/EN/TXT/?uri=COM:2021:82:FIN.

European Commission (2021d). The EU's 2021–2027 long-term Budget and NextGenerationEU, facts and figures. Luxembourg: Publications Office of the European Union. 73 p.

European Commission (2021e). Strategy for financing the transition to a sustainable economy. COM(2021) 390 final. Strasbourg, 6.7.2021. https://eur-lex.europa.eu/legal-content/EN/TXT/?uri=CELEX:52021DC0390.

European Commission (2022a). A European Green Deal (website). https://ec.europa.eu/info/strategy/priorities-2019-2024/european-green-deal_en.

European Commission (2022b). Draft General Budget of the European Union, Working Document Part I, Programme Statements of operational expenditure. Luxembourg: Publications Office of the European Union, 2021. 1349 pp.

European Environmental Agency (2022). EEA greenhouse gases — Data viewer. Data and maps. https://www.eea.europa.eu/data-and-maps/data/data-viewers/greenhouse-gases-viewer.

European Financial Reporting Advisory Group (2021). Proposals for a relevant and dynamic EU sustainability reporting. Brussels, 19.2.2021. https://www.efrag.org/Assets/Download?assetUrl=%2Fsites%2Fwebpublishing%2FSiteAssets%2FEFRAG%2520PTF-NFRS_MAIN_REPORT.pdf.

European Investment Bank (2020). EIB Group climate bank roadmap 2021-2025. European Investment Bank. https://data.europa.eu/doi/10.2867/503343.

European Investment Bank (2022). Climate Awareness Bonds. https://www.eib.org/en/investor-relations/cab/index.htm.

Frischmann, B. M., Marciano, A., & Ramello, G. B. (2019). Retrospectives: Tragedy of the commons after 50 years. *Journal of Economic Perspectives*, *33*(4), 211–228.

Furton, G. & Martin, A. (2019). Beyond market failure and government failure. *Public Choice*, *178*(1), 197–216.

Gabor, D. (2021). The wall street consensus. *Development and Change*, *52*(3), 429–459.

Gadenne, D. L., Kennedy, J., & McKeiver, C. (2009). An empirical study of environmental awareness and practices in SMEs. *Journal of Business Ethics*, *84*(1), 45–63.

Giglio, S., Kelly, B., & Stroebel, J. (2021). Climate finance. *Annual Review of Financial Economics*, *13*, 15–36.

Goldstein, A., Turner, W. R., Gladstone, J., & Hole, D. G. (2019). The private sector's climate change risk and adaptation blind spots. *Nature Climate Change*, *9*(1), 18–25.

Hardin, G. (1968). The tragedy of the commons: The population problem has no technical solution; it requires a fundamental extension in morality. *Science*, *162*(3859), 1243–1248.

Hockerts, K. (2015). A cognitive perspective on the business case for corporate sustainability. *Business Strategy and the Environment*, *24*(2), 102–122.

IFRS (2022). IFRS Foundation and GRI to align capital market and multi-stakeholder standards to create an interconnected approach for sustainability disclosures. https://www.ifrs.org/news-and-events/news/2022/03/ifrs-foundation-signs-agreement-with-gri/.

Intergovernmental Panel on Climate Change (2021). Climate Change 2021. The Physical Science Basis. Summary for Policy Makers. Working Group I contribution to the Sixth Assessment Report of the Intergovernmental Panel on Climate Change. https://www.ipcc.ch/report/ar6/wg1/downloads/report/IPCC_AR6_WGI_SPM_final.pdf.

Intergovernmental Panel on Climate Change (IPCC, 2022a). Climate Change 2022. Impacts, Adaptation and Vulnerability. Summary for Policy Makers. Working Group II contribution to the Sixth Assessment Report of the Intergovernmental Panel on Climate Change. https://report.ipcc.ch/ar6wg2/pdf/IPCC_AR6_WGII_SummaryForPolicymakers.pdf.

Intergovernmental Panel on Climate Change (IPCC, 2022b). Climate Change 2022. Mitigation of Climate Change. Summary for Policy Makers. Working Group III contribution to the Sixth Assessment Report of the Intergovernmental Panel on Climate Change. https://report.ipcc.ch/ar6wg3/pdf/IPCC_AR6_WGIII_SummaryForPolicymakers.pdf.

Islam, N. & Winkel, J. (2017). Climate change and social inequality. DESA Working Paper No. 152. United Nations, New York, October 2017. https://www.un.org/esa/desa/papers/2017/wp152_2017.pdf.

Joint Committee of the European Supervisory Authorities (2021a). Final Report on Draft Regulatory Technical Standards. JC 2021 03. 2.2.2021. https://www.esma.europa.eu/sites/default/files/library/jc_2021_03_joint_esas_final_report_on_rts_under_sfdr.pdf.

Joint Committee of the European Supervisory Authorities (2021b). Final Report on Draft Regulatory Technical Standards. JC 2021 50. 22.10.2021. https://www.esma.europa.eu/sites/default/files/library/jc_2021_50_-_final_report_on_taxonomy-related_product_disclosure_rts.pdf.

Jung, J., Herbohn, K., & Clarkson, P. (2018). Carbon risk, carbon risk awareness and the cost of debt financing. *Journal of Business Ethics, 150*(4), 1151–1171.

Kishan, S. (2022). ESG Pioneer Expects Shakeout for Funds Hyped by 'Fairy Dust'. Bloomberg. https://www.bloomberg.com/news/articles/2022-03-20/esg-pioneer-warns-funds-hyped-by-fairy-dust.

Krueger, P., Sautner, Z., and Starks, L. T. (2020). The importance of climate risks for institutional investors. *The Review of Financial Studies, 33*(3), 1067–1111.

Lade, S. J., Steffen, W., De Vries, W., Carpenter, S. R., Donges, J. F., Gerten, D., ... & Rockström, J. (2020). Human impacts on planetary boundaries amplified by Earth system interactions. *Nature Sustainability, 3*(2), 119–128.

Liu, Z., Deng, Z., Davis, S. J., Giron, C., & Ciais, P. (2022). Monitoring global carbon emissions in 2021. *Nature Reviews Earth & Environment, 3*(4), 217–219. https://www.nature.com/articles/s43017-022-00285-w#citeas.

Lockwood, M. (2018). Right-wing populism and the climate change agenda: Exploring the linkages. *Environmental Politics, 27*(4), 712–732.

Milanovic, B. (2016). *Global Inequality: A New Approach for the Age of Globalization.* Cambridge, MA: Harvard University Press, 299 p. Global inequality. In *Global Inequality.* Harvard University Press.

Mori, K. & Christodoulou, A. (2012). Review of sustainability indices and indicators: Towards a new City Sustainability Index (CSI). *Environmental Impact Assessment Review, 32*(1), 94–106.

Nolan, B., Richiardi, M. G., & Valenzuela, L. (2019). The drivers of income inequality in rich countries. *Journal of Economic Surveys, 33*(4), 1285–1324.

OECD (2011). OECD Guidelines for Multinational Enterprises. OECD Publishing. http://dx.doi.org/10.1787/9789264115415-en.

Ostrom, E. (2010). Beyond markets and states: Polycentric governance of complex economic systems. *American Economic Review, 100*(3), 641–672.

Pástor, L'. & Veronesi, P. (2021). Inequality aversion, populism, and the backlash against globalization. *The Journal of Finance, 76*(6), 2857–2906.

Persson, L., Carney Almroth, B. M., Collins, C. D., Cornell, S., de Wit, C. A., Diamond, M. L., & Hauschild, M. Z. (2022). Outside the Safe Operating Space of the Planetary Boundary for Novel Entities. *Environmental Science & Technology, 56*(3), 1510–1521. https://pubs.acs.org/doi/full/10.1021/acs.est.1c04158.

Platform on Sustainable Finance (2022a). Final Report on Social Taxonomy. February 2022.

Platform on Sustainable Finance (2022b). The Extended Environmental Taxonomy: Final Report on Taxonomy extension options supporting a sustainable transition. March 2022.

Rant, V. (2021). EU sustainable finance framework in the context of the European Green Deal. *The Journal for Money and Banking, 70*(11), 24–34.

Ravallion, M. (2018). Inequality and globalization: A review essay. *Journal of Economic Literature, 56*(2), 620–642.

Regulation (EU) (2018/841). Inclusion of greenhouse gas emissions and removals from land use, land use change and forestry in the 2030 climate and energy framework. European Parliament, Council of the EU. https://eur-lex.europa.eu/legal-content/EN/TXT/?uri=CELEX%3A32018R0841.

Regulation (EU) (2018/842). Binding annual greenhouse gas emission reductions by Member States from 2021 to 2030 contributing to climate action to meet commitments under the Paris Agreement. European Parliament, Council of the EU. https://eur-lex.europa.eu/legal-content/EN/TXT/?uri=celex%3A32018R0842.

Regulation (EU) (2019/2088). Sustainability-related disclosures in the financial services sector. European Parliament, Council of the EU. https://eur-lex.europa.eu/legal-content/EN/TXT/?uri=celex%3A32019R2088.

Regulation (EU) (2020/852). The establishment of a framework to facilitate sustainable investment. European Parliament, Council of the EU. https://eur-lex.europa.eu/legal-content/EN/TXT/?uri=CELEX:32020R0852.

Regulation (EU) (2021/1119). Establishing the framework for achieving climate neutrality (European Climate Law). European Parliament, Council of the EU. https://eur-lex.europa.eu/legal-content/EN/TXT/?uri=CELEX:32021R1119.

Richards, C. E., Lupton, R. C., & Allwood, J. M. (2021). Re-framing the threat of global warming: An empirical causal loop diagram of climate change, food insecurity and societal collapse. *Climatic Change*, *164*(3), 1–19.

Rockström, J., Steffen, W., Noone, K., Persson, Å., Chapin III, F. S., Lambin, E., ... & Foley, J. (2009a). Planetary boundaries: Exploring the safe operating space for humanity. *Ecology and Society*, *14*(2), 32.

Rockström, J., Steffen, W., Noone, K., Persson, Å., Chapin, F. S., Lambin, E. F., ... and Foley, J. A. (2009b). A safe operating space for humanity. *Nature*, *461*(7263), 472–475.

Rogge, E. & Ohnesorge, L. (2021). Europe's green policy: Towards a climate neutral economy by way of investors' choice. *European Company Law*, *18*(1), 34–39.

Sanderson, H., Irato, D. M., Cerezo, N. P., Duel, H., Faria, P., & Torres, E. F. (2019). How do climate risks affect corporations and how could they address these risks? *SN Applied Sciences*, *1*(12), 1–6.

Schoenmaker, D. (2017). *Investing for the Common Good: A Sustainable Finance Framework*. Brussels: Bruegel.

Schoenmaker, D. & Schramade, W. (2018). *Principles of Sustainable Finance*. New York: Oxford University Press.

Steffen, W., Richardson, K., Rockström, J., Cornell, S. E., Fetzer, I., Bennett, E. M., ... and Sörlin, S. (2015). Planetary boundaries: Guiding human development on a changing planet. *Science*, 347(6223), 1259855.

Stroebel, J. & Wurgler, J. (2021). What do you think about climate finance? *Journal of Financial Economics, 142*(2), 487–498.

Stulz, R. M. (2019). Fintech, bigtech, and the future of banks. *Journal of Applied Corporate Finance, 31*(4), 86–97.

Tan, C. (2022). Private investments, public goods: Regulating markets for sustainable development. *European Business Organization Law Review, 23*(1), 241–271. https://link.springer.com/article/10.1007/s40804-021-00236-w#citeas.

Toole, M. (2022). Sustainable finance continues surge in 2021. Refinitiv. https://www.refinitiv.com/perspectives/market-insights/sustainable-finance-continues-surge-in-2021/.

Troeger, T. H. and Steuer, S. (2021). The Role of Disclosure in Green Finance. European Corporate Governance Institute-Law Working Paper (604).

United Nations (2011). Guiding Principles on Business and Human Rights. United Nations, New York and Geneva. https://doi.org/10.18356/9ceabfd3-en.

United Nations (2015a). Transforming our world: The 2030 Agenda for Sustainable Development. https://www.un.org/ga/search/view_doc.asp?symbol=A/RES/70/1&Lang=E.

United Nations (2015b). Paris Agreement. https://unfccc.int/sites/default/files/english_paris_agreement.pdf.

Van Reenen, J. (2018). Increasing differences between firms: Market power and the macro-economy. CEP Discussion Papers dp1576. Centre for Economic Performance, LSE.

Venturini, A. (2022). Climate change, risk factors and stock returns: A review of the literature. *International Review of Financial Analysis*, 79, 101934.

World Bank (2018). From Evolution to Revolution: 10 Years of Green Bonds. https://www.worldbank.org/en/events/2018/11/16/from-evolution-to-revolution-10-years-of-green-bonds.

© 2024 World Scientific Publishing Europe Ltd.
https://doi.org/10.1142/9781800614451_0013

Chapter 13

Development of Sustainable Finance in the European Union: The Role of Public Policy

Anastasiya Luzgina

Belarusian Economic Research and Outreach Center (BEROC), Vilnius, Lithuania

luzgina0330@gmail.com

Abstract

The chapter describes the role of public policy on sustainable finance in the European Union (EU). Based on working and legislative documents, key aspects of public decision-making on sustainable finance development at the supranational level are analyzed. The research reveals incentives and legislative conditions for the development of green finance in the European context and concerns some aspects of national policies in the area. Special attention is paid to climate and environmental risks faced by banks. The chapter concludes by presenting the main results and recommendations in the sphere.

1. Introduction

Climate change and natural disasters create new challenges and obstacles for economic development. On the one hand, business should consider possible green risks. On the other, companies need to build new business processes in accordance with the goals of sustainable development. The financial sector is one of the main drivers of green development. Banks, investment companies, and other financial institutions determine which projects will be financed and under what conditions. But the introduction of new tools, evaluation methods, and green risk management require clear rules and legislation. Public policy plays a crucial role in green finance market development. As it is a new sphere for regulation, the development of absolutely new approaches and regulations are required. The European Union (EU) is one of the leaders in the process. But the creation of an effective legislative base is not an easy thing. The development of a sustainable finance market involves coordinated work by national and supranational authorities as well as calls for unified regulation adoption.

The chapter is based on the analysis of EU regulatory documents, discussion papers, plans, and strategies in the sustainable finance sphere. Among them are the European Commission (EC) Action Plan on Financing Sustainable Growth, Taxonomy Regulation for Sustainable activities, Proposal of European Green Bonds Standards, Sustainable Finance Disclosure Regulation, European Banking Authority (EBA) Action Plan on Sustainable finance, European Central Bank (ECB) Guide on climate-related and environmental risks, etc. The work also draws on documents describing green finance initiatives at the national level, including the Lithuanian Strategy and Action Plan on Sustainable Finance and the Riksbank's Climate Report. The research analyzes key issues of the German Sustainable Finance Strategy and examines the role of commercial banks in creating a green environment on the basis of German state-owned KfW Bank's official information and Pricewaterhouse Coopers' (PwC) survey on Green Finance in Poland.

The goal of the chapter is to explain the evolution of the green finance regulatory environment in the EU. Based on the documentation, official information, and surveys, the research highlights challenges and future activities in this direction. As green issues are a part of sustainable finance regulation, it is impossible to overview green aspects separately from other sustainable elements, such as social and governance issues. So, the chapter explains public policy in sustainable finance with a focus on green issues. The work helps to understand the logic and main aspects of the regulatory environment as well as its importance for sustainable financial markets.

In the first part of the chapter, main issues related to EC, EBA, and other EU policies on sustainable finance are described. This part analyzes more general documents, such as the EU Taxonomy, Action Plan on Financing Sustainable Growth, and the Green Deal, which became the basis for more specialized issues. The author shows the multifaceted nature of state decisions, their logic, and expected results. The second part of the chapter contains the ECB green policy with a detailed analysis of the central bank's actions regarding the regulation of environmental and climate-related risks. For a better understanding of the opportunities for the development of green finance at the national level, the third part of the chapter describes EU countries' initiations in the sphere of sustainable finance. The conclusion focuses on the main findings of the research and presents some recommendations for the further development of green/sustainable finance public policy.

2. EU public policy on sustainable finance

Green finance, as a part of a sustainable finance, has become one of the main drivers of a sustainable economy. European countries increasingly make significant efforts in this direction. The first steps were taken in 2015 when the United Nations (UN) *Agenda for Sustainable Development* was adopted, and the Paris Agreement on climate change was signed. Since that time the EU has started to build their economic policies in line with green goals. In March 2018, the *EC* published the *Action Plan on Financing Sustainable Growth (Action Plan).* The document became the basis of sustainable finance development and served as a guide for other EU authorities' policies in the field. The EC Action Plan includes areas of activities that are implemented by the EC and other European Union official bodies. Among them are the following: EU Taxonomy development; green bonds standards and green labeling for financial instruments' adoption; enhancement of green investments' popularity; development of methodologies that allow to incorporate green risks into the regulator's assessment; sustainable activities and green risks disclosure; consideration of sustainable aspects in consulting services, provided by financial intermediaries for their clients; sustainable factors' inclusion in ratings; unification and harmonization of climate transition; and Paris Agreement aligned benchmarks on the EU level and others (EC, 2020a). The document consists of three main parts.

The first part describes the EU Taxonomy, which is a system for classifying sustainable activities. The second part is devoted to information disclosure. Financial and non-financial companies should publish data on their ecological and social impact. Sustainability information is necessary for investors who are interested in green and social projects and want to make investment decisions on the basis of full true database. The last part of the Action Plan describes green standards and green labels' implementation. Investments in sustainable projects will be more effective if common rules and criteria of sustainable financial instruments are used, such as for green bonds, climate-related bonds, green mortgages, etc. Therefore, the Action Plan is one of the EU documents that aims to push investments in sustainable projects, create the basis of green financial risks management, and increase the importance of sustainable, including green, finance (EC, 2018).

One of the core sections of the Action Plan was devoted *to Sustainable Finance Disclosure regulation (SFDR)*. The Document was developed at the end of November 2019 (published on 9 of December 2019) and came into force in March 2021 (some articles became effective from December 2019, and Article 11(1) to (3), from the beginning of 2022) (European Parliament and the Council, 2019). The goal of the document is the development of sustainable investments by green- and social-related information disclosure as well as preventing greenwashing. Participants of the financial market will be obliged to publish several compulsory indicators, some optional indicators, the description of principal adverse sustainability impact assessment policy, and other information in the *Adverse Sustainability Impact Statement (ASIS)* (BIQH SFDR Team, 2021).

In April 2022, the European Commission adopted the final version of *Regulatory Technical Standards (RTS)*, which is intended for SFDR, and Taxonomy principals used in practice. RTS is a joint work of *European Banking Authority (EBA)*, *European Security and Market Authority (ESMA)*, and *European Insurance and Occupational Pensions Authority (EIOPA)*. The document describes the process of environmental, social, and governance (ESG) data disclosure on entity and product levels. On the entity level, companies will publish ASISs, which show principal adverse impacts on sustainable parameters. On the product level, financial entities will present information on sustainable-related products, their goals, and characteristics, results of using, and methodologies of assessment (EIOPA, 2021).

Considering that the RTS will come into force from January 2023, companies should publish ASISs with different parameters and explanations for 2022 no later than by the end of June 2023 (Lovells, 2022). The regulatory framework is aimed toward sustainable information disclosure by EU financial institutions such as banks, investment funds, insurance companies, pension funds, credit institutions, and other financial market participants.

In December 2019, the *European Green Deal* was adopted. As per the document, EU countries will strive to reach zero net greenhouse gas emissions by 2050, develop energy efficient buildings, support environmental protection, introduce high ecological standards, etc. Among numerous spheres of activities in the framework of the Green Deal, one of them is related to finance (EBA, 2021).

In the framework of the development of the sustainable finance sphere, the *European Green Deal Investment Plan* was published in January 2020. It is expected to spend around 1 trillion EURO for a decade on different sustainable projects. As follows from the document, *Just Transition Mechanism* was introduced. This tool is necessary for mitigation of negative socio-economic consequences in the period of transition to a sustainable economy for regions that depend on mining industries (EC, 2020a). For example, thousands of workers from such countries like Poland, Bulgaria, Germany, and Spain will lose their jobs because of coal mining reduction in coming years (World Resources Institute, 2021). At the same time, possible prohibition, or restrictions, to buy Russian natural resources could slow down the process of coal production reduction in Europe. This may have a negative effect on the environment but will limit social tensions.

In June 2020, the special *Regulation on green/climate-related taxonomy* was published. The aim of the document is classification development of sustainable activities, which will support direct financial flows into sustainable projects (it came into force in July 2020). The document uses the definition of "sustainable finance", but it is about green finance mostly. In particular, the document describes the main principals, criteria of climate change mitigation, and other green activities, requirements for sustainable financial products, and covers such areas as climate change accommodation, climate change prevention, circular economy development, biodiversity and water resources protection as well as describes environmentally destructive activities. Gradually, the EU social and governmental taxonomy will be developed. To improve the quality and expand the taxonomy process, a special *Platform on sustainable finance in EU* has been created. It presents the pool of experts who consult the Commission on possible changes/development of the EU Taxonomy and monitor capital flows to sustainable projects, based on the analysis of current trends and stakeholders' requests. The first meeting of the Platform was organized in the middle of October 2020. Although the current Taxonomy focuses primarily on "green" issues, the participants of the Platform are responsible for advising of taxonomy development in social spheres as well. For example, in February 2022 the Platform published the *Final Report on Social Taxonomy* (Platform on sustainable finance).

In October 2022 the Platform published a report on the results of observations of Taxonomy reporting by financial and non-financial entities. The report also keep the regulatory framework and recommendations (April 2022, PSF Oct. 2022).

In July 2021, the European Commission presented the new *Strategy for Financing the Transition to a Sustainable Economy (SFTSE)* (EC, 2021a). The document was based on the *Action Plan on Financing Sustainable Growth (2018)*, Feedback of the *Consultation on the Renewed Sustainable Finance Strategy (2020)* (EC, 2020c), and *Transition Finance Report of the Platform on Sustainable Finance* (Transition Finance Report, 2021). The SFTSE has six main areas of activity.

The first set of actions is related to the expansion of financing opportunities for building a sustainable economy. They include possible adoption of legal acts to stimulate financial injections into certain areas, which are important for sustainable development, including financing of energy projects. For example, the projects can be directed to greenhouse gas emissions reduction. The Commission also proposes widening the number of economically sustainable activities within EU Taxonomy by adding such areas like nuclear energy and agriculture. Finally, this block of measures includes the special green labels and rules for the development of sustainable financial instruments.

The second set of actions is devoted to *inclusiveness*. This topic covers methodology improvement of green expenditures' trackability and national governments' support from EU funds in the event that EU members would like to spend more resources on green goals.

One of the measures in the sphere of inclusiveness is related to green mortgages and loans. According to SFTSE, it is necessary to increase the access to financial green instruments among small entrepreneurs and the population. Also, the EC is going to ask the European Banking Authority to develop definitions of "green" financial instruments, enhance their popularity as well as improve the insurance cover for climate-related and environmental risks.

The third group of actions concerns the inclusion of sustainable risks in international reporting, credit ratings, and risk management of financial institutions. The European Commission considers that sustainable risks should be taken into account in the reporting forms of such organizations as the European Security and Market Authority, International Accounting Standards Board, and others. In collaboration with other European authorities, the EC will work on further identifying and minimizing sustainable risks at the system level. Moreover, rating agencies should integrate sustainability indicators in their methodology of credit assessment and reports on a transparent basis. Banks and financial institutions will be required to continue the implementation of solutions to environmental and climate-related risks in risk management.

The fourth group of actions is concentrated on *environmental, social, and governance (ESG)* information disclosure and increasing the quality of sustainable ratings. Large companies will have to publish sustainability-related information that covers the whole value chain process in the finance sphere. This data will help financial institutions get the necessary information for further sustainable transformation. The EC will also work on open database creation, which will be free to access and include sustainable aspects of companies' activities. Such information is important for investors who are interested in green and social sustainable projects. At the same time, banks and other financial institutions will be required to publish green social goals and strategies, as well as their efforts to transition to sustainable principals of work.

The fifth set of actions is directed to prevent greenwashing risks and cooperating within EU for the development of sustainable investments. The European Commission advocates for cooperation between authorities of member states, the European Central Bank, and financial supervisors for better understanding of the process of sustainable development in the financial sector, as well as successful achievement of green goals. Finally, the EC plans to organize a Sustainable Finance Research Forum. It will be a place for sharing knowledge on ESG aspects and will engage the academic and the expert community in the process of sustainable finance market development.

The sixth group of measures is devoted to international cooperation. The EC suggests an international sustainable finance structure creation with the standardized rules of work, new approaches in regulation, and monitoring. The Commission, together with partners from other countries, works on unified rules and instruments in the sustainable finance sphere as well as discusses green and social issues in the finance sector on international platforms and forums. For example, in 2019 the *International Platform of Sustainable Development* was created. Within its work, new taxonomies, sustainable instruments, and methods of information disclosure by financial entities are defined. Finally, the Commission will work to support low- and middle-income countries in attracting investments in sustainability-based projects.

As a part of the EU sustainable policy Proposal for a Regulation of the European Parliament and of the Council on European Union, *Green Bonds Standards (GBS)* were published in July 2021 (EC, 2021b). The standards are not mandatory. The document is aimed at increasing the quality of financial instruments in the European financial market as well as creating understandable and unified requirements for green and other types of sustainable bonds' emission and circulation. According to the document, sustainable debt securities can be issued by residents and nonresidents of the EU. Projects under which green bonds are issued should comply with the EU Taxonomy, be evaluated by independent experts that are registered with the *International Securities Market Authorities (ISMA*[1]*)* (EC, 2021c, 2021d). Possibly, after the final approval of the GBS, the regulation will become mandatory. The idea of mandatory regulation is not supported by the International Capital Market Association as it can lead to market fragmentation and capital outflow to less regulated jurisdictions (Geddes *et al.*, 2022). At the same time, understandable

[1]The Association adopted green bonds principals, which were taken as the basis for the European Green Bonds Principals.

requirements will create a uniform environment for further European financial market development.

The set of documents that were adopted by the European Commission and by other EU authorities in the sustainable finance sphere form a basis for further sustainable/green banking development. The *European Banking Authority (EBA)* is one of the main supervisory bodies in the EU finance system. The regulator pays much attention to sustainable finance and green risk mitigation. Several important steps have been taken in the sphere of ESG risk management and new regulation development in this area. For example, the *EBA Action Plan on Sustainable Finance* was published in December 2019. The document overviews the EBA's plans on working with ESG factors and risks. The EBA's activities under the plan include such areas as ESG information disclosure, regulation of ESG risks management, development of definitions of risks, and assessment methodologies. The whole process of the development of a sustainable financial environment should take about 6 years (from Q4 2019 till June 2025) (EBA, 2019).

One of the important steps of the EBA Action Plan was the publishing of the *Discussion Paper on Management and Supervision of ESG Risks for Credit Institutions and Investment Firms* (published in October 2020). The document includes ESG risk definitions, as well as definitions of risk appetite and describes how green and social factors give rise to ESG risks that influence the traditional financial risks (credit risk, operational risk, others). The EBA overviews several methods of ESG risk assessment and suggests incorporating the ESG factors into business strategies, risk management, and internal government. The discussion paper identifies several types of ESG risks. All ESG risks can be classified into *physical and transition environmental (green) risks, social risks, and governance risks.* The main issues of green risks are described in the ECB's "Guide on climate-related and environmental risks" (the Guide) (see in Paragraph 3). In many cases, green and social risks are interrelated. For example, changes in environmental policy can influence unemployment rate as new restrictions and tighter standards encourage the closure of hazardous industries, or worsen their financial results. At the same time, governance risks of financial institutions can be realized as a negative impact of the partners' activities/policies (because of bad reputation, avoiding the introduction of energy-efficient operating principles, etc.) on banks' financial results (EBA, 2020).

The main goal of the Discussion paper is receiving feedback from financial institutions on EBA suggestions. Based on the public discussions, the EBA Action Plan, and the EBA work in the sustainable finance segment, the Report on management and supervision of ESG risks for credit institutions and investment firms was published in June 2021. The Report includes such topics as sustainable factors and sustainable risk definitions; evaluation of sustainable risks' influence on financial institutions' work; green and social risks' management based on business strategies, stress testing, and risk scenarios; links between sustainable and traditional financial risks, etc. The report has a lot of recommendations for banks and national authorities on sustainable risks assessment. At the same time, sustainable risk management has not been included in Guidelines for common procedures and methodologies for the *Supervisory Review and Evaluation Process (SREP)*, *Investment Firms Directive (IFD)*, and *Capital Requirement Directive (CRD)* yet. Nevertheless, mandatory disclosure requirements and green risk regulation will become a norm in banking regulation in the near future (Loyens and Loeff, 2021).

In this regard, a key EBA document on ESG risks information disclosure is *Final Draft Implementing Technical Standards on Prudential Disclosure on ESG risks*, which was adopted in January 2022 (EBA, 2022). The document presents mandatory requirements for financial institutions on disclosure of sustainable risks and activities. The technical standards include a set of templates, tables with qualitative parameters of climate-related risks' assessment, business strategy, and risk management characteristics, as well as quantitative indicators of institutions' activities for client support to reach carbon neutrality and adopt climate change. The document also contains special *key performance indicators* (KPIs) for analysis of financial institutions' sustainable results of work, including *Green Asset Ratio (GAR)* and *Banking Book Taxonomy Alignment Ratio (BTAR)*. *GAR* refers to the share of green assets in banks' total assets. Sustainability reports should include information on loans, advances, securities, and other financial tools and can be disaggregated by environmental goals, clients, types of activities as well as present cumulative level of GAR. At the same time, BTAR refers to bank's contribution to achievement of European sustainable goals. According to the document, all large institutions issuing securities on the EU regulated market should publish ESG risk reports. For example, this provision has become mandatory for Deutsche Bank, UniCredit Bank, and other large banks (Huw Jones, 2022).

First reports for 2022 will be published at the beginning of 2023. At the same time, there is a transition period for some items (see Table 1). For example, GAR indicators will be disclosed from the beginning of 2024 and BTAR information will be available from the middle of June 2024 (EBA, 2022). Banks need some transition period for gathering necessary information and calculating KPIs.

Technical standards of EBA were developed considering *EU Taxonomy Article 8 delegated act (disclosures delegated act)*. The main goals of the act are information disclosure on sustainable activities and instruments by financial and non-financial large companies, as well as prevention of greenwashing risks in the market. In addition to *GAR*-indicator, the document also includes the following KPIs:

FinGar (green ratio of financial guarantees) — The share of financial guarantees supporting debt instruments on projects that meet the requirements of the taxonomy in total financial guarantees supporting debt instruments.

AuM (green ratio of assets under management) — The share of assets under management that meet the requirements of the taxonomy for all assets under management.

F&C (fees and commission income) — The share of commission and fees for banking services, other than credit fees, that meet the requirements of the taxonomy in total amount of bank's fees and commission, other than credit fees (EC, 2021e).

According to EU policy, taxonomy standards should be harmonized not only with EBA Technical Standards and SDFR but with Green Bonds Standards, Ecolabel for financial products, and other legislative acts and requirements as well (EC, 2021f). Consistency in the field of sustainable development will allow the construction of a harmonious regulatory environment in the EU and make the transition to a sustainable economy more effective. The analysis of the aforementioned documents shows the coherence and complementarity of EU regulations. To systematize the information reviewed, the evolution of EU legislative rhetoric in sustainable finance is described in Table 2.

Table 1. The features of templates and timing of adoption of EBA Final Draft Implementing Technical Standards on Prudential Disclosures on ESG Risks.

Climate change transition risk				Climate change physical risk	Sustainable activities		
Information will start to be published at the beginning of 2023, but data used in the numerator of the GAR will be available from the end of 2023; data used in the numerator of the BTAR — from the end of June 2024.	The data will start to be published from the beginning of 2023.	The data will be available from the beginning of 2023. Information disclosure will be mandatory from June 2024.	The data will start to be published from the beginning of 2023.		Information will start to be published since 2024.	Information will start to be published from the end of June 2024.	The data will start to be published from the beginning of 2023.
Template 1: The quality of credit disaggregated by sector, emissions, and residual maturity.	*Template 2*: Energy efficiency of the collateral.	*Template 3*: Data in relative terms on emissions based on International Energy aligned metrics.	*Template 4*: Institution's comparative analysis with 20 top carbon-intensive companies in the world.	*Template 5*: Information about the risks of banks because of the impact of climate change on the bank's clients; the information should be disaggregated by economic sectors and geography.	*Templates 6, 7, 8*: Information for GAR calculation.	*Template 9*: Information for BTAR calculation.	*Template 10*: Other climate mitigation measures and activities.

Source: Developed by the author based on EBA Final Draft Implementing Technical Standards on Prudential Disclosures on ESG Risks.

Table 2. Main elements of EU regulatory framework (approved/developed by EC and EBA) in the field of sustainable finance development.

Adopted/Developed/Published	Name of the regulation/act
	European Commission
March 8, 2018	European Commission Action Plan on Financing Sustainable Growth
December 11, 2019	EU Green Deal
January 14, 2020	The European Green Deal Investment Plan
March 2020	Taxonomy; Final Report of the Technical Expert Group on Sustainable Finance
June 22, 2020 (came into effect from July 12, 2020)	Taxonomy Regulation for Sustainable Activities
Adopted: July 6, 2021	Strategy for Financing the Transition to a Sustainable Economy
July 6, 2021	Proposal of European Green Bonds Standards (at the end of February 2023 the political agreement between the Council and European Parliament was reached on the EC's proposals about green bonds standards)
Presented: December 10, 2021 (came into effect from January 1, 2022)	First Delegated Act Supplementing Article 8 of the Taxonomy Regulation
Adopted: April 6, 2022	Regulatory Technical Standards (RTS) — were developed by EIOPA, EBA, and ESMA
	European Banking Authority
December 6, 2019	EBA Action Plan on Sustainable Finance
Published: November 3, 2020 (adopted October 30, 2020)	Discussion Paper on Management and Supervision of ESG Risks for Credit Institutions and Investment Firms
Published press release: June 23, 2021	Report on Management and Supervision of ESG Risks for Credit Institutions and Investment Firms
January 24, 2022	Draft Implementing Technical Standards on Prudential Disclosure on ESG Risks

Source: Developed by the author based on official information from EBA and EC.

Based on the aforementioned information, we can conclude that EU authorities do a lot in the sphere of sustainable finance market development. Nevertheless, most of the normative documents have a voluntary basis. Information disclosure on sustainable factors and instruments will be obligatory for financial institutions from 2023. At the same time, some issues and activities don't consider sustainable factors fully. In this regard, mandatory information disclosure has become an important step in sustainable finance regulation. Banks and other financial institutions operate in a highly regulated environment, as they work with attracted financial resources.

Climate change and other environmental issues create new challenges for banks. Legal authorities have to prepare the financial system for a new reality by timely introduction of the effective legislation. The creation of clear rules and requirements for banks and other financial institutions in such spheres as risk management, strategic planning, and business model development is necessary. The *European Central Bank (ECB)* plays an important role in the process.

3. ECB role in green financial market development

The ECB plays one of the central roles in green finance development in the EU. The regulator has accomplished a lot in the green sphere. It implements numerous ESG activities in the monetary policy framework. From the beginning of 2021, the ECB has started to accept bonds with coupons as collateral for monetary policy purposes if a company's emission is related to one or more objectives of the EU Taxonomy Regulation or the United Nations' Sustainable Development Goals (ECB, 2020a).

In the middle of 2021, a comprehensive Action Plan with a roadmap of climate change-related actions was presented. The document includes measures in such areas as macroeconomic modeling; climate-related risks data analysis; data disclosure for collateral and assets purchases; incorporation of climate-related risks in risk management by ECB and rating agencies; supporting innovations; and development of sustainable instruments.

The ECB emphasizes the impact of climate change on financial stability, the transmission mechanism of monetary policy, employment, investment, and interest rates. Given that the situation in the economy and financial sector affects price stability, it is very important to assess the impact of climate change on macroeconomic indicators and financial parameters (ECB, 2021a).

As part of the roadmap prepared for the period 2021–2024, the ECB intends to construct indicators for green instruments; implement climate-related physical risk indexes for information disclosure by financial institutions; collect statistical data for climate change analyses; develop base standards in the field of climate-related risk evaluation for internal credit ratings; prepare a legal environment for information disclosures as a base for collateral and asset purchases; and consider climate-related risks in regulator's macroeconomic forecasting and monetary policy implementation (ECB, 2021b).

Adoption of the ECB Climate Agenda supports fulfilling such objectives as data collection on climate-related risks, analyzing and using them in the field of the monetary regulation process, forecasting, stress-testing as well as implementation of activities to promote the development of sustainable finance (ECB, 2022a).

Based on the information above, the "green" policy has been an important component of the bank's activities in recent years. The first steps in the "green" direction were taken in 2007 when the environmental policy was adopted. Since 2014, the ECB has occupied a very modern, energy-efficient building. In 2021 ECB established the climate change center and till 2030 the bank has to decrease its carbon emissions by 46.2% (to base 2019) management infrastructure (ECB, 2022b).

Among other things, the Climate Change Center was created in 2021. It is a separate unit inside the ECB that is responsible for all green topics and accumulates information on green policy as well as manages the process of sustainable actions. Also, the ECB works in close collaboration with other institutions in the green sphere.

For example, the ECB has participated in the Eco-Management and Audit Scheme (EMAS) since 2010. This initiation helps to improve green management of the central bank and to reduce the negative impact of the ECB operations on the environment (EC, 2023).

Moreover, the EU monetary regulator, together with the national central banks of the Eurozone, cooperates with the European

Commission on sustainable financial strategy revision. This work is necessary as not all banks and other financial institutions understand the role of the financial sector in the sustainable development process. As estimated by the Commission, the European Union has to spend about 470 billion euros annually in order to fulfill climate-related and environmental policy objectives. In response to the EC's public consultation on the Renewed Sustainable Finance Strategy, the ECB prepared five key statements:

1. Financial institutions need to receive complete information on the "green" effect of possible investment projects to build their strategy in a sustainable direction. There is a lack of structured data in this area. Clear definitions of sustainable financial products will help banks run sustainable businesses as well.
2. In general, the financial market can support the transition process from a traditional to a sustainable economy, but banks and other financial institutions can't lead these changes. Climate policy and other government initiations can be a base of sustainable economic development.
3. Climate-related and environmental risks must be regulated. Banks need to work on green risk management as these types of risks can impact the realization of credit, operational and reputational risks, risk of liquidity, and others. Moreover, a weak banking sector can decline or change the effect of monetary policy transition.
4. International cooperation is necessary for the development of sustainable finance. Implementation of standards uniformly will shape the international market of sustainable finance. As European green legislation and policy are developed further, international cooperation will help other countries to push the process of sustainable finance market formation.
5. Work on the establishment of the sustainable finance market is to be synchronized with other European initiations, such as the *Capital Market Union (CMU)*. On the one hand, unified legislation and sustainable financial instruments will support capital market integration within the EU. On the other hand, a strong capital market will push the development of green/sustainable finance through access to different resources and risk insurance options (ECB, 2020b).

Finally, the ECB participates in the *Network for Greening the Financial System (NGFS).* This organization was established in 2017 and brings together central banks and supervisory bodies from different countries. The purpose of the NGFS is the exchange of expertise in sustainable finance and financial flows directing to green projects for the development of a sustainable economy. As of mid-February 2022, NGFS had 108 members and 17 observers. Besides the ECB, other European central banks as well as EU institutions, such as the EBA, European Insurance, Occupational Pensions Authority, and the European Securities and Markets Authority participated in the organization (NGFS).

The ECB pays a lot of attention to green risk management. According to the ECB, this group of risks is one of the most important in the banking sector. In 2020, the *Guide* was issued. The document is not mandatory but is more for discussion and new supervisory environment development.

Based on the Guide, climate-related and environmental risks are divided into physical and transition risks. Physical risk is a negative financial consequence for banks due to climate and environmental changes as well as natural disasters. This type of risk can be divided into acute and chronic risks. Acute risks result from sudden natural disasters, such as floods, forest fires, earthquakes, tornadoes, etc. On the other hand, chronic risks occur due to long-term natural changes, such as drought and melting glaciers because of climate change, biodiversity reduction, pollution, air quality deterioration, etc. All these environmental changes can have negative impacts on the economic activity. In this case, banks suffer from the financial problems of their clients (for example, agricultural companies' insolvency due to a dry summer) and/or physical losses (for example, destruction of a bank's building or other technical problems because of an earthquake).

Transition risk appears because of policy changes for sustainable economic development. National governments adopt numerous normative and legislative acts in the green sphere. Therefore, companies have to spend additional financial resources to fulfill new rules. Not all businesses can perform as per updated green requirements and continue to work effectively. Environmental policies can deteriorate the financial sustainability of clients, and, therefore, the efficiency of the banking sector. The transition risk is also related to reputational risk. Green rhetoric changes the population's attitudes toward harmful industries. If banking institutions continue to finance projects that are harmful to the environment, the banks' reputation will suffer.

One of the main features of green risks is that they can be realized as traditional financial risks, such as credit, operational, liquidity, and market risks. The ability to mitigate them depends on the consistency and elaboration of a bank's risk management policy. The willingness of a bank's customers to comply with sustainable development goals also reduces the likelihood of green risks materializing for banks. A few examples of what banks can do toward green risk reduction are presented as follows (see Table 3).

The main part of the Guide is devoted to the ECB's recommendations for risk mitigation. According to the document, banks' activities in that area are divided into four groups. The first group of measures is related to the banks' strategy and business models. Banks should indicate and underline possible green risks in the short and long term. It is very important to understand how climate changes or new green policies will affect the economic situation, and influence macroeconomic indicators, such as level of employment, GDP growth, level of taxation, migration, etc. The banks should analyze the actual and future business environment including the influence of green risks. These risks are expected to be considered in the banks' business strategy and stress-testing. For better preparation for the environmental and climate-related risks, it is necessary for banks to also develop a set of *KPI*s. For example, the indicators may include the share of green mortgages in the total mortgage portfolio and the share of green bonds in an investment portfolio.

The second group of ECB recommendations is related to the internal policy and management of the bank. The bank's executives should be responsible for the implementation of the green risk management, ensure that all activities are clear, organize the process properly, and distribute responsibilities correctly. If necessary, a special Department/Committee on Environment issues should be created. The experts of the Committee have to understand and take into account possible green risks and their impacts on the executives' decisions. The management should be responsible for the development of green policy in line with the main international ESG agreements such as the Paris Agreement and the EU Green Deal. At the same time, internal audits will verify the banks' compliance with the requirements, which are defined for green risk management, and assess their effectiveness and adequacy. A very important issue in this area is related to the data collection and preparation of information on green risks on a regular basis. The banks' IT systems should be reconfigured to collect and process the necessary data. Based on aggregated information, all possible green risks and their impact on the sustainability of the institution should be reflected in the banks' reports.

Finally, a block of recommendations in this part of the Guide is related to the implementation of risk management in the banks'

Table 3. Management of climate-related and environmental risks.

	Climate-related and environmental risks	
Examples	**Physical (Acute, chronic)**	**Transition**
1	Reducing the risk of bank's data center damages as result of tsunami or windstorm by relocating servers to a safe area	Risk management of clients' solvency deterioration due to necessity of adopting new energy efficiency standards including an assessment of the real creditworthiness of businesses, considering environmental requirements
2	Preventing massive withdrawal as a result of natural disaster by introducing term deposits without the right to early withdrawal or offering supported financial products to the suffering people	Reducing the losses of reputational risk by adopting green principles (when society begins to care about sustainable issues)
3	Risk management of clients' solvency deterioration due to natural disasters (in seismically active areas — compulsory)	Reducing financing of hazardous industries

Source: Developed by the author based on ECB, Nov. 2020a, Guide on climate-related and environmental risks, 52 pages.

appetite systems. It considers all significant risks and makes it possible to prevent losses by adjusting the banks' activities in a safer direction. For example, a bank may refuse lending to agricultural enterprises in regions prone to drought. As part of the implementation of risk strategy and risk appetite, a set of qualitative or quantitative green-risk assessment indicators should be developed. Specialists in green finance should define some limits (thresholds) for green risk indicators, which allow to fulfill sustainable policies. Financial institutions are expected to incorporate green risk management results into their remuneration process.

The third part of ECB recommendations is related to the influence of green risks on traditional risk management and its links to main financial risks. In this regard, financial institutions should identify, evaluate, and mitigate the impact of climate-related and environmental risks on the traditional risks such as market, credit, or liquidity risks. Green risks should be quantified. Sometimes, it is impossible to calculate the size of green risks. In this case, additional indirect scores can be used. So, green risks should be taken into account. For example, if there is a relationship between green and credit risks, the bank is expected to include green risk evaluation at all major lending stages. In addition, climate and environmental risks should be considered in the collateral and interest rate diversification process. Credit rates can be a very good stimulus for transition to a sustainable economy. For example, banks can decline the level of interest rates if clients have reduced carbon emissions in the previous credit reporting period.

Financial institutions are expected to assess the influence of green risks on operational risk also. Physical environmental risk has a negative impact on bank activity in the seismically active areas. Natural disasters can cause damages to banks' communications systems. Financial institutions have to develop additional measures to neutralize possible damages or hedge losses.

Another example is related to reputational risk when financial institutions work with companies that have a high negative ecological impact. In this case, the bank can check the level of pollution or other negative impacts on the environment from its clients' activities to estimate the size of reputational risks and their dynamics. This is extremely important for banks operating in countries with a strong green movement.

The relationship between green and market risks is based on the market participants' decisions. Banks should predict possible changes on the capital market, including demand growth for green and sustainable instruments (green, sustainable bonds, green lending). At the same time, investments in companies with high-carbon emission can not only be risky but also not very profitable.

Assessing the impact of climate-related and environmental risks on the liquidity situation requires the set of measures to predict money outflow from the bank. As an additional measure, a financial institution will be able to create a financial buffer. Liquidity risk regulation is very important for regional liquidity redistribution if a bank has branches or centers of activities in ecologically and seismically unfavorable areas.

Finally, part of the ECB Guide is dedicated to information disclosure. Banks should describe methodologies and metrics of green risk evaluation, present the approaches followed by institutions to estimate the materiality (or immateriality) of the risks. They are recommended to publish information on main green risks and their influence on the bank, as well as banks' green strategy. Such information can be very important as some banks are committed to taking part in green projects. Quantitative and qualitative information on achieving on green risks and green goals helps show banks' progress in the green sphere. Climate-related financial disclosure can include four main parts:

1. **Governance**: The part explains the main steps of management in the sphere.
2. **Strategy**: The information helps to understand material green risks, their influence on the bank's plans, strategy, and financial results.
3. **Risk management**: This explains how climate-related and environmental risks are estimated and mitigated.
4. **Metrics and targets**: These include the methodology of green risks metrics' development and the main goals that a bank plans to achieve in managing green risk.

It should be noted that as of today the Guide on climate-related and environmental risks is not mandatory, and published information on green risks are usually very fragmented. But in the future unified rules will be developed and disclosing details of climate-related and environmental risks will become a part of banking statistics (ECB, 2020c).

In early 2021, the ECB conducted a survey, asking banks to self-assess their management of green risks and follow-up plans in the area. The study analyzed the answers of 112 major financial institutions. The results of the survey showed some problems. Banks try to consider climate-related and environmental risks in their management, stress-testing, and business plans, but many of them are still on the first steps of the process. The worst situation is with internal documentation preparation, regulation of green risks' impact on the market, and liquidity risks as well as the consideration of green factors in stress-testing. About 50% of respondents think that green risks can be realized in the short and medium terms. From banks' points of view, implementation of green risks can have a high impact on strengthening credit, operational, and business model risks (ECB, 2021c).

So, green banking is one of the main spheres for the ECB supervision and regulation. Moreover, the monetary regulator participates in inter-institutional green activities and initiations as well as develops its work in line with ESG goals. The most important and complicated sphere of the bank's responsibilities in the area are related to supervising climate and green risks. There are no clear rules or approaches. Many European financial institutions take only the first steps in managing green risks. Thus, the ECB pays much attention to working with banks in managing green risks.

The process of transition to sustainability is complex for everyone, but for financial institutions it is accompanied by additional challenges. First, banks need to incorporate sustainability principles into their daily operations as legal entities. This includes such activities like reducing electricity and water consumption and switching to electronic document management. Second, banks have to develop green products and consider the sustainability issues in working with customers. Finally, financial institutions will have to incorporate green risks into their risk management process. The achievement of these goals is a complicated task as the European Union is one of the pioneers in sustainable financing. Therefore, regulators and banks have to rely on their own experience and expertise. Moreover, within the European Union, the development of sustainable financing is not homogeneous.

4. European experience in sustainable finance on the national level

European legislation stimulates national central banks and national authorities to implement new rules in the finance sphere. At the same time, the process of sustainable development of finance is unequal and depends on national monetary policy, private initiatives, and the level of financial market development in each EU country. For example, Lithuania is not a leader in sustainable finance. But national initiations will contribute to the development of the sector in the future. The European Union project on Lithuanian Strategy and Action Plan on Sustainable Finance (Strategy) deserves attention. The project was developed by Sorainen and Richard Kemmish Consulting Limited with the support of Linklaters LLP for the Ministry of Finance, *European Bank Reconstruction and Development (EBRD)*, and the EC, and supports sustainable finance market development.

The project focuses on climate and environmental goals, as well as the development of a special base for achieving other ESG goals. The Strategy includes three main groups of actions: (1) Private sector sustainable finance development; (2) Public sector sustainable finance development; (3) Different actions on sustainable environment building, including creation of special databases, the Green Finance Institute, labeling sustainable finance products, etc. In the framework of the project, the report with main recommendations, timing, and responsible authorities was published in December 2021.

The Green Finance Institute will be an advising body and educational center for private companies and the public sector in the sphere of sustainable finance. Also, the Institute will support development of affective financial instruments, which will be attractive for sustainable projects — potential recipients of funds. The authors of the report underline the importance of competent public policy, well-developed strategies' implementation together with the creation of the Institute that will be able to develop the market of sustainable finance. As part of the Lithuanian Strategy and Action Plan of Sustainable Finance, there are important recommendations, including: the development of public–private cooperation in the infrastructure sustainable projects; an increase the share of sustainable bonds in the total volume of government bond; growth in the share of loans for sustainable related projects to state-owned enterprises; incorporating definitions of green loan covered bonds in national legislation (the peculiarity of this type of bonds is that they are issued for financing/refinancing loans for sustainable projects (for example, energy effective project)); *compensation of costs for small and medium enterprises (SMEs)* that are related to the use of green instruments (sustainable bonds or green loans) to raise funds; the development of an open database on sustainability-related information in line with EU requirements; the development of the methodology of evaluating projects on sustainability; creation of special environment for labeling service providers development; organizing an educational process on sustainable finance for government officials, personnel of financial and non-financial companies, and the general population; the reinforcement of cooperation in the sustainable finance sphere in the Baltic Region (EBRD, 2021).

The Central Bank of Lithuania has started the process of transitioning to sustainable development also. For example, the institution is going to publish a report about its investment portfolio with the assessment of climate-related and environmental impact after some preparation work is done. Moreover, the Bank is a member of the *NGFS*, which brings together European central banks and supervising authorities on a voluntary basis (Bank of Lithuania, 2021; NGFS, 2019).

At the same time, the *Central Bank of Sweden (CBS)* prefers to buy sustainable debt instruments as part of its purchase program. These securities include government green bonds, corporate green bonds and target treasury bills (Gondijan and Merle, 2021). Since 2021, CBS has started to purchase corporate bonds for monetary policy purposes if they correspond to international sustainability standards and include not only environmental characteristics but such issues like human rights and anti-corruption activities/measures.

According to the CBS investigation, there is a correlation between natural disasters and long-term real interest rates. So, long-term interest rates should be included in inflation targeting. In this case, the influence of environmental factors will be considered in inflation forecasting. Another very important issue, which is of interest to the Central bank, is the influence of weather on prices and output. The bank also publishes quarterly reports on CO_2 footprint emissions of its corporate bonds' portfolio. The regulator plans to calculate the size of carbon footprint of foreign reserves and government bonds. The institution also conducted a study that showed the significance of environmental risks if banks invest in companies with high or medium CO_2 emissions. It mentioned that about a quarter of loans for enterprises with harmful production go to firms with bad financial conditions.

Payment issues are also a part of the Swedish monetary regulator's work in the sustainable sphere. For example, the coins that are put into circulation today are lighter and made only from steel, which has a less harmful mining method compared with mining of nickel and other materials. At the same time, organic cotton is used for banknotes production. Another new feature in the payment sphere is that CBS introduced more possibilities for financial institutions to make instant payments on the basis of RIX-INST service, that is connected to the EU instant payment platform *TIPS (Target Instant Payment Settlement).* The service is more green compared with cryptocurrency transactions or operations with payment cards. Besides CBS's internal policy and cooperation with ECB and EBA, the bank is also involved in sustainable finance projects in partnership with international organizations such as Basel Committee, NGFS, *International Monetary Fund (IMF), Financial Stability Board (FSB),* and others (Riksbank, 2021; Riksbank, 2023).

Despite the fact that a lot of activities on sustainable finance development were undertaken, there are some problematic issues, such as information disclosure and lack of reliable data and legislation. SBC mentions that 3 main Swedish banks publish information in accordance with *Task Force on Climate-related Financial Disclosures (TCFD).* TCFD recommendations were developed by an international organization — *Financial Stability Board (FSB).* In 2021, more then 2600 financial and non-financial companies adopted TCFD. But it is difficult to assess the reported climate-related information because of the lack of uniform rules of publication, templates, and tables as well as the absence of the necessary complete database. There is a question as to why Swedish banks don't use European legislative acts, such as SDFR and RTS for disclosing sustainable issues. Possibly financial institutions will be guided by the EU regulation on the national level when it is fully adapted. The same situation holds true with green bonds. Sweden has a significant green bond market. At the same time, there is lack of clarity on the unified requirements of issue and circulation. The EU's adoption of green bond standards will contribute to financial market development in accordance with the principles of sustainability.

The importance of a well-developed sustainable finance regulation is not only a Swedish or Lithuanian issue. As follows from PwC's survey on Green Finance in Poland, one of the main challenges for polish banks in the process of implementing ESG factors in their risk management is "absence of final, transparent regulation". ESG risk management and sustainable strategy development are new activities for financial institutions. Therefore, banks must be given clear instructions on how to operate in the context of prioritizing sustainable factors (PwC, 2021).

Lack of information and underdeveloped legislation effect not only management of green risks but also restrict investments in sustainable projects. For example, Germany has one of the biggest financial markets in the world. But the country is not a leader in green finance. One of the main obstacles in the area is absence of clear rules of projects assessment. In May 2021, the Government published German Sustainable Finance Strategy, which aims to meet current problems and provide further development of the sustainable financial market. In the strategy the following operations can be underlined: development of a "traffic light" system for identifying sustainability-related projects; credit support for export-oriented green projects; continued issuance of green bonds; widening the practice of publishing non-financial reports; development of sustainable finance on the EU level; and increase in the role of KfW bank in the process of sustainable finance development. The last point is based on the KfW banking group mandate.

State-owned KfW bank and other participants of the bank's group developed *Paris Compatible Sector Guidelines* that support achievement of climate-related goals. There are some areas that are prohibited for the bank's financing, including production of pesticides or other substances hazardous to nature (KfW IPEX-Bank, 2023c). Moreover, the bank applies Equator principals in project financing and develops its volume-based mapping of sustainable development goals, which is a financing plan that describes the volume of financing for each ESG goal annually (KfW IPEX-Bank, 2023a,b).

Therefore, EU countries like Lithuania, Sweden, or Germany are engaged in the process of sustainable financial market development by creating clear recommendations and understandable labeling methodologies, forming a green bonds market, working on rules for climate-related and environmental risk management, and creating incentives for financial institutions to invest in green and social projects. Although the countries have implemented various green finance initiatives, in some areas they are still in the early stages. Further development and improvement of sustainable finance public policy at the EU level will support the creation of the sustainable finance sphere in all EU countries.

5. Conclusion

The research shows the crucial role of public policy in the field of green finance. Today, European regulators are able to ensure consistency between numerous legislative acts. The effectiveness of European green finance policy is enhanced by the ongoing dialogue between regulators and market participants. Over the past few years, a number of important documents in this area have been adopted. But there is still a lot to do in such areas as risk management implementation and organization of green financial market. Moreover, the establishment of a sustainable finance system must include the development of the legislation for sustainable finance, implementation of modern green requirement and information disclosure in other sectors of the economy.

One more problematic issue is related to mandatory legislation adoption. Today, banks and other financial companies prepare sustainable reports, which are based on their understanding of international principals and EU recommendations. The regulatory environment that operates on a voluntary basis with flexible interpretation of main issues limits the development of sustainable finance, as some banks may not fully comply with the rules or may misunderstand them. This, in turn, restricts the creation of a comprehensive database. In this regard it is reasonable to adopt clear and detailed legislative acts on sustainable information disclosure, green risk management, sustainable labeling, and unified green bond standards. Some of them should be mandatory, making the European financial system an important part of a sustainable economy.

Risk management plays an important role in the financial sector. As banks work with attracted or borrowed resources, they have to ensure the safety of the money. Financial institutions should consider not only traditional but climate-related and environment risks as well. Special legislation adoption will increase the financial sector's resilience.

For speeding up the process, EU countries define special institutions in the sustainable finance area. They include the Green Finance Institute in Lithuania or the KfW Bank in Germany. European countries on the national level also work on management of green risks, acceleration of sustainable investments, etc. Important issues in this direction are related to disclosure of public–private partnership creation. Supranational regulation should be a basis for the national policy on sustainable finance development.

Finally, the effect of the public policy is higher if regulators demonstrate the transition to sustainability through their own activities. For example, the ECB has created the Climate Change Center, cooperates with other supranational and international institutions in the green finance sphere, and incorporates the principles of sustainability in its work. At the same time, the CBS buys sustainability-related corporate bonds for monetary policy issues.

Thus, creating a well-functioning system of sustainable finance requires development of new rules, policy recommendations, and decision-making on the national and supranational levels. This work is obligatory for the development of a sustainable economy.

References

Bank of Lithuania (2021). Bank of Lithuania to manage its financial assets based on sustainable investment principles. Available at: https://www.lb.lt/en/news/bank-of-lithuania-to-manage-its-financial-assets-based-on-sustainable-investment-principles.

BIQH SFDR Team (2021). Sustainable Finance Disclosure Regulation [SFDR]: The indicators in details. Available at: https://www.biqh.com/blog/sfdr-the-indicators-in-detail/.

EBA (2019). Action plan on sustainable finance. Available at: https://www.eba.europa.eu/sites/default/documents/files/document_library/EBA%20Action%20plan%20on%20sustainable%20finance.pdf.

EBA (2020). Discussion paper on management and supervision of ESG risks for credit institutions and investment firms. EBA/DP/2020/03. Available at: https://www.eba.europa.eu/calendar/discussion-paper-management-and-supervision-esg-risks-credit-institutions-and-investment.

EBA (2021). Report on management and supervision of ESG risks for credit institutions investment firms. REP/2021/18. Available at: https://www.eba.europa.eu/sites/default/documents/files/document_library/Publications/Reports/2021/1015656/EBA%20Report%20on%20ESG%20risks%20management%20and%20supervision.pdf.

EBA (2022). Final draft implementing technical standards on prudential disclosures on ESG risks in accordance with Article 449 a CRR. EBA/ITS/2022/01. Available at: https://www.eba.europa.eu/sites/default/documents/files/document_library/Publications/Draft%20Technical%20Standards/2022/1026171/EBA%20draft%20ITS%20on%20Pillar%203%20disclosures%20on%20ESG%20risks.pdf.

EBRD (2021). Lithuanian strategy and action plan on sustainable finance. Available at: https://finmin.lrv.lt/uploads/finmin/documents/files/Strategy_and_Action%20Plan_2021-12-30_small(2).PDF.

EC (2018). Communication from the Commission to the European Parliament, the European Council, the Council, European Central Bank, the European Economic and Social and the Committee of the region. Action plan: Financing sustainable growth. COM/2018/097 final. Available at: https://eur-lex.europa.eu/legal-content/EN/TXT/?uri=CELEX:52018DC0097.

EC (2020a). Financing the green transition: The European green deal investment plan and just transition mechanism. EC press release. Available at: https://ec.europa.eu/commission/presscorner/detail/en/ip_20_17.

EC (2020b). Regulation (EU) 2020/852 of the European Parliament and of the Council on the establishment of a framework to facilitate sustainable investment and amending regulation (EU) 2019/2088. June 18, 2020. Available at: https://eur-lex.europa.eu/legal-content/EN/TXT/?uri=CELEX:32020R0852.

EC (2020c). Consultation on the renewed sustainable finance strategy. Available at: https://ec.europa.eu/info/consultations/finance-2020-sustainable-finance-strategy_en.

EC (2020d). Commission action plan on financing sustainable growth. Available at: https://ec.europa.eu/info/publications/sustainable-finance-renewed-strategy_en.

EC (2021a). Strategy for financing the transition to a sustainable economy. Available at: https://ec.europa.eu/info/business-economy-euro/banking-and-finance/sustainable-finance/overview-sustainable-finance_en.

EC (2021b). Proposal for a regulation of the European parliament and of the council on european green bonds. COM/2021/391 final. Available at: https://eur-lex.europa.eu/legal-content/EN/TXT/?uri=CELEX:52021PC0391.

EC (2021c). Commission put forward new strategy to make the EU's financial system more sustainable and proposes new European green bond standard. EC press release. July 6, 2021. Available at: https://ec.europa.eu/commission/presscorner/detail/en/ip_21_3405.

EC (2021d). Communication from the commission to the European parliament, the council, the European economic and social committee, and the committee of the regional strategy for financing the transition to a sustainable economy. COM/2021/390 final. Available at: https://eur-lex.europa.eu/legal-content/EN/TXT/?uri=CELEX:52021DC0390.

EC (2021e). Commission delegated regulation (EU) 2021/2178 of 6 July 2021 supplementing Regulation (EU) 2020/852 of the European Parliament and of the council by specifying the content and presentation of information to be disclosed by undertakings subject to Articles 19a or 29a of directive 2013/34/EU concerning environmentally sustainable economic activities, and specifying the methodology to comply with that disclosure obligation. Available at: https://eur-lex.europa.eu/legal-content/EN/TXT/?uri$=$uriserv:OJ.L_.2021.443.01.0009.01.ENG.

EC (2021f). Frequently asked questions: What is the EU taxonomy article 8 Delegated Act and how will it work in practice? July 6, 2021. Available at: https://ec.europa.eu/info/files/sustainable-finance-taxonomy-article-8-faq_en.

EC (2023). EMAS in the European Institutions. Available at: https://ec.europa.eu/environment/emas/emas_registrations/emas_in_the_european_institutions_en.html.

ECB (2020a). ECB to accept sustainability linked bonds as collateral. ECB press release. Sept. 22, 2020. Available at: https://www.ecb.europa.eu/press/pr/date/2020/html/ecb.pr200922_482e4a5a90.en.html.

ECB (2020b). Eurosystem reply to the European commission's public consultations on the renewed sustainable finance strategy and the revision of the non-financial reporting directive. Available at: https://www.ecb.europa.eu/pub/pdf/other/ecb.eurosystemreply europeancommissionpublicconsultations_20200608_cf01a984aa.en.pdf.

ECB (2020c). Guide on climate-related and environmental risks. Supervisory expectations relating to risk management and disclosure. Available at: https://www.bankingsupervision.europa.eu/ecb/pub/pdf/ssm.202011finalguideonclimate-relatedandenvironmentalrisks 58213f6564.en.pdf.

ECB (2021a). ECB presents action plan to include climate change considerations in its monetary policy strategy. ECB press release. July 8, 2021. Available at: https://www.ecb.europa.eu/press/pr/date/2021/html/ecb.pr210708_1_f104919225.en.html.

ECB (2021b). Annex: Detailed roadmap of climate-related actions. Available at: https://www.ecb.europa.eu/press/pr/date/2021/html/ecb.pr210708_1_annex_f84ab35968.en.pdf.

ECB (2021c). The state of climate and environmental risk management in the banking sector. Report on the supervisory review of banks' approaches to manage climate and environmental risks. Available at: https://www.bankingsupervision.europa.eu/ecb/pub/pdf/ssm.202111guideonclimate-relatedandenvironmentalrisks~4b25454055.en.pdf.

ECB (2022a). ECB climate related agenda. Available at: www.ecb.europa.eu/press/pr/date/2022/html/k~cb39c2dcbb.en.pdf.

ECB (2022b). Environmental protection at the ECB. Available at: https://www.ecb.europa.eu/ecb/climate/green/html/ecb.environmentalstatement202207~dedabd566b.en.html#toc2.

EIOPA (2021). The three European supervisory authorities publish final report and draft RTS on disclosures under SFDR. Available at: https://www.eiopa.europa.eu/media/news/three-european-supervisory-authorities-publish-final-report-and-draft-rts-disclosures_en.

European Parliament and the Council (2019). Regulation (EU) 2019/2088 of the European parliament and of the council of 27 November 2019 on sustainability-related disclosures in the financial services sector. December 9, 2019. Available at: https://eur-lex.europa.eu/legal-content/EN/TXT/?uri=celex%3A32019R2088.

Geddes, E., de Longeaux, L., Jackaman, J., & Shah, M. (2022). The EU green bond standard. Will compulsion fragment the market? Available at: https://www.herbertsmithfreehills.com/insight/the-eu-green-bond-standard-will-compulsion-fragment-the-market.

Gondijan, G. & Merle, C. (2021). Integrating sustainability criteria into central bank's asset purchasing programs — The Swedish Central bank as a first mover. Available at: https://gsh.cib.natixis.com/our-center-of-expertise/articles/integrating-sustainability-criteria-into-central-banks-asset-purchasing-programs-the-swedish-central-bank-as-a-first-mover.

Huw Jones, H. (2022). Top EU banks to publish "pioneering" climate data. Reuters. Available at: https://www.reuters.com/business/cop/top-eu-banks-publish-pioneering-climate-data-2022-01-24/.

KfW IPEX-Bank (2023a). Paris-compatible sector guidelines of KfW Group. Version Feb. 2022. Available at: https://www.kfw-ipex-bank.de/Sustainability/#:~:text=Sustainability%20mission%20statement%20of%20KfW%20IPEX%2DBank&text=We%20provide%20viable%20long%2Dterm,of%20life%20of%20future%20generations.

KfW IPEX-Bank (2023b). Sustainability mission statement of KfW IPEX-Bank. Available at: https://www.kfw-ipex-bank.de/Sustainability/#:~:text=Sustainability%20mission%20statement%20of%20KfW%20IPEX%2DBank&text=We%20provide%20viable%20long%2Dterm,of%20life%20of%20future%20generations.

KfW IPEX-Bank (2023c). Sector guidelines — Steering KfW's new financing activities in particularly greenhouse gas-intensive sectors according to the targets of the Paris Climate Agreement. Available at: https://www.kfw.de/nachhaltigkeit/About-KfW/Sustainability/Strategie-Management/Sustainable-Finance/Sector-guidelines/.

Lovells H. (2022). EU sustainable finance disclosure regulation and EU taxonomy; regulatory technical standards update. LEXOLOGY. April 7, 2022. Available at: https://www.lexology.com/library/detail.aspx?g=4357c4ce-1447-40c4-985e-aa52c2ab6e96.

Loyens & Loeff (2021). Quoted. The IFR and IFD: The new prudential regime for investment firms. Available at: https://www.loyensloeff.com/globalassets/02.-publications-pdf/01.-internal/2021/quoted-ifr-and-ifd-the-new-prudential-regime-for-investment-firms.pdf.

NGFS (2019). Available at: https://www.ngfs.net/en/about-us/governance/origin-and-purpose.

PSF (Oct. 2022). Platform recommendations of data usability, October 2022, Available at: https://finance.ec.europa.eu/system/files/2022-10/221011-sustainable-finance-platform-finance-report-usability_en_1.pdf.

PwC (2021). Green finance in Poland. How will ESG change the banking sector and corporate financing? Available at: https://www.pwc.pl/pl/pdf-nf/2021/Green_finance_in_Poland_PwC_ESG_report.pdf.

Riksbank (2021). Climate risks in the policy work. The Riksbank's climate report. Available at: https://www.riksbank.se/globalassets/media/rapporter/klimatrapport/2021/the-riksbanks-climate-report-december-2021.pdf.

Riksbank (2023). Overall discription of RIX-INST. Available at: https://www.riksbank.se/globalassets/media/rix/rix-inst-rtgs/engelska/rix-inst-overall-description.pdf.

Transition Finance Report (2021). Available at: https://ec.europa.eu/info/sites/default/files/business_economy_euro/banking_and_finance/documents/210319-eu-platform-transition-finance-report_en.pdf.

World Resources Institute (2021). European Union's just transition mechanism: Transnational funding and support for a just transition. April 1, 2021. Available at: https://www.wri.org/update/european-unions-just-transition-mechanism-transnational-funding-and-support-just-transition.

© 2024 World Scientific Publishing Europe Ltd.
https://doi.org/10.1142/9781800614451_bmatter

Index

F

G

H

I

www.ingramcontent.com/pod-product-compliance
Lightning Source LLC
LaVergne TN
LVHW011657200926
848484LV00004B/977
* 9 7 8 1 8 0 0 6 1 4 4 4 4 *